Hero of Fort Schuyler

Hero of Fort Schuyler

Selected Revolutionary War Correspondence of Brigadier General Peter Gansevoort, Jr.

PETER GANSEVOORT, JR.

Edited by DAVID A. RANZAN *and* MATTHEW J. HOLLIS

McFarland & Company, Inc., Publishers
Jefferson, North Carolina

Library of Congress Cataloguing-in-Publication Data

Gansevoort, Peter, 1749–1812.
Hero of Fort Schuyler : selected Revolutionary War correspondence of Brigadier General Peter Gansevoort, Jr. / Peter Gansevoort, Jr. ; edited by David A. Ranzan and Matthew J. Hollis.
p. cm.
Includes bibliographical references and index.

ISBN 978-0-7864-7948-1 (softcover : acid free paper) ♾
ISBN 978-1-4766-1680-3 (ebook)

1. Gansevoort, Peter, 1749–1812—Correspondence. 2. United States—History—Revolution, 1775–1783—Personal narratives. 3. New York (State)—History—Revolution, 1775–1783—Campaigns. 4. United States—History—Revolution, 1775–1783—Campaigns. 5. Generals—United States—Correspondence. 6. Fort Stanwix (Rome, N.Y.)—Siege, 1777. I. Ranzan, David A., editor. II. Hollis, Matthew J., editor. III. Title.
E207.G26A4 2014 355.0092—dc23 2014029544

British Library cataloguing data are available

On the cover: Peter Gansevoort, Jr., engraved by J. F. E. Prud'homme based on a 1794 painting by G. Stuart (Gansevoort-Lansing collection; manuscripts and archives division; The New York Public Library; Astor, Lenox and Tilden Foundations)

Printed in the United States of America

McFarland & Company, Inc., Publishers
Box 611, Jefferson, North Carolina 28640
www.mcfarlandpub.com

To Kelly, Eric and Ashley

Table of Contents

Preface

The American Revolution has its share of great leaders from all sectors of society. Scholars and history enthusiasts alike have explored innumerable primary and secondary sources, studying the great men who had been inspired by Greece and Rome to engage in the greatest democratic experiment in history. Most are familiar with the exploits, both mythic and real, of George Washington, John Adams, Patrick Henry, and other revolutionaries. The American memory is rich with epic tales of the maligned Benedict Arnold turning to the British in exchange for wealth and opportunity, and of Nathan Hale making the ultimate sacrifice to protect the Revolutionary cause.

As historians of the American Revolution delved deeper into its history, they discovered contradictory evidence that had the potential to alter our understanding of the war. Did Nathan Hale truly say he had but one life to live for his country when confronted with his imminent doom? Did the demonization of Benedict Arnold dehumanize a complex and ultimately tragic figure? Only since the 1970s has there been a trend of historians shifting their focus from the main figures of the American Revolution to those lesser-known participants. The advent of social history brought with it another level of analysis of the men who were at the forefront of the Revolution. These were common men of American society from various walks of life who left their families and the comfort of their homes to enlist in either the Continental Army or their respective local militias.

As many social historians have accurately described, these common soldiers in the American military suffered hardships very different from those suffered by modern soldiers. Often without shoes and clothes, medical supplies, and food, these men fought valiantly on the battlefield with little more than courage, a vague faith in the Revolution, and inspiration from the gallantry displayed by their commanding officers. Primary sources written by these men are incredibly rare. With the discovery of the memoirs of Joseph Plumb Martin, as well as those of other former soldiers, we obtain a precious glimpse into not only the trials and tribulations they experienced during their service, but also the beginnings of a common American memory.

Is it enough to say that by focusing on the common soldier and the officer of privilege and noble upbringing that the American people have gained as concise a knowledge of the American Revolution as possible? Or is it possible that, as many historians at the turn of the twentieth century sought to discredit the deification of the founding fathers, that the same could be said for the other parts of Revolutionary society? Instead of being condemned to an eternal circle of myth and deconstruction, another pathway into a deeper understanding of this era may be found in the middle.

Neither landed gentry nor lower class citizens, junior officers of the Revolution were at the crossroads of these historical viewpoints. Many of these junior officers were born into relatively wealthy families, wielding considerable influence in their townships, counties, or colonies. These officers had, in a sense, been bred to experience both worlds of American society. These families had the considerable respect of their colleagues. Yet their social status was not considered equal to that of the Virginia planters or the rich New England shipping merchants. Many of them did not have titles indicative of "gentlemen."

When word of revolt and revolution against Britain spread throughout the colonies, many of these men were appointed to lead their local militias. With little to no military experience, lack of qualifications precluded them from the possibility of a senior rank. However, the influence of their families often earned these men higher ranks in state militias than they could have achieved in the Continental Army. Others joined the Continental Army in the hope that their service in battle would lead to promotion into the top ranks.

Peter Gansevoort was one of these peculiar individuals that occupied the middle ground of the Revolutionary military. Born to a wealthy brewing family in Albany County, New York, Gansevoort saw the Revolution as an opportunity for influence as much as independence. It is in his correspondence, along with the correspondence of many others of his ilk, that historians can further discern the relations between the upper and lower classes of the Revolution. As a junior officer, Gansevoort would essentially serve as a conduit of communication between the soldiers on the march and the superiors commanding them. Gansevoort's correspondence acts as a narrative device; the generals' initial orders are followed by Gansevoort's response, detailing the condition and readiness of his men to comply. Gansevoort also acts as a filter for bias and ambition that otherwise may not have been hinted at by other primary sources. By reading his correspondence with his brother and other close relatives, we can discern Gansevoort's political ambition, sympathy for his troops, and the occasional ire towards both his superior and subordinate officers.

The letters also hint at the nature of other relationships both in the hierarchy of the military and at home. There are confrontational and occasionally combative letters between Gansevoort and his superior, General Horatio Gates, illustrating that there was far more at stake to the officers of the American Revolution than independence. Descriptions of scouting missions, and diplomatic meetings with the Iroquois Confederacy show how Gansevoort treated friend and foe.

Ultimately, this collection of Gansevoort's writing reveals, through both his letters and the letters of his correspondents, fears and hopes unique to Gansevoort and his family, those of his subordinate officers, the men he commanded, the villages he maintained watch over, his commanders, natives, and the enemy. This book will hopefully become a tiny yet important piece of a vast puzzle, one that we have only begun to invest large amounts of research. Regardless of political or academic climate, the American Revolution has always remained a cornerstone of American historians.

The editors hope that the contents within are found enlightening to the reader or researcher, and to place a springboard before a new concerted effort in uncovering new angles of historical interpretation. At the very least, we hope that this publication provides some homage to one of the many forgotten patriots of the American Revolution.

The military papers of Brigadier General Peter Gansevoort, Jr., are part of the Gansevoort-Lansing Collection, which is housed in the Manuscripts and Archives Division at the New York Public Library. Most of Gansevoort's military papers are bound together in nine volumes and concern his service during the American Revolution; this includes muster rolls, returns, ration accounts and letters from prominent individuals in the military. A selection of the documents are transcribed *verbatim, literatim et punctuatim.* The illustrations reproduced are also from the volumes.

Catherine Van Schaick Gansevoort, the wife of Peter Gansevoort, Jr., bequeathed the papers to their son, Peter Gansevoort, in 1831. Subsequently, the papers were passed through the hands of Brigadier General Gansevoort's grandson, Henry S. Gansevoort, Bvt. Brigadier General, U.S.A., and then to Henry's brother-in-law Honorable Abraham Lansing. Catherine Gansevoort Lansing, Brigadier General Gansevoort's granddaughter, arranged them into nine volumes during the years 1899–1905 and bequeathed them with other manuscripts and printed books to Victor Hugo Paltsits, an archivist and librarian who was, at one time, head of the Manuscripts Division of the New York Public Library, who gave them to the New York Public Library in 1919.

Although Brigadier General Gansevoort is the focus of the publication, the significance of his papers goes beyond the man himself. The reader can gain a detailed understanding of the northern campaign, including the fortification and supplying of the Champlain-Hudson-Mohawk Valley forts of New York during the American Revolution as well as the battles fought in the area. The depth, quantity, scope, and diversity of these documents make them of long-term value not only to American Revolution enthusiasts but also to a wide range of scholars and students.

The letters have been transcribed as accurately and literally as possible in the hope of preserving the spirit of the eighteenth century. Nevertheless, the physical format of the letters has been standardized and when possible, dates and addresses are supplied in square brackets whenever omitted within the letter and/or present on the envelope. Because the transcriptions retain the inconsistencies of spelling of the originals, this may cause potential problems for the reader. Where there was any doubt about the interpretation of a particular word, that word was followed by a question mark and enclosed in brackets. Interlineations were brought down to the line of the text at the place indicated as well as addition in the margins. Omitted text was indicated with a blank space within square brackets [ ] and crossed-out words and phrases were retained when legible with the deleted passage placed in the text with a strike-through bar.

Chronology

1749	July 17	Born in Albany, New York, son of Harman and Magdalena Douw Gansevoort
1775	May 4	Obtained a lieutenant's commission in a militia company in the Albany third ward
	July 19	Appointed by Congress with a commission of major in the Continental Army in charge of the Second New York Regiment
	late August	Took command of the Second New York Provincial Battalion at Fort Ticonderoga
	November 5	Stationed at Chambly during the Montgomery's Montreal and Quebec campaigns and participated in the assault on St. Johns and Montreal
1776	March 19	Promoted to Lieutenant Colonel and assumed command of Fort George
	November 18	Moved to Fort Saratoga
	November 21	Promoted to colonel in charge of the Third New York Regiment
	winter	Back to Albany to recruit for his depleted regiment
1777	March 15	General Schuyler ordered Gansevoort to leave Fort Anne for Fort Schuyler
	May 3	Assumed command of Fort Schuyler
	August 2–22	British Colonel Barry St. Leger laid siege to Fort Schuyler
	October 4	Recognized Colonel Commandant of Fort Schuyler by Congress
1778	January 12	Married Catherine Van Schaick, daughter of Wessel and Maria (Gerritse) Van Schaick in the Van Schaick Mansion located on Van Schaick Island
	late May	Returned to Fort Schuyler after honeymooning in Albany
	winter	Stationed at Schenectady and Fort Saratoga
1779	May 12	Assembled at Canajoharie with the late Livingston's, Dubois's, Alden's & Butler's Regiments for Sullivan's expedition.
	June 17	Left the Mohawk River and marched across the country to Otsego Lake
	July 2	Reached the head of Otsego Lake
	August 9	Marched down the Susquehanna River
	August 22	Joined General Sullivan at Tioga
	September 12	Son Herman was born

	September 20	Sullivan ordered Gansevoort to the Lower Mohawk Castle and arrest every male Mohawk and take them prisoner to Albany
1780	July	Stationed at West Point
	August	Took command of the York Brigade (HQ at Orange Town)
	fall	Took command of the post at Fort Saratoga; remained until the realignment of the New York Line in January 1, 1781, when his position was eliminated
1781	April 3	Succeeded General Abraham Ten Broeck, assumed command of the First Brigade of militia in Albany County as Brigadier General, a position he kept until the end of the war
	November 23	Son Wessel was born
	December	Attempted to quell an insurrection in the regiments of Colonels John and Henry K. Van Rensselaer near the towns of Schaghticoke and Hoosick caused by the New York-Vermont controversy involving the New Hampshire land grants.
1782		Dealt with deserters, spies and Tory sympathizer. Petitioned for a higher commission in the newly organized Continental Army. Kept his militia brigade in readiness in case of an attack.
1783	Summer	Accompanied Washington on his tour through the northern battlefields of the Mohawk Valley (from Schenectady to Fort Schuyler)
	October 15	Son Leonard was born
1788	December 22	Appointed Indian Commissioner
	September 29	Son Peter was born
1790	April 6	Served a two-year term as Sheriff of Albany
1791	December	Daughter Maria was born
1799		Visited Mount Vernon to paid homage to the late George Washington
1802	April 29	Appointed Military Agent for the Northern Department of the United States
1803		Appointed one of the first Board of Directors of the New York State National Bank of Albany
1808	March 11	Appointed Regent of the University of New York
1809	February 15	Appointed Brigadier General in the U.S. Army, commanding the Northern Department of the Army
	March 25	Resigned his commission as Major General of the 4th Division of Infantry of New York—a position he held for nearly twenty years
1811	June	Appointed President of General James Wilkinson's Court Martial; trial was in session from September 2 to December 25
1812	July 2	Died in Albany, New York, age sixty-two

Chapter One

1775: Invading the North

"Thus a war has begun." Joseph Warren penned this phrase upon hearing the news of Benedict Arnold[1] and the Green Mountain Boys' capture of Fort Ticonderoga.[2] Two weeks after the British marched on the towns of Lexington and Concord, a war cry sounded throughout the countryside compelling the colonists to set their allegiance with either the new revolutionary fighters or hold true to the rule of King George III. Many men heeded the call for freedom as the newly assembled Continental Congress put forth resolutions concerning the arrangement of the troops. In New York's Albany County, individuals from the lower classes enlisted in the militia and continental regiments, while those from the more prominent families sought commissions of higher status. One such patriot was Peter Gansevoort, Jr.

Born on July 19, 1749, the eldest son of merchant and brewer Harme Gansevoort[3] and Magdalena Douw, Peter came from one of the most influential families in the city of Albany. Harmen Gansevoort, Peter's great-grandfather, immigrated to America before 1657, and settled at Beverwyck, on the Hudson River. Harmen moved to Albany in 1677, where he bought a lot at the southeast corner of Brewer's Street and Maiden Lane. He built his home and a brewery on the spot. It was here that Peter Gansevoort was born.[4]

Peter Gansevoort, Jr., joined the Albany militia with a rank of lieutenant when the war began and when the resolution to raise troops in New York was approved Peter sought admission into the new Continental Army. On June 12, 1775, he contacted his uncle and vice president of the New York Provincial Congress, Volkert P. Douw,[5] to assist him in obtaining a commission in the Revolutionary Army.[6]

1—To Volkert P. Douw

Albany June 12th 1775

Sir In Consequence of the offer you was so obliging as to make when I was at New York to recommend me for a Commission in the Service of the Province, I must acquaint you that I have expostulated with my Parents and Friends on the subject who have no objections to my accepting a Genteel Post in the said Service I should be glad if you would ~~be glad~~ speak to your Friends on the subject and get me appointed if my Person should be approv'd my Conduct and Political Sentiments I doubt not but would be Vouch'd for by some of your Board

Your Nephew & Very Humble Servt

Peter Gansevoort Junr

[Letter to my Uncle at New York requesting an execution of his Influence to obtain for me a Commission in the Revolutionary Army]

The mention of a "Genteel Post" suggested that Gansevoort wished an immediate position befitting his family's stature. Although many in the Provincial Congress wished to deny Gansevoort's enlistment, General Schuyler's need for fresh officers placed Peter Gansevoort in a prime position for appointment.[7] On June 30, 1775, Gansevoort received the commission of Major in the Second New York Regiment under the command of Colonel Goose Van Schaick.[8]

Peter Gansevoort, Jr. Engraved by J. F. E. Prud'homme based on a 1794 painting by Gilbert Stuart (Gansevoort-Lansing collection. Manuscripts and Archives Division. The New York Public Library. Astor, Lenox and Tilden Foundations).

The year 1775 saw the beginning of Gansevoort's military career that would span almost forty years, yet the year would end with quite a few personal and private challenges. Not only a fresh recruit but a lower ranked officer of the Continental Army, his participation in the Canadian invasion of 1775–1776 had him witness the gaps in his command's weaponry, supply system, and ability to scout through the rough Canadian wilderness in the cold of winter. His correspondence exposed other problems seemingly inherent in the fledgling Continental army; some of these problems included troop desertion, inability to deal with the amorphous nature of diplomacy with Indian tribes, and inefficient communications between higher ranked officers and Gansevoort himself. By the end of the campaign, Gansevoort would no doubt employ these valuable lessons within his own command of the Third New York Regiment during the siege of Fort Schuyler, his expedition with Generals Clinton and Sullivan into Indian borderlands, and at his New York militia post during the later phases of the war.

His enlistment and rise through the military ranks is understood through an analysis of his family history. The Gansevoort family had acquired wealth from ownership of a popular local brewery,[9] and was widely acknowledged as part of the Albany patrician class by the 1750s.[10] It is important to note that by the time of Peter's enlistment, the Gansevoorts had intermarried with other esteemed families, such as the Ten Eycks,[11] the Douws, the Cuylers in 1749, and with Peter's marriage to Catherine Van Schaick in 1778.[12] The Gansevoort families' participation in local politics formed a bond with the politically active Schuyler family, beginning with the formation of a merchant coalition in the 1730s.[13] Many Continental Army officers working in conjunction with Peter Gansevoort, Jr. included General Philip Schuyler,[14] Colonel Goose Van Schaick, and Cornelius Cuyler.

As a newly enlisted major in the Continental Army, Gansevoort was given orders to head immediately to Fort Ticonderoga.[15] Preparations were then to be taken to join General

Schuyler and Colonel Benedict Arnold (later to become a general in 1776) to capture British Quebec. Many of the authorities in the military and in the rebelling colonies assumed that Quebec was lightly defended, and had discovered that British General and Canadian Department head Guy Carleton's attempts to rally the citizens of Quebec in its defense had little effect.[16]

2—From Goose Van Schaick

Albany 19th Augt 1775

Sir You'll take under your Command the four companies now in Camp at the Patroons Mills and proceed with them to Ticonderoga without delay in the following Order. On your arrival at Half Moon[17] *you will dispatch to Genl Schuyler or Officer Commanding at Ticonderoga a letter by way of Fort George*[18] *acquainting him of the number of men you have under your Command the day you march from Half moon and on what Day you Expect to arrive at Skeensborough.*[19] *The Baggage & Camp Acquipage to be sent forward from Fort Edward*[20] *by way of Fort George under a Sufficient Escort & yourself with the men under your Command to proceed to Skeensborough where Boats will Undoubtedly be ready to receive you on your arrival. At Ticonderoga you will produce these your orders to the Genl or Officer Commanding at that Station. I must intreat you to inforce good order. that individuals may not suffer in their property let no pains be Omitted to impress the men with Just notion to Society & how infamous it would be in us who have arms in our hands for the protection of our Country to betray that trust by a Violation of their rights*

Goose Van Schaick Coll

To Majr Peter Gansevort [Order's to Maj'r Peter Gansevoort by Goose Vn Schaick]

Even in the first months of his military career, Gansevoort's involvement with the doomed campaign had hit upon the first stumbling block. Whereas General Schuyler was meant to be in charge of the thrust to St. John's north of Lake Champlain, he had fallen sick and was forced to turn command over to General Richard Montgomery in mid–September.[21] After participating in the capture of nearby Fort Chambly[22] on October 20, Gansevoort had also succumbed to sickness. In a letter from his brother, Leonard,[23] Peter was moved from Chambly to the camp near St. John's for treatment of a severe fever.[24]

3—From Leonard Gansevoort

Dr Brother I can hardly express my Distress upon receiving a Letter from Mr James Van Rensselaer[25] *acquainting me with your indisposition and that you in consequence thereof had been obliged to leave Chamblee and that you was then in Coll: Biddels*[26] *Camp on the North side of St John's; every thing seem'd to conspire to confirm me in the Opinion that you must have been very Ill you cannot be ignorant of the Emotions in my Breast when you consider that Fraternal Affection which has always subsisted between us, and in what Manner I must have also felt when ~~my Duty~~ (prompted by Duty) I communicated the Contents of the Letter to our Joint Parents, I was oblig'd to meliorate the News by telling them that your indisposition was the Fever Ague but do assure you that upon reading the Letter from the same Gent. to Mr Philip Van Rensselaer*[27] *that tho' you was then yet pretty Weak you was greatly recovered, I seem'd to be rais'd from the lowest Abyss of dispondence to the highest pinnacle of Hope and I will leave you to reflect how industrious I was to communicate it to the old people—I beg my Dear Brother as you Love your Friends who are under the greatest uneasiness yet that you will write us a Line if you are able, and if not procure some one to write for you—and beg further that if you are not recovered on receipt of this that you will apply for leave to come down and write me before you set out that I may meet you on your Way—I should have been up with you already If I could possibly have obtained leave of Hetty*

We are all well I am Your loving Brother

Leonard Gansevoort

Albany Octr 31st 1775

To Peter Gansevoort Junr Esqr [Provincial Camp at St Johns]

Leonard Gansevoort. Etched by Max Rosenthal, 1885 (Gansevoort-Lansing collection. Manuscripts and Archives Division. The New York Public Library. Astor, Lenox and Tilden Foundations).

Histories of the Canadian invasion suggest that sickness in the Chambly camp was a feature common in other American camps due to inadequate supply and a particularly harsh Canadian winter. Following the failure of the second siege of St. John's, almost half of General Montgomery's forces were sick.[28] This was also evidenced by large desertions of Continental soldiers: "Rather than longer endure the hardships of the camp, the deserters preferred to face the dangers of starvation in the wilderness bordering on the sides of the lakes."[29] Desertion, sickness, and bad supply would be a large problem for the invaders and for Gansevoort's career through 1776.

Major Peter Gansevoort apparently recovered from the life-threatening malady within the space of two weeks, judging from his father's November 16th letter.[30]

4—From Harme Gansevoort

Albany 16th Nov: 1775

Dear Peter Yours of the 3d Instant Received Eight Days After Dated thereof Assure you with great pleasure to hear of Such Important affair that St John was Fallen and that Without much Bloodshed and more in particular of your recovery So far as to Testify it with your own hand. Which was the greatest and best tydings that I Could Expect from any matter in this world. So that have only to Recommend you to give thanks to him that [with?] the Whole world and kept you from your Illness and Relieved the Army from Suffering any Longer. as to news Referr you to your Brothers Letter and newsPapers. Shall only acquaint you that we are all in good Helth thank God [first?] and hope this may find you in the Same Your Mother Sister and miss maggy Joyn with me In our kind Love to you and Mr John Livingston[31] *familie if you should have the happiness to Come to Montreal, Where I hope you will find em in good Helth Am*

Your Loving Father

Harme Gansevoort

PS our Neighbour Isaac Smith was Buried Last Saturday

[Peter Gansevoort]

His brother's November 30 letter contained some foreboding information; Colonel Arnold had joined up with General Montgomery's forces outside of Quebec far later than expected.[32] The disease and winter weather fatigued both forces and Arnold's army had slowed in their progress due to inaccurate maps of the territory.

Arnold's troops also lost a number of transport ships across the St. Lawrence rapids. One particular October night saw Arnold and his men rush to save gunpowder, fallen victim to a sudden flooding of the Dead River.[33] There were reports within the same timeframe from Forts Chambly and Ticonderoga that the garrisoned men were speaking of abandoning their post in refusal to travel in similar conditions.[34] The British seizure of these forts would mean the annihilation of supply routes to the front lines.

5—From Leonard Gansevoort

New York November 30th 1775

Dr Br I should accuse myself of Inattention did I remain as silent as yourself—I now sit down to acquaint you that I arrived here safe on the 23rd Inst and am in good health Capt Henry Livingston[35] *arrived here last Sunday who brought us the agreeable News of the surrender of Montreal*[36] *to your Arms I ~~give~~ congratulate you on the Occasion and ~~it~~ the Circumstance of the Surrender of that Garrison as well as that of St John's reflects the greatest Honour on Genl Montgomery—by a Copy of a Letter from Genl Schuyler we learn that Arnold is arrived at Quebec and he supposed that he was then or soon would be in Possession of the Town which Event I sincerely wish has taken place before now—*

We have great hopes here, that an Accomodation may take place soon from a Letter of Capt Effingham Lawrence[37] *to a Gent. in this City who writes that he expects to come over in the Spring with the Olive branch in his Hand—*

Capt. Livingston also informs me that he had din'd with you in Montreal the Day before he left it and that you were quite well again which afforded me great pleasure. Persevere to the last in fighting for those Rights and Prividges which are deriv'd to us from God & the Constitution and which our Posterity have a right to demand from us unsullied & unimpair'd—let neither Danger nor Ambition divert you from the Course you ought to Steer—keep the two massive Pillars which support the noble Fabrick of the British Constitution always in View and determine to Succeed or die in the attempt—excuse me

I am in haste Your Friend & Hum Servant

Leonard Gansevoort

To Peter Gansevoort Junr Esqr [Provincial Camp in Canada]

After the capture of Montreal, Montgomery and Arnold had decided to initiate the siege on Quebec in a desperate attempt to win over Canadian locals and seize British supply trains. Evidence of the two General's desperation was contained within a letter from Major Gansevoort to John Van Schaick[38] one day before the siege.

6—To John G. Van Schaick

Montreal Decemr 30th 1775

Dr Fd By an express which arrived a few days ago from Quabec we are informed that Genl Montgomery lyes before the City has erected Batterys and Bumbarded the place for some hours after which he sent a Flag of Truce with a Letter to Genl Carleton demanding a surrender of the place as soon as the Flag drew near the Wall an Officer appear'd on the Wall's and desired to know his errand he returned for answer that he was sent by Genl Montgomery with a Letter to Genl Carlton sometime was taken up in returning their answer which was they should immediately leave the Wall's that no Letter or Message would be received and unless they departed without hesitation the would be fired upon the fatel die is now Cast and nothing remains but the most Sanguary measures to be taken Genl Montgomery has rallied his Troops informed them he found it necessary to storm The Town and offered them as a reward for their service that they shoud be plunder Genl Carleton and all his Adherents and every person found in arms against us their effects would become a prey to the Soldiers except one Hundreth part which would be reserv'd as a reward for such as distinguish themselves most in the service of their of this Contrey

By a another express which arrived Yesterday we are informed that Genl Montgomery was ready to Scale the Walls last Wednesday at two OClock in the Morning. The Weather not being favorable, Postponed the attack till a more convenient Opportunity

I hope you will not Censure me for not Writing to You before now. I beg you will present my Compliments to Mrs Annatie Van Schaick[39] And believe me that I am with the sincerest Sentiments of Love

You Affectionate Friend and Very Hum Servt
Peter Gansevoort
P.S. Please to deliver the Inclosed
[Mr. John G. Van Schaick—Albany]

Although the invading armies performed with vigor despite fatigue and Arnold's rally temporarily inspired his men with "invincible courage,"[40] General Montgomery had been fatally wounded by grapeshot fired by retreating Quebec sailors.[41] With the British defenses still intact, their armies streamed out of the city's fortifications in full force, necessitating a gradual retreat for the invaders back to the Lake Champlain valley.

In the coming year, the Americans in the Lake Champlain valley would find themselves in a quagmire of lost provisions and a perpetual state of undersupply, the death of one of the most talented and reputable American officers, and a rough retreat from Canada back into American territory. Gansevoort would slowly learn the logistics, procedure and conduct befitting an experienced officer. He also experienced the bitterness of a stinging defeat at the hands of the British only a few months into his service.

Chapter Two

1776: Defending the Lake

In 1776 the invading Continental army was in low spirits. The failed siege on Quebec and the death of General Montgomery threatened not only the organization and morale of the men, but the entire operation as a whole. A letter from Leonard to Peter mourned the loss of General Montgomery and sought "to endeavor to revenge his Death."[1] In addition, Leonard remarked on not seeing Peter's name in the "Public prints." He expressed his understanding of the vacancy due to Peter's illness and not from a "want of Spirit" to distinguish himself. He also announced that in the near future there might be a chance of promotion due to the raising of the regiments.

7—From Leonard Gansevoort

Albany Feby the first 1776

Dr Br I condole with you the loss of the gallant the great and the amiable Montgomery, but be not dismayed consider that the greater the loss is which the Cause sustains by his sudden and unhappy exit, the more his survivors are to endeavour to revenge his Death—I am extremely sorry I have not yet discovered your Name in the Public prints which I am convinced has not been owing to a want of Spirit but of an Opportunity to distinguish yourself which has been prevented by your indisposition during the Siege of St John's[2]*—*

We have just now heard ~~that~~ from Lieut Mudge[3] *that you was gone to forward to Quebec—I wish you health and Success in the Campaign—*

Many Troops are now on their March to Join you at Quebec—2200 Men from Philadelphia are daily expected who the General tells me began their March the 21st of January—

We are all well—your Letters by the Post are come to hand—Miss ____ is very well—I set out for N York again next Week to Join Congress—Many new Regiments to be rais'd in this Province you stand a great chance of Promotion—20,000 Men are to be station'd at New York under the Command of General Lee[4]*—your Brother in Law Ten Broeck's Family is very well he is elected a Member of the Genl Assembly with A Yates—they go down next Week also*

Your's &

Leonard Gansevoort

[PG Major of the 2nd Battalion of the New York Forces—Canada]

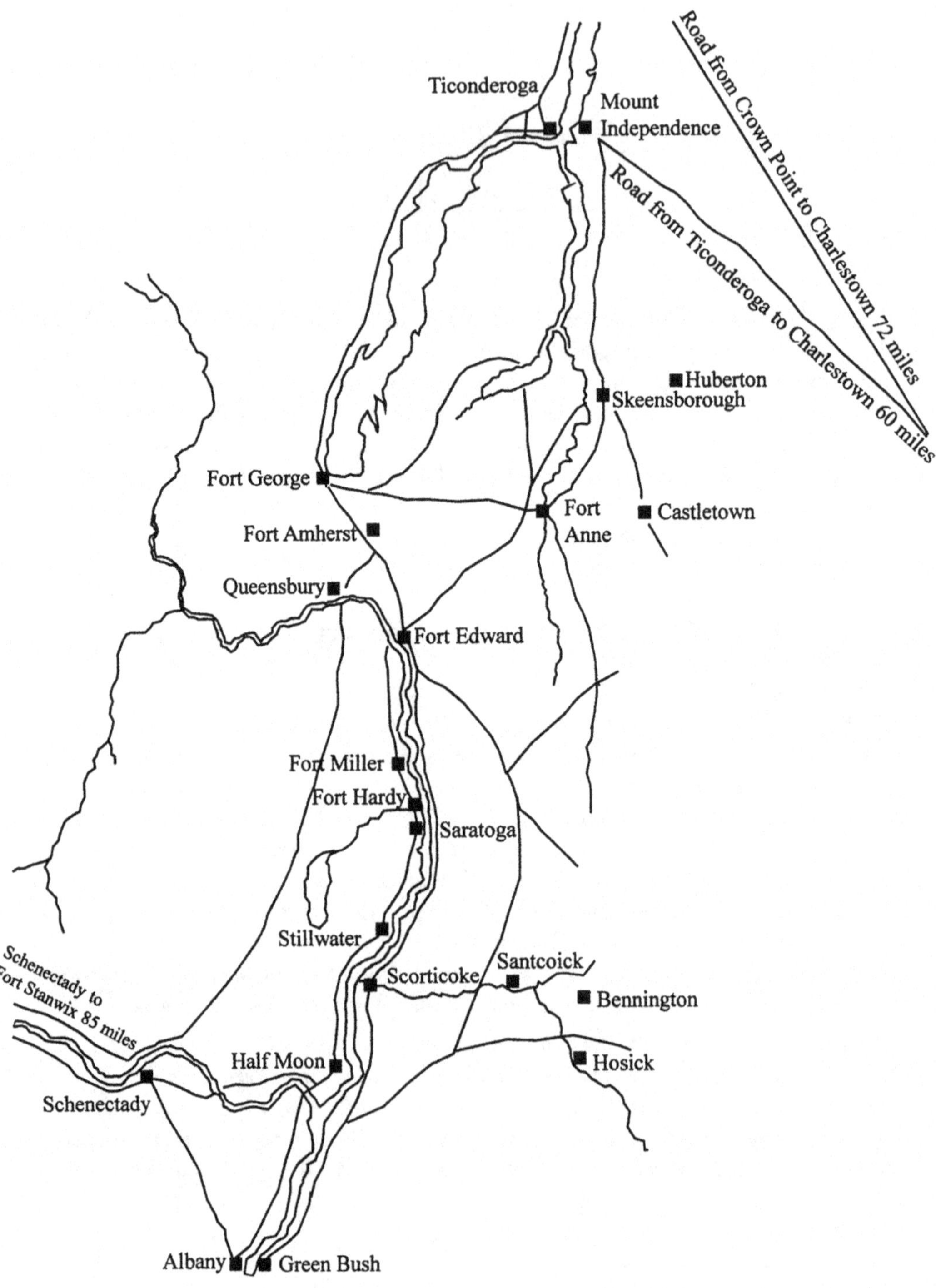

Line drawing based on "Part of the Counties of Charlotte and Albany, in the Province of New York" by Thomas Kitchins, Sr., 1778 (Gansevoort-Lansing collection. Manuscripts and Archives Division. The New York Public Library. Astor, Lenox and Tilden Foundations).

Fortunately, the winter was set to dissipate over the next few months, allowing valuable time for the Continental Congress to push for reinforcements. Despite the Gansevoort brothers' yearning to avenge Montgomery, they had neither the manpower nor the equipment to do so.

In a February letter to the Committee of Albany, the Continental Congress ordered the raising of five companies for New York's defense.[5] Equipping this new army would not be easy. Many of the citizens in the area were still supporting the Loyalist cause; some secretly confiscated arms, others simply refused to sell arms to the new soldiers. This was to be a consistent problem throughout most of the Revolutionary War; in August of the same year, Peter Gansevoort was alerted to a "Sutler ... trading with Some Soldiers for their Guns offering to give them Liquors...."[6] A new recruit was expected to "furnish himself with a good Gun and Bayonet, Tomehawk, Knapsack or Haversack and two Bills." If unable to procure these items, the recruit would receive the items by credit and the "payment of which small Stoppages will be made out of their Monthly Pay till the whole are paid for." This was an example of colonial wage garnishment.

8—Nathaniel Woodhull[7] to the Committee of Albany

In Provincial Congress New York Febt 18th 1776

Gent The Congress having determin'd that your County shall have the Opportunity of raising five Companies in the four Regiments to be rais'd by Order of Continental Congress for the difence of this Colony have resolved that blank Warrants for the Officers of the same should be sent to your Committee you will observe by the inclosed Resolve is that you are restrained in the Appointment to give the preference to such Persons as have served their Country in the last Campaign—but it is not be any Means the Design of Congress that Men who have misbehaved themselves should be any further employed—

It is expected that each Man furnishes himself with a good Gun and Bayonet, Tomehawk, Knapsack or Haversack and two Bills, but those who are not able to furnish themselves with these Arms & Acoutriments will be supplied at the public Expence, for the Payment of which small Stoppages will be made out of their Monthly Pay till the whole are paid for, when they are to remain the Property of the Man

It is expected that the People will readily inlist in these Regiments as they are rais'd for the express purpose of defending this Colony and unless we raise them from among ourselves in all probability they will be sent from other Colonies which will be to our everlasting disgraces—

We have great Confidence in your Zeal for the Common Cause and trust you will exert yourselves that these Levies be compleated with all possible Dispatch

We are Gent Your very Humble Servants By Order

Nathll Woodhull Presid

To The Committee of Albany

Guns were not the only scarce items needed by Gansevoort's camp and the threats to his position were increasing as the months went by. General Schuyler noted that goods and other assistance should be expedited in a May 13 letter to the Sub-Committee of Albany, noting that after raising the fateful siege on Quebec, the armies abandoned two hundred incapacitated soldiers, cannon, and much of their meat supplies.[8] Schuyler directly stated that unless his need for reinforcements, fresh artillery batteries, and supplies were met, a potentially disastrous and crippling situation would befall the entire war effort.

Philip Schuyler. Engraved by H. B. Hall & Sons based on a painting by Gilbert Stuart, c. 1860s (Gansevoort-Lansing collection. Manuscripts and Archives Division. The New York Public Library. Astor, Lenox and Tilden Foundations).

9—Philip Schuyler to the Sub-Committee of Albany

Fort George May 13th: 1776

Gentlemen Some Ships of War with Troops arrived on the fourth Instant at Quebec which obliged our Troops to raise the Seige—We lost about 200 of the Sick who were too ill to be moved and a few others who were out in detached parties Guards some of our Cannon and most of our provisions, so that our Army suffers for Want of Meat, as none is to be had in Canada—and notwithstanding the proper and immediate Measures you took to procure Carriages in Consequence of the last Letter I had the Honor to address you, very few indeed are as yet come up and the Army must absolutely come out of Canada unless immediately supplyed—Let me therefore intreat you to try one more—perhaps if the principal Gentlemen of the City were to go to the different Districts it would have a good Effect, and possibly be the Means of Preventing the Evacuation of Canada by our Troops. I am Gent Pray send to Esopus[9] for Carriages Your most obedient hble Servant

Ph: Schuyler

The Sub-Committee of the City & County of Albany

Schuyler transmitted the severity of the situation to Gansevoort almost a month later on June 3, demanding that Gansevoort's group immediately send "Whatever Powder and Artillery Stores [that] may Come to this [Fort George]."[10] It would appear through this correspondence that the people of Albany were able to raise very little in comparison to General Schuyler's needs and forced him to divert resources from other regiments. Schuyler was also desperate for some form of currency to reimburse the now ragged and fatigued Continentals to prevent desertion; this was evidenced by General Washington's dispatch of $300,000 to the Canadian forces.[11] Despite Washington's quick action, Gansevoort's own command would not see any of this money until almost two months later at the end of June.[12]

10—From Philip Schuyler

Fort George June 3d 1776

Sir, If during my absence from this Place any Troops Should arrive that are destined for Canada, now will immediately Send them on allowing one Batteau to every thirty Men

In each Batteau you will put ten Barrels of Provisions and the Troops that are to go in the Batteaus are to be victualled for twelve Days—Each Batteau is to have eight Oars

If any Small cannon arrive, They are to be Sent to Col: Wynkoop[13] *for the Use of the Vessels on Lake Champlain—*

Whatever Powder and Artillery Stores may come to this Post you will forward without Delay—If any Dispatches from Congress or General Washington arrive for me forward them by the Way of Skeensborough—I am Sir Your most Hum Servant

Ph: Schuyler

To Col: Gansevoort

As General Schuyler left Fort George to rally the political bodies in Albany for support, he appointed Gansevoort to take command of the post. Schuyler emphasized the importance of quickly forwarding any flour or clothing received from Albany for the benefit of the soldiers.[14] A huge undertaking had begun at Cheshire's near Fort Anne[15] in preparation to defend Lake Champlain. Schuyler instructed Gansevoort to forward all necessary manpower and supplies to support this effort. Gansevoort, recently promoted to Lieutenant Colonel on March 19, was allowed "Two Carpenters of Miltons and two Wheelrights of Van Der Bogert's Company" to repair the barracks at his post.

11—From Philip Schuyler

Fort George June 9th: 1776

Sir The Public Service requires my immediate Presence at Albany, you will therefore take the Command here and I doubt not but you will diligently attend to every Thing conducive to the good of the Service.

Whatever provisions comes from Albany is to be forwarded without the least Delay, giving the preference to the Flour until seven hundred Barrels are gone on and then you will send equal Quantities of pork and Flour.

If any Cloathing for the Troops in Canada arrives here that must be sent in preference to every Thing.

Let the Carpenters know that they are not to build any Batteaus after Thursday next and that on Friday, they are to prepare and set off on Saturday for Cheshire's near Fort Ann—You will order Mr Yates the Waggon Master to provide Carriages for them—They are to take with them ten Days provision and be employed in cutting Timber for a Saw Mill, for which I shall give Directions by the Time they arrive at Cheshire's

You will send with the Carpenters a Grind Stone and three Casks of Nails of different Sizes—twenty felling axes—six Pick axes four Shovels three Spades two Crow Bars—and a Tent to every five of them

You will be particularly careful to guard against Accidents.

If any Letters from Canada arrive for me forward them to Albany, even tho' you should learn that I was in Tryon County, as my Stay at any place is very uncertain.

The working Cattle at this place with the Carts are to be sent to Cheshire's to remain there and they may carry part of the Carpenters Baggage.

Two Carpenters of Miltons and two Wheelrights of Van Der Bogert's Company are to remain here—They may be employed in repairing the Barracks or other necessary Work.

I am Sir Your Most Obedant & Humble Servant

Ph: Schuyler

Lieutenant Colonel Gansevoort [Fort George]

Repairs went slowly as word of nearby British movement required several scouting parties to be sent out,[16] and influx of British prisoners required the precious little supplies to be further rationed.[17] Gansevoort soon began to experience desertion once again but this time, the desertion would occur under his own command. Schuyler offered Gansevoort his condolences that "so Many of the Troops desert...," however in such cases Gansevoort's priority would then be to "Send all such Except of Colo Wynkoops & Yours, in Irons to General Sullivan."[18]

12—From Philip Schuyler

Albany June 17th 1776

Dear Sir I am sorry to learn by a Letter from Mr Lansing[19] *that so Many of the Troops desert. If You can apprehend any Send all such Except of Colo Wynkoops & Yours, in Irons to General Sullivan.*

Please to Make me a Weekly Return of that Part of Your Regiment which is at Fort George, Crown Point[20] *or any where Except those gone to Canada without the least Delay & be very particular, & You will not forget to Make me a Monthly Return on the last Day of Every Month—*

Let whatever Men You can spare from Duty & the Batteaus, put the Fort into as good Order as possible & Mount the Six Pounders

I am Dr Sir Your Most Hble Servt

Ph: Schuyler

Lt Colo: Gansevoort [Fort George]

It would seem almost impossible in light of these circumstances that any adequate repairs were completed. With his workforce split into scouting parties for deserters and British detachments, guards for prisoners, and guards for supply trains, Gansevoort's initial orders to repair the barracks were practically at a standstill. This was not an isolated incident. The garrison at Fort Montgomery[21] experienced manpower deficiency in establishing chains and diverting river passages. At Fort Ticonderoga, soldiers' attempts at boom modification resulted in a loss of ten months worth of labor, food, and wood.[22] With these resources wasted on rebuilding defenses along the New York side of the Hudson River, the forts on the Canadian front lines were left particularly vulnerable to attack.

These attacks were assumed by many officers to be primarily from the British armies, but word of Indian scouting parties in the area caused apprehension. Early reports in late June and early July indicated a rising amount of Indian activity within range of Gansevoort's position. Colonel Cornelius Wynkoop, the commander of Fort Ticonderoga, noticed that "several Indians had been Seen near the fort last Night," and that this information be immediately passed onto General Schuyler, for the fort was "...Very Weak having not more than One Hundred Men at present."[23] Wynkoop's aide, John Wendell,[24] added on June 25 that "14 of our Men were Scalp't & kill'd at Point Au Fare[25] by the Damn'd Indians & some Canadians."[26] One day after this letter was a response from John Lansing, Jr., General Schuyler's aide, dated June 26, addressed directly to Peter Gansevoort, ordering him with utmost caution to keep at least fifty men on active garrison duties.[27]

13—From Cornelius Wynkoop

Ticonderoga June 19 1776

Dr Sir I send a Letter in Company with this for the General Informing him that Several Indians had been Seen near the fort last Night which you will Send to him if he Should not be at Fort George Immediately we are Very Weak having not more than One Hundred Men at present I likewise Desire'd of the General not to Send any more provisions at present as they must have Alare Stock by them And it is not Certain wether they Can keep their Ground or not and If they have too march it will be lost—Should they Retreat—if you Can Spare any men please to Send them Over for I want to put this place in Some Posture of Defence if possible

From Sr Your Huml St

Cornelius Wynkoop

To L. Colo Peter Gansevordt [Fort George]

14—From John H. Wendell

Ticonderoga June 25th 1776

I send you herewith a letter from for Genl Schuyler which I have this Moment received from Genl Sullivan, who writes me from Isle aux Noix,[28] *to send him all the Boats, that are here or at Crown Point, & as I am but weakly Mann'd at this place, with that you would send me, some Men to send of with Boats, I have of the Number which I have with me Sent of Capt Wendell with 12 Boats, 2 Men in a Boat to Crown Point, in Order to Send Men from that place forward with the Boats to Isle at Noix. I have at present but the Guard in Garrison—the Officer who brought the letter to me, mentions of 40 Boats which must go down if no more—14 of our Men were Scalp't & kill'd at Point Au Fare by the Damn'd Indians & some Canadians I am Sir Your Humble Servt By Order*

Jno H Wendell

Corns D Wynkoop Commanding Officer

To Lieut Collo Peter Gansevoort Esq [Fort George]

15—From John Lansing, Jr.

Dear Colonel I arrived here this Morning and notwithstanding your prognostications brought your Sulky safe—I found the General much reduced by the Ague, He is now in Bed under a severe Fit.

Tho' the General does not think that there is any great Danger of an Attack, yet he wishes you to take every precaution prudence can suggest to guard against a Surprize

Colo: Wynkoop has Directions to send you five Carriages as soon as you receive them you are desired to have the six pounders mounted on the Fort—The General also desires you to convoy the Musquet Balls now in the Store into the Fort: to lay in a few Barrels of Water to supply your Garrison in Case of Necessity—to keep out a scouting party constantly, and to ~~keep~~ give them Directions to be very vigilant and alert in the Night approaching your post toward Day and to be very careful to endeavor to make Discoveries: to continue to forward all the Batteaus you possibly can; but not on any Occasion to reduce your Garrison to less than fifty Men.

You will in a few Days be reinforced by a Body of Men draughted from the Militia.

The General has ordered a Ton of powder to your post [incomplete]

[John Lansing Jr Albany June 26th 1776]

[PG Fort George]

The cautious yet aggressive stance towards the Indians was for good reason. Alliances within the Six Nations and outlying tribes were constantly shifting. As the tribes in Western New York became increasingly convinced of the American colonists' hostile intentions, the Oneida appeared to be the only tribe willing to stay out of confrontation since their declaration of neutrality in June 1775.[29] General Schuyler had previously accepted a belt from the Six Nations announcing their neutrality in the face of the more militaristic members of the Mohawk and Iroquois camp in December 1775,[30] but the efforts of pro–British Mohawks under the rabble-rousing Sir John Johnson[31] required a punitive expedition by militia in January 1776.[32] Under these circumstances the neutrality agreements on both sides seemed to have been violated regularly.

Gansevoort's first involvement as a fort commander with Indians occurred in early July. Major James Van Rensselaer ordered Gansevoort to provide clothing and provisions to two natives traveling through the fort destined for Albany.[33] One week later on July 14th, Gansevoort would receive a letter from General Horatio Gates,[34] who claimed that thirteen Indians from Crown Point were being transported as prisoners by an outfit of Continental officers to Albany. Gates was very adamant to "see them safe to General Schuyler; though they are considered in the light of Prisoners, I would recommend that their imprisonment by made as easy as possible."[35] Making it "as easy as possible" for these prisoners included smallpox inoculations and medical examination of the prisoners, as well as detaching a further escort for the remainder of their trip. These thirteen must have been of diplomatic significance; a July 24th letter to Gansevoort noted that three colonials infected with smallpox were traveling the same route, and had neglected the need for a doctor's examination.[36]

16—From Horatio Gates

Tyconderoga 14th July 1776

Sir The Bearer Lieut Ten broek has the Care of thirteen Indians sent hither from Crown Point with a Letter to Major General Schuyler The Small Pox is broke out upon one of the Young Indian Lads; you will Order the Surgeons at your post to give all the Assistance in their Power to recover him—when the Indians incline to go on to Albany, you will send an Escort with them to see them safe to General Schuyler; though they are considered in the light of Prisoners, I would recommend that their imprisonment by made as easy as possible. you will Order them to be supplyed with such refreshments, & accomodation, as your Post Affords—I am Sir Your most Obedient Humble Servant

Horatio Gates Majr General

/Lieut Col. Gansevoort/ [Fort George]

Horatio Gates. Engraved by H. B. Hall & Sons based on the painting by John Trumbull, c. 1850s (Gansevoort-Lansing collection. Manuscripts and Archives Division. The New York Public Library. Astor, Lenox and Tilden Foundations).

The month of August meant a reorganization of regional priorities. While continually being aware of natives in the area, General Schuyler told Colonel Elias Dayton,[37] commander of Fort Schuyler, to begin felling trees into nearby Wood Creek, to "considerably retard their progress, if they mean an attack upon your post."[38] The tactic of felling trees became the most important use of the heavily forested terrain for impeding British invasion from the Northern Hudson; this tactic would later be used to considerably stall and frustrate General Burgoyne's[39] campaign one year later. The rest of August continued with relatively little excitement, at least in comparison to the first apprehensive half of the year. The colonists focused on restocking forts with ammunition, constructing of "bateaus" or transport ships, and requesting reinforcements throughout the Hudson River Valley area.

17—Extracts of Letters and Orders from General Schuyler to Coll Dayton While Commanding at Fort Schuyler

Extract from letter of July 18th.

If you Should get certain intelligence of the approach of an enemy thro Lake Ontario you will then cause the Timber on the banks of Wood Creek to be felled into it in Such a manner as to give the greatest obstruction to the enemy.

This Letter is dated at the German Flats40 Extract from letter of August 8th.

In my letter of 18th Ultimo I directed you upon the receipt of certain intelligence of the approach of an enemy thro Lake Ontario that you Should cause the Timber on the banks of Wood Creek to be felled into it &c. You will please to observe that before you fall the Timber into the Creek, I mean that your intelligence Should be Such as to give you the Strongest reason to believe that any enemy crossing Lake Ontario, intend to come your way, this will be best deter-

mined by their coming to Oswego or landing in Some other part of the Lake in the vicinity of that place. In Such case, any roads by which cannon could be conveyed, Should also be rendered as impassable as possible Should you at any time gain intelligence of the approach of an enemy, you will not only dispatch an express to me describing the rout they take or you judge they may take but also Send the Same information to the officers commanding here & at Johnstown[41] *& to the Committee of this county.*

From letter of August 18.
Let all the horns of the cattle killed at your place be saved and made up

From letter of August 20.
Let me intreat you to keep Scouts constantly out towards Oswego & Oswegatchie[42] *that you may have the earliest intelligence of the approach of any enemy. A Sum of money is Sent you for defraying contingent expences. Mr. Thomas Spencer*[43] *who resides at Cayuga as a Blacksmith & is a very intelligent man has promised the Commissioners to transmit you, intelligence; as he is well beloved by those Indians, his information may be useful; you will therefore please to pay attention to what he may communicate*

From Letter of August 2d.
You will distribute the rum at Such times & in Such proportions as you may think proper to fatigue men not exceeding a gill per day unless upon very extraordinary occasions. The pay to Carpenters & persons who are good workmen to be one fourth of a Dollar per day. other artificers one eighth of a dollar. It is impossible to ascertain what the contingent expences to which the commanding officer will necessarily be put, will be, Such Aconomy is to be used as will be consistent with the good of the Service

From letter of Septr 7th:
Do not forget to fill Wood Creek with Timber, as that will considerably retard their progress, if they mean an attack upon your post. I do not by any means think you ought to comply with the request of the Indians not to Send any white people to gain intelligence as in that case we must entirely depend on what accounts they are pleased to give, which may be attended with the most dangerous consequences; I would therefore have you by all means, mix Some of your officers and men with any parties you may Send, & also Send Small parties entirely composed of your corps.

The hard money left with the commanding officer by General Schuyler's orders is to be expended only for Such purposes as other money will not answer.

Coll Dayton begs leave to recommend it to Coll Elmore[44] *by no means to Suffer the Indians to get too much rum at this place, for if they get drunk he will find them very troublesome nor Suffer them to run in & out of the fort as they please and also to keep a watchful eye over the Toreys & dram Sellers here else they may do great mischief among the Indians & men.*

The above Extracts are taken verbatim from General Schuylers Letters

Elias Dayton Colo commanding Fort Schuyler

the House that formely belonged mairs the Barn with Hay a Stack of Oats in the field belong to the public after paying to Mairs upwards of Ten pounds

The reconnaissance reports from Continental scouts revealed little threat to the immediate area from August into September; a surgeon named Stephen McCrea aboard the sloop *Enterprise* suggested to Gansevoort that the British were holding back a possible advance inland until fairer weather permitted.[45] Given the apparent break in inherent military threats, Gansevoort dealt with far more trivial matters such as receiving several petitions concerning a bartering for a horse gone awry. McCrea had apparently attempted to sell some of his horses to civilians near Lake George; one particular horse became the focus of a heated argument, in which McCrea apparently left the horse to the civilian, who then promptly let the horse wander off on its own.[46]

On September 18th, a speech from the Five Nations was delivered, declaring that any harm shown by the Americans towards the Mohawk in the Hudson Valley would be considered a breach of neutrality agreements and that the Five Nations would then be swayed over to support the British cause.[47] Apparently Schuyler's determination to cease loyalist activity by arresting John Johnson and other loyalists had the opposite effect. The Five Nations were still neutral, but the majority of the tribal leaders were now at a consensus that if further harassed by any of Schuyler's men, they would join the British in driving the Americans from the frontier. Although the hindsight of history shows that there was no major engagement by Indians or Continentals until the next year, Gansevoort must have been under the impression that the entire Western frontier was now teeming with armed and volatile Mohawks.

18—Speech from the Five Nations

Niagara 18th Septemr 1776

A speech delivered by the Hurins, Ottowas, Chippawas, Pottowatorries Missagoes, Senekus, Cayugaes, Onnondages, Oniedes, Tuskorories, Mohawks, Delawares, Annaticots, Connoys, Squaghkies, being in Council in presence of Lieut Colo John Caldwell Commandant[48]

Colo John Butler[49] *Eng Depty Agt*

Lieuts Matthews

Burnitt

Phinvesly

Ensn Butler

Sastarilze, speaker, he spoke as follows Adressing himself to us desired we would lisen to what he would Say, And Commit it to writing to Accompany a Belt which is now to be sent down to their Brothers Oniedas Tuskarorees, and Mohawks By one of their Brothers A Mohawk

We now Aquaint you by this Belt, that we are all unanimously and fully determined to fullfill our Engagements with the King. we speak for ourselves, as also our western And Southern allies. which are all of our opinion We have Sent you a Message of 3 days ago,, desiring you to quit the Bostonians, And we now By this Belt desire you to be Strong and determind to fullfill your Engagements and not suffer yourselves to be forced Bullied by those Drunken people all our Eyes as well as the Eyes of our Western Brethren are fixed of on the Mohawk As the head of the 5 nations & whatever hurts them will be Equally painfull to the whole of us and will be the means of disturbing the peace between us and them who should pretend to disturb you upon the first Call, shall fly to your Assistance being willing and fully determind to share our Fate with you We desire that some of you will Immediately rise and come to this Great Counsil fire, with your Answer that we may transmit it to our western Bretheren Should you delay your Answer long, we Shall Immagine that our Road of peace is Entirely Stopped and it will oblige us to act accordingly we desire and Expect that the Shechems and Warriors will take the Above speech into their most Serious Consideration A Belt

the under Namd are the shechems and Chief warriors of the Difene nations now Assembed

Hurin Chiefs—De wat ont, Wan dan dy jong, Stawaing shong, it tongwaraing, La Saussage
Ottoway chiefs—Chamintawa, Orange, Otowakie, Mishimemduk, Shawanagijick
Chippawa Chiefs—Recontkeejeck, Warin akum, Sagutchuwaon, hesh kee bug isee
pottowatomie Chiefs—Paimamakitam, Peenash, Milai catchi, nowagota
Sineka Chiefs—Siowea, Adon goat, Sawetoo, Cienlakereah, Ra sats tie, oan un ties
Caywgo Chiefs—tyagoraghtake, Ojakeghte
Anondage chiefs—Dayaweronte, kaghkaghkatye
Oniada Chiefs—Shagoghnatskeehawe
Tuskorores chiefs—Shagogh
Mohawk chief—Aaron, Kanonraron
Deleware chief—Gwar bess son
Annanticot Chief—Maghgirawas, No tsigh Cel

All of these preparations in light of low supply, little reinforcements, and a breakdown in communication culminated in a written confrontation between Gansevoort and General Horatio Gates. Gates first lectured Gansevoort in July over a "wanton waste of Powder."[50] Apparently despite the lack of gunpowder, Gansevoort saw it fit to fire off multiple salutes in the course of the day, perhaps to improve morale or keep idle hands busy. Another letter from the same day required a shipment of "Spare Oars" from Gansevoort's camp to supply freshly built bateaus north of his position. Gates also put emphasis on Gansevoort's apparent lack of attention to deserters and other infringements of the soldier's personal property:

19—From Horatio Gates

Ticonderoga July 17th 1776

Sir, I understand that there is a Wanton waste of Powder, at your Post, in firing a Morning and Evening Gun, & in unnecessary Salutes

It is my positive Orders, that this practice be Immediately Discontinued and no Ammunition expended on any Account, except in Opposition to The Attacks of The Enemy,—

I am, Sir, Your Humble Servant
Horatio Gates Majr Genl
Commanding Officer at Fort George
[PG]

20—From Horatio Gates

Tyconderoga July 17th 1776

Sir On the Receipt of this, you will Send what Spare Oars you may have, to Mr Daniel, Qr Mr at the Landing on this Side of the Lake;—The Oars will be wanted here, therefore by you will send them, as soon as possible—

You will be very Carefull Sir! to prevent any Desertion of those who are or may be sent to the Genl Hospital; Some Villains, perhaps Seign themselves Sick merely with Design of gaining an Opportunity of Deserting,—The utmost Care will be necessary to prevent this Evil—

There is great Complaint among the Officers here, that their Letters, both going & coming are frequently interrupted & broke open;—I beg, Sir! If anything of this kind has hap'ned at your post, an immediate Stop may be put to it;—& if any person can be discover'd either to retard or Open any Letters either to or from the Army, apprehend him immediately, & let him be try'd—a Crime of this Nature cannot be too Severely punish'd—

The utmost Care for the public good & the Security of your post, in every particulars is at this Time peculiarly requisite—

I am Sir Your Obedt Hble Servt
Horatio Gates Majr Genl
[PG Fort George]

The correspondence seemed to suggest that Gates questioned Gansevoort's ability to manage his command and comply with the most basic requests. Although there was no direct evidence, it was apparent that Gates' targeting of Gansevoort might have been due to his struggle over control of the Northern Department with General Schuyler. As Schuyler had close family connections with Gansevoort, replacing Gansevoort with an officer more in sync with Gates' objectives may solidify and centralize his control over the Department. Gates's stringent instructions may have also been indicative of reservations regarding the junior offficer's capabilities. A seasoned veteran, Gates had already served as a British officer; Gansevoort, a colonist of Dutch descendant, was practically a fresh recruit with no experience. Gates certainly therefore saw himself as socially and militarily superior to the Lieutenant Colonel.

Even Gansevoort's younger brother, Leonard, was using his influence as a member of the Provincial Congress to mend relations between Gates and Peter.

21—From Leonard Gansevoort

Ticonderoga August 2nd 1776

Dr Colo General Gates has informed me while ~~you~~ here that it has been represented to him that you have made it a practice to give furlows to people in the Army who pretended to be sick which ~~he~~ conduct he said he could not but censure and reprobate I mentioned to him what had passed between you and Lieut Spencer[51] *upon his application for his Friend, ~~which~~ with which he was well pleased—*

He also told me that he had desired you to make a Weekly return of the Garrison in which you had been remiss as he had received but one from you as yet and was at a loss to Account for the neglect—I told him the Multiplicity of Business you had on Hand and the Variety of Application foreign to your Department he says he is willing to grant you all the Assistance in his Power and has begg'd me to write you assuring me that from his acquaintance with me he conceiv'd he might confide in you.

I must beg you to be particularly attentive to every Matter that shall be recommended by the General here and General Schuyler and I am so well convinc'd of your Zeal to Serve the Public with Dispatch and punctuality that I presume it is need less for me to expatiate on the Subject.

Your good Sense will suggest to you how necessary it is to be careful in avoiding all practices which may be reprehensible in you or lead to sacrifice my Riputation should General Gates invest you with any further Powers in consequence of my Acquaintance with him

The General will now write you for a Return of the Garrison you at present Command, and permit me to beg from you that you will be industrious to get an accurate return of all the Men Sick and well the Number of Battau Men Carpenters Ordnance and Military Stores as a true Copy thereof will be delivered to us to be transmitted to Congress and the necessity of the Measure is a sufficient Agreement with you to be particularly careful in this Matter

I Shall be with you again the latter End of next Week—we this Day set out for Crown point we shall return to morrow and go to Skenesburough next Monday

My kind Remembrance to Doctor Potts,[52] *your Aide de Campe, Sawny, Vrooman and the other Worthy Gent of your Mess—*

I am Dr Sir Your's very sincerely

Leonard Gansevoort

To Colo Gansevoort [Fort George]

The suspicions of Colonel Gansevoort's disorganized command may have been well-founded; Jonathan Trumbull's[53] review of the troops at Fort George showed many gaps in Gansevoort's officer ranks.

22—From Jonathan Trumbull, Jr.

Sir I Recd a Return of the Troops at your post, this Morning—Which I now Enclosed to have Corrected—I have Corrected Several parts of it myself—

The principal Errors—are—that the Officers of all Ranks are included in the Number of—Totals of the Rank & File—that Column is intended Solely to Shew the Numbers of Rank & File Effective—The Columns of Wanting to Compleat are incorrect—not Comparing with the Totals of each Rank—I here are always as many wanting in a Company as While Compleat it to 1 Capt—3 Subt 4 Sergts 2 Drums—& 80 R & F. ~~What to~~ Each Rank to be returnd under their own head—

There is no occasion of Returning to me each Company but the diferent Corps, of which the Garrison is Compos'd—

I have made a form & Inclos'd, which you'll order the Adjutants to send to Carefully & regard the Columns of Absent, & Vacant Officers &c—underneath as well as the other parts of the Return Correctness & Neatness are necessary as I send to Congress the Same Returns which are Sent me

I am Sir Your very Obedt Humble servt

J. Trumbull Dy Adjt Genl

H Qtrs Ticonderoga

August 6th 1776

Lt Col Gansevoort [Fort George]

Sir Your Bror: Was Mistaken as to the Returns, they have been regularly received the only fault is your Adjutant not being correct—J: T

How many of these accounts of disorganization could truly be applicable to Gansevoort's supposed incompetence? With orders to have at least one officer under his command to accompany soldiers on Indian scouting parties, these parties may not return for many hours or days. It was also not known when exactly these accountings of officers were to take place; it was possible that the scouting parties had not returned at that point in time, making it impossible to know of any casualties.

In August, General Gates requested that three thousand barrels of flour be shipped from Fort George to Ticonderoga and to take inventory of his exact supply so as to ship any surplus to other forts in need.[54] This order was most likely either not complied with, or delivered far after General Gates's request. Apparently the content of the order was enough to warrant a response from Gansevoort in defense. The affront on Gansevoort's honor was finally addressed in a letter to Gates dated August 12.[55] In it Gansevoort claimed Gates had personally hurt and afflicted his honor, and that General Schuyler's best judgment deemed him worthy of his station. Gansevoort questioned Gates' request to remove Colonels Van Schaick, Wynkoop, and Siskes from service, and that their regiments be disbanded for "they impos'd upon the Public."[56] As the majority of these officer's families were closely related to the other Albany patricians, it reinforced the idea that Gates saw fit to "clean house," by removing many loyal Schuyler officers from his new command.

23—To Horatio Gates

Fort George August 12th 1776

Hond Sr I have just now been informed by Lieut Low in Capt Evan's Company & Colo Visscher Regt[57] *that your Honor had said that the Regiment's of Van Schaick Wynkoop and Siskes ought to be discharged for that they impos'd upon the Public*

by this Assertion I must beg leave ~~to acquaint~~ to acquaint you that I conceive my~~self~~ Honour Hurt ~~and~~ Wounded and Injur'd as Lieut Colonel of Colonel Van Schaick's Regiment and as a Gentleman and the more so as Genl Schuyler has placed the Confidance in me of appointing me Commanding Officer of this Garrison both Honour to myself and Justice to the Public therefore Demand that I should immediately (appreize your Honour that I shall beg leave from Genl Schuyler that some other more worthy Officer than I am supposed to be may be appointed to the Command of this Garrison at least one whom your Honour will not have Reason to suspect, and that I may have an Opportunity of Clearing myself of that imputation, I shall beg that a Court of Inquiry maybe called and should I be convicted of the Charge I shall be content with receiving the Punishment adequite to the demerit and laying Under the imputation of being a Scoundrel and a Villian and not worthy of being in the Public Service but should I on the contrary (as I ~~shall expect~~ make no doubt but I will) be acquitted, I shall expect that your Honour will do me the Justice of giving me the names of those Persons who have so maliciously endeavoured to sully my Character (which I hold most dear) that I may have an opportunity of doing that Justice to myself which my Honour as a Gentleman Demands

Hints and precautions from a Superior officer in my duty I always have and ever shall take kind, so have I taken the Hints in your first Letter's but when I perceived that I scarce received a line from your Honour but contained some implied censure upon my conduct as Commanding officer here I confess it Created some Jealously in me that your Honour was diffident of me as an Officer and a Gentleman which I attributed either to your not knowing me or from the misrepresentation of my Conduct by some malignant Person's, And I cannot conclude without observing to you that I had before conceiv'd my Honour somewhat attak'd by a Passage in your Honours Letter of the 17th July last which came to hand 4th Instant And is in these Words—"Thare is great Complaint among the Officers here that their Letters ~~are~~ both going and coming are ~~frequen~~ frequently interrupted and broke open, I beg Sr if anything of this kind has happened at your post

"Post an immediate stop may be put to it."

This passage in my Humble opinion speaks this Language that Your Honour suppos'd that such practices might be done here and that it could not be done without my privity or knowledge I beg your Pardon if I have misconstrued the Passage but I declare to your Honour as a Gentleman it appeared so to me

[PG]

[Gates Ticonderoga]

The usage of "Scoundrel and Villain" certainly suggested that General Gates had made particularly damning accusations of Gansevoort to other officers and perhaps even public circles. Even despite this, the clearest evidence of personal confrontation between the two officers was most evident at the end of the letter:

"...I have taken the Hints in your first Letter's but when I perceived that I scarce received a line from your Honour but contained some implied censure upon my conduct as Commanding officer here I confess it Created some Jealously in me that your Honour was diffident of me as an Officer and a Gentleman which I attributed either to your not knowing me or from the misrepresentation of my Conduct by some malignant Person's, And I cannot conclude without observing to you that I had before conceiv'd my Honour somewhat attak'd by a Passage in your Honours Letter of the 17th July."[58]

Depending on the speed of message delivery given the two officers' locations, a letter dated two days later from General Gates speaks absolutely nothing in regards to the Gansevoort's defensive response letter and instead continued to demand supplies from Gansevoort's store.[59] On August 17th, Peter received word from his brother Leonard announcing that he had reported the dispute to General Schuyler, who made a convincing defense on Peter's behalf.[60]

24—From Leonard Gansevoort

Albany August 17th 1776:

My Dear Friend & Br I have just Time to inform you that I have spoke to Genl Schuyler respecting your affair with Genl Gates he is exceedingly happy of your spirit and the appearance of the rectitude of your Conduct by desiring it to be scrutiniz'd and enquir'd into I also shew'd him the draft of your Letter which I told him I expected you had sent forward, he says that it will be best that you make a representation of the Matter in Writing to him but that you therein cautiously avoid giving up the Command longer than untill you are cleared of the Charge, get our good Friend Dr Potts to give you his Assistance and tell him he must pardon my not writing to him before alledging that the Loss of my Dear little Son & your Friend Abraham Cuyler Gansevoort[61] *and the consequent distresses of my Family has prevented me assuring him that I will chearfully embrace every opportunity of communicating all Occurrences worthy of Attention in our Quarter in exchange. In the mean Time I beg my kind Remembrance to him and all the good Gent of your Mess.*

I am with Sincere Love Your's very Sincerely

Leonard Gansevoort

Colo Gansevoort [Fort George]

turn over

The Genl thinks it will be best to leave after taking in the Words—Honor to myself and Justice to the Public demand that I should immediately then leave out all untill you come to—beg that a Court of Inquiry may be called &c

A September 12th letter from Captain Benjamin Egberts,[62] storekeeper at Fort George, revealed that the troubled Gansevoort was preparing to leave Fort George in order to preserve his honor and best serve the New York community.[63] Judging by the continued correspondence afterwards between Gansevoort and other officers, his post was saved by General Schuyler's interference. Regardless, these interactions did not change the fact that Gansevoort had been labeled as a disorganized and inexperienced officer.

25—From Benjamin Egberts

Ticonderoga Sept the 12th 1776

Dear Sir/ I hear'd a while ago that you was to leave fort George which I was very Sorry for but under Stood Since you keep the Command there which pleases me much in hopes of being Sent as Ordered there Soon as I understand that the Commissary of Artillerry from mount Independance is Coming on this Side I then Shall applie to him to Get a Conductor in my Stead, I understand that General Gates has wrote to you & General Schuyler about Shepherd's Sending things over to this Pace very irreguler the General I believe wants to know by whome Shepherd is put in that Office. If he is turn'd of, I hope you will get me to Come to fort George in his stead in so doing you will Oblidge Sir your most Obedient & humble Servt

Benjn Egberts

PS I enclose you a letter to Mr P Van Rensselar which I hope you will forward as Soon as possible it's concerning my being sent to fort George & Some artikles much Wanted my Compliments to Brother Jacob & all our friends at fort George Rum &c is very skarce & dear at this Place Some times I cannot get a drink of tody in a whole day unless I go to the Generals & beg one

B.E. Store keeper Gnl

[PG Fort George]

[on the envelope] Some old Junk is wanted very much if you have any at fort George I will be very glad you'll it pr first Boat

In the fall, evidence of a budding relationship between Peter and Catherine Van Schaick, his regimental commander's sister, was becoming apparent as they started to exchange correspondence. Her "agreeable epistle of the 27th August" requested a rendezvous in September. Unfortunately, Peter feared it would be unlikely for him to obtain liberty from Fort George until the fate of Fort Ticonderoga was settled. Gansevoort had received information regarding Guy Carleton's plans to raid the Champlain Valley fortifications in the coming months. He concluded his correspondence by expressing his "sincerest sentiments of love" to her.

26—To Catherine Van Schaick

Fort George 24th Septr 1776

Dear Caty I was Honor'd with your agreeable Epistle of the 27th August three or four days since inclosed in your Brother Johns

I was much surprized at your Brother in forwarding your Letter sooner

I should think myself very ungratefull had your Letter been received soon after the above date not to have answered it till now

You conclude in yours with the thoughts of seeing me this Month I dread much that we shall not have the pleasure of seeing each other till the Latter and of next month—I dont Expect to obtain Liberty to leve this post till the fate of Ticonderoga is Determined, if Genl Carleton means to attack the last Mentioned post it will be within One Month, how long and tedious will that month ~~Needs~~ Needs prove till I shall have the pleasure of seeing her ~~in~~ in whom my future Happiness depends, but I shall indeavor to pass away the time in Contemplating my past happy Moments I have had in in your Agreeable Company

I beg that you will Deliver the inclosed by the first Opportunity I must concludue with the Sincerest Sentiments of Love

Your affectionate and Sincere Friend

P: Gansevoort

PS I must beg an answer to this by the first convenient opportunity

To Miss Caty Van Schaick

The remainder of 1776 continued unabated. Reinforcements were finally beginning to trickle into Gansevoort's camp and General Schuyler issued specific instructions for the enlistment of new officers. Following the official Declaration of Independence in July, Gansevoort had taken the Oath of Allegiance to the United States in late October.[64] By October, Congress had issued a mandate for all "non commissioned Officer and Soldier who shall inlist in the Service of the united States" to take an oath of allegiance.

27—The Oath of Allegiance

I Swear to be true to the united States of America, and To Serve them honestly and faithfully against All their Enemies or Opposers Whatsoever and To Observe and Obey the orders of the Continental Congress and the orders of the Generals and officers Set Over me by Them

28—Jacob Cuyler[65] and Robert Yates[66] to Cornelius Wynkoop

Albany October 28 1776

Sir The above is the form of the oath which Congress require to be administered to every non commissioned Officer and Soldier who shall inlist in the Service of the united States upon the new Establishment, ~~of~~ and you will be pleased to furnish the recruiting Officers of our State with Copies there of

We are Sir your most Obedt & humble Servts

Jacob Cuyler Rob Yates

Coll Wynkoop

[Sent to PG at Fort George]

Meanwhile, the confrontation with Gates continued. A November 9th letter from Ticonderoga implied Gates' growing anger over Gansevoort's apparent insubordination; this letter in particular showed Gates had been "astonished" that more bateaus had not been sent from Fort George. Opposite Schuyler's messages that there may be British troop movement north of Gansevoort's position, Gates insisted "there was not an Enemy within a hundred Miles of your Post."[67]

29—From Horatio Gates

Tyconderoga November 9th 1776

Sir I am astonished at your keeping all the Batteaux at the South End of the Lake, and not Sending forward the Flour. By your last Return, exclusive of the Militia, you had 231 Officers included fit for duty at Fort George. I am convinced there is not an Enemy within a hundred Miles of your Post, so, you need not have any Apprehensions upon that Account.—It is my Positive Orders you dispatch immediately every Boat you have full of Flour to this Landing, fifty Men is more than Sufficient for your present Garrison. The Bearer takes Sixty Men with him to assist in bringing over the Flour, and I have been obliged to carry the Boats over this Carrying Place, to transport him and his Party, not having one at this End of Lake George. Dispatch the large Vessells as quick as Possible and continue to keep the Batteaux going as long as the Navigation is open. I desire you will See the Batteaux full Freighted, and as it grows late in the Season Order Seven Men into each Batteau.

I am Sir Your most Obedt Humble Servant

Horatio Gates

[PG Fort George]

The close of the first chapter of Gansevoort's military career during the War of Independence seemed to end on a foreboding tone. He had experienced the rough trek into Canada, along with the sickness of his first commanding officer, and many of his fellow men at the Quebec siege. After experiencing the sickness, desertion, and disorganization of his ranks, the Gates' correspondence called into question as to whether this experience had transformed Gansevoort into a soldier worthy of his post. Had the letters ended here, any researcher would be led to believe that Gansevoort's military career was essentially over, if not in stagnation. Luckily, Gansevoort managed to obtain a transfer to Saratoga by mid–November, temporarily escaping Gates' criticisms.[68]

30—From John Lansing, Jr.

Head Quarters Fort George Novr 18th: 1776

General Orders Lieutenant Colonel Ten Eyck, with that part of Colo: Van Dyck's Regiment[69] *now at this post to march immediately to Fort Edward and join the Regiment.*

Lieut: Colonel Gansevoort, with that part of Colo: Van Schaick's Regiment now at this post to march to the Barracks at Saratoga, as soon as Waggons can be procured to carry their Baggage to Fort Edward—Their Baggage to be their embarked in Batteaus and conveyed from post to post to Saratoga.

Colo: poor[70] *with his Regiment to follow Colo: Van Schaick's to the same place.*

No Officer, Non commissioned Officer or Soldier by any Means or on my account whatever to take a Waggon or Cart, without first applying to the Waggon Master for the same who will deliver Carriages to those that ought to have them.

Colo: Starks's[71] *and late General Reid's Regiments to remain at this post until further orders*

The Hospital to be removed to Albany as soon as Carriages can be procured to convey the sick & Stores

By Order of the General

John Lansing Junr Secy

In a letter received, his brother Leonard laid out for Gansevoort the rules of commanding a regiment in preparation for his upcoming promotion. On November 21st 1776, Gansevoort was given the command of the re-established Third New York Regiment with the rank of Colonel. His regiment consisted of eight companies. For the remainder of the year, he corresponded with many individuals, including newly appointed Lieutenant Colonel Marinus Willett,[72] Major Robert Cochran[73] and Pay Master Jeremiah Van Rensselaer,[74] concerning a mass recruiting campaign throughout the countryside to build up the regiment. It was the task of the officers to recruit for the regiment and for companies they commanded.[75]

31—From Leonard Gansevoort

Dear Br I expected to have had Time & perhaps an Opportunity before ~~I~~ now to have paid you a Short Visit or to have Seen you ~~before I go down~~, but now begin to dispair of doing myself that Pleasure I have a few thoughts upon my Mind which I beg leave to communicate to you by Letter, which as you are honoured by Your Country with the Command of a Regiment respect only yourself

1. That you keep proper Accts of all the Money by you paid to the Officers of your Choir

(2) That you make a receipt Book in which have all your receipts drawn specifying the Uses for which the Money is intended then will your Accts be at once always perspicuous and Clear—

(3) If any of your Officers refuse to accept their Commissions immediately and without Loss of Time recommend others—

(4) pick out Some young Fellows to recommend for Ensigns as requested by Mr Yates's Letter

(5) Recommend your pay Master Surgeon & Mates—

(6) Tho' much out of Fashion in those Days I would recommend to you by all Means to procure a good Chaplain, and consider that a proper Sense of Religion and the Duties of your Men will thereby be preserved and promulgated

(7) I wish you would signify to me by Letter where you incline to Serves whether in the Southern or Northern Departments as I Shall endeavour to get it settled with General Schuyler

There are many other Matters which I could wish to have an opportunity to confer with you about—

Col: Van Dyck is appointed L: Col: to Col: Van Schaick—

The Congress have down you amble Justice—

Adieu Your's very Sincerely &c

Leonard Gansevoort

Albany Novr 27 1776

Col: Gansevoort [Saratoga]

32—From John Lansing, Jr.

Head Quarters Saratoga Decemr 10th 1776

General Orders The recruiting officers appointed to enlist Men to serve during the War may recruit from any Corps now in the Service not engaged to serve during the War makeing a return to the commanding officer of the day on which the Recruit reinlisted that he may be borne on the pay Roll of the Corps he was formerly enlisted and no longer—All recruiting officers to make Weekly Returns to the Commander in Chief of the Northern Department of the Men enlisted by them, specifying the Day when the Corps the recruit belong to if their former Inlistment is not expired or the Corps they last belonged to, if the Term of Inlistment was expired at the Time of their Reingagement

Such Non commissioned officers & Privates who are now at any of the Garrisons in this Department and shall engage in the new Levies will after their respective Garrisons are ~~releved return~~ Relieved be Permitted to come down on Furlows for a Month

By order of the Genl

John Lansing Junr Secty

I certify that the Above is a true copy of an Original Order Sent to me by Genl Schuyler

P Gansevoort Colonel

33—To Marinus Willett

[December 11th 1776]

Sir Mr Jacob Cuyler one of the Committee of Arrangement having informed me that you had accepted of your Appointment as Lieut: Col: to my Battalion and that he had paid you £1800 ~~to be~~ to be distributed among the Officers of my Battalion down below—I beg you will inform me by the first Day of January ~~who~~ which of the~~m~~ officers ~~you have~~ have accepted ~~&~~ or declin'd the Cash advanc'd them respectively for the purpose of recruiting, and the Numbers of Men by them Severally inlisted, I must also beg your Strict Attention that the Officers are kept faithfully to do this Business ~~as the Season advances very fast~~ that we may be ready to take the Field as early in the Spring as may be necessary—The Officers in this Quarter ~~he~~ meet with very good Success

I am Sir Your Hum Servant

[PG]

Refers to Willette

Marinus Willett. Engraved by J. Rogers, c. early 1860s (Gansevoort-Lansing collection. Manuscripts and Archives Division. The New York Public Library. Astor, Lenox and Tilden Foundations).

34—To Robert Cochran

[December 1776]

Sir I enclose you a Copy of the Arrangement of the third Battalion of Troops to be raised in the State of New York to Serve during the War by which you will perceive that you are appointed Major to the said Battalion—

The Bearer hereof Capt. Aorson[76] *is also appointed Capt in the said Battalion and has my Orders to repair to Fort Schuyler for the purpose of recruiting, should you have it in your power by your Influence ~~to be~~ among the Men of Colo: Elmore's Regt to assist him, I make no doubt but he will receive it—you will observe that recruiting officers have by a Resolve of Congress a right to inlist 2 Men of any Corps or State (who are not already engag'd to Serve during the War.*

I must also desire you to inform me by the earliest Opportunity whether you accept of your Appointment,

I am with great respect Sir Your very Huml Servant

[PG]

To Major Robert Cochran

PS. When you conceive yourself of no longer use at Fort Schuyler in assisting Capt. Austin to recruit you have my permission to return to Albany—

35—To Jeremiah Van Rensselaer

Sir I give you this Notice of your Appointment as Pay Master to the third Battalion of the Continental Army raising in the State of New York, and for your acting in that Station this shall be to you a sufficient Voucher—I have it not in my Power to give you any particular Instructions as they are not yet promulgated by the Honorable the Continental Congress You will therefore only observe such Orders ~~such Orders~~ as you shall receive from me or the Commanding Officer ~~Amidst~~ present

I am Sir Your Hum Servant

[PG]

[December 1776]

Refers to Jeremiah Van Rensselaer

Chapter Three

1777: The Siege of Fort Schuyler

Out of all the years Gansevoort would serve during the American Revolution, 1777 would come to define him as a soldier and an officer. His defense at Fort Schuyler was the climax of his military career; his actions ultimately redeemed him in the eyes of both New Yorkers and other more experienced Continental officers. Just a year before, he had fallen under intense criticism from General Horatio Gates, who appeared convinced that Gansevoort was an irresponsible and inexperienced young officer appointed to his post purely out of family connections in New York. Certainly considering Gates' reputation as a seasoned commander, other officers in the Continental Army became wary of Gansevoort's character themselves.

British General John Burgoyne was proving himself the same year albeit to the disadvantage of the American forces. With native scouts and small bands of Hessian mercenaries, Burgoyne planned to sail down the Hudson River into central New York. Along the way, Burgoyne would capture any forts overlooking the river passage to secure a supply line, as well as confiscate the precious little armaments the defending Americans possessed. From there, Burgoyne's forces would then march into central New York, capturing key cities and ultimately cut off the northern American colonies from their southern counterparts. If this strategy were to prove successful, the British could then initiate a massive offensive with troops coming from the Canadian border to the north, and the Mohawk River Valley to the west and southwest. As Gansevoort would be placed in charge of the defense of Fort Schuyler on the Mohawk, he would sooner or later meet Burgoyne's forces in a desperate attempt to hold the line. If Gansevoort were to fail, Continental forces would be required to send a brigade to recover the fort, while fully aware that their thinned forces would have to eventually face the fury of Burgoyne's main army.

Orders issued from General Schuyler concerning the defense and upkeep of the fort were sent throughout March. General Schuyler sent men to maintain any engineering repairs the fort would require; he also indicated a "New Moddle" of the fort, most likely to reposition heavy artillery towards Burgoyne's advance.[1]

36—Extracts of Letters and Orders from General Schuyler to Colonel Samuel Elmores While Commanding at Fort Schuyler

Extracts from Letter March 6th: 1777
It is a Matter of much Moment to the United States that no Officer or Soldiers Should on

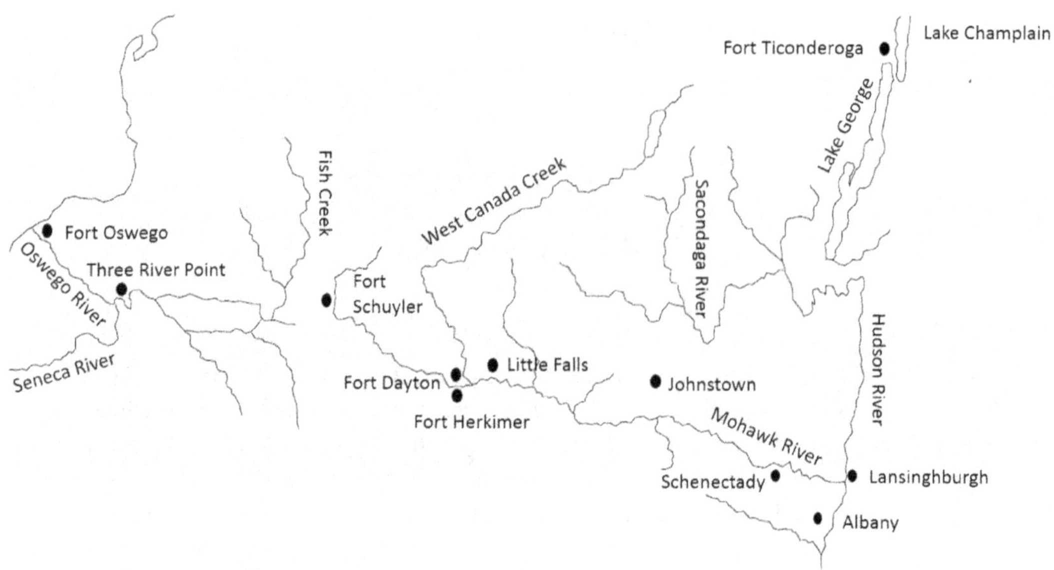

Line drawing based on the "Map of the State of New York, with its Counties" by Hoffman and Knickerbocker, 1788 (Gansevoort-Lansing collection. Manuscripts and Archives Division. The New York Public Library. Astor, Lenox and Tilden Foundations).

any Account Trade with them, and you will therefore Publish as my Orders that None Presume to do it, on Pain of being Punished for Disobedience of Orders, Should any however be so Audacious as to contravene the Orders, you will if an Officer, Immediately put him Under Arrest, if a Noncommissioned or Soldier confine him and Report to me that proper Measures may be Taken to bring them to Punishment—If an Officer has Occasion for any thing Immediately for his own Use Mr Hansen will Purchase it and Deliver it at First Cash

Extract from Letter March 19th: 1777

Captain Marquizee[2] *has in Charge from the General to New Moddle Fort Schuyler and Make Some additional Fortifications at that Place: You will afford him all the Assistance in your Power to Effect that Necessary work, and comply with Such Requisitions as he Shall make to Enable him to Do it with Dispatch*

The Above Extracts are Taken Verbatim from General Schuylers Letter

Samuel Elmore Col Commanding Fort Schuyler

Colo: Elmore would Recommend to Colo: Garnsworth For to be Friendly to the Indians as it is of Consequence and helpfull to the Cause

In June 1776, after the suggestion by General Washington of a potential threat from Canada, General Schuyler sent Colonel Elias Dayton to repair the works at Fort Stanwix. He accomplished little but renamed it Fort Schuyler.[3] In October 1776, Colonel Samuel Elmore's Connecticut regiment had replaced Colonel Dayton's Third New Jersey Regiment, the first American troops to occupy Fort Schuyler.

Fort Stanwix, named after its builder, General John Stanwix, was built in 1758, during the French and Indian War to replace Fort William, which was built in 1746. Amidst the wilderness thirty miles from civilization, a square fort, "having four bastions surrounded by a broad ditch, eighteen feet deep, with a covert way and glaces [sic] was positioned between

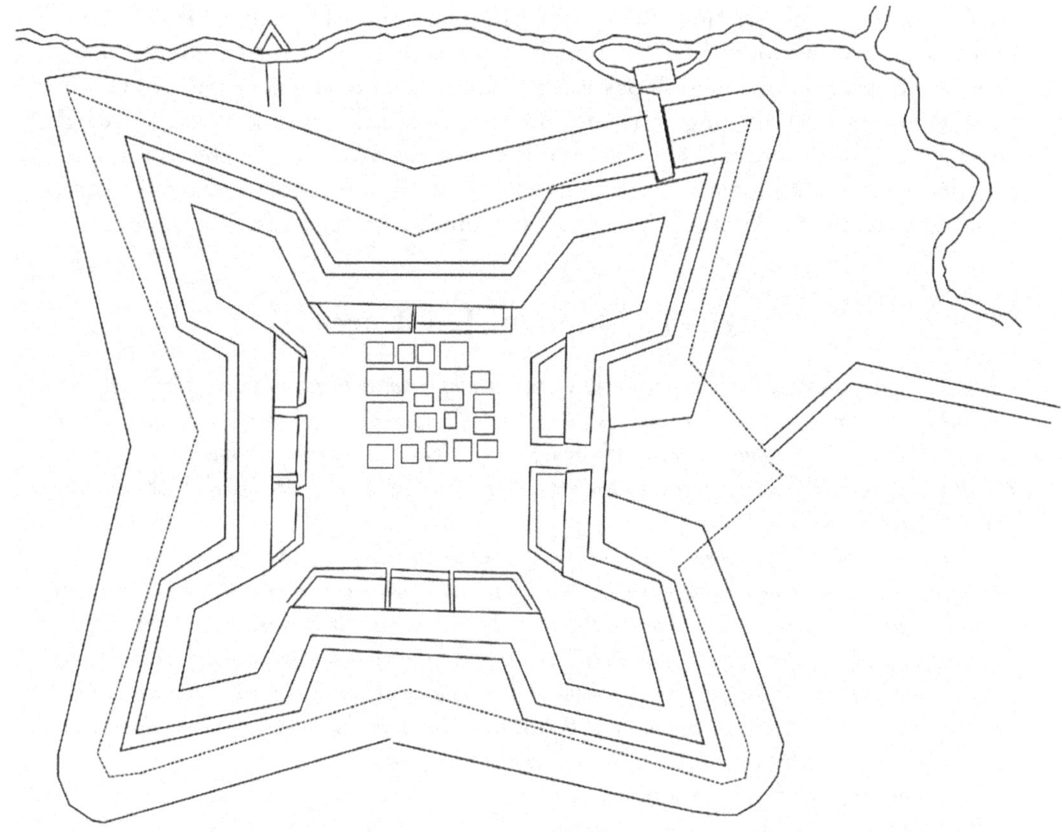

Line drawing based on the plan of Fort Stanwix, built at Oneida Station, by provincial troops, in 1758 (courtesy Library of Congress).

the navigable waters of the Mohawk River and Wood Creek." With a "row of perpendicular pickets was placed in the center of the ditch, while another horizontal row was fixed around the rampants," this post guarded the eastern end of the Great Oneida Carrying Place (De-o-wain-sta). It was erected for £60,000 but left in ruins after the French and Indian War came to a close when Sir William Johnson made the Treaty of Stanwix in 1768 with the Indians. The treaty defined the land boundary between the Indians and the white settlers in central New York.[4] "On November 5, 1768, Sir William Johnson took deed to all the lands of the Six Nations south of the settled boundary line and paid the Six Nations $10,000 for their interests. The boundary as adjusted ran from the mouth of the Tennessee, followed the Ohio and Allegheny rivers to Kittaniny and thence to the west branch of the Susquehanna to the east branch of the Susquehanna northeastward to the junction of Canada and Wood Creeks, its northern boundary. The north of this line lay the land of the Six Nations. South of it they ceded their interests to the Crown. Thus did they barter away their birthright."[5]

Gansevoort's correspondence in the early months of 1777 do not seem to indicate such a formidable confrontation on the horizon. Ordered to Fort Schuyler, Gansevoort sent word to the leader of the Albany County Militia and President of the New York Provincial Congress, Abraham Ten Broeck,[6] expressing concern regarding his regiments being dispersed throughout the region. He also regretted and stated that he "must once more apologize to the Convention for not sending a Return of my Regiment agreeable to their Order."[7] In spite of this setback, Gansevoort defended himself by saying the very decentralization of the soldiers in the area made it almost impossible to construct a correct regimental return. It was possible that General Washington would consider this lack of response in a negative light, as Gansevoort made sure to "beg ... Interposition with his Excellency George Washington" in order to settle this problem once and for all.[8] Ironically, the problem of greatly delayed regimental returns would haunt Gansevoort as a militia commander later in the war.

37—To Abraham Ten Broeck

Sir I must once more apologize to the Convention for not sending a Return of my Regiment agreeable to their Order ~~but~~ The dispersion of my Officers upon the recruiting Service has prevented me but as I am now under marching Orders for Fort Schuyler with that part of my Regiment which is here I have ordered all the Officers in with their Recruits I shall Soon be able to transmit you the Return Requested—

It gives me great Pain ~~to be~~ that part of my Regiment is separated from me and wish for nothing more than to have them ~~together~~ Joined, it gives me little Concern what department I Serve in, but when Corps are so divided they can do little Honor to themselves or the State they belong to, and believe me that my utmost Exertions ~~will~~ would not be wanting to make them usefull—permit then to beg your Interposition with his Excellency General Washington that we may be Joined and as I said before I am indifferent where we Join, but conceive it would contribute to the Credit of the State if all the Regiments could be together

I am most respectfully Sir Your very Hum Servant

[PG]

The Honble Abraham Ten Broeck Esqr President &c

[March 17th 1777]

In a March 29 letter to Lieutenant Colonel Willett, Gansevoort announced that all soldiers on leave must immediately join with their regiments in anticipation of a new campaign.[9] Gansevoort received immediate orders to secure a house and farm field near a swamp and adjoining "Brodthacks Field" with the intention of securing hay, vegetables, and to make small repairs to the fences.[10] The Marquis de Lafayette[11] implied that Gansevoort's men needed to prepare for a possible siege and with the supervision of engineer Colonel Gouvion,[12] they would accomplish this task. Surely Burgoyne had begun his movement down the river[13]; full repairs on Fort Schuyler and outlying defensive positions needed to be completed as soon as possible.

Gansevoort's correspondence of March 31 to Chairman of the Committee of Arrangement Robert Yates recommended William Colbreath[14] to the rank of lieutenant when a vacancy appeared in his regiment. A journal, attributed to Colbreath, would provide vital information on the daily events during the siege.

38—To Marinus Willett

Albany 29th March 1777

Sir. As the Season for opening the Campaign is near at hand, the General Commanding the Northern Department has desir'd in General Orders that all Soldiers now on Furlough do immediately Join their respective Regiments and that no more furloughs be granted which you'll please to See executed.

You will have a Force run from ~~the House where~~ Swamp [Casp] ~~place~~ Stefanus the Frenchman's House formerly stood to the River and another from the Crippelbush at the lower End of Brodthacks Field[15] *to the River ~~which will~~ with a Swinging Gate in Each these two Fences will be enclosure sufficient to supply with Grass and Hay and secure the Garden—as ~~it~~ there is too much Work to be done at present to have the fences made ~~at present~~ as they formerly were*

As Soon as the Season will permit you will have the Garden put in Seed, that the Garrison may not be without Vegetables in their Season—

Colo Gouvion the Engineer who is with you at present the Marquis de Lafayette informs me will be ordered to the Southward Soon, you will therefore receive from him every necessary Instruction to compleat the Fort ~~that we may not be in~~ for a Seige—

You will constantly make returns to me of every Necessary wanting at the Fort, that I may procure them.—

I am Yours &c

[PG]

You will order the Quarter to send Down the Account of Rations and parts of Rations which may be due to the Regt

[Copy of a Letter sent Lieut Colo. Willett]

39—To Robert Yates

Albany March 31 1777

Sir William Colbrath who is appointed Ensign to the 8th Company of the third Regiment I must ~~recommend~~ beg leave to recommend to the Committee of Arrangement as an exceeding good officer he has been indefatigable in the recruiting Service ~~and as much that I believe he has inlisted~~ and deserves the attention of his Country, ~~I am~~ should any Vacancy offer for a Lieutenancy in my Regiment would be happy of his appointment thereto it being but the Rank he held in Col: Nicolson's Regiment[16] *last Year.*

I ~~now~~ must inform you that I am under marching Orders for Fort Schuyler with that part of my Regiment which is here ~~without Commissions~~ and should be very happy to receive the Commissions of my Officers before we begin our March

I am most respectfully Sir Your and the Committees Very Hum Servant

[PG]

Robert Yates Esqr Chairman of the Committee of Arrangement

General Gates sent orders to Gansevoort on the 24th declaring that the Continental Congress had appointed Gates commander of the army in the Northern Department replacing General Schuyler. Gates had accused Schuyler of dereliction of duty following the blunder at Fort Ticonderoga. Therefore, Gansevoort would be placed under his direct command.[17] Gates demanded an immediate troop return, and an exact return of all provisions held by the respective regiments. These orders would be in effect on the first and 15th of every month thereafter. Whether or not this policy was put into effect due to Gansevoort's delay of his previous returns, this new policy put more pressure on Gansevoort to act with the punctuality befitting his rank.

40—From Horatio Gates

Albany 24th: April 1777

Sir The Honorable the Continental Congress having thoughts proper to Appoint me to Command The Army in the Northern Department of America:—You will please to Transmit by the Bearer, a Return of the Troops under Your Command, agreeable to The Inclosed Form, which I desire you will Sign with Your Name, Rank, and Regiments; You will also order the Commissary or Commissaries, at your post, to send me an Exact Return of all provissions, Ordinance Stores, Intrenching Tools, and Stores of every kind, belonging to the United States, now in His, or their Charge or posession, and this I expect to have regularly Comply'd with, on the 1st: & 15th: days, of every Month hereafter ensuing: You will also please constantly to inform me, of all Extraordinaries that happen, and of such undoubted Intelligence as you may from time to time receive, of the Motions of the Enemy's Troops, and the Conducts of those, disaffected to the Freedom of America.

I am Sir Your humble Servant

Horatio Gates

To Collo Gansevoort

The Officer Commanding at Fort Schuyler

Two days later, Gates ordered Gansevoort to move to Fort Schuyler, in order to relieve the fort's commander, Colonel Samuel Elmore, and to take the utmost care in relaying any intelligence to both Gates and the militia forces stationed in Albany.[18]

41—From Horatio Gates

Orders for Colonel Peter Gansevoort, going on Command to Fort Schuyler.

You will proceed directly to Fort Schuyler, and take the Command of that Post, relieving Colonel Elmore, whose time of Service is expired:—You will receive from him the Orders, & directions given by Major General Schuyler, which you will Strictly Obey.—You are from time to time, to acquaint me, and the Commanding Officer in Albany, with all extraordinary Occurrences at, or in the Vicinity of the Fort: and regularly make Returns, agreeable to the Forms & directions now Deliver'd to you.—Given at Head Quarters in Albany, the 26th: of April 1777—

Horatio Gates Major General

[PG]

A detachment of the Third New York Regiment under the command of Major Robert Cochran arrived on April 17, 1777. Gansevoort arrived on the third of May and informed Schuyler that the works were "untenable" and in no condition for defense. The ditch was filled in and the pickets had rotted away and fallen down. Two days later, Gansevoort wrote to John Van Schaick to inform that he had arrived safely and found "it here extreemly pleasant and Agreeable."

42—To John G. Van Schaick

Fort Schuyler 5th May 1777

Dear Sir, I have just time to acquaint you of my safe Arrivel at this post on the 3d Instant.

I find it here extreemly pleasant and Agreeable—I have nothing particular to write to you, I beg if any thing Transpires worth communicating you will write me You may be assured I shall always be very happy to receive a line from you You will be good enough to deliver the inclosed and you'll much oblidge

Sir Your friend and Very Hum Servt

Peter Gansevoort

To Mr John G. Van Schaick

On May 7, Gates reminded officers on the frontier that no bartering with natives was allowed on penalty of imprisonment.[19] The adjutant of the fort was ordered to make three copies and to hang them at the fort's headquarters, the fort gate and at a neighboring house belonging to German-native John Roof.[20]

43—From Horatio Gates

Fort Schuyler 7th May 1777

Garrison Orders Parole Ward C. Sign Schuyler

All Officers and Soldiers, the Militia The Inhabitants and Every Person Whatever, wether Living, or Having only a Temporary Residence at this Place are Strictly forbid by Colo Gansevoort—in Pursurance of General Gate's orders to him. To Buy or Sell any article or thing whatever of any Indian or Indian's that may come from Time to Time to this Post, Should any Person Whatever be so daring As to Preservance. To have the least dealing or Traffic Whatever, with any of them. They may Depend on being Proceeded against, and Punished agreeable to the General's orders on that Head All officers non commissioned officers and soldiers belonging to this Garrison wheather Continantel or Militia are ordered to attend the Parade in the Fort this Evening at the Beating of the Retreat to hear the Above Orders read

The Adjutant is Ordered to take three copies from the Above Orders Ralitive to Indian affairs and fix one at Head Quarters one at the Fort Gate and the other at Mr Rouf's

Peter Gansevoort Colonel

Orders for Colonel Peter Gansevoort, going on Command to Fort Schuyler

The middle part of May revealed that the needs for repairs to the fort were moving at an incredibly slow pace and that supplies needed to conduct the repairs were unable to be provided by other sources. Unfortunately, Engineer Bernard Maussac de La Marquisie had been denied extra bateaus by General Gates. Gansevoort, needing the necessary supplies, requested another company of bateaux men to carry supplies down the river. Assistant deputy-quartermaster Henry Glen[21] replied on May 14 informing Gansevoort that Gates denied his request as he could not spare them from the fortifications on Lake Champlain and Lake George. Glen reassured Gansevoort that Captain Myndert Wemple[22] would continue his route between Little Falls and Fort Schuyler carrying boards and limestone for de La Marquisie, who was in charge of repairing the fort. Probably in response at Gansevoort's inquiry, Glen also mentioned that Marinus Willett had gone with General Arthur MacDougal to "Denbury" [Danbury]. Danbury had been raided and burned by British General William Tryon.

44—From Henry Glen

Schonectady 14th May 1777

Dear Sir Whereas the Engineer at your post Mr B. D. Marquizie has occasion for some men to carry boards from the upper part of the Settlements for the use of the Garrison. I have accordingly applyed to Genl Gates for another company of Battoemen; but he tells me he can not spare them as yet I have ordered Captn M. B. Wimple of the Battoemen to continue between the little falls and your post in carrying boards for the Engineer for one trip and would be much obliged to you if you could let Mr Marquisie have as many hands as will man the 4 battoes that were brought to your post by Captn Arson to carry boards, Lymestone &c. I shall pay them 21 pr day till such time as I can be furnished with more Battoemen from Hudson River. You will be pleased not to detain Wimp longer than one trip as I want to send flower to your Garrison. Nothing new. No news from Jersey lately. The Last Acct of Col. Willoot was he was gone with General MacDougal to Denbury.[23] *I have given Your grid Irons to Mr Wimp hope they will answer the purpose.*

I am Dear Sir Your Humble Serv.

Henry Glen

P.S. my Compliments to Captn Arson and the Rest of the Garrison

To Colonel Peter Gansevoort

Apparently the orders issued months earlier were having little effect on the men, who were bored by inactivity and in want of supplies or other things to occupy themselves. It seemed that many of the soldiers and lower officers were regularly violating these orders in secrecy. This emphasis on past orders came at an important point regarding Indian diplomacy. Gates's letter only a day after announced that Major Jean Arthur de Vermonet[24] was to pass through Fort Schuyler with the intention of negotiating with the Six Tribes.[25] Apparently this excursion was successful as Leonard Gansevoort congratulated his brother for "the marks of Friendship ... from the Aborijines of America."[26]

45—From Leonard Gansevoort

Dear Brother —My Father just now Shew'd me a Letter he had received from you by Express who is to return to morrow—

I congratulate you upon the marks of Friendship which you receive from the Aborijines of America, your good sense will point out to you that it is not only your Interest but Duty also to cultivate their Friendship for give me leave to tell you, that I believe it will be the only Thing in which you will be able to render any service to your Country this Campaign because removed with your Regiment from the Seat of Action and there being no probability of any descent from the Westward you will be obliged to cast about in your Mind in what respect you can contribute to the Welfare of your Country, and permit me farther to suggest that it is an Object of the greatest moment not to this State in particular but America in general to maintain Peace and amity with them—and whoever can in the least contribute thereto is loudly called upon to leave no means unessayed to accomplish that great End.—

I would advise you to confer with them according to their Custom and from Time to Time to transmit Copies of your proceedings upon this Head to the Commissioners here and the Command in Chief of the Department Mr. Hansen may be of infinite Service to you in this matter and I am persuaded from his benevolent disposition will with Alacrity will afford you all the Assistances in his power

We have nothing material new from Head Quarters except that Genl Washington's Army is increasing very rapidly and that he was advancing upon the Enemy's Lands, the Enemy have thrown up very extensive Lines, a Strong Indication of their Weakness—

Lieut: Col: Willet arrived here Yesterday Morning with about 200 men he will March on Monday Next.

Lieut: Tap of your Regiment and another Gent: named Rip who came up with him have informed me severally that they have seen and convers'd with a French Gent: at Fish Kill[27] *who ~~informed~~ said that he was a General in the French Service that he had left a French Fleet and 12,000 Troops in the River St. Lawrence that he was going to congress to acquaint them therewith, that he came to Fishkill escorted by a Number of New England Troop and was from thence escorted by a Troop of light Horse to Philadelphia what think you of the Congress now?*

Your Mother sends you pr. Mr Edward S Willet[28] *your Silver Spoon and Camp Stool*

—I have the happiness to inform you of the Welfare of all your Friends—Adieu and may God bless and prosper you and your Corps

I am in Sincerity Dr Brother Your's very affectionately

Leonard Gansevoort

Albany May 17. 1777.

Remember me kindly to Van Veghten. Hansen Cochran Aorson Staat[29] *&c &c*

On May 18, because of rumors of a British invasion from the west, Lieutenant Colonel Willett was ordered to remove the remainder of the regiment stationed at Fort Constitution[30] to Fort Schuyler. He and his regiment set sail to Albany on three sloops, arriving on May 21. He proceeded to Schenectady[31] and from there to Fort Schuyler, arriving there on May 29. As soon as the Third New York Regiment arrived, Gansevoort began to repair the fort.[32]

On May 23, Gansevoort attempted to explain the numerous difficulties his regiment was experiencing in maintaining their defenses to Gates.[33] The one hundred silver dollars left by Colonel Elmore, the fort's former commander, had almost run out; whether this was due to unnecessary bartering with native tribes or farmers was unknown. The majority of the money was set aside to be used in further negotiations with the natives and without it they would be unable to offer the natives anything in return for their wares and good standing. In addition, he requested two horses to be provided in case natives lodging with Gansevoort's regiment were in need of emergency transport.

Rum supplies were short despite Gansevoort's commissioning of some less than a month earlier. He noted that the men had not indulged in any quantity of spirits for almost a week, and that may severely affect morale and the current work rate.[34] He finished by warning Gates that the undersupplied men in charge of the bateaus and transporting repair materials to the fort were moving in a "Slow Manner ... Between this and Schenetay [Schenectady]."[35] He believed that at least another company of men would be required to hasten the transport, and that another ten bateaus were needed to transport vital boards for repairing the men's barracks.

46—To Horatio Gates

Sir Colo Elmore Before his Departure from this Garrison duly Deliv'd me the Difflt orders from Genl Schuyler with 100 Silver Dolears Being the Whole of the Money he had in Hand Belonging to be, united States as he informed me—The Hard Money which Genl Schuyler Sent Last year To this Post is now Nearly Expended—

It was solely intended for any Sudden occasion with the Indians—

I have found Since my arrival here that I Cannot well doe with and a Some of Moneys in Paper—for the Public use here—& Some Silver Solely—for the Indians to be Lodged with me for which To acct for when Caleed upon—I conceive it allso Necessary that Two Good Horses be kept at this place for any Sudden Emergency—

I would allso Request yr Honor that a Quantity, of Rum might be Sent out Immediately—as our fatigue & work men have already been 7 days without it what Little is Left Being Referred for the Indians—who Daily Come & go from this Place I shall afford the Engineer have Every assurance in My Power to Promote the Speedy Completion of the Works—which ~~this he is sent To are~~ are Intended at this Fort this Season But I must inform yr Honor that Every Man Belonging To my Regt here will be obligd to be in Fatigue Except the Necessary Guard & Scouts—The whole of which it is my opinion will not be near Enough to Compleat the Extensive work which are to be made here—as the whole of the Fort & Barracks is to be new Moddelled I have thought proper to advise your Honor of this—& In Case your Honor Should think Proper—To order more troops this way—that the sooner it is done the Better—

I Must not omit to acquaint your Honor—in what Slow Manner the Battoemen Ply Between this and Schenetay—I have Now Looked for the above Seven Days what can be the Reason of their not coming I do not know—

When they arrive here I Dispatch them Back the Same Day—or Next Morning—

I think they ought not to be allowed to Stay above 48 Hour in Schencty—

I think anothr Co will be wanted for we will want Boards from the Mills Between this & ~~Canajohary~~ Caughnewauga[36]*—I shall be undr Necessy of Having at Least Ten Battoes to fitch Lime & Boards = for the Barracks etc*

Copy of a Letter to Genl Gates at Albany May 23th 1777

[Thomas Spencer]

Leonard Gansevoort's letter to Peter mentioned events taking place in other states and abroad. According to Benjamin Franklin's account in Europe, the British Parliament was only able to raise 1,500 extra troops to support the northern theater of the American War. A seizure of over ten thousand muskets was initiated by a select group of Boston privateers; the muskets were said to be en route to Quebec. Certainly this capture of such a large number of guns would significantly delay the already delayed men in Burgoyne's camp. The French had also sent thousands of shirts and other assorted clothing to Philadelphia and Maryland ports; whether any of this would be distributed to Gansevoort's men was not made clear. Another bit of good news in respect to the Colonel was mentioned at the end of the letter. Leonard claimed that Schuyler was immediately ordered to resume duties of the Northern Department at Albany headquarters, and that if Gates "would not serve under him he should be recalled."[37] A later letter from Leonard indicated that Schuyler had regained command of the department on June 2nd.[38] Schuyler's reinstatement must have greatly alleviated the pressure put on Gansevoort to maintain high performance in executing fort repair duties, while simultaneously bereft of raw materials to achieve any significant repairs.

47—From Leonard Gansevoort

Dear Brother Notwithstanding your remissness in Writing I cannot forbear Sending you another Scroll to Shame you, and tell you of your Indolencd—

Since my last we have received Intelligence here from Doctors Lee & Franklin in France that the Court of Great Brittain connot procure more than 1500 foreign Troops which together with a detainment of one Thousd Men if they can be spared are all the reinforcement which the Tyrant of Brittain can spare his Workers of Evil in America this Year—

A Vessel bound to Quebec loaded with dry Goods and 10,000 Stands of English Muskets was taken at Sea by one of the Boston privateers and carried into that Post.

50,000 Suits of Cloathes and 8,000 Stand of Arms are arrived at Chisepek Bay between Maryland and Philadelphia from France—

Lee[39] *is at Madrid—Franklin*[40] *at Paris & Deane*[41] *at the Hague—The Empress of Russia ~~is arrived at~~ has applied to Congress to have an American Ambassador at her Court*[42]*—*

A Letter from Brigadier Genl Parsons[43] *to Governor Trumbull informs that Col: Meigs*[44] *with a Detachment of 160 Men had crossd over from Sachems head to Tagg Harbour where he had surpriz'd a party of the Enemy who were stationed there killed and captivated the whole, the killed not ascertained 90 prisoners among whom were 1 Capt. 2 Commissaries—Mr Chew and Mr Bell—he destroyed about 100 Tons of Hay a Quantity of Grain burnt 15 Vessels lying in that Harbour and took 10 [Hhds] of Rum and other West India produce—without the loss of a Man killed or wounded—remarkable a Providence who can forbear being an Enthusiast—I have not the paper or would be more particular—*

Mr John Carter Yesterday returned from Philadelphia says that last Monday a Week the Board of War to whom was referred the Case of Genl Schuyler—reported "that Genl Schuyler should be directed forthwith to return to the City of Albany and resume the Command of the Northern Department and that if Genl ~~Schuyl~~ Gates would not serve under him he should be recalled—I have the pleasure to inform you that Genl Schuyler has given Congress the greatest Satisfaction and has received many public Testimonials thereof both from Congress and Genl Washington a great vicissitude in affairs with respect to this Gentleman.

Mr Carter further says that Genl Washington had with him by his returns to Congress 43 Battalions of Continental Troops averaging 400 Men to each Battalion

We hear from Kingston that Genl George Clinton[45] *has with him about 1400 Men in fort Montgomery well Arm'd & tolerably disciplined plenty of Provisions Artillery Stores and Provisions—*

Genls Putnam Green McDougall and Knox[46] *are at Peekskill*[47] *with about 6,000 Men*

The Col: of the Irish Brigade Serving in France is safely arrived at Head Quarters with the Appointment of Brigadier General by Congress, he has his permission to come over and serve in America under the Sign Manual of the King of France—

The two Frigates built at Poughkeepsie[48] *are fitting but by order of Genl Washington in the Highlands—happy for this State*

Yesterday there was a Meeting of Some Gent: of this place to consult who they should hold up to fill the officers ordered to be Elected for in this Country when they agreed as follows.

Ph: Livingston as Governor
Abm Ten Broeck as Lieut Govr—disputed in behalf Vol: P. Douw.
Senators
Genl Schuyler
Ry: Mynderse[49]
Mr Douw
Mr Yates—Genl Hercamer[50]
Representatives in Assembly[51]

Jacob Cuyler	*William B. Whiting*
Wal: Livingston	*Stephen J. Schuyler*
Rob: Van Rensselaer	*John Van Rensselaer Junr*
John Ten Broeck	*Peter B Vrooman*
John Taylor	*Anthony Van Bergen*

Major Jon: Lawrence[52] *one of the Senators for the Southern is appointed one of the Commissioners for Carrying on the Works of Manufacturing Salt Sulphur Flints &c. above and will probably call upon you at Fort Schuyler he is an intimate Aquaintance of mine and a Friend of all Mankind—You will please to Shew him every Mark of Friendship on my Account and his own Merit*

Your Friends are all well here—particularly Miss Van Schaick—

Your Friends the Oneidas &c. are very Neighbourly both here and at your Fathers—he has them every Day at Dinner—

My kind Remembrance to my worthy Friends Hansen Van Veghten Rensselaer Willet &c &c &c

Adieu Your's very Sincerely &
Leonard Gansevoort
Albany 30 May 1777

The summer correspondence involved the local natives and the rumors surrounding their intentions. Colonel Gansevoort sent a letter to John Van Schaick on June 1st, claiming that Colonel John Butler had brought five hundred natives to Oswego, and that a scouting party was sent to ascertain their motives.[53] Though Gansevoort had received intelligence saying Butler's movements were unfounded and false, he nonetheless advised Van Schaick to take precautions in case the force was to suddenly appear with hostile intentions. On June 5, Gansevoort wrote a quick note to Catherine Van Schaick expressing his frustration that he could not leave his post, per General Washington's orders. "No officer is to leave his post or Choir without Permission in Writing from a Genl Officer Commanding in the Department." This would mean Gates would have to grant Gansevoort his leave. This would have been unacceptable in a time of war in Gates' eyes.[54]

48—To John G. Van Schaick

Fort Schuyler 1st June 1777

Dear Sir We had an Account here a few days since by some Indians that Colo Butler was arrived at Oswego with five Hundred Indians, and that his intention was to pay us a Visit, in consequence of which I immediately Dispach'd a Scouting party to Oswego to gain what intelligence they can—I must inform you that while I was writing this I receiv'd a Letter from Mr

Spencer at Onoyda a very intelligent Man and a warm friend to our Cause, He informs me that the above report is false and groundless—However, I shall know the particulars by the return of the Scout. if they bring any news worth Communitating I shall Let you know—If any News Transpire's not your plan I beg you will let me know

You will deliver the Inclosed—Remember me to Mrs Van Schaick.

I am in Sincerity Your's very affectionately

P Gansevoort

To Jno G Van Schaick

49—To Catherine Van Schaick

Fort Schuyler, 5th June 1777

Dear Caty Your Agreeable receiv'd Letter was handed me by Mr. Edward S. Willett

You mention in yours that you will be glad to hear of coming Down soon, I must observe to you that since my Arrival at this post, I have receiv'd an Order Publish'd by his Excellency General Washington, that no officer is to leave his post or Choir without Permission in Writing from a Genl Officer Commanding in the Department—By this order you will find that I shall not have it in my power to pay you as many Visits, this season as I expected—You may be assur'd that I shall indeavor to get have to go down as soon as possible

I must inform you that I have exceeding good living here plenty of Veal Pigion's and Fish of Different Sorts—

The Express is just going off I must therefore conclude Adieu and may God bless and Prosper you

I am in Sincerity Dr Caty Yours very affectionately

Peter Gansevoort

Remember me kindly to your Sister Mary and your Friend Mary Ganset

P.S. I shall glad to hear from you by the first convenient opportunity

On June 6, a resolution from the New York Council of Safety recommended the commanding officers at the forts throughout the state to permit their soldiers, who had the right to vote, to go to their respective polling places.

50—Extract of the Minutes of the New York Council of Safety

State of New York

In Council of safety June 6th: 1777

Resolved that it be recommended to the commanding officers, at the several Forts and Garrisons throughout this State, that they permit such of the Militia at their respective Forts and Garrisons who have a right to vote; to go to the next places of Election to give their votes.

Provided Nevertheless that the same shall in the opinion of such commanding officers be perfectly consistent with the safety of the said Forts and Garrisons respectively

Extract from the Minutes

Robt Benson Secry[55]

Copy J. Lansing Junr Secy to the Honble Major General Schuyler

The reinstated General Schuyler issued his orders for the summer in a June 9 letter to Gansevoort.[56] Within the letter, Schuyler demanded an update on all concerns with the rebuilding and repair of Fort Schuyler; emphasis was placed on the report being "very particular."[57] An exact return of troops was needed, and a count of any and all men charged with supplying labor for construction not formerly involved with the military. Continued friendly diplomacy with native tribes was emphasized, but it was stressed that only members of the Indian Department should conduct direct negotiations or speeches; following that, a detail of the speeches or words exchanged should be transcribed and sent to Schuyler for review.[58]

One particularly interesting aspect of these orders was Schuyler's emphasis on health inspections of the camp. He advised that one officer analyze the quality of the food in the camp, the men's quarters were to be regularly swept, and bedding to be "frequently aired."[59] In all of Gansevoort's military papers, this is the first, and with regards to the Revolutionary War period, the last mention of anything regarding regular duties to ensure the health of the men. Details on powdering hair, distribution of blankets, and the cleaning of arms seem overly involved. Yet these men had just recovered from the Northern winter and spring months involving harsh cold; the coming months were sure to bring a large amount of uncomfortable humidity and the spread of disease. Insects and unhealthy bacteria could manifest themselves inside of the soldier's bedding and wigs, and constant contact with native parties risked the spread of disease and hygiene conditions that the American settlers would deem particularly abhorrent.

Another letter from General Schuyler requested that Gansevoort attend to the needs of a traveling party; the party consisted of Major Vermonet, a "French Gentleman" and a "Company of Some Indians."[60] They had recently concluded discussions with the Six Nations Coalition and needed supplies and a possible detachment to protect them from any British or spies in the area. Schuyler does mention that Gansevoort, in consort with James Deane (one of the Indian Department interpreters), should consult the traveling party on the shortest and safest route possible so as not to "give suspicion of their Intention."[61]

June 13 saw a particularly long and involved letter from Leonard Gansevoort. With his usual mixture of veiled sarcasm and frustration, Leonard once again berated his brother for "breaches of Correspondences." Leonard continued to "absolve" and forgive his brother's lack of correspondence in his usual wordsmith fashion, but also sent news of a possible revolt in the St. John's and Montreal regions of Canada against the British. Apparently, low stores of food were pushing the inhabitants to refuse to bear arms, a shocking reversal of their mindset during the Canadian offensive in late-1775 to early-1776.

51—From Philip Schuyler

Albany June 9th 1777

Dear Sir You will please without delay minutely to inform me what advance are made in fortifying Fort Schuyler and also how that work is conducted—I am advised that all the Economy is not made use of that ought to be and that the Engineer employ a greater Number of barriages than are necessary—pray be very particular in your Report on this Intend

You will make me an exact Return of the Troops that compose your Garrison, and of the Artificers and others employed about the Works, and to do this Monthly.

You will keep up a friendly Intercourse with the Indians and suffer no Speeches to be made to them by Capt: Marquisie or any other person, not employed in the Indian Department, and when you have occasion to speak to them, let your speech be written and a Copy transmitted to me, that the Commissioners may be informed of every Transaction with those people.

You will be very careful and attentive to preserving the Health of your Garrison, and to their Discipline—Let one officer daily inspect into the Cooking and see that the Utensils be kept clean another to see that their Quarters be kept clean and sweet and their Bedding frequently aired—Suffer no officer, Non commissioned officer or privates to use any Bedding or blankets, when on Guard, and obliged the officers always to remain with their Guards; nor must your Adjutant bring any person to the parade for Guard whose Hair is not powdered; his person perfectly clean; his Cloathe in good Order; his arms bright and accoutrements in compleat order—I wish your closest attention to these particulars, and doubt not but you will give it, as it will redound so much to your Credit to introduce good Order and Discipline into the Corps you have the Honor to command.

Inclose you a Resolution of Convention which you will please to attend to.

My Compliments to the officers of your Garrison, and to Mr. Hansen. I am Dr Sir Your most obedient humble Servant

Ph: Schuyler

Colonel Gansevoort

52—From Leonard Gansevoort

Dear Br I congratulate you on General Schuyler's return to Albany with the entire Command of the Department, by the Papers inclosed you will perceive with what Honor he is acquitted and the public Testimonies he has received

I did not Imagine you capable of such breaches of Correspondences as you have been guilty of since our parting; could I have believed that you would be Six Weeks at Fort Schuyler and not write me a Line to inform me of your State of Health, when it is not of your to plead the want of opportunity and depriv'd of the Excuse of multiplicity of Business, and more especially as I have immers'd you so deep in Debt that without I mitigate the Rigous of the Rules of Correspondence you are almost incapable of exonciating your self from the immense load you have contracted by your Indolence and reimissness (paid on my Freedom I mean it as a rebuke)—I have sollicited most pathetically hopes of an ample Compensation—I now once more tend a you my willingness to maintain a Correspondence with you; and that you may not sink down under the Wieght of your Debt and may with the more facility execute your part. I do hereby remit the Debt you owe and for Even discharge you of and from all Letters due me paid pardon and release you from all breaches of Correspondence with which you stand convicted in your Mind and freely absolve you from your Indolence and remissness ~~with reprobating you~~ and as your remorse & compunction of Heart must be the severest torment I can inflict I must have you in that state of penance untill you make expiation ~~therefore~~ for your Wanton transgression—

The Frenchmen whom Genl Schuyler sent into Canada before he went to Philadelphia are returned ~~and~~ they confirm the News of the Conflagration that consumed the Twen Storehouses between St John's & Montreal—they say that the Canadians are ripe for a Revolt and manfully refuse to bear arms against us—That Genl Carleton has ordered all the Inhabitants out of the Town of Quebec that has not Six Months provision in store, and was removing his Army thither what does this indicate but an Expectation of being attack there—A very agreible piece of Intelligence is it not?

Our Army down below continues in the Same good situation as when I last wrote you—

Lieut McClallen has desired me to inform you that he has drawn out of the Store sixty good new French Muskets and the like Number & Quantity of Bayonets Cartoriet Boxes and Bayonetbells—Also 76 Coats blue with Red facings and white lining just your Uniform together with the like Number of Infantry Hats—

I dine today with Doctor Potts he has desired me to present you with his kind Remembrance—he tells me he is preparing Doctor Williams[62] *to repair to Fort Schuyler with Medicines and Hospital Stores, and assures you he will not forget the Marks of Friendship you have sheiving him—and what will undoubtedly please you but intends to send you some Wine Claret Shrub &*

What in the Name of Fort Schuyler is become of my old Friend John Hansen is he still alive or is he wasted upon the Wings of Death to the Eternal World has he taken up his abode among the silent and peaceful and left this tumultuous wicked world if he has let me know his exit, or what Else is become of him I am wearied being in Suspence respecting him—if he be still in the Land of the living till him he could make me supremely happy by indulging me with three Hours private Interview—

Genl Gates and his Family set out last Monday for Morristown—

Brod is in Town and longs to hear from you and his other Friends at Fort Schuyler

I lik'd to have forgot my Friend & Br Van Veghten how does he do?

Huzza for Genl Schuyler Govn & Genl Clinton Lieut Govn there will be no incongruity in the Posts—

Remember me to Col: Willet Major Cochran Capt Aorson Lieuts Staats && I forgot Ed Willet—

Adieu—Your's most faithfully &
Leonard Gansevoort
Albany June 13 1777
Col: Gansevoort

Gansevoort sent a letter to General Schuyler on June 15th acknowledging native affairs occurring near the fort. He also mentioned sending additional orders for cleanliness to other officers in the area to reinforce regular inspection of food and cleanliness of the barracks. Rations were to be increased for the carpenters working on fort repairs, something the men surely appreciated since the lull or lack of additional funds in the spring season. Gansevoort concluded his letter by mentioning that a few of the men regardless of these health regulations had fallen sick. Gansevoort believed that part of this was due to the men "...and others Toasting their Boors On Sticks..."[63] and avoiding the usual pan cooking of foods due to the spread of sickness. Finally, Gansevoort declared that there was still a large shortage of bateaus for material transport and that more were necessary for the transfer of lime, something not previously mentioned in the other letters. It was possible that the engineers had experienced problems strengthening the stone fortifications surrounding the area and now needed to fill in gaps.

Another letter sent the same day claimed that despite the increased pay rate, the carpenters and other workers were suffering from fatigue, further slowing down the rate of repair.[64] Gansevoort seemed to be frustrated in the slow work rate, claiming in the letter that "...the Fortification ... at present little more then the Name of a Fortification ... the Barracks at present being Bad and insufficient to contain the fine Men we have here."[65]

53—To Philip Schuyler

Fort Schuyler June 15th 1777

Sir Your Honor Lettr of the 9th Inst Duly Rec'd by Major Hubbele[66]*—I have noted the Contant of Same—I Shall now give yr Honour the Best State of affairs atr this Place I am able—Notwithstanding all In Regard that yr Honor is advised that not all Occonomy is used at this Place that Should be I will inform you that Just Before my arrival here the foundation of a Small House—was Laid for one Stephanis DeGrau a frenchman who is married To an oneida Squaw [from] here that the House might have been Something Smaller—Still it is [Cut] a Small one indeed—The Engineer has had about Twelve Waggens—I Can assure yr Honor—if he had had Twenty he would have had Employment for the whole The Engineer appears To me To Diligent in his Business—*

I now enclose the Genll Return of the Troops which Compose this Garrison allso a Return of the artificers De-Employd at the Public works here—which I will Continue To Send monthly agreeable To order—

I Shall Pay the Strictest attention To yr Honors orders in Regard To Indian affairs—I Suffer no one To make any Speeches—To them with in the Verge of my Command—

I have given the Necessary orders in Regard To refitting the Barracks—&c—for the Preservation of Health as will as the Severall other Matters which yr Honor Recommended To me—which I will at all Times See Put in Execution—

Sir I would Suggest To yr Honor the Necessity of having Two Good Horses at this Post with Saddles & Bridles on any Sudden Emergency

I have Since my arrival here given orders to the Commisy To Victuall the Carpenters here with one Ration & an Half pr man a day—The Mastr Carpenter Having Produced me the Contract he made with Coll Lewis—for Same—I was allso Necessitated To give orders for Victualling the other artificers with a Ration & an Half Each—& Day—for which I hope To Receive yr Honor approbation as make as order To Continue the Same—Coll Elmore never Delivd me any order To Victualate Indians—nothwithstanding I have Continued the mode adopted by him & Coll Dayton for which I would be allso Glad to Receive yr Honors orders—We have been Two days without any Rum I have ordered the Commsy here to apply To Mr Avery for Some Which Informs me he has done I hope yr Honr will ordr Some To be Sent immediately as the Men Seem Sulky without having the upscale allowance when they Return from Fatique—

We are in want of a Guide To our Scouts here—I would be Glad To Know—what I might allow or Pay John Mathews pr Day when he is upon that Business as he is Verry usefull & well acquainted as far as Oswego—& farther in good Connection with the Indians by the Bank I until have Learnt Since I have been here I Beg Leave To Inclose yr Honor Coppy of a Letter I Sent To Genll Gates Some Time ago To which I Never Recd any answer—

I would be Glad of Some Paper Many at this Post as I am frequently Obliged To advance Some

By the Inclosed Return you will find—that we have a Number of Sick here I am sorry To inform yr Honor that this Garrison in So Destitute of Utensils for Cooking—The men frequently Obliged To wait the one for the other & in the Mean Time Some useing Pans—Just Boiling of it up & others Toasting their Boors—on Sticks—To which I impute the Number of Sick being So Large as it is—I therefore Beg we may have a Sufficient Supply—allso Spare utensils—in Case of the Militia Being ordered up here any Time this Summer We Shall have Occasion here for a Number of Battoes—To Bring Boards & Lime—I have been Obligd To Send for Boards as far as forts at Canajoharry[67]

The Lime I Expect we will be able to get at this Side of the Little falls—

These are the Principal matters that have occurred To me at the fort

I Shall from Time To Time give your Honor Every information of our Situation & Condition at this Place—I ~~will from Time~~ Take the Liberty To make Requisition for Every Thing I may think Needfull & absolutely Necessary for the Good & Preservation of Same

[PG]

[Philip Schuyler]

54—To Philip Schuyler

Copy of Letter Sent to Gen Schuyler 15 June 1777

That not withstanding all the Men who are fit for duty which are not on particular command or on Guard and every day in Fatigue the Works go on very Slowly there are about Two thousand Pickquetts laying around the Fort which we have Drawn out of the Swamp through which we have been obliged to make Roads for that purpose and will ~~be~~ soon be able to compleat that part of the Business—Nothing of any importance as yet been done towards the Strengthening the Fortification which at present has little more ~~than~~ then the Name of a Fortification, The Engineer ~~at this place~~ has just laid the Foundation of a Saliant angle before the Gate and the Carpenters are employed in framing a Barracks to be raised just before the Glasic opposite the South Bastion the Barracks at present being Bad and ~~the whole of works being~~ insufficient to contain the fine Men we have here, the Whole of the Works while appear to me to be Necessary and which Capt. Marquerzie tells me are to be done at this place undoubtedly require more strength then we have here at present, I therefore Humbly request that that part of my Regiment—which is at present stationed at Fort Dayton[68] *maybe ~~with~~ Relieved and ordered to this place for our assistance pleased with such other help as the Genl may be pleased to afford us that the Works may be compleated in due time—*

Because of the incompetence of the French engineer Bernard Moissac de La Marquisie, who was employed by Schuyler, the fort did not resemble its original condition until late July. The engineer began to erect buildings outside the fort, destined to be barracks. (They would be set on fire on August 5 between 4–5 p.m. by the enemy.) He mistakenly ordered large parties to the surrounding swamp to cut pickets that were seventeen feet long, instead of the required ten feet. Instead of placing the pickets in the center of the ditch, which was the original design, they were displayed in the covert way. He also began to "erect a salient angle to cover the gate, with 2 embrasures in it." "He was also engaged in erecting pickets along the covert way. The pickets were placed about three feet from the parapet of the glacis. Two of them were framed together with cross pieces and formed a land of port-holes, which were intended to be placed opposite the embrasures." "The portholes in the pickets did not correspond with the embrasure of the fort" but would come opposite to the neck of the embrasures. By this means, the salient angle would be rendered "wholly useless." Because of these blunders, Gansevoort ordered Marinus Willett to arrest the engineer and set him back to Schuyler. Major Nathaniel Hubbell was assigned to superintend the works. Gansevoort had been reluctant to discharge de la Marquisie because Schuyler appointed him. By August 1, 1777, "the walls around the fort were repaired; the parapets nearly raised; the embrasures made on three sides of the bastions; horizontal pickets extending over the ditches from the embankment, the perpendicular pickets were erected around the covert way and the gate and bridge made secure." The fort was stocked for a long siege by late July with six weeks of ammunition and provisions and musket cartridges, and was resembling its original condition. To help the defense, Gansevoort "put a detail of axemen to filling Wood Creek with a tangle of felled trees."[69]

On June 23, Gansevoort relayed information on the enemy's "Southward" intentions to Catharine Van Schaick and expressed his appreciation that Caty would not be driven from her home by "that Vile Burdening Banditts." He would try to obtain a leave of absence for a few days in late July or early September to pay her a visit as he believed "this Campain will be to me an Exceeding inactive one."

55—To Catherine Van Schaick

Fort Schuyler 23rd June 1777

Dear Caty I avail myself of this opportunity to inform you that I am still in good Health and Usual Spirits

I am informed that three French Officers taken at Sea, by an English Vessel and Carried into New York, Some time ago, and have since made their Escape, they inform that it is the avowed Intention, of the Enemy to carry on their Operations, to the Southward; If this information be true, I am of opinion that the Inhabitents at your place are not so much Alarm'd as they ware when I left you—You must needs think when this report reach'd me it must have given me the greatest Satifaction

I now flatter myself that you with rest of the good Cityzens will not be driven by that Vile Burdening Banditts from your peaceable Habitations—We are likewise inform'd that Genl Howe will not move until their Reinforcement arrives from Canada—hence I infer that Nothing threaten's from the North and Consequintly that this Campain will be to me an Exceeding inactive one

I am confident that the State of New York can not produce of so Eligent a Garden as we have here at present, with two fine Summer Houses, and a Stream of Water which runs round the Whole.

The Bearer of this will be Mr John Hansen Commissary at this post—I shall also write by him a Letter to Genl Schuyler to Obtain Leave of Absence from him for a few days about the last of July or the first of September; at which time if I should get Permission, shall do myself the pleasure to pay you a Visit

I am Dear Caty Your affectionate Friend and Very Hum Servant

Peter Gansevoort

To Miss Caty Van Schaick

June 26 saw the beginning of a flurry of correspondence between Gansevoort and Schuyler. In a letter to Schuyler, Gansevoort reported that intelligence had gained word that Colonel

Butler planned to "Soon be about this Place," which significantly affected the unprepared fort and settlement laborers.[70] Gansevoort also informed Schuyler that an ambush by hostile natives in the morning resulted in the death of Corporal Samuel Madison and the scalping of Captain James Gregg.[71] Gregg and Madison proceeded two miles from the fort to hunt pigeons between Forts Newport and Bull.[72] Believing their guns would not be heard, they began to fire. They were soon discovered by a scout from the enemy's Indians, and both were shot and tomahawked. The men were later discovered by a dog and two men fishing and went to the fort for help; a party was led to the spot. The corporal was dead but the captain was alive. When he was shot the ball entered his side and ran along near the middle of the back. It then passed near the spine and exited just beyond. He was also struck on the head with a tomahawk and scalped. Gregg had pretended he was dead when the Indian approached. After the Indians left, he crawled to Madison, finding him dead. He then laid his head on Madison's body and waited for help. Doctor Hunloke Woodruff[73] dressed Gregg's wound which led to a miraculous recovery and miraculously he recovered three weeks later. Gansevoort responded by immediately sending out a reconnaissance party to find the natives.[74]

General Schuyler sent word to Gansevoort on the 30th that Sir John Johnson was preparing an attack on Fort Schuyler and that scouts should be sent out to the Oswego region to search for any sign of movement. Schuyler informed Gansevoort that General Nicholas Herkheimer [Herkimer] of the Tryon County militia would be ordered to reinforce the fort if such an attempted ambush was to take place.[75] Gansevoort issued general orders to his men on the July 1 detailing battalion and regiment formations.[76] One day later, Gansevoort sent a message to the Six Nations notifying them of his preparation for battle. It was expected that Gansevoort would directly address the Six Nations given Schuyler's insistence that only the Indian Department conduct diplomacy. Gansevoort also restated his dedication to the wellbeing of the tribes:

"...be assured of my good affection towards you, and the Whole Confederacy of the Six Nations and will always be glad to see you and the more so because I am one of your old and Near Neighbour's being Borne in the City of Albany—Where the Six Nations have been acquainted Even since the Arrival of the first White folks, in the Country..."[77]

In this letter Gansevoort seemed to imply he and the natives shared a kinship beyond that which would be expected, apologizing for the "lies told Every Day by the Tories."[78]

56—To Philip Schuyler

Fort Schuyler, June 26, 1777

Sir I have Recd a Letter from yr Honor's Secretary dated the 20th Inst in Relation to Thomas Mair—allso a Lettr To Colo Elmore dated on the 20th Day of March Last Regards To the Same man. I have made the Strictest Enquiry about his affairs in my Power & have found that ~~Since his Residence here for Some Time~~ he has been a great Enemy To our Cause Ever Since Coll Dayton arrival here Last Year who Obligd him to Leave the place Colo Elmore ~~allso~~ forbid him allso To Remain on this Ground—Indians before my arrival have have Requested that he Should not Remain at this Place—Whom he has frequently offended by his Behavior Towards them He was here a few weeks ago when he Reportd that Butler would Soon be about this Place—Which gave Great uneasyness amongst the Carpanters &c—who were obliged To goto the woods Every Day

In Short I think he has Endeavourd To impose upon yr Honor & it is my opinion—he ought not on any Pretence be Suffered To Remain at this place as To his Barn It was but a Trifleing one & has been Taken Down—The New Barracks are Building on the Same Spot—his Dwelling House Stand on the Glacis of this fort—The Engineer has informd me that it must be Taken Down—it is a House of But Little Value—

This Man is Strongly Suspected of Being a Great Villain—he had Three Thirty dolear Continetl Bills By him which I susseed was counterfiet—I had him Confined during the Examination of the Bills—The Gentn of the Garrison Diffd in their opinion—Some thought they were Really Counterfied but the Majority thought not—on which I Let him go—& Desired him Never To appear again on this Ground which Doubt not but yr Honor will approve of—

I am Sorry To inform yr Honor That Capt Greggs & Copl Maddison of my Regt went out a gunning yesterday morning Contrary To orders—

It seems they went out Just after Breakfast & about Ten o Clock—Corpl Maddison was killd & Scalped—Capt Greggs was Shot threw his Back—Tommyhawkd—& Scalped & is still alive[79]*—he informs me the misfortune Happend about Ten o Clock in the morning—he Looked at his watch after he was Scalped he saw But Two Indians he was about 1½ mile from the fort—he was not discovered Till Two o Clock in the afternoon—I immediately Sent out a Party—I had him Brought in the fort—Just after three o Clock—allso the Corps of Maddison—He is Perfectly by his Senses & Speaks Strong & hearty—notwithstanding his Recovy is Doubtfull—*

I have been Obligd To Detain Some Battoes To Bring Board from the Mills Below & have got Some of my men To work them—they Complaind that they could not work on one Ration of Proviss I have orderd the Commsy To Issue one Ration & an Half—during the Time they may Remain in that Service which hope your Honor will approove of—& sign by To me by the first oppy

[PG]

57—From Philip Schuyler

Albany June 30th: 1777

Sir A Report prevails that Sir John Johnson intends to attack your post: you will therefore put yourself in the best position of Defence you possibly can—Keep out Scouts continually towards Oswego and every other Quarter from which the Enemy may approach—Be very watchful and alert that you may not experience the Disgrace of a Surprize.

I have written to General Herkimer to support you with the Militia in Case you should be attacked—Give him therefore the most early Intelligence if any Enemy should approach you—Direct your Scouts, if they discover any Enemy to try to learn their Numbers, and if they are British Troops Canadians & Indians on which of them.

I shall write you again as soon as I can find a Moment's Time At present I am wholly engrossed in preparing to march with the Militia to the Northward as the Enemy are got to Crown point.

I am Sir Your humble Servant

Ph: Schuyler

Colo: Gansevoort

Verte

P.S. You will please to send down immediately Hugh Fothergill a soldier of Captn Austin's Company with Directions to repair without Delay to me P S.

58—General Orders

Fort Schuyler July 1st 1777

The Military Club being open'd at the Hour appointed Proceeded to business in Order to Consider the Exercize & Maneuver which is to be preform'd on Field Days by our Regimt after some Disputes it was Again

Noted When the Battallion is form'd the men is to be Siz'd from the Right and left to the Centre, allso Agreed that the first Sub Division from the Right to be sent as an escort for the Colours; Commanded by the Oldest Captn Eldest first & Second Lieutenant the five youngest Ensigns to Carry the Coulours the youngest of which is to Care the Standard—

the Colours to be escorted Agreeable to the Instructions Given in Simms Millitary Journal When the Battalion is Drawn up the Drums is to be plac'd in the Rear of the Centre in a line with the Sergeants that all the Drums is to go with the Escorting party Except thru which is to Remain with the Battalion, ~~two~~ one on the Right and left and ~~one in~~ the Other in the Centre, When the ~~Officer~~ Escorting party arrives to the Battallion with the Colours The Major gives the Word for the Officers to take their posts in the Battalion The Receiving Offr to be Recd with Open Ranks and the Battalion to perform the Motion of presenting their Arms

When the Drummers Call is beat; the Officers who is to carry the Colours is to repair with the Drums to the Right of the Battallion

[PG]

59—To the Six Nations

[July 2 1777] Brothers Schems & Warriors of the Six Nations

The time for Which Colo Elmores Regiment was to serve being Expired about 28 Days ago—

Genl Schuyler knowing that time—gave me Orders to Prepare & to come to this Place to Relieve Colo Elmore Accordingly I sett out with only a few men of my Rigt who you now see with me in 8 or 9 Days I Expect Remainder of the Men of my Regt Genl Schuyler has Recommended me to Live in Friendship with you and all the Six Nations—

I am now happy to see so many of you at this place and you ma be assured of my good affection towards you, and the Whole Confederacy of the Six Nations and will always be glad to see you and the more so because I am one of your old and Near Neighbour's being Borne in the City of Albany—Where the Six Nations have been acquainted Even since the Arrival of the first White folks, in the Country—When Ever I get any News from Genl Washington and our Armies, in The Service of the American States, I will let you know it; I hope you will also Continue to give me what News you may have from Time to Time from our Enemies

I am Sorry that so many lies are told you Every Day by the Tories, I am told it is now Reported that Genl Schuyler, is gone to New York, It is the greatest Lie that Ever was told it is like all the rest they tell you every Day—Genl Schuyler is now in Philadelphia with the Great Congress on Business of the Greatest importance which the Commissioners of Indian affairs will tell you, when you git to Albany

Brothers Sachems and Warriors

I desire such of you as are going to Albany to call and See my Old Father he will be glad to see you—& tell him that I am well Taking an interpreter with you

Gansevoort's speech seemed to be in a desperate though ultimately wise attempt to cement the Six Nations' support in the future. It was ironic that on the same day of the declaration, Gansevoort received a letter from his brother describing General Washington's operations in New Jersey. Washington had taken Brunswick despite previous intelligence acknowledging British fortifications, and that the British forces in the area had retreated near Crown Point. Leonard mentioned that the natives allied with the British had scalped multiple men in the camp; he also does not hesitate to call them "Aborigines" and "copper colored Sons of Lucifer."[80] The two men from the same family within one week had developed incredibly different perceptions of the natives.

The early days of July brought increasing news of coming hostilities. Gansevoort's July 3rd letter to Schuyler detailed the restocking of food supplies in case of a siege. While there appeared to be sufficient food for the soldiers save for a meager few barrels of rum, the Indian Department was notably bereft of supplies.[81] Gansevoort personally assured Schuyler that with large quantities of artillery batteries and ammunition, that "...nothing in (Gansevoort's) power shall be wanting to Maintain this important post."[82] Despite such large depots of ammunition, Gansevoort still required a "proper Supply" of musket powder and grapeshot. The letter ended with good news; Gansevoort's letter was well received as members of the Six Nations had given him a belt as a token of continued friendship.[83] Gansevoort sent another letter to Schuyler a day later informing him that an annual review of the garrison was conducted.[84]

60—To Philip Schuyler

Yours of the 30th of June is come safe toe hand I shall be carefull in complying with your directions by keeping out proper scouts and hastning to put this place in the best posture of defense I can and by every other means in my power guard against the disgrace of a surprise at the same time I beg leave to remind you that the Number of men here are small; yet sufficiently at present large for the Quantity of Provisions at this Post at present having only Barrels of Beef and Pork which is the total of all the meat (tho the Flower and peas are considerable larger in proportion) and the demands for the Indian department are considerable; we have likewise no more then Barrells rum—

I inclose you a return of the Artiliry & Ammunition by which you'll pereceive that Should we be invested we will require a considerable supply of Ammunition which together with a proper supply of Provision I beg your Honour will order this way with as much dispatch as possible and you may assure yourself nothing in my power shall be wanting to Maintain this important post.—

besides the above I think the Commissary should be pressed to hurry a supply of Provision and the Conductor Urged to send a proper Supply of Powder Ball Grap shot & what else may be wanting agreeable to a return to be obtained from Capt Savage[85] *for that Purpose—I have yesterday had a Meeting with Some of the Chiefs & Warriors of the Six Nations—who delivd me a Belt ~~and~~ as a farther token of their Friendship and Confidence and desired that I should inform you of it—they likewise requested me to inform you that Major Fonda*[86] *at Caughhawaga falls has ~~sold~~ Rum to some Indians for One Dollar in Silver pr Quart or Two Dollars in paper money which is Depresiating the paper ~~Money~~ Currency, and if that should be Looked over they are Determined not to take any paper Money for the future which they have reported thro the Different Castle and Create's a great Uneasiness amongst them*

[Copy of a Letter sent to Genl Schuyler Dated Fort Schuyler July 3rd 1777]

61—To Philip Schuyler

Fort Schuyler July 4th 1777

Sir Having taken an annial review of the State of the garrison, I think it is incumbent on me to inform your Excellency by Express of our present circumstances. Every possible assistance is given to Capt Marquizee to enable him to carry on such works as are deem'd absolutely necessary for the defence of the garrison—The Soldiers are constantly at work—even such of them as come off guard are immediately turned out to fatigue. But I cannot conceal from your Excellency the impossibility of attending fully to all the great objects pointed out in the orders issued to the commanding officer on the station with out farther assistance. Sending out sufficient parties of observation felling the timber into Wood creek clearing the road from Fort Dayton which is so embarrassed in many parts as to be almost impassable and prosecuting at the same time the internal business of the garrison are objects of the greatest importance, which should if possible be immediately considered. But while no exertion compatible with the circumstances now are in and necessary to give your Excellency satisfaction with respect to all these interesting matters shall be ommitted. I am very sensible it is not in our power to get over some capital obstructions without a reinforcement. The inclosed Return and the difficulties arising from the increasing number of hostil Indians will shew to your Excellency the grounds of my opinion—One hundred and fifty men would be needed speedily and effectually to obstruct Wood creek—an equal number will be necessary to guard the men at work in falling and hauling of timber. Such a deduction from our number together with smaller deductions for scouting parties & would scarcely leave a man in the garrison which might therefore be easily surprised by a very contemptible party of the enemy. The number of inimical Indians increases. In the affair of last week only two made their appearance Yesterday a party of at least forty supposed to be Buttlers Emissaries attacked Ensign Sporr[87] *with 16 Privates who were out on fatigue cutting turf about three quarters of a Mile from the Fort. One soldier was brought in dead and inhumanly mangled—two were brought in wounded—one of them slightly and the other mortally. Six privates and Mr Sporr are missing. Five parties were immediately sent to pursue the enemy, but they returned without being able to come up with them—This success will no doubt encourage them to send out greater numbers and the intelligence they may possiblly require will probably hasten the main body distinated to act against us in these parts. Our provision is greatly diminished by reason of the spoiling of the Beef, and the quantities that must be given from time to time to the Indians—It will not hold out above 6 Weeks Your Excellency will perceive in looking over Capt Savage's Return of the State of the Artillery that some essential articles are very scarce. As a great number of the gun bullets do not suit the firelocks, some bullet molds of different sizes for cooling others must be of great advantage to us. Our stock of powder is absolutely too little. A [Time?] in addition to what we have is wanted as the lowest proportions for the shot we have on hand. We will not withstanding every difficulty exert ourselfes to the utmost of our power and if your Excellency will be pleased to order a speedy reinforcement with a sufficient supply of provision and ammunition to enable us to hold out a siege we will I hope by the blessing of God be able to give a good account of any force that will probably come against us*

[Copy of a Letter Sent Genl Schuyler]

The soldiers were still reconstructing parts of the barracks and the fort, and they seemed to be suffering from fatigue. Gansevoort was concerned that if a surprise attack or siege was attempted, the men would be disoriented and would not possess the high morale required to defend the fort. Reconnaissance had been faulty; the passes into the neighboring forest were impossible to cross. Gansevoort further stated that reinforcements (in his words at least one hundred and fifty men) would be absolutely necessary if the multiple logistical problems hampering the fort were to be addressed. He also noted that increasing amounts of Indians were spotted around the settlement, but due to the slow nature of the scouting parties, it was unknown whether they were members of the Six Nations or hostiles.

Whereas earlier mentioned the fort was in good supply, Gansevoort now noted that the stocks of salted beef had spoiled, and that some of the ammunition was not the correct size to be used in the artillery pieces. The amount of gunpowder in the fort was at the absolute minimum required. He determined that unless they were supplied within six weeks, they would be completely unable to defend themselves. What happened in the day between Gansevoort's two letters? Most likely, he was relying on orders rushed to him at his request by officers far more concerned with the siege preparations. His letter to Catherine Van Schaick on July 5 further complicated the question; within it he finds himself more than able to conduct a siege in relative safety.[88]

62—To Catherine Van Schaick

Fort Schuyler 5th July 1777

Dear Caty I have just time to acquaint you that I am well, and hope to hear the same from you by the return of this Express which will have Albany one or two days after his Arrival

You will undoubtedly hear of some mischief done again by some Indians to a Party of our Men who whare at Work about three Quarters of a Mile from the Fort—I hope this will not occasion the least uneasiness in you, with respect to my safety, I can assure that I think myself as safe ~~as~~ in this Fort, as I would in any post of America and shall not upon myself by stroling about the Garrison—The Express is waiting for this and must conclude

I am Dr Caty Your Sincere Friend

P Gansevoort

To Miss Caty Van Schaick

The day before, a party of forty unknown men had attacked Ensign Spoor's men before disappearing into the woods; one was found dead and "inhumanly mangled."[89] It is possible that, in preparing for the siege the British sent scouting parties to enrage and intimidate the fort's defenders. A July 6th letter to General Schuyler claimed that there were sounds of cannon fire not far off from the scouting parties in the Oswego region; intelligence indicated that the arrival of Colonel Butler's party in the area would be announced by such a volley.[90]

63—To Philip Schuyler

Copy of a letter from Colonel Gansevoort to M General Schuyler, dated Fort Schuyler, 6th July, 1777.

Sir we have just received an Express from Mr Spencer at the Oneida Castle, which is forwarded to your Excellency by this conveyance. This Day several of our People heard a firing of Cannon, supposed to be at Oswego. This circumstance concurs with the advise which Mr Spencer sent us some time ago, upon his return from a visit to the six nations, that he was informed by the Indians that Colo Butler was expected ~~by~~ at that place soon, and that his arrival would be announced by the firing of Cannon, as a Signal for the Indians to meet him, for the purpose of entering into a Treaty; upon the breaking up of which, it was said a visit might be expected at Fort Schuyler. This new occurrence with the necissity of sending a strong scouting Partys, on account of the number of Indians in the woods, which We cannot possible spare, will, we doubt not be considered by your Excellency as one additional Argument of great Weight, sending us a speedy Reinforcement, with such a Supply of provision & ammunition as will enable us to hold out a Siege.—

I have the Honor to be, Your Excellency's obed humble Servt

Peter Gansevoort

[available from the Papers of the Continental Congress]

The cannon fire was to also indicate that natives would meet with Butler's party to make some sort of treaty that may well have endangered the neutrality and friendship between Schuyler's force and the surrounding tribes. Gansevoort needed to send more scouting parties in hopes of intercepting such a meeting, but had no men to spare and once again emphasized the need for reinforcements.

A July 7th letter from the Commissary of Fort Schuyler, John Hanson, contained ominous news concerning the American evacuation of Fort Ticonderoga. Major Robert Cochran was ordered to hastily move his men to meet Gansevoort at Fort Schuyler in preparation for an attack; Hanson intended to return a few days later.[91]

64—From John Hanson

Albany July 7th 1777

Dr Sir This you will Receive by Major Cochran who Leaves this Immediately we have heard that our Troops have Evacuated Tionderoga & brought off their stores with them to Skeensbourough—it is believd by some and others not—I inclose you a Letter from Head Quarters in New Jersey to the Convention of this State at Esopus—Genll Schuyler has Recd a Letter from Genll Washington dated 2d Inst—in which he writes that the whole Province of N Jersey was Evacuated by the Regulars & that the whole army were on Staten Island—a Report presants that They are all Embarkd—Since & Sailed out of Sandy Hook[92]*—an other Report is that they are coming up the North River*

Major Cochran is ordered to Proceed with all Speed—To Fort Schuyler—so that I have not time to send you a Long Epistle—This Days Post Not arrivd—I inclose you the Last Paper in Town: Jacob Cuyler Esqr is appointd Dy Commy—Genll of Purchase for the Northern Army by the Honle Continental Congress with the Rank Colonel in the Army—Yr friends are all well. I have Genll Schuylers Leave of absence for a few Days more I shall come up in Compy with Colo Varick[93]*—I am with my Compts to Colo Willitt and all the officers & Gentn in yr Garrison—Your Real friend & most Obed. & Huml Servt*

John Hanson

The fort had fallen to General Burgoyne's men and would be used as a rendezvous point for British reinforcements and supply routes. The capture of the heavily fortified military post also meant that most of the remainder of the Hudson River was protected from

Continental artillery fire, as Fort Schuyler was one of the few forts left in Burgoyne's path.[94] A later letter sent from Leonard Gansevoort on July 9th declared that a large number of supplies and cannon were captured and that Fort Schuyler would come under attack before the season was over. He ended the letter begging his brother to achieve victory to preserve the prestige and high standing of the "New York Arms," and sent word regarding the resolve of not only their friends at Albany but the family as well: "Your Fellow Citizens put great Confidence in you and your Father flatters himself that you will Conquer or die."[95]

65—From Leonard Gansevoort

Albany July 9th 1777—

Dear Br Your two Letters I have received and condole with you in the Misfortunes they communicate—

Ticonderoga and Mount Independence are in the possession of the Enemy[96]*—they were evacuated by our Army but in what Manner I am ignorant of—without fighting and with the Loss of all the Stores Baggage &c. a most shameful affair indeed—but as we have not the most authentic Intelligence suspend your Judgement till you hear—but give me leave to suggest to you that I shall be extremely Sorry to hear that you / in case the Enemy should invest you / had left the Garrison I beg you / and depend upon you and your Regiment /will not be a disgrace to the New York Arms—you may prepare yourself for I expect something will be attempted with you—fight and maintain or gloriously fall then your memory will at least be bless'd and held in Remembrance and may God support you and grant you Victory—Your Mother is very uneasy and I am going to bring her with Mrs Gansevoort to Great Barrington*[97] *Mrs Gansevoort is so far advanced in her pregnancy*[98] *that I have conceiv'd it precedent to carry her off—when she will at least be out of the Way in Case the Enemy should penetrate—*

Our Army is collecting at Fort Anne when we shall in a few Days have a very respectable Army a Letter from Genl Schuyler to Genl Ten Broeck which arrived this Morning says that the Enemy had attacked our Troops at Fort Anne but were repuls'd and that a party of our Men had surrounded a Number of the Enemy and that a reinforcement was marched to sustain the officer who had surrounded the Enemy Genl Nixon's Brigade[99] *arrived here Yesterday on their Way to the Northward—*

Your Fellow Citizens put great Confidence in you and your Father flatters himself that you will Conquer or die—

I can give you nothing about the Army below some say their Intentions ~~is~~ are up the North River others to the Eastward others to the Delaware and some to the West Indies—

The whole Militia of the County are on the move up

Adieu in great haste Your's very affectionately &c.

Leonard Gansevoort

Col: Gansevoort—

On July 12, Gansevoort answered Catherine Van Schaick's letter expressing his concern over the abandonment of Ticonderoga. Very busy in fortifying his own garrison, he would give the enemy a "warm reception" when they arrive. Schuyler had ordered General Herkimer to send a reinforcement of two hundred militiamen to Fort Schuyler.

66—To Catherine Van Schaick

Fort Schuyler 12th July 1777

Dear Caty I Received yours by the Express yesterday and was very sorry to hear that you was so much distressed on the Account of our Army having Evacuated Tyconderoga

I have Yesterday Received a Letter from Genl Schuyler who informs me that he has ordered Genl Harkimer to send me a Reinforcement of Two Hundred Men of the Militia, I doubt not but we shall be perfectly secure when they arrive, I could wish that you and the rest of my Friends ware as secure as I shall then think Myself—We are very Busy in Fortifying this Fort, and doubt not but shall ~~be~~ give them a warm Reception if they should pay us a Visit

I am Dr Caty your Sincere Friend

P Gansevoort

To Miss Caty Van Schaick

Further details on provisions needed by Gansevoort's command were listed in a July 15th letter from Jacob Cuyler.[100] Multiple heads of cattle were sent with one of them intended as a gift for the local natives. In preparation for enemy attack, Cuyler confirmed that it was now more than ever in his best interest to receive constant correspondence from the fort so that the garrison may be well provided. Colonel Goose Van Schaick, who was in charge of the First New York Regiment, was given command over the forces amassing in Albany.

67—From Jacob Cuyler

Albany July 15th 1777,

Dear Conl Twenty one head of Cattle are now ordered to Fort Schuyler, for the use of the Garrison, one of the number is however intended for the indians If they Assist and Deliver Same the rest (as a Gratuity for their Service's) those are the Sent Provisions transmitted by me to your Garrison—

I have Given directions to Mr Hansen or the Person Acting for him, how to proceed with what they do in my Department,

It will be well for you at all times to Give me timely notice Either by yourself or throw your Commissary of your wants—

It will be my Constant Study to see the Army will Provided, at least I flatter my Self nothing shall be wanting on my Part—my friends & Countrymen I have near at heart—

Give me leave Colonel to recommend to you to hasve a Quantity of Grass Cut and made into hay, in Case the fort shuld be Invested by the Enemy, It would do to feed your Cattle which In my Opinion you will be Oblidge to Inclose Shuld that be the Case, at any Rate you shall want it in Winter, turn over

The Sooner this work Can be done the more use you may Perhaps have of It, how Does my Couzin Mr Van Veghten Do, he will be usefull to you I Imagine in Time of Action tho it may be ~~ought~~ out of his Department, yet Gentlemen Who have a Naturale military fondness love to see armies drawn up in Order—

Our friend Sarahmus John remains Still in town, but vary Anxcious to go to his Post more Especially as in his Opinion he belives the Enemy Will Come to pay you a Visit, and Sir you know a good officer is fond of Promotion, & is always willing to under the greatest Danger

My Complyments To Whose Gentlemen of the garrison, with Whom I have the Pleasure to be Acquainted Shake Oata's hand of friendship for me, the Town has been much Alarmed but People after they Came to Reason now look up again, the Girles Dress look Better & more Butifull then Ever,

I am Dear Coll your most Obedt & humble Servt

Jacob Cuyler

D.C. Genl of Purchases

To Colln Peter Gansevort

Comdg Officer at Fort Schuyler

I shall give you my ~~little~~ Letter between you & me

P.S Since writing the Within I have been under the Necessity to order the Cattle refered to. To the army at Fort Edward & have by this Conveance sent order To Mohawk River to Purchase Cattle and to have them forwarded

Your &c

Ja: Cuyler

A letter sent on the 21st ordered Gansevoort to start felling trees to disrupt enemy movement.[101] This had been incredibly effective against Burgoyne's campaign; at certain points Burgoyne was traveling less than a mile a day, and traversing the harsh wilderness in the summer season saw many British soldiers falling ill to malaria and other diseases.

Reinforcements and supplies had not yet arrived during the last days of July. Gansevoort wrote to Schuyler on the 26th out of what must have been frustration. Gansevoort claimed that General Herkimer's reinforcements have still not yet appeared, nor had any correspondence informing Gansevoort of his arrival.[102]

68—To Philip Schuyler

Copy of a Letter from Colonel Gansevort to Gen Schuyler dated July 26 1777.

Dear Sir your Honor wrote me some time since that you had sent orders to General Herkimer to reinforce this Garrison with two Hundred of ~~this Garrison~~ his Militia. You will find by inclosed return, that your Orders have not been complyed with. The Militia which are here at present have orders to be absent only fourteen Days In Consequence of which Orders, they will leave us in two days time. I was yesterday informed of Colonel Butlers arrival at Oswego, with a number of Indians and Canadians, and that Sir John Johnston was on an Ilse Land near Oswego, with a number of Tories; in Consequence of which information, I have this morning sent a party of one Hundred and Thirty Men to obstruct Wood Creek.

I must inform your Honor that I have not yet Received any Provisions or amunition, since I have applyed for them, Except a few Barrels of Flower.

I am, Dr Sir, your most Obed Hum Sert

Peter Gansevoort

[available from the Papers of the Continental Congress]

69—To Catherine Van Schaick

Fort Schuyler 26th July 1777

Dear Caty I again take the pleasure of writing you a few lines, to inform of my being still in good Health and usual Spirits, and hope to hear the same from you by the first opportunity—I expected Eir' now to have done myself the pleasure of paying you a Visit

I have yesterday received an Account by an Indian that Colo Buttler has Kindled a Council Fire Oswego with Indians of Different ~~Tribes~~ Nations and that this Numbers are not like to be so large as was Expected

You will not Expect me down till some time in Fall; as I cannot consistent with my Honor and the good of the Service leave my post, till we know in what the Treaty will Terminate at Oswego

I am Yours Sincerely &c &c
Peter Gansevoort
Miss Caty Van Schaick

The letter also announced the arrival of Colonel Butler and John Johnson's men to Oswego, attempting to conscript loyalists in the area. In a last ditch attempt to further prevent British advances towards the fort, a detachment of one hundred and thirty men were ordered to Wood Creek to obstruct any paths or waterways.

Part of the memorandum of British Lieutenant Henry Bird[103] observed that up to a week before the Fort Schuyler siege occurred, many scouting parties were aware that a siege was imminent. Bird's July 28th entry observed a number of "Savages" along with a large group of Seneca Indians. He claimed that "the Savages hinted an intention to send parties to Fort Stanwix [Fort Schuyler] but to proceed in a body no farther."[104]

70—From the Memorandum Book of Henry Bird

"Tuesday, 28th July, 1777

After going two miles, & no Savages following, waited two hours for them. 16 Senecas arriving I proceeded to the three Rivers—waited there two hours—seventy or eighty Messesaugers coming up I proposed moving on—they had stolen two oxen from the drove of the army—would not advance—but stayed to feast—I advanced without Indians 7 miles farther—in all nineteen miles four Centries all night from a Sergeant's guard of 12 men—relieved every hour—visited every half hour—all fires put out at 9 oClock.

Wensday

Set off next Morning at 6, having wailed for the Savages till that time, tho none arrived—Order'd the Boats to keep 70 yards behind each other—half the men kept their arms in their hands—whilst the other half rowd. Ordered, on any of the boats being fired on the men arm'd to jump on shore—the rest to support them with all expedition—rowd all night. encamped near nine mile point.

~~30 July~~ with 27 Senecas & nine Messesaugers—joined Mr. Hair's Party on thursday. Many Savages being ther with us and Messesaugers We proceeded to the Wood creek a march of fifteen miles—orderd the Rangers to compleat our party to 36 men—divided them into three Watches of 12 each—6 Centries one hour and a half 6 another—at the end of the 3 hours the first watch reliev'd by the second so on either Mr Clerges or myself up all night

Friday

the Savages hinted an intention to send parties to Fort Stanwix—but to proceed in a body no farther—I calld a Council of the Chiefs told them I had orders near the Fort that if they would accompany me I should be content but If they would not go I should take the white people under my Command—in all 60 and proceed myself. The Messesaugers declared they would go with me The Senecas said I had promised to be advised the the chiefs—that it was their way to proceed with caution—I answered I meant as to fighting in the bush that I had communicated my intentions to them in the former camp of preventing them stopping the creek—and investing their Fort but I had promised to be advised by them I would take it so far as to wait till next morning—but would then certainly march at daybreak—they after some counselling seemd pleasd with what I had said said they would sent out large scouts to prepare the way accordingly 18 or 20 set off this evening guard the same as before

Saturday

[No 2 Memonandum Book of Lt Bird on his approach to the Fort][105]

This and several of the following Papers were found in the Port folio of Genl St Ledger in his Marque after his raising the Siege or precipitate Flight

The phrase of "no farther" suggested that the hostiles were planning to meet up with a British detachment. Perhaps another reason for their early excursion was to convince the defenders of Fort Schuyler that the majority of Indian locals were planning to join.

A letter from Gansevoort's brother on July 28th noted that hostilities were increasing near his camp. Jenny McCrea and Mrs. Sarah McNeil were carried out of their houses and "cut to pieces, her breasts ripd open and scalped."[106]

71—From Leonard Gansevoort

Albany July 28 1777—

Dear Br I am returned from Claverack[107] *where I have left our Mother, my Wife & her Mother the former is at Capt: Phillips's & the latter are at Coll Robt V Rensselaer's. I enclose you two Letters for Adjutant Say this which respect the Goods of Ensign Spoor give him all the Assistance in that Matter in your Power your Mother lodges in the House where he was bred up—Your Father & Sisters are in Town: well—the Fish you was so kind as to Send is come to hand but all spoiled—Lieut. Tob: V. Veghten*[108] *is killed and scalped at Fort Edward together with one Serjeant & four Men—Miss Jenny McCrea & Mrs. McNeal are carried out of the House and the former cut to pieces her breasts ripd open and scalped She was found Mrs McNeal is not yet found—Genl Glover's brigade*[109] *is arrived here and march this Day for Fort Edward—Genl Lincoln*[110] *is arrived also he says that the Enemy are sailed from New York out of the Hook that part of them were landed at New castle about 45 miles below Philadelphia and that Genl Washington was on his March to Philadelphia with his Army—the Enemy have left only Genl Skinner's brigade*[111] *at New York God grant you Success inspire you with true Courage and Save your & your Regiments Life—Adieu*

[Leonard Gansevoort]

[Collo. Peter Gansevoort Fort Schuyler]

This incident would later be immortalized in John Vanderlyn's 1804 painting entitled "Death of Jane McCrea" and would serve as a horrifying reminder of why Americans were fighting against the British and their allies. Leonard also detailed the movements of the British army landing in New Castle below Philadelphia and that Washington was en route to meet them. Washington had long been expecting such an attack; Admiral Howe[112] had constantly threatened a landing through naval intimidation. Such intimidation tactics may have also acted as a distraction from Burgoyne's plan to strike Fort Schuyler and Albany. If Washington sent his men to fight at New Castle, they would be tied up and unable to send any possible reinforcements to defend the Hudson and Mohawk River valleys.

A letter from an Oneida scout named Thomas Spencer warned Gansevoort that the British force in Oswego would cross through Wood Creek by the 30th; a night crossing of the Oneida River to bypass land obstructions was more than likely.[113]

72—From Thomas Spencer

Oneida July 28 1777

Sir Just now came heere an Indian Named Cannawerjyandos has told a friend of his that he Left oSwago falls 2 Days past that the Troops are on this Side Oswego & some of them Over the falls & the otheres in haste: they are a mind to git to wood creek before it is Stoped he Thinks they Will be heere in two Days They are to Cross the Onoida Lake in the night he says the River is full of boats from Oswego to the falls: the Indian Lives in Old onoyda & is one of Brants Party[114] *that was in oquage he Say, there Will be some boddy Left At Swego to Attend If treaty there was Some Strings of Wampom heere to Day to Acquaint the Ind. the Treaty is to be at the 3 Rivers Yours &c*

Please to Pay the Messenger

Tho Spencer

a Party of 80 Indians is to come by way of Rehoehage who will come a cross fish creek at the fishing place at the Indian field.

Despite this harrowing news, General Herkimer demanded the release of his two hundred militiamen sent to reinforce Fort Schuyler as they had originally agreed to stay no more than sixteen days.[115] Herkimer agreed to extend their stay to three weeks but his men needed to return home to tend to the harvest.

73—From Nicholas Herckheimer

Conajohary Dist. July 29 1777

Sir As the Time of my Militia now stationed under your Command at Fort Schuyler will be expired this Week, I beg of you, not to detain them longer; The

Joseph Brant or Thayendanegea. Painted by G. Cullin from the original of E. Ames, 1805 (Gansevoort-Lansing collection. Manuscripts and Archives Division. The New York Public Library. Astor, Lenox and Tilden Foundations).

County Committee promised them not to Stay longer but Sixteen days but I prolong'd the Time to three Weeks from Home to home, which I assured them under my hand. They will long for the Time in Regard to their Hay and Wheat Harvest, as their presence at home is most ~~when~~ ecessary at this Season; I hope therefore, that you'll grant them their Discharge next Thursday, that they may reach home at the Three Week's End, especially as one hundred and Sixty Men Continental Troops are set off to day for Fort Schuyler to reinforce your Garrison,. In case of detaining them longer as promised, I really fear, that it will cause a Disturbance and an unwillingness for their future Service, when wanted and besides they perhaps would desert from their Station, to the dishonor of our County—I have procured twenty fat Cattle for your Garrison agreeable to your Request, they are ready and waiting for to be drove along under a sufficient guard—I am always with Respts—

Sir Your obed. Humble Servt

Nicholas Herckheimer

PS. Colo Waston, as I understood of him, is ready and willing to march up with his Men to Fort Schuyler, as soon as you will Require the same otherwise he is to stay at Fort Dayton

Colo Peter Gansevoort

Commandt Fort Schuyler

Thomas Spencer wrote again on the 29th; according to reconnaissance efforts by the allied tribes in the area, the British force would arrive at Fort Schuyler no less than four days time.[116] A militia force was being prepared on orders of the Albany committee with the expectation that they might delay part of the force along the Three Rivers area.

74—From Thomas Spencer

Oneida July 29th 1777

Sir At a meeting of the Chiefs they tell me that there is but four Days remaining of the Time set for the Kings Troops to come to Fort Schuyler and they think it likely they will be here sooner the Chiefs desire the Commanding Officers of Fort Schuyler to exert themselves in their Defense not make a Ticonderoga of it but they hope you will be couragious they Desire Genl Schuyler may have this with speed and send a good Army here there is nothing to do at New York we think there is men to be spared we expect the Road is stopped to the Inhabitants by a Party through the woods we shall be surrounded as soon as they come This may be our last Advice as their Soldiers are past those that are to hold a Treaty Send this to the Committees as soon as they receive it Let the Militia rise up and come to Fort Schuyler To morrow We are a going to the 3 Rivers to the Treaty we expect to meet the Warriors and when we come there & declare we are for Peace we expect to be used with Indifference and sent away Let all the Troops that comes to Fort Schuyler take Care on their March as their is a Party of Indians to stop the Road below the Fort—about 80 or 100. we hear they are to bring their Cannon up Fish Creek we hear there is a 1000 going to meet the Enemy we advise not the Army is too large for so few men—Defend the Fort we send a Belt of 8 Rows to confirm the Truth of what we say It looks likely to me the Troops are near—hope all Friends to Liberty and that loves their Families will not be backward but exert themselves as one Resolute Blow would secure the Friendship of the Six Nations and almost free this Part of the Country from the Excursions of the Enemy—

Your very humble Servt & Well Wisher

Tho Spencer

Copy

On July 31, Caty Van Schaick sent Gansevoort a letter, which unfortunately did not arrive until August 6. The courier of the letter was killed at the battle of Oriskany. In the letter, she expressed her pleasure upon hearing that he was in good health. She shared her opinion about the trustworthiness of the Indians, friend and foe. Caty and her family were relocating to Esopus, as the war was getting too close to home in Albany.

75—From Catherine Van Schaick

Albany 31th July 1777

Dear Sir I received yours of 26th Instant it gave me pleasure to hear of your being in good Health—I was glad to find your Letter so peaceble it was to me as Cordial to a Faint Heart, but of Short duration I have Since ben informed that an Express arived here from your Fort who brings an account that a party of Regulars Canadians and Indians to the Amount of three Thousand are by their way from Oswego, I hope you not put much trust on Our Indians they are a Sett of people not to be trusted on, All my fear is that you will be blocked up in the Fort and will be forced to Surender for the want of provision and left to the Mercy of those brutes,—

I have yet hope that the Lord is with us although he hides his face as it ware for a moment and puts us to trial, to hear See and experience things we never toght of, and if the Lord is with us who will be against us, may he dwel in the midst of your Councels, may he who is Strong in battele go out with our Armies may give us help from trouble, for vain is the help of man, Through god we shall do valiantly for he it is that shall tread down our Enemies, this is my trust Through god only we shall be saved, I must Coclude with this long but Inocent stile—See the other Side

I must inform you of our going to move down to Eusopus and from thence we now not as yet, my Brother Gerrit[117] *is gone down last week with some goods is to Look out for a Place, we received a Letter from him he is arived there the peopele being much afraid of the Indians if the ragulars Should get in Posesion of this Place*

I am sory to leve this place I hope it is for the Best, I Content myself with the thoughts of hearing from you as often as poseble, I Tremble to hear that our army is at Stilwater[118] *I have more to say but my heart is overvelmed may I once more see you is my sincere Wiches may the Lord give serve us all I remain*

Your Sincerest

Catherine Van Schaick

Sister Remembers her love to you

[The carrier of this letter was killed in the Battle of Oriskany and the letter was later recovered in Lt Col Willett's Raid on the Indian Camps near Fort Stanwix on August 6, 1777]

Marching orders with intent to seize the fort were finally given by British commander Barry St. Leger on August 1st.[119] Under the supervision of British officers, allied Indians were to march as the front of the main force with the rear guard consisting of the British troops. Indians were to guard both flanks and sixty marksmen under the command of Captain Stephen Watts, brother-in-law of Sir John Johnson, would join the rear guard formation. The Indians in front were to intimidate the defenders and to take the attention off the marksmen preparing to fire behind the lines. Another letter from St. Leger to Henry Bird was sent on the day when the siege began, indicating that the operations underway were "sensible and spirited," and that another corps of Indians under Joseph Thayendanegea [Joseph Brant] were on the way to replace any fallen natives comprising the first attack.[120] St. Leger's own men would move on the fort itself by midday. The siege of Fort Schuyler was officially underway.

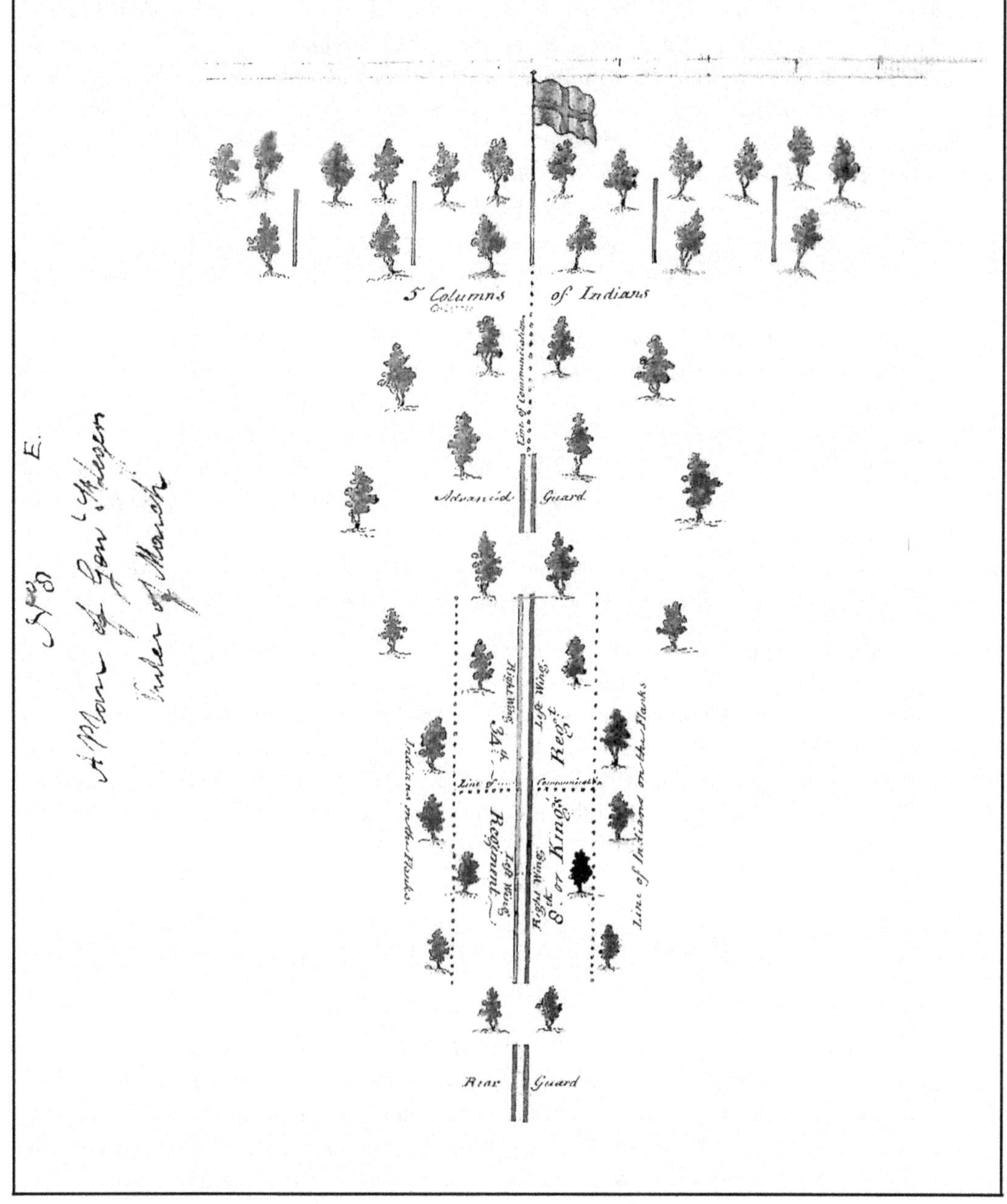

A Plan of St. Leger's Order of March 1777 (Gansevoort-Lansing collection. Manuscripts and Archives Division. The New York Public Library. Astor, Lenox and Tilden Foundations).

76—St. Leger's Line of March

(According to Lossing Vol. 1 page 241. this date is Aug. 1. 1777.)

(St. Leger & his Rangers)

Line of March

A Body of Indians properly officer'd, marching in Line of their own sort of Columns, at large intervals form the San, at 460 paces in the front of the Line; they will stretch a file of Indians from their body at ten paces from each other, to form a line of communication with the advanc'd Guard of the Line; which is to be 100 paces in the front of the Column; The right and left flanks will be covered by Indians at 100 paces, stretching likewise files of communication with the main Body.

The rear Guard at 100 paces, will be formed of the Troops.

The King's Regt. will move from the left by indian file, while the 34th will do the same from the right.

Capt. Watts with 60 Marksmen from the K. R. R. of N. York, will form the advanc'd and rear Guards.—

A general Line of battle for any attack on the March

The Van Guard of Indians will form a line entire to their front, those on the flanks will face outwards.

The advanced Guard will form to the front; the rear Guard to the rear—

The left Wing of the King's Regt. will form to the front, the right wing will face outwards and dress square with the left; while the right Wing of the 34th Regt. will form to the front and it's left facing to the left, will dress square with the right.

Each Corps will have ten chosen Marksmen in different parts of their line, to be pushed forward to any quarter if occasion requires to reinforce or countenance the Indians.—

As the British-Indian alliance positioned around the fort, things did not go according to plan. Felling trees at Wood Creek would retard St. Leger's movement. The large artillery forces meant to shell the vulnerable eastern side of the fort were stalled and the troops were forced to make improvisational shelters.[121] This effectively cut off all the heavy guns from Henry Bird's advance party and St. Leger's marksmen, leaving them incredibly vulnerable to volleys from the defenders. Sir John Johnson's men were busy themselves with cutting path to the southwest of the fort.[122]

77—Henry Bird to Barry St. Leger

August 2d

Sir I take the earliest opportunity of sending Mr Wilson[123] to you—who as I have advanced appears to be so well acquainted with the country that his informations—with respect to advancing the Cannon & baggage as where it may be drawn~~gdd~~ where landed &c (if there are not people well acquainted with the road ; in the army)—maybe of great service—Ten men with axes two days employ'd may clear the road, or make it fit for cannon as far as I have advanced—

No Savages would advance with me except Henrigues a Mohawk and one of the Six nations—an old acquantance of mine Those two Sir I hope to have the honour to present to you

a ~~Man~~ Savage who goes by the name of Commodore Bradly was the Chief cause of the Savages not advancing to day—twelve Messesaugers came up two or three hours after my departure those with the scout of fifteen I had the honour to mention to you in my last—are sufficient to invest Fort Stanwix if you honour me so far as not to order the contrary

I am Sir with respect Your most obed

Henry Bird

Barry St. Leger. Published by H. Hinton, 1794 (Gansevoort-Lansing collection. Manuscripts and Archives Division. The New York Public Library. Astor, Lenox and Tilden Foundations).

78—Barry St. Leger to Henry Bird

Nine Mile Point Aug 2d 1777

Sir, I this instant received your letter, containing the account of your operations since you were detached, which I with great pleasure tell you have been sensible and spirited, your resolution of investing Fort Stanwix is perfectly right, & to inable you to do it with greater effect, I have detached Joseph [Thayendanegea] and his Corps of Indians to reinforce you—you will observe that I will have nothing but an Investiture made and in case the Enemy, observing the discretion and judgment with which it is made, should offer to capitulate, you are to tell them that you are sure I am well disposed to listen to them: this is not to take any glory or honor out of a young Soldier's hands, but by the presence of the Troops to prevent the barbarity and carnage, which will ever obtain when Indians make so superior a part of a Detachment—I shall move from hence at eleven oClock and be early in the afternoon at the entrance of the Creek.

I am, Sir, Your most obedt. humble Servt

Barry St. Leger

Lieut. Bird 8th Reg. [(on His Majesty's service) HHKing's Regt. command of a Detachment &c at the entrance of Wood Creek or elsewhere]

St Ledger's anxiety encreases lest the Garrison should surrender & Lt Bird orders him not even to treat of a surrender under the plausible pretext of preventing Act of barbarity

Inside the fort, Gansevoort was doing his best to reduce unintentional loss of life. Already aware of the enemy's arrival weeks in advance, he requested all the women, wounded and sick away from the garrison on 28 July.[124] On July 30, reinforcement arrived from Fort Dayton totaling 150 men of Colonel James Wesson's Ninth Massachusetts Regiment under Major Stephen Badlam.[125] At 5 p.m. on August 2, one hundred more men of the Ninth Massachusetts Regiment arrived on four batteaus under the command of Lieutenant Colonel James Mellen[126] of Van Schaick's Island docking at the Upper Landing with provisions. Knowing more men were arriving, Gansevoort ordered one hundred men under Captain Benschoten[127] and three subalterns to reinforce the guard and the batteaus. Just as the supplies entered the fort, Indians began to fire upon them near Fort Newport, which was less than a mile from Fort Schuyler. Gansevoort ordered a party of thirty men with a field piece to set fire to two barns, under cover of two cannons on the southwest bastion. On August 1, Gansevoort assigned detachments to the four bastions when the alarm sounded—Major Badlam's detachment to the southeast bastion, Captains Aaron Aorson and Cornelius T. Jansen's[128] detachments to the southwest bastion, Captains Thomas DeWitt, Abraham Swartwout and Leonard Bleeker's[129] detachments to the northeast bastion, and Captains Elias van Benshoten, Jr., and Henry Tiebout's[130] detachments to the northwest bastion.

On 3 August, at 3 p.m. St. Leger paraded his force around the fort and sent a "flag [of truce] brought up [by] Captain [Gilbert] Tice,[131] came into the Fort with a Proffer of protection if the Garrison wou'd Surrender, which was Rejected with disdain." A makeshift Continental flag was hoisted on the southeast bastion with the drummer calling the assembly and the regimental adjutant, Lieutenant Christopher Hutton,[132] who then read the Congressional resolution ordering the flag.[133] Upon hearing the resolution, Gansevoort ordered the white stripes to be made from strips cut from army shirts, the red from bits of scarlet cloth from petticoats, either from the garrison or from a captured British cloak and the blue ground for the stars, from either a cloak belonging to Captain Abraham Swartwout of the Dutchess County, NY, regiment (the camlet cloak taken from the enemy at Peekskill) or from the petticoat of Anna Roof.[134]

The next two days, continuous firing of small arms by the Indians killed two men and wounded six. Gansevoort ordered the house and barn belonging to Mr. Roof to be set on fire. Without the artillery, St. Leger was forced to concentrate fire on the surrounding mechanisms of the fort. The recently constructed barracks situated one hundred yards outside the garrison were also set on fire.[135]

Forenoon on the 6th, three militiamen, John Adam F. Helmer, Hans Marcus Demuth and Johan Jost Folts,[136] arrived at the fort. Sent by General Herkimer, the leader of the nearby militia, they delivered a letter announcing his approach to the fort with one thousand militia. From Herkimer's letter, Gansevoort was ordered to fire three cannon to signal the messengers' arrival and prepare a sortie once the militia neared the fort. If Gansevoort heard small arms fire east down river, he was to send a party to quickly reinforce them.[137]

Soon after, St. Leger had received word that Herkimer's militiamen were fast advancing towards the siege. Sir John Johnson's men were ordered to split up, with Johnson's half to meet up with the main infantry force firing directly upon the fort. The split of Johnson's forces effectively meant that the British would be unable to flank Gansevoort's defensive positions; they had to maintain a direct frontal attack in the desperate hope that they could force surrender before American reinforcements arrived.

After a thunderstorm, Gansevoort detached 250 men and one field piece under Lieutenant Colonel Willett with orders "to proceed down the road to meet the General's party." Willett marched to the direction of the militia and came upon an encampment of the enemy a half-mile away from the fort. The sortie killed approximately twenty men and took four prisoners (three wounded). Willett seized seven wagons between the two camps of Johnson and the Indians, including "several bundles of papers and a parcel of letters" for the garrison.[138] Other letters found were correspondence between Johnson and other British officers containing revealing information on the enemies' positions. Among the bounty returned to the garrison, four colors were hoisted as trophies of victory.[139]

Willett wrote a letter to the men of the Third New York Regiment[140] professing a sincere belief that his mission would help annihilate the direct threat on the fort. He closed the letter informing the troops that like good soldiers, they should not fear the enemy force as "they are truly a Contemptable pack their designs are of the most baraberious kind, but their power is not sufficient to put their Diabolical purposes into execution."[141]

79—Marinus Willett to the Officers of the Third New York Regiment

My Dear Brother Officers and Soldiers

My Secret and unexpected Departure[142] *from the Garrison by order of Colo Gansevoort will undoubtedly Surprise you and I dont doubt you will believe me when I assure you that the thoughts of parting with you tho: but for a few days afflicts me ~~grieviously afflicts me~~ at this Critical time; with you I have hitherto with pleasure endured & fatigue and Encountered Dangers and it is as well for your sakes as in support of the glorious Cause in which we are all embarked that I have now undertaken to encounter new Dangers & fatigues, Let no mans heart fail him tho he is surrounded with a Sett of Cruel Savage Enemies there Cruelty & Vengeance should cause to double our Fortitude & Diligence—The Enemies we have to encounter with one by no means [ ] as they are cruel and those Cruelty ought Undoubtedly to make us the more determined ~~and~~ nor is there any reason to fear that with the Blessing of Heaven—you will in a very few days be delivered from those [direfull] Enemies with which you are now Surrounded you will Easisly perceive the Propriety of my keeping my design a secret from you as it is impossible to Mention it without being in danger of being counteracted in it by its coming to the knowledge of the Enemy for [Maloncholy?] as the Consideration is it is true that there have been Villains among you Wretches who void of the obligations they are under to there God and there Countrey have barely deserted to our Cruel and Unatural Enemies—May God almighty preserve any more of you from this shamefull and abandoned Crime for my own part I assure that not a step than it is possible for me to take for your Speedy deliverance shall be omitted nor am I without the most Sanguin hopes that I shall soon Enjoy the pleasing sight of seeing you again on this possible & Congratulating you on a Glorious Deliverance from your Present Enemies and in assisting you to divide their Spails among you In the mean time I beseech you by all the love and regard you have for yourselves for Your Countrey and all the regarde you have for me to perservere in doing your Duty Like good Soldiers dont be afraid of your Enemies they are truly a Contemptable pack their designs are of the most baraberious kind, but their power is not sufficient to put there Diabolical purposes into execution do your duty and fear not keep God Almighty will bless you with success eaqual to your most Sanguin hopes—*

I am my Dr Br Officer & Soldiers yours Most Affectionately

M Willett

[August 5th 1777]

It would seem by Willett's letter to the men that the British inclusion of their Indian allies in the front ranks not only failed to deprive the defenders of their morale, but that the defenders now would believe that there would be no surrender and instead would be left at the mercy of the "baraberious" Indians. This must have hardened their resolve; a force faced with either complete victory or a cruel death would be guaranteed to fight with a viciousness not seen in other battles.

On the 8th, St. Leger's adjutant-general, William Ancrom, and Colonel John Butler were permitted access inside the fort to deliver a letter from militiamen Colonel Frederick Bellinger and Major John Frey,[143] who were captured during the battle of Oriskany, "begging us to surrender, telling us our Communication was cut off, that the Enemy had a large parcel of Fine Troops and an Excellent pack of Artillery and farther that they expected General Burgoyne was in Albany and could see no hopes of our having any succor as the militia had many killed and taken."[144] Ancrom had also verbally delivered a request for surrender.[145] St. Leger claimed the siege was initiated under the premise of holding forth "security not depredation to the Country." He also claimed that if there was such a surrender, that the inhabitants of the nearby settlers "remain quietly at their houses that they do not suffer their Cattle to be removed nor their corn or forage to be secreted."[146] After hearing the word of Jane McCrea's murder, the inhabitants would not see this as a genuine offer of peace, and the soldiers could certainly expect far worse. His last sentence in the request for surrender carried the suggestion that the policies in New Jersey and Pennsylvania would continue unabated at Fort Schuyler: "The messengers of Justice and of wrath await them in the field add devastation, famine and every concomitant horror that a reluctant but indispensible prosecution of military duty must occasion will bar the way to their return."[147]

80—From Barry St. Leger

By Barry St Leger Esqr

Commander in Chief of a chosen body of Troops from the Grand Army, as well as an extensive ~~of~~ Corps of Indian Allies, from all the nations, &c &c

The Forces entrusted to my command are designed to act in concert and upon a common principle, with the numerous Armies and Fleets which already display in every Quarter of America, the power, justice, and when properly sought the mercy of the King—

The cause in which the British Arms are thus exerted applies to the most affecting interest of the human heart, and the military servants of the Crown at first called forth for the sole purpose of restoring the rights of the Constitution, now combine with love of their Country and duty to their Sovereign the other extensive incitements which spring from a due sense of the general privileges of mankind. To the eyes and ears of the temperate part of the public, and to the breast of suffering thousands in the Provinces be the melancholy appeal whether the present unnatural rebellion has not been made a foundation for the completest system of Tyranny that ever God in his displeasure suffered for a time to be exercised over a froward & stubborn generation

Arbitrary imprisonment, confiscation of property, persecution & torture unpredented in the inquisitions of the Romish Church are among the palpable enormities that verify the affirmative—These are inflicted by Assemblies & Committees who dare to profess themselves friends to Liberty upon the most quiet subjects without distinction of age or sex for the sole crime often for the sole suspicion of having adhered in principle to the government under which they were born and to which by every tie Divine and human they owe allegiance, To consummate these shocking proceedings the profanation of religion is added to the most profligate prostitution of common reason, the conscience of men are set at nought and multitude are compelled not only to bear arms but also to swear subjection to an usurpation they abhor

Animated by these consideration; at the head of Troops in the full powers of health discipline and ~~ardour~~ valour determined to strike when necessary and anxious to spare when possible, I by these Presents invite and exhort all persons in all places where the progress of this army may point, and by the blessing of God I will extend it far to maintain such a conduct as may justify me in protecting their lands habitations & families The intention of this address is to hold forth security not depredation to the Country—

To those whom spirit & principle may induce to partake the glorious task of redeeming their Countrymen from dungeons and reestablishing the blessings of legal government, I offer encouragement and employment and upon the first intelligence of their assocations I will find means to assist their undertakings. The domestic, the industrious, the infirm and even the timid Inhabitants I am desirous to protect provided they remain quietly at their houses that they do not suffer their Cattle to be removed nor their corn or forage to be secreted or destroyed that they do not break up the bridges or roads; nor by any other acts directly or indirectly endearous to obstruct the operations of the kings troops or supply or assist those of the enemy—

[x] The Forces entrusted to my Command are designed to act in concert and upon a common principle with the numerous Fleets and armies [x]

Every species of provision brought to my Camp will be paid for at an equitable rate and in solid coin—If notwithstanding these endearous and sincere inclinations to effect them the phrensy of hostility should remain, I trust I shall stand acquitted in the eyes of God and men in denouncing and executing the vengeance of the State against the willful outcasts. The messengers of Justice and of wrath await them in the field add devastation, famine and every concomitant honor that a reluctant but indispensible prosecution of military duty must occasion will bar the way to their return

By Order of the Commander in Chief Barry St Leger

Will: Osb: Hamilton[148]

[This was handed by the Adjt Genl & Coll Butler[149] *on the 6th of August to Col Gansevoort 1777]*

Gansevoort, Willett and Massachusetts Lieutenant Colonel James Mellen were present and after a discussion, Gansevoort delegated Willett to respond. Gansevoort feared his Albany Dutch accent would either hinder negotiation or be subject to ridicule. The garrison's reply: "I will answer no verbal summons but at the mouth of the cannon, unless delivered by Colonel St. Leger himself."[150] At one in the morning, Willett and Lieutenant Levi Stockwell[151] went on a secret expedition to reach General Schuyler. Two days later, they reached Fort Dayton, situated near the German Flatts. They then arrived to Stillwater, to the house of Dirck Swart, headquarters of General Schuyler.[152]

After receiving St. Leger's written request the next morning, Gansevoort sent his reply, and the plain and immediate wording surely deflected St. Leger's attempts at intimidation.

81—To Barry St. Leger

Your Letter of this days Date I have Receiv'd, in Answer to which I say, that it is my Determined resolution with the Forces under my Command to defend this Fort ~~& Garrison to~~ the

Gansevoort's reply to St. Leger's correspondence, 9 August 1777 (Gansevoort-Lansing collection. Manuscripts and Archives Division. The New York Public Library. Astor, Lenox and Tilden Foundations).

last Extremity in behalf of the United American States who have placed me here to Defend it against all their Enemies

I have the Honor to be Sir your most obt Huml Servt
P Gansevoort Colo
Commanding Ft Schuyler
[Copy of our Answer to Genl St. Leger Summons on 9th day of August 1777]

Upon receiving Gansevoort's reply, St. Leger began to bombard the fort, which sustained little damages. Gansevoort, fearing the provisions would be damaged if a shell set the barracks on fire, moved them upon the parade. He had also secured public papers and money in the hands of John Hanson and papers of Hansen Van Veghten belonging to the paymaster, Ensign Jeremiah Van Rensselaer, in the bomb proof in the southwest bastion. Again, at 10:30 p.m. the enemy began to bombard the garrison and continued until daylight, which was "very well directed" killing one and wounding another.

The next day, the enemy tried to trick the garrison in believing they were abandoning their siege but Gansevoort thought otherwise, ordering the "guard & piquet doubled and the troops to lay on their arms." The fort was heavily bombarded from 1 a.m. until dawn.

Schuyler sent word to Gansevoort that forces were currently en route to raise the siege (these forces would be ambushed by a British detachment at Oriskany), and that "Great Reinforcements" were being prepared to face General Burgoyne's main army at Fort Edward.[153]

82—From Philip Schuyler

Albany August 10th: 1777

Dear Colonel A Body of Troops left this Yesterday and others are following to raise the Siege of Fort Schuyler—Every Body here believes you will defend it to the last, and I strictly enjoin you so to do.

General Burgoyne is at Fort Edward[154]*—our army at Stilwater—Great Reinforcements coming from the Eastward, and we trust all will be well and that the Enemy will be repulsed.*

General Howe[155] *landed at New Castle in Delaware, but was soon obliged to reimbark—It is said he means to land on the Jersey Shore and try to get opposite Philadelphia and bombard it.*

Mr. Watts who was wounded in the Engagement with General Herkimer died the next Day.

I am Dr Sir Your most obedient humble Servant

Ph: Schuyler

Colonel Gansevoort

On 11 August, St. Leger decided to implement more extreme tactics to win back the Indians' support. Ultimately, it seemed that the Indian morale was so low due to the loss of several key chiefs during the Battle of Oriskany as to necessitate a desertion from the British forces.[156] St. Leger ordered the river's course to be altered. Gansevoort, in anticipation of this, ordered two wells to be open inside the garrison.[157] From the start of the siege to 15th, the enemy launched 137 shells at the fort. They would continue to bombard the garrison day and night until they departed. On 19 August, the enemy began digging a trench towards the northwest bastion, and were within 150 yeards of the fort's peripheral ditch by the end of the siege.[158]

Gansevoort's leadership and Willett's venture and capture of enemy supplies fell on many ears outside of the siege. An August 15th letter from Leonard congratulated his brother's performance, and that according to Willett himself that his "Enemies even speak well of you."[159]

263—From Marinus Willett

The following is a narrative of part of the transactions at and near Fort Stanwix since the investiture of that place by the enemy, given in Manuscript by Lieutenant-Colonel Willet of that Garrison, which appeared in the Massachusetts Spy, August 29, 1777.

On Saturday Evening August 2d, five battoes arrived with Stores for the garrison. About the same time we discovered a number of fires a little better than a mile from the north west corner of the fort. The stores were all got safe in, and the troops which were a guard to the battoes marched up. The captain of the battoes and a few of his men delaying their time about the boats, were fired on by a party of indians which killed one men and wounded two the captain himself was taken prisoner.

Next morning the enemy appeared in the edge of the woods about a mile below the fort, where they took post in order to invest it upon that quarters, and to cut off the communication with the country; from whence they sent in a flag who told us of their great power, strength and determination, in such a manner as gave us reason to suppose they were not possessed or strength sufficient to take the fort. Our answer was a determination so support it.

All day on Monday we were much annoyed by a sharp fire of musketry from the Indians and German rifle men, which as our men were obliged to be exposed on the works killed one and wounded seven. The day after, the firing was not so heavy, and our men under better cover, all the damage sustained by us this day was one man killed by a rifle ball. The evening indicated something in contemplation by the enemy. The Indians were uncommonly noisy; they made most horrid yellings great part of the evening in the woods hardly a mile from the fort. A few cannon were fired among them.

Wednesday morning there was an unusual silence. We discovered some of the enemy marching along the edge of the woods downwards. About eleven o'clock three man for into the fort, who brought a letter from General Harkeman of the Tryon county militia; advising us that he was at Ercsks (8 mile off) with part of his militia, and purposed to force his way to the fort for our relief. In order to render him what service we could in his march, it was agreed that I shou'd make a sally from the fort with 250 men consisting of one half Gansevoorts, one half Massachusetts ditto and one field piece (an iron three pounder.) The men were instantly paraded, and I ordered the following disposition to be made thirty men for the advance guard, to be commanded by Capt. Van Benscouton, and Lieut. Stockwell's thirty for the rear guard under the command of Capt. Allen,[160] *of Massachusetts troops and Lieut. Dauffendorfs*[161] *thirty for flank guards, to be commanded by Capt.—from Massachusetts, and Ensign Chase.*[162] *The main body formed in eight subdivisions commanded by Captain Blacker, Lieutenants Comine, Begardus, McClenner, Costrander; Ensigns Bagley,*[163] *Lewis and Dennison; Lieut. Ball*[164] *the only supenumory officer, to march with me. Capt. Janson to bring up the rear of the main body, Captain Swartwoudt with Ensigns Magee, Ament*[165] *and 50 men to guard the field piece, which was under the direction of Major Bedlow.*[166]

Nothing could be more fortunate than this enterprise. We totally counted two of the enemy's encampments destroyed all the provisions that were in them, [breaste] off upwards of 50 brass kettles, and more than 100 blankets, (two articles which were much needed) with a quantity of muskets, tomahawks, spears, ammunition, cloathing, dearskins, a variety of Indian affairs and five colours, (the whole of which on our rear turn to the Fort were displayed on our flag staff under the continental flag.) The indians took chiefly to the woods, the rest of the troops then at these rafts to the river. The number of men left by the enemy is uncertain; 6 lay dead in their encampments, 2 of which were Indians; several scattered about in the woods; but their greatest loss appeared to be in crossing the river and no inconsiderable number upon the oppeson shore. I was happy in preventing the men from scalping even the indians, being desirous if posable to teach even the savages humanity but the men were much better employed, and kept in excellent order. We were out so long that a number of British regulars accompanied by what Indians, etc. could be rallied, had marched down to a thicket at the other side of the river, about 50 yards from the road we were to pass on our return; near this place I had ordered the field peice;—the ambush was not quite formed when we discovered them, and gave them a wall directed fire. Here especially Maj. Bedlow with his field piece did considerable execution --- Here also, the enemy were annoyed by the fire of several cannon from the fort as they marched round to form the ambuscade. The enemy's fire was very wild, and though we were very much exposed; did no execution at all.

We brought in four prisoners, three of which were wounded.

One of the prisoners is a Mr. Singleton of Montreal,[167] *who is a Lieutenant in a company of which Mr. Stephen Watts of New-York (brother in law to Sir John Johnson) was Captain, and who was himself killed in the engagement with the militia about two hours before. Mr. Singleton told me that Sir John Johnson was with him when we attacked their camp, and that he thinks he ran to the river. It is said by some of the Oneida Indians that he is killed, which does not appear unlikely. From these prisoners we received the first accounts of Gen. Harkeman's militia being ambushed on their march; and of a severe battle they had with them about two hours before, which gave reason to think they had for the present given up their design of marching to the fort.*

I should not do justice to the officers and soldiers who were with me on their enterprize, if I was not in the most positive terms to assure their countrymen that they in general behaved with the greatest gallantry upon this occasion, and next to the very kind and signal interposition of divine providence, which was powerfully manifested in their favour, it was undoubtedly owing to that noble intrepidity which discovered itself in this attack, and struck the enemy with such a panic as disembled them from taking pains to direct their fire, that we had not one man killed or wounded. The officers in general behaved so well that it is hardly right to mention the names of any particular one for their singular valour: But, so remarkably intrepid was Capt. Van Benscouton, and so rapid was his attack, that it demands from me this particular testimony of his extraordinary spirit.

Among other things taken from the enemy were several bundles of papers and a parcel of letters belonging to our garrison, which they had taken from our militia but not yet opened, here I found one letter for myself, there was likewise papers belonging to Sir John Johnson and several others of the enemies officers, with letters to and from General St. Leger their commander, these papers have been of some service to us. On the evening of the next day the enemy fired a few cannon at us from high ground about half a mile north of the fort where they have erected a small battery. Next day, being Friday the 8th, they threw a parcel of shells from the same battery, none of which did any execution. This evening they sent us a flag, with which came their Adjutant General; Capt Armstrong, Col. Butler, and a Surgeon,[168] *the Surgeon to examine Singleton's wounds; the principal business of the flag was to acquaint us that Gen. St. Lager had with much difficulty prevailed on the indians to agree that if the commanding officer would deliver up the fort, the garrison should be secured from any kind of harm, that not a hair of their heads should be touched, but if not, the consequence to the garrison, should it afterwards fall into their hands, must be terrible; that the indians were very much enraged on account of their having a number of their chiefs killed in the late action, and were determined, unless they got possession of the fort to go down the Mohawk river, and fall upon its inhabitants, Our answer was that should this be the case, the blood of those inhabitants would be upon the heads of Mr. Butler and his employers, not upon us, and that such proceedings would ever remain a sigma upon the name of Britain; but for our parts we were determined to defend the fort.*

That evening it was agreed by the field officers that I should undertake with Lieutenant Stockwell (who is a good woodman) to endeavour to get down into the country and by making a proper representation of our affairs endeavour to procure such force as may be sufficient to accomplish this important piece of business. By the best accounts the loss of the indians must be very considerable, and they are quite sick of the expedition.

Marinus Willet
German-Flats, Aug. 11, 1777

83—From Leonard Gansevoort

Albany August 15 1777

Dear Sir I congratulate you on your Success in the Sortie[169] *made on Thursday the 6th Inst as related by Lieut Col Willet your Friends are very happy to hear it and your Enemies even speak well of you—Colo Willet has given us an Acct also of the Conference between you and ~~the~~ Adjutant Genl the Surgeon Genl & Colo Butler which has redocinded much to your Honor. Adam Helmer agreeable to his promise called at your Father and related the Matter exactly as Colo Willet does he is an honest Fellow*

Your Mother is at Claverack very well—Anatje goes to Esopus today with John Ten Broeck's Family—

This will be delivered you by Genl Arnold who goes to raise the Siege of Fort Schuyler with a fine Body of Troops God grant him success

Miss [ ] is at the great [Imbogt] with her Father—My Love to Harry John &c &c &c &c &c &c

Your's very Sincerely
[Leonard Gansevoort]
Col Gansevoort

He finished the letter with the news that General Arnold was personally taking men to raise the siege once and for all. Arnold had been desperate to prove his capacity for heroic leadership after being reprimanded by Horatio Gates at Saratoga. While Arnold was heading towards the fort, militiamen and civilians under General Stark in Bennington had ambushed and taken hundreds of British prisoners and multiple artillery pieces.[170] On August 22, Gansevoort informed Arnold that St. Leger had retreated "with the utmost precipation."

Benedict Arnold. Engraved by H. B. Hall, 1863 (Gansevoort-Lansing collection. Manuscripts and Archives Division. The New York Public Library. Astor, Lenox and Tilden Foundations).

84—To Benedict Arnold

Dear Sir This morning at eleven o'clock I began a heavy cannonade upon our enemy's works, which was immediately returned by a number of shells and cannon. About three o'clock seven deserters came in, who informed me that Gen. St. Leger with his army was retreating with the utmost precipitation[171];

soon after which I sent out a party of about 60 men to enter their camps, who soon returned, and confirmed the above accounts.

About seven o'clock this evening, Hanjost Schuyler[172] *arrived here, and informed me that General Arnold with two thousand men were on their march for this fort, in consequence of which I send you this information.*

I am, dear Sir, yours, & c.

Peter Gansevoort, Col.

To General Arnold or the Commanding officer of troops marching to Fort Schuyler

[appeared in the Connecticut Courant, September 1, 1777 and Early American Imprints, Series 1, no. 43384, 1777]

Arnold's reputation, not his actual task, drove the British army and Indians. According to the *Military Journal of Dr. Thatcher*, it was due to the actions of Lieutenant Colonel John Brooks, a savvy officer from Massachusetts, in the advance of Learned's regiment. He suggested using a messenger to spread the alarm about Butler's capture and the large force of Arnold in hopes to put the enemy to flight. Arnold quickly approved it. Lieutenant Walter Butler, with approximately eight soldiers and ten Indians, were taken prisoners at Shoemaker's house, about two miles from Fort Dayton. Shoemaker was a justice of the peace, and was later apprehended by Colonel Wesson.[173]

Benedict Arnold wrote to Gansevoort on the same day, informing that he will be arriving at the fort in only a few days.[174]

85—From Benedict Arnold

German Flatts 22d Augt 1777

Dear Colonel I wrote you the 19th Instant that I should be with you in a few days since which your Express is arrived and informs me you are in high Spirits and under no Apprehensions at present, I have been retarded by the badness of the Road, waiting for some Baggage and Ammunition Waggons & for the Malitia who did not at first turn out with that Spirit I expected, they are now joining me in great Numbers, a few days will relieve you, but under no kind of Apprehensions I know the Strength of the Enemy & how to deal with them.

Inclosed are Several Letters and Papers which will announce to you a Signal Victory gaind by General Stark over the Enemy, you will accept my congratulary Compliments on the Occasion

Howe with his shattered Remnant of his Army are on board Ship. The last Acct was the 4th Augt he was in the Gulph Stream becalmd—Burgoyne, I hear this Minute is retreating to Ty—I make no doubt our Army which is near Fifteen Thousand will cut of his Retreat

Adieu & Believe me to the Dr Colonel Your Sincerely

B Arnold

Colonel Ganzevort

Although the enemy had already vacated their positions around Fort Schuyler, Arnold was still en route to Fort Schuyler to relieve Gansevoort. Burgoyne's main force had attempted a retreat back to Ticonderoga following the disastrous battle at Bennington but instead faced off against the Continental Army at Saratoga. Arnold also sent a letter to General Gates on the 23rd, happily informing him that the enemy forces were in retreat from Fort Schuyler with "great precipitation."[175]

86—Benedict Arnold to Horatio Gates

Mohawk River, 10 miles above Fort Dayton, August 23t, 1777 5 o'clock P.M.

Dear General, I wrote you the 21st instant from the German Flatts, that from the best intelligence I could procure of the enemy's strength it was much superior to ours. at the same time inclosed you a copy of the resolutions of a council of war, and requested you to send me a reinforcement of 1000 light troops, as the enemy had made their approaches within 200 yards of the fort. I was determined at all events to hazard a battle rather than suffer the garrison to fall a sacrifice This morning I marched from the German Flats for this place.—The excessive bad roads and necessary precautions in marching thro' a thick wood, retarded us so much that we have but this moment reached this place, where I have met an express with the enclosed letter from Col. Gansevoort, acquainting me the enemy had yesterday left Fort Schuyler with great precipitation. I am at a loss to judge their real intentions, whether they have returned home or retire with a view of engaging us on the road. I am inclined to think the former from the account of the deserters, and from leaving their tents and considerable baggage, which our people secured. I shall immediately detach about nine hundred men to make a forced march to the fort, in hopes of coming up with the rear and securing their cannon and heavy baggage. My artillery, tents Etc. I shall leave here. The battoes with provisions follow me. As soon as the security of the post will permit, I shall return with as many men as can be spared. As I came down in battoes shall be able to make great dispatch. I have sent an order to the light troops if you have sent any, to return to you immediately, and the militia to go home.

I am, &c

B. Arnold

Hon. Major General Gates. (copy)

A gentleman from Number Four informs, That two families ([?ately] resilient in the neighbourhood of Bennington) arrived there and inform, that Gov. Skeene died of a wound[176] *he received in his thigh at the late battle with Gen. Starks.*

[appeared in the Connecticut Courant, September 1, 1777]

Arnold would send nine hundred men in front of his main force to secure Fort Schuyler and made preparations for the supply train's arrival. The next day Arnold informed Gates that Gansevoort had anticipated Arnold's nine hundred men, and had instead dispatched his own party to capture any remnants of the fleeing British army. The result was the confiscation of British tents, ammunition, and other provisions.[177]

87—Benedict Arnold to Horatio Gates

Fort Schuyler, August 24, 1777. Ten o'Clock at Night.

Dear General, I wrote you yesterday, that the enemy had retreated from this place; at five o'clock this evening by a forced march of twenty-two miles, through a thick wood, I reached this place, in expectation of harrassing the enemy in their retreat, Colonel Gansevoort had anticipated my design, by sending out a small party, who brought in four royals, and a considerable quantity of baggage, with a number of prisoners and deserters, the enemy went off with the greatest precipitation, leaving their tents; standing, their provisions, ammunition, &c. &c. which have fallen into our hands.

I am, Dear General, Your affectionate
B. Arnold
Honorable Major General Gates
[appeared in the Early American Imprints, Series 1, no. 43384, 1777]

According to a journal contributed to an officer at the fort, William Colbreath, eighteen men were wounded, seven were killed and nine had deserted during the three-week siege of Fort Schuyler.[178] In addition to all the drama of the siege, on August 22, a woman who stayed in the garrison gave birth to a daughter despite being wounded in the thigh the day before.[179]

After St. Leger's dismantled the siege, Gansevoort addressed the men of the Third New York Regiment who bravely thwarted the enemy advancement. In somewhat humorous fashion, Gansevoort wrote on the end of the transcribed speech "A laconic Address to my fellow Officers and Soldiers."[180]

88—To the Officers and Soldiers of the Third New York Regiment

I should be wanting in Justice to you, if I did not give Some Testimony of your good Conduct during the Time you have been in this Garrison and especially while we were besieged by our Enemy, believe me that I am impress'd with a proper Sense of the Behavior by which you have done essential Service to your Country and acquir'd the immortal Honour to yourselves—nothing can equal the pleasure I have experienced Since my Absence in hearing and receiving the public approbation of our Country for our Services, which is and must be to every Soldier a full and ample Compensation for the Same, permit me to congratulate you upon the Success of the American Arms both to the Southward and Northward every Day terminates with Victory to America, and I make not the least doubt but in this Campaign we will effectually establish the Independence of the United States and thereby Secure to ourselves the Spirits and Liberties for which we have so nobly stood forth

No 36 A laconic Address to my fellow Officers and Soldiers after our success at Fort Stancoise
[PG]

After hearing the successful news of Fort Schuyler, John Adams, the president of the Board of War, wrote to his wife, Abagail on September 2: "Gansevoort has proven it is possible to hold a fort." This was different from his response about the disgraceful evacuation and retreat of Fort Ticonderoga by General Arthur St. Clair: "I think we shall never defend a post until we shoot a General."

There was little pause in the Continental forces following Peter Gansevoort's victory. His brother Leonard sent word to the New York Delegates that all available forces turned their attention to the north of Albany in anticipation of a "very decisive Blow," noting that Burgoyne was losing sufficient supplies and river transports; he would in all likelihood be forced to directly confront the nearby armies of Generals Gates and Lincoln.[181]

89—Leonard Gansevoort to the New York Delegates

Sept 18th: 1777 Kingston
Gentlemen, *The Flurry of Business occasioned by calling out the Militia for reinforcing*

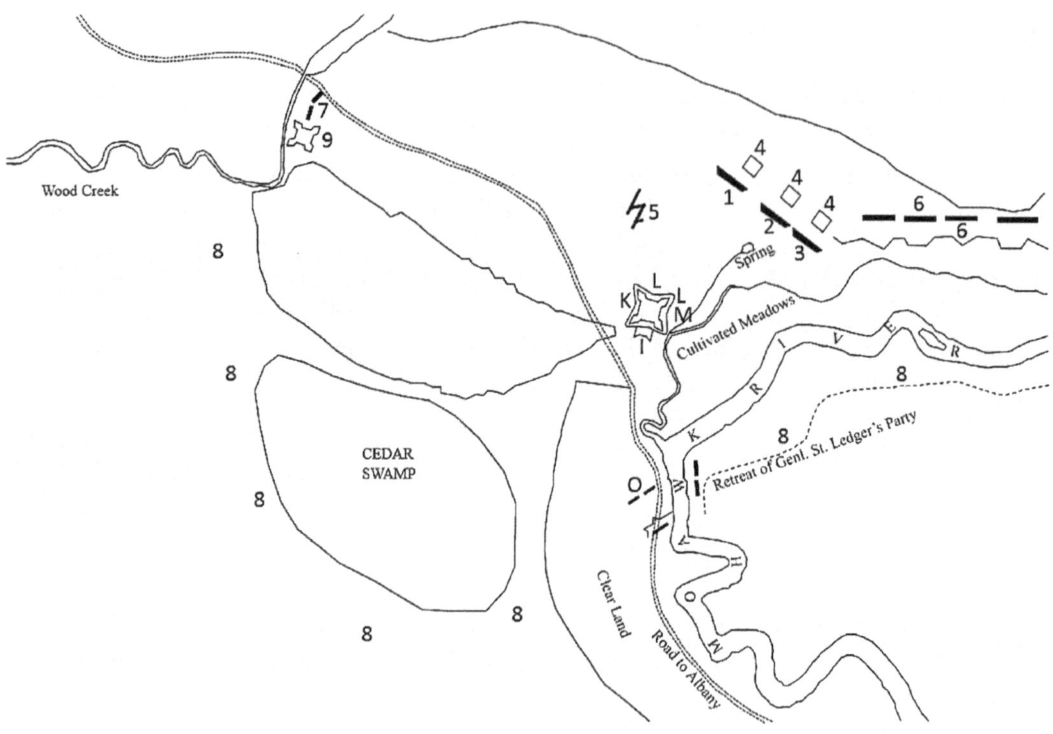

The Siege of Fort Schuyler, based on Francois Louis Tesseidre de Fleury's sketch, 1777.

1. Battery of 3 Guns
2. Bomb Battery of 4 Mortars
3. Bomb Battery of 3 Guns
4. Redoubts to cover the batteries
5. Line of approaches
6. British encampment
7. Loyalists
8. Indians
9. Ruins of Fort Newport
I. Horn work begun
K. Covered way
L. Glacis
M. Sally port
O. Willet's attack

our Northern Army & the ~~convening~~ meeting of the Legislature has prevented my answering your Letter of the 8th Ult: as early as I could have wished—The ~~raising of the Seige of~~ late Successes attending our Exertions to the Westward having ~~drove relieved Fort Schuyler and drove the~~ obliged the Enemy to raise the Seige of Fort Schuyler and abandon their Attempts in that Quarter with Loss and Disgrace and the strong Reinforcements which already have and are daily joining the Armies under Generals Gates and ~~General~~ Lincoln has greatly changed the Face of Affairs to the Northward which ~~when I you wrote me~~ not long since were truly critical and alarming—Genl Gates has advanced with the Army under his immediate Command which is from the best Accounts I have been able to gather about 10,000 strong to the North of Stillwater where he is ~~busy~~ throwing ~~up Works~~ a Bridge across the River and laying out Works to defend that Pass—Genl Lincoln with about 5,000 lies to the Eastward ~~some when~~ in the Grants at ~~or near~~ a Town called Pawlet[182]*—The Enemy's advanced Party is at Van Veghten's in or near Saraghtoga ~~at which Place where they be~~ & Same Body between that & Fort Edward where they have also ~~thrown~~ ended a Bridge across the River and have their Boats. ~~in a~~ By the latest Accounts ~~Genl Burgoyne appears to be upon the~~ of the Disposition of Genl Burgoyne's Army it appears as if ~~they~~ he intended speedily to move forward and before this reaches you it is highly probable that some very decisive Blow will be struck it is said and credited that Burgoyne has destroyed his own Boats in the Lake for which* *if true there is no accounting ~~but by Attributing it to his cutting off his own Retreat~~ unless he means to render his People desperate by Cutting off all Possibility of a Retreation—Which ~~in a~~ however in my Opinion is more likely to ~~produce~~ occasion Desertions than to produce the respond ~~intended~~ supposed Effect—*

The Failure of the Enemy to the Westward has lost them the Confidence of the Indians the Warriors of whom ~~had who~~ (the Oneidas excepted) had pretty generally joined St Leger ~~within~~ Within these few Days past a Member of the Sachems ~~of the~~ and warriors of the different Tribes of the six Nations have come to Albany to hold a Treaty ~~of~~ with our Commy and it is said to ... make a Tender of their services and join our Army most of them being well armed. ~~On Friday and~~ I am informed by Letters by Express from Genl Putnam that a large Number of the Enemy with several Peices of Artillery had crossed from Speten Devil on Friday and Saturday last to Fort Lee[183] *and marched to Hackinsack that they were joined ~~by a~~ there by another Party from Staten Island who took their Rout thro' Elizabeth Town Newwark & that by the last Accounts they were encamped at Lobiseski's Mills about 4 Miles West of Hackinsack on the Road to Paramus and amounted to About 5000—Genl McDougal crossed the River to ~~oppose them and~~ prevent their penetrating into the Country and I have ordered out eleven Regiments of the Militia ~~at~~ of this State to strengthen the Posts in the Highland ~~and~~ to reinforce the Army under Genl Putnam and ~~to strengthen Genl McDougal~~ the better to enable Genl McDougal to oppose the Enemy. ~~It is~~ Genl Putnam also inform me that he is advised and believe that the Enemy have recd a considerable Reinforcement lately at New York which must be the Case or their Numbers in ~~the~~ Jersey much mistaken what their Designs are Time only can discover. ~~I am exceedingly anxious~~ Our Anxiety now is chiefly about our Affair to the Southward we fear for the Fate of Philadelphia and of our public Stores near Swede's Ferry And we still dread more that by too strenuously contending to save the former we may lose what is of much more Importance our Army tho' we repose in the greatest Confidence is the Prudence of our General:—*

Our Legislature have been upon Business for a Week past both Houses are pretty full and I have the greatest Hopes that the new Machine will work well.—

The first Team of our Supreme Court ended last Week on Saturday it was held with great Order and Decorum and I have the Pleasure to assure you that the People seem happy under ~~the~~ a proper Organized Governmt

It is impossible to put in Execution in this State under its present Circumstances the Resolve of Congress for recruiting our Continental Regiments—The Militia being chiefly in the Field it would answer no Purpose to attempt it—I wish the Allowance for recruiting ~~had~~ been made to the Officers ~~to be~~ who should be appointed ~~for that Purpose~~ out of the different Regiments. Men will always choose to engage with Officers who are to serve with them and Persons properly qualified for the recruiting Service are to be found now in the Army only.—Some time since the Council of Safety wrote you for the ~~All~~ Pay & Allowance /made to Militia Troopers of the State of Connecticut last summer to which they have not as yet recd your Answer We have not been able to pay our Horsemen who were also in Service at that Time & since not knowing what allowance to make them. They are discontented for want of their Pay it is right they should have it I must therefore beg you will forward me ~~an account as the Estable~~ an Account of the Pay allowed by Congress for that service and Army

To the Delegates

[LG]

90—From Marinus Willett

Albany Sep: 30th 1777

Dear Colo/ Not till Yesterday evening did I arrive here Colonel Varick who conveys this will give you a Genuine state of affairs in this Quarter. it is therefore unecessary for me to say any thing on that head.

I believe I shall pay our armey a Visit before I go to see Mrs Willett[184]—have heard from the Major who was well two days ago may every thing thats Clever attend the garrison at Fort Schuyler—my kind respects to all our Gentlemen

I am Dr Sir Your Affectionatly

M. Willett

Colonel Gansevoort [Fort Schuyler]

91—To Horatio Gates

Fort Schulyer Octr 1st 1777

Sir I have the Honor to inclose you the Return of the State of this Garrison, and the Artillery & Stores wanted ~~to compleat~~ at this Fort—which I should be very glad to have up this Fall, that we may be ready early the ensuing Spring to make a respectable Defence as we have Reason to expect another Attack—

Notwithstanding I am little of an Engineer myself I perceive ~~beg~~ that the Works carried on here ~~that they~~ are altogether irregular & will ultimately require Attention × Major Hubble the present Engineer is now busy to lay the Foundation of Bomb Proof Barracks, the Timber he has brought in for that purpose in my Opinion ~~is not~~ will not be sufficient against a 18 Inch Shell—and for a Number of other Reasons ~~therefore I should~~ I imagine it for the good of the Service ~~that am~~ and I request of your Honor, to Send an experienced and able Engineer up to finish the Fort as soon as possible—The Season being so far advanced is my only Reason for pressing this so hard—My Zeal for this Service of my Country & the Defence of the Post intrusted to my Care are the Motives that I wish my Request may be complied with

I also beg Leave to offer it as any opinion that there should constantly be three months Salt Provisions in this Fort which ought never to be touched unless we were visited by the Enemy

[Copy of a Letter Sent Genl Gates]

92—From Marinus Willett

Fish Kill October 6th 1777

Dear Colonel/ it is now Eleven days since I left you & have not yet had the pleasure of seeing Mrs Willett nor is it likely I shall see her for some days. the Enemy are now at Peeks Kill & this Countrey in Alarm. I shall go down to our Armey at Peeks Kill this afternoon it is thought there will be some pepering work going on there. We have nothing of particular importance from Genll Washington my kind respects to all the officers. we had a very tedious passage down to this place tell Doctor Woodruff he must not lay too much in bed for fear of growing too bulkey.

I am Dr Col; Your affectionately

M. Willett

Colonel Gansevoort [Fort Schuyler]

Gansevoort continued to ask for materials to help rebuild Fort Schuyler, which sustained significant damage during the three weeks of siege. He sent word to General Gates on October 1, saying that despite his lack of engineering knowledge, he saw the work being carried out as "altogether Irregular" and that a more experienced engineer should be sent to inform the current workers of how to best proceed.[185]

General Gates recalled Gansevoort to Albany in mid–October to take command of fresh recruits; his eldest officer, either his second-in-command, Lieutenant Colonel Willett, or if he did not return in time, Major Cochran, would take control of Fort Schuyler's repairs.[186] Gansevoort would receive formal congratulations for his "personall Bravery" during the course of the year.[187] On October 4, 1777, the Continental Congress appointed Gansevoort Colonel Commandant of the fort "for the bravery and preseverance which they have so conspicuously manifested in the defense of Fort Schuyler."[188]

93—From the Officers of the Third New York Regiment

Hond Sir From a just sense of that Conduct which has hitherto so conspicuously been shown, to advance the Third New York Regiment to Honor, and Public notice,

We congratulate you that those Characteristics which so eminently point out the Gentleman and Soldiers have by your Personall bravery been deservedly noticed by our Bleeding Country.

Altho' we rejoice at your Promotion yet we cannot but regret the loss of so worthy a Patron.

That the prosperity which has crown'd your Conduct with Victory, may still be continued is the sincere Wish and Prayer of Hond Sir

Your Honor's Most Obedient and Very Hble Servant

Fort Schuyler 12th October 1777

Aaron Aorson Capt, Thos DeWitt Capt, Corns T. Jansen Capt, Leond Bleeker Capt, Henry Defendorff Lieut, John Ball Lieut, Philip Conine Lieut, John Welch Lieut, Nanning Vander Hayden Lieut,[189] *Isaac Bogert Lieut, William Tapp Lieut, George Sytez Adjt, Prenkin Bowen Lieut,*[190] *Jer V Rensselaer PM, H Woodruff Surjn, John Elliott PM,*[191] *Gerrit Staats Lieut, Thomas Warner Lieut, Benj. Bogardus Lieut, Thomas Ostrander Lieut, T Williams Junr QM,*[192] *Wm Colbrath Ensign, Christopher Hutton Ensign, Josiah Bagley Ensign, Samuel Lewis Ensign,*[193] *Eldert Ament Ensn*

To the Honorable Brigr Genl, Gansevoort

94—To the Officers of the Third New York Regiment

Gentlemen Your polite Address to my Promotion Merits my Sincerest thanks ~~Justice &~~ Gratitude I hope Shall never be Wanting in me to the third NY. Regiment who have by their firmness & dcipline been the Cheif Author of my Promotion. Therefore Gentlemen please to Except my Warmest wishes for the persperity of the Corps that all their Virtious Endevours in the defence of their Bleeding Contery may be Crowned with Honour & Success which ~~in the~~ will allways be Earnest prayer of Gentlemen

Your most Obliged Humbl Servt
[PG]
[Copy of a Letter Sent to the Officers of my Regt October 12th 1777]

The last two months of 1777 were best summarized in a December 5 letter from Henry Glen: "Nothing particular has happened Since your departure from this place."[194] The somewhat awkward confrontational nature of correspondence between Gates and Gansevoort would continue unabated. The difference this time would be Gates having to publicly acknowledge Gansevoort's outstanding performance against a numerically superior force with higher morale, better supplies, and perhaps to Gates, a better officer core.

95—To Horatio Gates

Fort Schuyler 12th Decemr 1777

Dear Sir In my last Letter of the first Inst I gave your Honor the State of Provisions at this post—This morning a Man arriv'd from the Little falls, of whom I inquired wether he had seen any provisions on the way between this and that place for this Garrison he told me he had not—In consequence of which I determin'd to send an Express to Your Honor to acquaint you that on the 19th Instant our Beef and pork will be wholly Expinded

This matter gives me much concern as I can assert that since my Command at this place since the 6th ~~May of Last~~ Day of May last I have been only Supply'd from hand to Mouth And during the Seige obliged to Kill Milch Cows Hogg's pig's &c which I had retain'd in the Fort Ditch ~~when the Enemy~~ being the property of the late Inhabitants at this place when the Enemy opened the Seige; from where this neglect proceed I cannot tell—I hope & wish Your Honor will order a Speedy and ample Supply—This will be handed you by Mr Williams Quarter Master of my Regiment I just now receiv'd a Letter from Lieut Nichols from Fort Dayton whi inform'd me that Capt Hansen was gone down to Albany, and did not expect him this four Weeks, wether he has left his post by your permission I know not

I am Dr Sir Your Very Hum Servant
Peter Gansevoort
[Genl Gates]

Gansevoort's victory surely gained the admiration and respect of his family friend General Schuyler and that of the inhabitants of New York. However insurmountable the pressure of Washington and Gates seemed to appear, Gansevoort's experience with the logistical failures of the Canadian invasion carried over and applied to Fort Schuyler; this time Gansevoort was in the advantageous position. Gansevoort had sent Willett out to harass and eradicate enemy camps while felling trees to delay British artillery, all while keeping flanks and potentially vulnerable areas of the fort safe from a direct threat, forcing the British to desperately attempt a constant light fire directly in front of reinforcements. The retreat of the British resulted in the capture of ammunition, blankets and tents needed for prolonged enemy offensives. To other officers, Gansevoort had unexpectedly ensured enough time for reinforcements to arrive before completely running out of supplies.

While the event in August 1777 would certainly remain among Gansevoort's greatest military accomplishments, he would continue to suffer under accusations of laziness and misconduct for the rest of the war. By the late phases of the war, Gansevoort would be relieved of his Continental position due to downsizing. However, Gansevoort would soon after accept a position as brigadier general of the New York militia. Gansevoort would spend the majority of the war still overcoming what he experienced before his shining moment; seasoned officers' high expectations on a fresh officer given his post by family connections instead of military conduct. He would become synonymous with the defense of Fort Schuyler and remembered to many as the "Hero of Fort Stanwix."

Chapter Four

1778: News of the War

Gansevoort's participation in the American Revolution during 1778 reflected that of a somewhat muddled and ambivalent crossroads. General Benedict Arnold was in an Albany hospital recovering from a serious leg injury sustained at Saratoga. General Horatio Gates was in the midst of a power struggle between General Schuyler, General Washington and the Continental Congress. Washington himself was still hoping to retake the former capital, Philadelphia, and was in the midst of reorganizing and improving the morale of the armies under his command following the disastrous winter in the Valley Forge camp.

The massive surrender of General Burgoyne's army at Saratoga in October 1777 meant the most direct threat against New York was defeated; Gansevoort's efforts at defending Fort Schuyler indirectly changed the outcome of that battle, and he was recognized as "Colonel Commandant" by the Continental Congress for his valiant performance. Gansevoort would leave for Albany in January of 1778 to marry and honeymoon with Catherine Van Schaick[1]; following the celebrations he was once again put in command of Fort Schuyler. Gansevoort had little to do other than to continue repairs to the fort and hear about the trials and tribulations of other officers. For Gansevoort, the majority of 1778 was business as usual: adhering to the rigidity and regulatory transmissions of garrison and supply returns, and settling local disputes as well as the occasional infractions against the local natives.

In Gansevoort's January 26 correspondence to Governor George Clinton, Gansevoort sent a return of the garrison at the fort, and forwarded news that another British army equipped with more heavy artillery than St. Leger's detachment may be moving towards his area.[2] Gansevoort sincerely believed that if another attack on the fort was to occur, the "Consequence must then be the loss of the Fort inevitably."[3] Shortages of clothing forced Gansevoort to request the state legislature to raise funds and send supplies, as the shortages would severely affect the troop's morale in face of a second siege. He even went so far as to state that the condition of his troops was critical, and that they were "not paid and half naked."[4]

96—To George Clinton

Albany Jany 26 1778

Sir I have the Honor to transmit you, a Return of the Garrison of Fort Schuyler in which is included a Return of my Regiment—I have this written to Congress this Day urging that Same heavy Artillery might be sent me—they must be Sensible that should another attempt be made against that Fort ~~they~~ the Enemy will be carefull to bring with them heavier Artillery ~~that~~ than they had last Year and ~~that~~ the Consequence ~~will~~ must then be the loss of the Fort inevitably—I wish you to mention the ~~Matter~~ Necessity of ~~theirs~~ Congress's ~~ordering~~ complying with my request in this Matter—

You have inclosed a Return of Cloathing wanting for my Regiment, ~~I hope our Legislature will turn their Attention towards their Troops~~ I doubt not but our Legislature will do every Thing in their power to have their Troops will Cloathed, but permit me to beg you to turn your Attention to this essential Business and urge the Legislature to ~~relieve the~~ endeavour to relieve the Distresses of their Troops in this particular as Soon as possible—Troops not paid and half naked can be but little expected from—this is our Case in ~~the northern~~ this Department—

I have the Honor to be Sir Your most Obedt Hum Servant

[PG]

His Excellency George Clinton Esqr &c &c &c

George Clinton, unknown artist (Gansevoort-Lansing collection. Manuscripts and Archives Division. The New York Public Library. Astor, Lenox and Tilden Foundations).

Apparently the same requests for new artillery batteries were made to General Gates, who had either not received word of the request or ignored it altogether. This may have been due to worries that the transport of such batteries would have been incredibly risky over snowy roads; a broken axle or frozen artillery piece would have been a dire loss to a fledgling army with heavy weaponry already spread over the entire northern region of the United States. Gansevoort mentioned the happy news that he had been formerly appointed "Colonel Commandant" of Fort Schuyler and made an inquiry as to whether he would receive any extra compensation for the new title.[5] Ostensibly the request for extra funds was not to benefit his men; Gansevoort complained that he was running low on "Table Liquors," and that such depletion was "Something considerable of a Commanding officer."[6]

97—To Horatio Gates

Albany Jany 26 1778

Sir permit to urge the Necessity of ~~sending Some~~ ordering the Heavy Artillery &c contained in my return to you wanting in Fort Schuyler ~~before~~ to be Sent up before the ~~Winter breaks up~~ Spring as it will be impracticable almost to carry them in Carts when the Roads are bad as they usually are in the Spring—you are Sensible ~~that without them~~, if an~~other~~ attempt ~~should be~~ is made against the Fort next Campaign, the Enemy will not come without heavy Cannon and should it be the Case the Fort must inevitably Fall—

I have the Honor to be with the greatest Esteem—
Your very Huml Servant
[PG]
The Honble Major Genl Gates

98—To William Duer[7] and Gouverneur Morris[8]

Albany Jany 26 1778

Dr Sir Some time last fall I made a return to Major Genl Gates of heavy Artillery Necessary at Fort Schuyler ~~which he informed~~ but as I have heard nothing of it Since and the Spring approaches I am somewhat apprehensive that he has forgot the Matter I beg you will urge the Necessity of having some heavy Cannon and Mortars Sent up there as Soon as possible, as it will be almost impracticable to get them up when the Snow is off the Ground—not a Moment ought to be lost—as it is obvious if the Enemy should come against ~~the Fort~~ us ~~in~~ from that Quarter with heavy Artillery the Fort must fall—

Congress have done me the Honor of appointing me Colonel Commandant of Fort Schuyler I should Esteem it as a Favor if you would inform me whether I am to receive any pay for that Commission other than as Colonel of the third Regiment of New Yorkers—and if not I should be Glad that you would endeavour to get something allowed me as my present pay will not ~~off~~ reimburse my Table Liquors which you may well conceive to be Something considerable as Commanding officer—I am not sollicitous to make Money by my Commission but I could wish not to sink ~~more than~~ by it—which I am oblig'd to do now—

The Commission which Congress ~~have~~ have Sent me as Commandant of Fort Schuyler subjects me as will to the Command of my Superior Officers as any former if that was the Intention of Congress the ~~Commission~~ Appointment is nugatory, if not I wish Congress to alter the Commission—

I have the Honor to be Your most Obedt Hum Servant
[PG]
The Honble Wm Duer & Gouverneur Morris Esqr

It would seem that following the defense of the fort, Gansevoort's superiors were all but ignoring his garrison even in regards to basic needs of clothing and blankets. This was evident not only in these letters, but others sent to Gates and South Carolina Continental Congressman Henry Laurens[9] on the same day almost repeating verbatim the former requests for artillery batteries.[10]

99—To Henry Laurens

[January 26th 1778]

Sir I beg leave to request of Congress that Some Heavy Artillery ~~might~~ may be Sent to Fort Schuyler The Enemy sensible that their disappointment last Campaign is chiefly to be attributed to the Want of heavy Cannon will be carefull to bring them along if they should ~~be~~ make another attempt against us ~~from that Quarter which can will avail them but little if we have the Same~~ which must be attended with the loss of the Fortress unless we have Some to defend ~~the~~ it—I have last fall made a Return to Major Genl Gates of the Artillery Necissary for another Siege ~~which~~ and I beg that no Time be lost to ~~forward~~ Send them up—as it will be exceedingly difficult to get them there in the Spring when the Snow is off the Ground and the Road bad—

I do myself the Honor to thank Congress for the Honor conferrd upon me in appointing me Commandant of Fort Schuyler

I have the Honor to be Your very Huml Servant

[PG]

The Honble Henry Laurens Esqr

In a February 26 letter from the officers of the Third New York Regiment, the officers complained of "perpetual Fatigue" and a wish to leave their station.[11] The officers did not necessarily wish to visit their homes; the letter mentioned the need to participate and serve in the "Manouvres of a Grand Army" several times.[12]

100—From the Officers of the Third New York Regiment

Fort Schuyler 26th February 1778

We the Subscribers Officers of the Regiment under your command, being very desirous of taking the Field, this ensuing Campaign—

Inasmuch, as we have already been one Year in this Garrison, secluded from those opportunities which are reaped by those Corps, who have the honor to serve with the Grand Army, and in a manner condemned to perpetual Fatigue, which may be conceiv'd rather a disgrace than honor to a Soldier especially whilst the Fields of America give so frequent opportunities, for him to display his Patriotism and Valour—

And also as we are young and inexperienced in the Manouvres of a Grand Army, where alone we may expect to learn, that Art of War, so essential for the Accomplishment of every good Officer

We therefore humble request, your Approbation and Interest, that our desires may be gratified. We have the honour to be, Your most Obedient and very Humble Servants—

M. Willett Lieut Colo:
Aaron Aorson Capt
Thos DeWitt Capt
Corns T Janson Capt
Leond Bleeker Capt
Henry Tiebout Capt
George Sytez Adjt
Nanning Vander Heyden Lieut.
Philip Conine Lieut
William Tapp Lieut
Gerrit Staat Lieut
Thomas Warner Lieut
Benj. Bogardus Lieut.
Moses Yeomans Lieut[13]
Wm Colbrath Lieut
Christ Hutton Ensign
Peter Magee Ensign
Josiah Bagley Ensign
Samuel Lewis Ensign
Geo Denniston Ensign
Matthew Potan Ensign[14]
Hunloke Woodruff Surgeon
John Elliot S. Mate

To Peter Gansevoort Esqr
Colonel of 3rd New York Regt & Commandant of Fort Schuyler

The men were increasingly bored and perhaps even hostile to their own surroundings, wishing instead to achieve success and higher rank within the Continental Army. It would appear that by remaining stationed in the fort they feared a never-ending season of morose drilling and begging for supplies. The officers of more privileged families wanted an opportunity to further enhance their prestige on other campaigns, or at the very least embark on another adventure.

A letter from the Marquis de Lafayette in General Washington's camp sent to Gansevoort in early March stressed the need to capture a nearby British officer.[15] Colonel Christopher Carleton,[16] brother of Guy Carleton and incredulous British commander that repulsed American forces during the siege of Quebec, was said to be in the area conducting various espionage activities. Apparently his activities were a significant threat; the Marquis personally promised fifty guineas to anyone that can relay solid intelligence leading to his capture.[17]

The Marquis de Lafayette, unknown artist (Gansevoort-Lansing collection. Manuscripts and Archives Division. The New York Public Library. Astor, Lenox and Tilden Foundations).

101—From the Marquis De Lafayette

Johnstown the 5th March 1778

Sir As the taking of Colonel Carleton is of the greatest importance, I wish you would try every exertion in your power to have him aprehended—I have desired Colonel Livingston who knows him to let you have any intelligence he can give, and join to them I hope I have got by one other spy about the [ ] and figure of Carleton—you may send as many partys as you please and every where you'l think proper, and do every convenient thing for discovering him—I dare say he knows that we are after him and has nothing in [wim] but to escape which I beg you to prevent by all means—you may promise in my name fifty guineas hard monney besides every monney Oi they can find about Carleton, to any party of Soldier or indians who will bring him alive—as every one knows now what we Send for there is no inconvenience to ~~pre~~ Scater in the country which reward is provided in order to stimulate the indians

I have the honor to be Sir Your most obedient Servant

the Mr de lafayette

Colo Gansevoort Comt Fort Schuyler

A letter from General Schuyler, as Commissioner of Indian Affairs in the Northern Department, to Gansevoort on March 10 ordered that anyone in charge of supplies or other provisions should be more than willing to distribute to Indian visitors any procurement they want in consequence of their pledged alliance with the Americans. On March 12, Gansevoort ordered Captain Leonard Bleeker to York Town, Pennsylvania to deliver "your Dispatches for the Board of War to the Honorable Major General Gates." The dispatches included "a Return of the Garrison of Fort Schuyler together with a Return of Cloathing wanting for the third NYork Regiment." In Bleeker's letter of introduction Gansevoort informed General Gates that his regiment was almost completely naked; half of the troops were without shirts.[18]

102—From Philip Schuyler

Caghnawaga March 10th 1778

Sir Where as It is necessary that the Indians of the Six nations In Alliance with us Should be furnished with provisions when Ever they come to Fort Schuyler on public Business, or their way to or from the Commissioners of Indian affairs, You will therefore In such cases please to Issue your orders to the Commissary of provisions for such quantitys as you may think necessary—

I am Sir Your Humble Servant
Ph: Schuyler
by order of the board of Commissioners
To Colo: P. Gansevoort
Commandant of Fort Schuyler

103—To Leonard Bleeker

Albany March 12 1778

Sir You are to repair without delay to York Town in Pensylvania, when you arrive there you will deliver your Dispatches for the Board of War to the Honorable Major General Gates. You will personally wait upon ~~that~~ the Board of War ~~who~~ and urge the Necessity of granting the Cloathing contained in the Return, and obey such Orders and Directions as you Shall receive from the Board for procuring the Same as they shall order—

I am Sir Your very Hum Servant
[PG]
Capt Leonard Bleecker

104—To Horatio Gates

[March 12th 1778]

~~Sir,~~ Dear General I have the Honor to transmit you by Capt Leonard Bleecker of my Regiment a Return of the Garrison of Fort Schuyler together with a Return of Cloathing wanting for the third NYork Regiment—It gives me pain to inform you that ~~we~~ my Regimt is almost naked, ~~which in so inclement a Country~~ insomuch that not more than half have Shirts, ~~which is terrible~~ which is exceeding discouraging to Troops in so inclement a Country let me by you Sir to ~~intirpose in~~ interest yourself in their behalf—you can easily conceive my Situation with Troops so naked—and I dare affirm without arrogating any Honor to myself that ~~the~~ America has not better Soldiers in the Service—

The Indians are at present way pacific and Friendly, hence I believe I shall be enabled without interruption to compleat the Fort—I my Men are but Cloathed to go on Fatigue—

I am with Sentiments of the greatest Respect Your very Hum Servant

[PG]

The Honble Major Genl Gates

President of the Board of War

Gansevoort's grievances continued unabated as his April 4 letter to General Gates urged for any spare artillery to be sent to the fort; Gansevoort specifically mentioned that only half of a normally functioning battery remained and his garrison undermanned.[19]

105—To Horatio Gates

Albany April 4. 1778.

Sir, From the return of the Garrison of Fort Schuyler furnished you this Day, you will ~~perceives the Strength of the~~ the Number of Troops there, which is not half sufficient to man the internal Works, ~~not less one thousand Men are wanting farther~~, tho' I conceive that four Hundred Men in Addition to those already there, might be sufficient ~~against the Teams that Number~~ to hold the Fort if well supplied—

There ~~are~~ is at present but half a Company of Artillery at the Fort I beg that I may have a full Company commanded a good active and Experienc'd Officer—

Johnstown and Fort Dayton have hitherto been Garrison'd, Colo Livingston's Regiment being ordered down leave those places without Troops—I Submit to you the Necessity of having ~~Your Troops~~ there as will to protect the Inhabitants of Tryon County, as to march to the relief of the Fort ~~with the Militia should it be invested~~

I am Sir with Sentiments of the greatest Respect Your very Huml Servant

[PG]

~~Should~~ when I Shall See Cause to order them—they are not wanted to the Fort untill the Enemy approach and it will be less expensive to supply them with provisions at those places than ~~the~~ Fort Schuyler—and they Serve as Guards upon the Communication for the supplies to the Fort this is the plan which was pursued last Campaign—

[Copy of a Letter sent to the Honble Major Genl Gates]

A separate letter sent to Major General Thomas Conway[20] on the 19th claimed that though state legislation had ordered the delivery of eight artillery pieces to the fort, Major Ebenezer Stevens[21] refused to send them unless he received a direct order.[22] With Gansevoort subsequently claiming that all of his previous requests had been met with silence, it would be unlikely that the artillery would arrive until the fall, if at all.

106—To Thomas Conway

Sir I have Early last fall made a return of Artillery and Stores wanting at Fort Schuyler to Genl Gates Since which I have from Time to Time written to Congress Genl Gates and Governor Clinton upon that Subject, but have never been honourd with an Answer from either—Colo Lewis now informs me that he has Orders from the Board of War to forward Eight pieces of Heavy Cannon to Fort Schuyler, and that Major Stevens refuses to grant them unless by the Order of [ ] these punctilios I conceive might be easily dispens'd with in cases of such great Importance—I am wearied with applications upon this Subject, but I take this Opportunity to declare to you that if you the Garrison is not supplied with the Necessaries wanting for a Siege I cannot be answerable for the defence thereof—You must be convinc'd Sir that had the Enemy come attended last Campaign with a few Eighteen and twelve pounders the Fort must inevitably have fallen the Enemy sensible of this will not come without them Should they ~~again~~ make another attempt against it—Your own Knowledge will suggest to you the great Consequence Fort Schuyler is to us, and the bad Consequences that would ~~attend~~ result from a loss Thereof Colo Gouvion the Engineer that is now at Fort Schuyler the Marquis de lafayette has informed, is to return in a ~~little~~ Short Time to the Southern Army, if so I beg ~~thro'~~ that I may be furnish'd with another—

I am Sir with the greatest Esteem Your very Hum Servant

[PG]

The Honble Major Genl Conway

[Copy of a Letter sent to the Honble Genl Gates April 19th 1778]

Still honeymooning in Albany, Gansevoort received correspondence on April 15 from Marinus Willett at Fort Schuyler concerning the supplies needed by the troops. The situation seemed to be extreme as Willett asked Gansevoort for permission to allow certain men to use nearby land for a makeshift farming effort, and that "We have nothing material."[23] Five days later, Willett reported that a small supply of shirts and shoes arrived but stressed that the supplies given "were not sufficient to enable every man to be supplyed with two." Willett also requested permission from Gansevoort to begin a recruitment campaign for the benefit of Captain DeWitt's company.[24]

107—From Marinus Willett

Fort Schuyler April 15th 1778

Sir/ Inclosed is a return of sundry articles wanting in this Garrison, with which it ought to be supplyed—I shall take care to comply with your directions relating to fencing in, Grassland; and Gardening—several officers have asked permission to fence in small spots for gardens for themselves, as they dont interfere with the ground you have ordered to the fenced in, I have given 'em permission agreable to there several requests—

The Gentlemen who have subscribed to pay for a Post to go weekly from this place to Albany, think the Post ought not to be detained by any one except the Post Master, who has permission in particular casses to detain him twenty four houres—as this Post is employed and paid by a few individuals who have often business which requires regular and timely answers, besides the expectations of being gratified with accounts of what may transpire below, there appears to me a propriety that the Post ought not to be liable to be detained except in very extraordinary cases—I should however be glad to have your sentiments upon this subject—

We have nothing material here I rejoice to hear that we ~~have~~ are like to have a supply of Cloathing for our men—

I am Sir your Very Hum: Servt

M. Willett

Colonel Gansevoort [Albany]

108—From Marinus Willett

Fort Schuyler April 20th 1778

Sir/ This day we had the pleasing satisfaction of receiving a number of shirts Shoes &c for our soldiers, the shirts however are not quite sufficient to enable every man to be supplyed with two; I dare say this supply will not slacken your endeavours to procure such farther supplys as we may require—dont you think the men ought to have each a Napsack of some kind or other in case anything should turn up to require us to march, as well as canteen; the latter I purpose to get our Coopers to try to make against a time of need—we are in want of garden seed, I understand you have some in store, please to inform me If they can be come at as the gardeners say the sooner we sow the better

Mr Colbreath comes with this, and at the desire of Capt DWitt I send Mr Bogardus to you for permission and Instructions to go a recruiting, Capt DWitt's Company is very small all the officers are present and Mr Bogardus has formerly acquited himself well in the recruiting business—I have nothing material to add at present—I am in want of writing Paper and so are the officers of our Regt in General—should be glad of a supply from the Q. M. Genlls Store—in haste I am Sir your Humb: Servt

M. Willett

Colonel Gansevoort [Albany]

The official reorganization of the new American infantry was established with an April 30 declaration. Each battalion was noted to contain nine smaller companies with at least one of light infantry. Specific numbers and groupings of ranks were listed; Gansevoort would be the commander of such battalions, with Willett ready to relieve him if he became incapacitated, killed, or retired.[25]

109—From George Clinton

Poukeepsie April 30th 1778

Sir I am requested by the Committee of Congress, for making a new Arrangement of the Army, to form the several Regiments raised in this State (excepting such of them as are with the Grand Army) upon the new Plan agreed to by that Committee; a Model of which for a Battallion you have enclosed. You are therefore desired with the Advice of your field Officers to return to me; without delay, The Names of the Gentlemen of your Regiment who are best qualified to serve the Public agreable to the present Establishment; And as this Plan is calculated to diminish the number of Officers in the Army, several must of course be left out; many of whom may be Merit. It is the Desire of the Committee therefore that the Names of such be transmitted to them; and for this Purpose you will please to furnish me with a List of such deserving Officers as by this New Arrangement may be left out; And it will not be amiss to note in what new Employment, you conceive they are best qualified to serve their Country.—

I am Sir Your most Obedient Servant

Geo Clinton

Colo Gansevoort [Albany]

110—Model for the New Arrangement of the Infantry of the American Army

[April 30th 1778]

Establishment of the Infantry of the American Army

That each Battalion shall consist of nine Companies of which one shall be of light Infantry to be kept compleat by Drafts from the Battalion and organized during the Campaign into Corps of light Troops

	Number	***Rank***
Each of the field Officers to Command a Company, and Lieut. of the Colos Compy to have the Rank of Captain	*1*	*Colonel*
	1	*Lieut Colo*
	1	*Major*
	6	*Captains*
	1	*Capt Lieut of Colo Compy*
	8	*Lieutenants*
	9	*Ensigns*
These Officers to be taken from the Line, the paymaster chosen by the Corps, the others officd on Recom. of field Officers from among the Subalterns		*PayMaster*
		Adjutant
		Qr Master
	1	*Surgeon*
	1	*Mate*
	29	***Com. Officers***

Whenever a Regt shall become vacant by the Promotion, the Resignation or the Death of a Colo, the Lieut Colo to take the command, but no promotion to be made in the Regiment so that in time there will be but Two field Officers to a Regimt.—

Because of the new arrangement of the Third New York Regiment, Gansevoort had to inform several of his company's officers that they were relieved of duty. Lieutenant Levi Stockwell was one of the officers that was left out. Stockwell, with Willett, bravely embarked on a secret mission while St. Leger laid siege on Fort Schuyler.

111—To Levi Stockwell

Fort Schuyler May 30th 1778

Sir, *You may observe that in the new Arrangement of the third New York Regiment, made in Consequence of Orders received from his Excellency Governor Clinton, You are left out.— This, Sir, was not occasioned by any Fault or Misconduct of Yours, but because of the Necessity of reducing the Number of Officers.—*

We lament that no Provision can be made for You in the Regiment & Esteem It our Duty to Express to You, our united Thanks, for the Service You have rendered Your Country and for Your Exemplary braves, Spirited & Solderlike Behaviour, during Your Service at this Garrison.—

We are Sir Your Most Obedt Servt

[PG]

To Lieut Levi Stockwell of Colo Gansevoort Regt

Gansevoort's orders would not be his last. The financial strain to maintain the Continental Army in the northern United States required many lower officers such as Stockwell to be either transferred to a militia post, or removed from military service altogether. The benefits in way of payment and prestige accompanying Stockwell's former rank in the Continental Army certainly caused consternation for his family, and other officers fearing for their status. On June 1, Gansevoort, with Lieutenant Colonel Willett and Major Cochran's consul, sent to Governor Clinton his recommendations for Captain Swartwout, Lieutenants Warner, Stockwell, Yeomans, Bogert and Mr. Williams, all officers who were dismissed from his regiment.

112—To George Clinton

Fort Schuyler 1st June 1778—

Sir In compliance with Your orders I have Jointly with Lieut Colo Willett and Major Cochran adjusted and made out a list of the names of those ~~Officers~~ of my Officers who are best Qualified to serve ~~on~~ the public ~~and~~ on the present Establishment as also the names of those left out, ~~most of which~~ some of whom have ~~either~~ Resign'd ~~or are~~ & Others are ~~dis~~unqualified for in serving to Advantage for any particulars ~~Issues~~ Office Except~~ing~~ Lieuts Thomas Warner and Levi Stockwell Lieut Moses Yeomans who if any post should offer in the Naval Department I do believe ~~they~~ would be very Suitable ~~for said~~ to be Employ'd in the Command of some of the Craft Built for the defence on the Hudson's River—Lieut Levi Stockwell's Merit will be explain'd to your Excellency by Lieut Colo Willett who is well acquainted with his Abilities.—~~if~~he is a Galls brave Officer ~~Let me~~ & Excellent woods man & if he can be employed in the Service as a Capt of Rangers I doubt not but that he will be able to execute that Office with Advantage to his Country & Honor to himself.—

Let me also beg Leave to recommend to Your Excellency Lieut Bogert & ~~Quarter~~ Mr. Williams my Quarter ~~or Forage~~ Master, to be employed in the Quarter or Forage Master Departmt They are good Pensmen & I believe them to be Very honest Men ~~&~~

Lieuts Deffendorff & Ball & Ensn Polang have long service made Application to resign & Lieuts Ostrander & Van Der Heyden, tho brave and willing to remain in the Army, are not ~~qualified~~ well calculated to Serve to Advantage in the Military or any other public Line.—

Capt Swartwout whom I esteem as a brave Officer, I beg Leave to recommended to Your Excellency for such Office as You may think proper to be conferred on him

I must in Justice to all the above mentioned Gentlemen, say that since they have been in my Battn they have acted like ~~gallant~~ Spirited brave Americans and honest men.—It gave me pain to dismiss any of them, but I trust that the other Field Officers as well as myself, ~~know not,~~ in the Execution of the Duty imposed on us, in Choosing the Officers have not been swayed by any Other Motive than the Real Good & Advantage of our Country—

As the New Arrangement is compleated and my Regiment already mustered agreeable to such Arrangement, I am at a Loss ~~for~~ What is to be done with those Officers who are left out; I Shall Venture on giving them Leave to ~~quit the Garrison till further~~ go-to the places of their Abodes in Hopes of receiving Your Excellency's Orders on the Subject in very few Days.—

[PG]

[George Clinton]

113—From Henry Glen

Schonectady 6th June 1778

Dear Sir Serjant Heareing with a Pariel of Recruits is detained are till Such time the Boats Goes off with the opinion of Mr Duane who is town of Duanburghs its tought Best to detain them a feiw days on Account of the alarm up the River Nothing Very Particular the Enemy have Burnt a Place Called Mayfield & Some hoses Neare that Place Called Sacondage[26] *By what I Care learn by [awcomen?] thats has been Prisiner with them who they let Go Their is about 60 or Seventy But majer Fonda writes of Some Hundreds they have taken severel prisiners But dont take women & Children they militia have Intirly left Johntown & Assembled at Conayaga in the Church & Great Cry for Assistant Part of the Tryon Militia are at Chervelly this morning Col. Van Alstyn*[27] *& Majer Henry Renselier Left this with 214 Militia to Relif of Tryon County I was at Alby yesterday for an Hour or two Report Privaite of two devisions from head Qur Exspectd at New Wincor at High lands in hast Yours Sincerly*

H Glen

To Colonel P. Gansevort [Fort Schuyler]

PS. Mr Mathew Warmout is Kiled & Schalpd Near Cervally[28] *my Compliments to Mr Turcker*

Despite receiving a small amount of cattle and flour in mid–June,[29] Gansevoort sent word to Deputy Commissary-General of Purchases Jacob Cuyler warning him that only two months of provisions were left in the fort and that the increasing disbursements to traveling Indian parties were putting extreme stress upon the little amount left.[30] The last paragraph of the letter hinted at Gansevoort's continued frustration regarding the army's ignorance of Fort Schuyler's plight; he emphasized that the fort held "...great consequence of this post in particular to this State No doubt remains with me."[31]

114—From Jacob Cuyler

Albany June 15th 1778

Dear Colonel, By the middle of Next month or Parhaps Sooner, I intend to send you the first drove of Cattle for the use of the Garrison. It may also be Necessary to forward Some more Flour and other Stores, I shuld be Glad to Remove If you will furnish me with a Proper Convoy, from this flatts to your Garrison when such Supplies Shall be ready—off which You shall have Timely notice—

I am Your most Obdt & most humble Servt

Jacob Cuyler

D.C.S.P—

Col. Gansevort

Commandg officer [of Fort Schuyler]

115—To Jacob Cuyler

Fort Schuyler 23rd June 1778

Dear Sir Yours of the 15th Inst is come to hand, Your request respecting the convoy shall be comply'd with

Major Cochran and myself have made a calculation, and find that we have no more than about two Months Provision at this post for the Garrison, ~~and~~ including the Indian Depart

It is impossible for you to conceive what Quantities of Provisions is Issue'd from time to time to the Indians, in particular to those whose Husbands, Brothers ~~and~~ &c &c are gone to Genl Washington ~~with this French Major whose name~~ It will therefore be Nesasary ~~to send a~~ that a Drove of fat Cattle ~~to this post~~ be sent to this post as soon as possiable as well as a Quantity of Salt, as ~~there is not quite two Barrels~~ we have not two Barrels left—~~I doubt not but the Wellfare of this~~

As you are well acquainted with the great consequence of this post in particular to this State No doubt remains with me ~~that~~ but every ~~thing~~ nerve in you~~r Power~~ will be ~~done~~ exerted towards supplying it every nesasary ~~in your~~ in Your Departments. This Morning Lieut Garrit Stats and a Sergt of my Regt—~~went on~~ left this on a Scout to Oswagachie to take a few prisoners in order to gain some intelligence—No Other News in this Quarter worth communicating—if any with you shall be ~~to w~~ to receive a line from you

I am Dr Sir with great Regard Your Obedt Servant

P Gansevoort

[Jacob Cuyler]

June 17 saw a court martial of John Henry under Gansevoort's orders. Henry served in the artillery regiment of Colonel Lamb[32] and had been accused of desertion, which he denied. Pleading not guilty against the charges, Henry faced an onslaught of testimony from his fellow officers claiming his involvement with a group of saboteurs within his command.[33] A private in Captain Aorson's company claimed that there was a spy in the the area; Major Daniel Hammill[34] had apparently corraborated this, claiming members of the artillery battery were being encouraged to desert and join the British army with any supplies they could escape with. Gansevoort had received word of the possible espionage and ordered the men to "sift it to the Bottom," starting with discussion with Samuel Geake to ascertain his motives.[35] At some point, Geake was held prisoner by the British and was offered a large sum of money by a Lord Rodnam[36] in exchange for enlisting himself and other possible loyalists in the area to a British artillery brigade. The duties placed on Geake with regards to Fort Schuyler were as follows: "...Lord Rodnam desired him to enquire into the State of the Garrison ... particularly as to Ammunition, Provisions, Number of Men, and to get as many Men as he could there to join him."[37] The ultimate goal was to join up with a larger force and move to retake Philadelphia. Henry later admitted that he was ordered to "furnish a Quantity of Powder."[38] After a number of recesses, Geake was called to the trial to confirm Henry's statement and also named a number of other officers including a Major Hammill. The end of the court martial does not reveal whether Henry was found guilty. A letter sent by General Washington to Gansevoort on August 13 requested that Samuel Geake be spared in exchange for his appearing as a witness against Major Hammill in a second trial; Gansevoort would detain Geake until the trial date and location could be determined.[39]

116—Garrison Court Martial of John Heny

A Garrison Court Martial held by Order of Peter Gansevoort Esqr Colonel Commandant of Fort Schuyler the Seventeenth Day of June 1778

Capt James Gregg President

Members—Capt Lieut Savage Artily, Lieut McClelan,[40] Ensign Spore, Ensign Bagley

The Court being duly sworn by the President and the President by Capt Lieut Savage, proceeded to the Tryal of John Heny of Col Lambs Regt of Artillery and Capt Walkers Company for a suspicion of attempting to desert to the Enemy.

John Heny being sent for by the Serjeant Major appeared, his Crime being read to him, to which he plead, Not Guilty.

Serjeant Kartele being sworn, deposeth, That on the 16th of June Inst Col Gansevoort sent for him, and told him that he suspected, John Geak a private of Capt Aorson's Company to be a Spy sent on some bad design by the Enemy, that having received a Letter from Col. Varick informing him that Major Hamill had been secured on the like Suspicion, it being well known that they came out together from New York and that Col. Gansevoort wanted to know as much of this plot as possible (if any he had) Ordered this Deponent to try to sift it to the Bottom & if necessary to pretend to ingage and join with him [Geak] and afterwards to discover the whole Matter to Col Gansevoort. That the Deponent denied that Serjt Jackson might assist him to which to which Col. Gansevoort assented. The Deponent then went to the said Geak & after pertending some Dissatisfaction told him, that he believed they were both of the same mind, and after some further Discourse, Geak said to him, that he had been a prisoner in Livingstons Sugar House in New York, That Lord Rodnam sent for him and gave him a Sum of Money, and sent him out of New York with Major Hamill and one Serjeant Hamilton who Geak told him, went all on the same Intention, that Lord Rodnam advised him to inlist in the Artillery and endeavour to engage as many Men as he could (particularly Irishmen) to desert, That Lord Rodnam intended to raise a Brigade of Irishmen in which Hamill was to be one of the Colonels, after which Lord Rodnam gave him his liberty, ~~and~~ upon which he came out of New York in Company with Major Hamill in his way coming along he spoke to many Soldiers informing them of Lord Rodnams Intentions & at Poughkeepsie he inlisted with Capt Swartwout of the 3d N.Y Reg. (he said) promised to enter him in the Artillery at this place, and further that Lord Rodnam desired him to enquire into the State of the Garrison of Fort Schuyler particularly as to Ammunition, Provisions, Number of Men, &c and to get as many Men as he could there to join him and when he that it wou'd do to spike up the Cannon, and push for Philadelphia, where he was to receive a Sum of Moneney from Lord Rodnam and a Lieutenancey in his Brigade for his service & further the Deponent says that Geak told him, that he intended to go off The next provision Day, and that Heny the Prisoner and Thomas Taylor had agreed to go along with him.—And afterwards at Tatterbeating, this Deponent Geak Heny (the prisoner) and Serjeant Jackson met behind the Barracks in a little Room where they agreed to stand true to ~~one~~ each other, and signed a Paper drawn up for the purpose which paper was produced to the Court whereon was written as follow vizt. "We the undernamed promise to be true to each other and never to devulge to any person Whatover unless with each others consent in Deserting the America Army until we join the British Forces Philadelphia, as Witness our Hands this 17th Day of June 1778."

Francis Jackson
John Kertill
Saml Geak
John Heny his Mark

John Heny the prisoner, (this Deponent further says) promised to furnish a Quantity of Powder to carry off with them—And lastly it was agreed by them all to bind themselves to each other by a Solemn Oath on the Bible to stand by one another, and Serjeant Jackson was sent out for *a Bible, but he went to the Guard for a file of Men and took Heny (the prisoner) and Geak to the Guard House.*

Serjeant Jackson being sworn Deposed, That at the meeting aforesaid befor the paper was signed, the said Geak told him that he came out of NYork as a Spy in the same Boat with Major Hamil and that it was agreed between them to pretend they had made their escape from the Enemy, and that Hamil charged him to be faithful and not devulge his mind to anyone and to entice as many Men as he could to Join him & that Hamil farther told him that he was to have a Commission in Lord Rodnams Brigade in a Regt of which he was to be Colonel—And Geak told the Deponent he (the Deponent) shou'd have as good a Commission as he (Geak) wou'd have, and that he intended to go to the Southward and then to Philadelphia. That said Geak spoke highly in favour of Lord Rodnam said that he was an Irishman, one of their own Country, and that a certain Paper was signed by them all in which they promised to stand true by ~~one~~ each other, that the prisoner promised to go along and gave his hand to the Deponent to confirm it, and that it was agreed to bind the agreement with an Oath. upon which the Deponent says he went (as he pertended) for a Bible, but brought a File of Men and took them Prisoners to the Guard.

The Court adjourned for half an Hour.

The Court met according to adjournment.

The Prisoners Geak & Heny & evidences being sent for appeared.

Serjt Jackson asked the Prisoner Heny who was the first enticed him to Desert. To which he answered Geak was the first.

Serjt Kartile ask'd Geak whether he did not know of 30 Men going next provision Day. To which Geak answered that he did not know of any more than Stevens Heny and Taylor.

Adjourned to 2 oClock P.M.

Samuel Geak was sent for by the Court at the desire of John Heny prisoner under Tryal, says that Lord Rodnam when he set him at Liberty desired him to go from New York through the Jersey's towards Philadelphia, and to speak to all the Irishmen as he went along, and acquaint them, that Lord Rodnam was going to raise an Irish Brigade; That he Lord Rodnam desired him to persuade them to join him at Philadephia, that he had sent a Gentleman on the same Business who would meet him at Greewich and go with him, And further says, that he promised to do every Thing that Lord Rodnam desired of him but without any Intention of performing ~~it~~, upon which he says he was set at Liberty, and went to Greenwich where he met Major Hamill and knew him having seen him when he was on Parole, and spoke to him saying "How do you do Major Hamill?" That after a little pause Major Hamill said, "I am not the Man you mention."—However they both went over the River together in a Canoe with four Green Coats and landed at Wehawke Ferry, that the Green Coats went back again After travelling some Distance together he [Geak] told Major Hamill that he knew him & the Business he was going upon, that it was the same as his own, and say's that Major Hamil acknowledged it was, but denied in having any Intention of going through with it, Upon which he the said Geak say's he advised Major Hamill to lay the whole Matter before the Governor, but that Major Hamill said, "They had better let the matter rest and say nothing about it," after which they went together to Poughkeepsie where Major Hamill put Geak to board at Hendricksons.

May it please your Excellency, A few days past I Recd A Letter from Colo Varrick & Willett Giving Information of one Saml Gates At Soldier in this Garrison being in League with Major ____ in Treasonable Conspirices Against the United States by Certain measures I have taken: find the Aforsaid hint to be Well Grounded therefore for the present have only to Acquaint your Excellency that the Next part Will Convey I belive Ample Testimony Againts Said Major Respecting the Crime he Stand Charged With—the Court Martial not having finished their Buisenss is the Reason of my Not forwarding the perticulars

I am

Samuel Gake at present under Confinement for Attempting to desert With Some Others from the 3d NYork Regt Being Examined and declares that While he was Confined in New York he had there Seen Major Hamill Serving out Cloathing to the prisoners. Some time After he the Said Gake was Inlarged on parctive that he Might Earn his Bread at the Sailmaking Buisiness But upon his Release he was brought to Lord Rodman and was by him Requested to Make his way towards philidelphia and Engage into the British Service All the Irishmen he Could and for his Reward he Should have a Lietes Commiss in his Brigade and he Was Accordingly Sent by Lord Rodman With A Letter directed to A German Officer at Grenwich Which Sd Officer Informed him that the Letter directed him to Convey the deponent Over the River but before he Left NYork Side he Mett Major Hamill and Calling him by his Name but was answered by Sd Major that he was Mistaken in the Man upon which he the deponent with Major hamill went into a Boat and was ferried Our Shore Sd Major Hamill Confessed himself to be the person for Which the deponent took him to be and Informed him that their Buiseness was the Same for Which the Said Hamill was to be Rewarded With a Lt Colonelcey in Said Ld Rodmans Corps: but that he the Said Hamill Never Meant to do A thing of the Kind Whereupon the dependent prepared to go and Acquaint the Governor With the Matter but Major hamill thought it Advisable not to Say any thing about it—but Requested the deponent if he was Questioned how he Made his Escape he was to Say that he the Said Deponent and Major Hamill was Confined on Board one of the Vessels and was to be taken on Shore to be Examined Concerning the Escape of Some prisoners & being Gaurded by A Hessian Serjt and two privates and Made a halt at the Corner of New Street at A publick house Keep by a Woman Who Understad no German Neither did ~~Either of~~ the Hesians Serjt Understand English but ~~was~~ he Requested by the Serjt to go in with a dollar Which he the Sd Hamill presented him with to buy Some Liquor but he the Said Serjt Understanding no English or the Woman no German he desired the two Hesians to go in and Interpet for the Serjt Which they did and Gave the Examinant and Major Hamill an Oppertunity to Escape Which they Affected and hid themselves until Night Among the Ruins of the Burnt houses and as Soon as it was dark the proceeded Alon Shoud found a Canoe at Grenwich With Which the Crossed Over to the Jersey Shore

Saml geake

Sworn before me at Fort Schuyler 27 June 1778

Peter Gansevoort Colo Commdt

117—From George Washington

Head Quarters, White Plains[41] *Aug 13th 1778*

Sir, *I have received the proceedings of a Court Martial held by your order respecting Samuel Gake. As neither the articles of war, nor any resolves of Congress authorise the constituting General Courts Martial by any other, than the commander in chief, the commanding officer in a Separate department, or a General—Officer commanding in a particular State—I Should have been under the necessety of ordering a Second trial, and appointing a Court for the purpose if it had been judged expedient to bring Gakes to punishment. But as his confession contains infor-*

mation very pointedly against Major Hammel, which concurs with other accounts I have received, I think it of more importance to the public to Save Gakes as a Witness against Hammel than to make an example of him. You will therefore keep him in such a kind of confinement, as will effectually prevent his escape till matters are ripe for the prosecution of Major Hammel, and at the Same time, will be as little rigorous as the nature of the case will admit. He need how ever know nothing of my intention.

I am Sir Your most Obed Serv

Go Washington

[PG—F Schuyler]

A report of enemy activity from Indians in Gansevoort's area coerced him into announcing a possible attack.[42] Emphasis on the escalation was implied in a July 19 letter from Colonel Peter Bellinger[43] claiming that a hostile Indian force had burned down the Andrews Town [Andrustown] settlement near the German Flats.[44] Caleb Stark[45] even stated that the enemy might go so far as to directly attack Gansevoort's garrison, warranting General Schuyler to do "Every thing in his power, to Raise the Siege."[46] Henry Glen's letter on the 24th of July expressed frustration over the movement of some bateaus for transport with the intention of arriving at Fort Schuyler.[47]

118—From Peter Bellinger

German Flatts, July the 19th 1778

Honoured Sir Yesterday we received the melancholy news, that the Indians have burn'd Andrews Town, about eight miles South of this place, and have killed 4 Men, and taken most of the rest Prisoners, and another place call'd Springfield.[48]

I have wrote several times to Albany but can never get any assistance And as the indians are continually destroying our back Settlements, the poor People are obliged to move here, and if we can get no reinforcement, to withstand the enemy, we shall be forced at last to leave this Place.

Therefore hoping You will take our Case, into Your serious Consideration, and if You can spare us some of Your Troops, to lay at Fort Dayton, You will very much oblige the inhabitants of this Place, and none more, than

Your most Obedient huble Servt

Peter Bellinger Colo

P.S. The Indians at Andrews Town, did not hurt to the Women and Children, but after talking to them, told them to come out to this Place.

[Peter Gansevoort—Fort Schuyler]

119—From Caleb Stark

Albany 19th July 1778

Sir I am Directed by the General, to Inform you that for Certain Reasons, he has Thought Proper, that Colo Aldens Regiment[49] *should Return to Cherry Valley,*[50] *(that is) in Case there is no Appearance of the Enemy making Preparation, to Attact you in your Garrison, which if they should, Rest Assured that the General will do Every thing in his power, to Raise the Siege, & has not the Least doubt, of his Influence with the other General officers, to Carry his point, Especially where Self Interest, & the Interest of the United States so much Depends,—I have the pleasure to Inform you, that there is a French Fleet on our Coast Consisting of 12 Sail of the Line, 6 Frigates, & four Zeabecks,*[51] *that they sunk one 26 Gun Ship, of the Enemies, on their way—this Account comes so well Authenticated, as leaves not the Least [?] Room for a Doubt, they are Bound Durectly to Sandy Hook, something Important I think soon comes to hand*

I am Very Humbl Servant
Cal Stark MB to B Genl Stark
Col Gansvoort [F. Schuyler]

120—From Henry Glen

Schonectady 24th July 1778

Dear Sir, As the Situation of the cummunication between this and Fort Schuyler is So alarming of the Savages &c that I cannot with propriety order the Captains of the Battoemen to go on to Fort Schuyler unless a guard from F. Dayton to F. Schuyler, I have Sent off 9 boats last night loaded with Stores &c for your garrison under the command of Capt Peters, the Loading is exceeding necessary for your garrison 11 Barrels of Rum 5 do Salt, Cloathing for Capt Savages company & Stores for Capt Tucker with Some Flour. I Shall expect there will be a guard at Fort Dayton by ~~Wednesday~~ Thursday—next while will be the thirtyeth day of the Month if it is in your power to Send one. I have given Capt Peters orders that in case there can be no guard obtained from your garrison on acct of Some alarming news you perhaps may have, that he will then Store the Loading with the Comy at Fort Dayton & turn back for another Load to this place, I have no particular news to acquaint you off, I Suppose ur now you have heard that two Small villages Springfield & Andrew town back of Cherry Valley are burnt & Some people killed—this moment an acct from the German Flatts all of one man killed & are taken prisoner—

I am Dr Sir Your Humble Servt
Henry Glen
Col. Peter Gansevoort [F. Schuyler]

Apparently the "Savages" in the area were up to their usual tricks, and Glen was afraid to move any of his men further to the fort unless a guard was secured. The same natives had burned the Cherry Hill settlement to the ground, with civilian casualties dead. Glen also mentioned that the bateaus were holding a large amount of supplies destined to the fort: eleven barrels of rum along with salt and more miscellaneous clothing.

On August 12, Gansevoort sent a request to Governor Clinton for his regiment to be relieved from their garrison duty at Fort Schuyler. After last fall's exciting adventure against St. Leger's forces, the rest of the time in the western wilderness had been mundane. Hearing the romanticized tales of George Washington's Continental Army fiercelessly repulsing the British invaders, the regiment wanted "an opportunity of serving ... to distinguish themselves."

121—To George Clinton

Fort Schuyler 12th Augt 1778

May it please your Excellency Beg this conveyance goes a Patition from the Officers of my Regiment to his Excellency Genl Washington that we may be relieved from this, It would be Acknowledged as a particular favour if your Excellency would interceed that our Patition may be gratified, And can at the same time Assure your Excellency that our desire of being relieved proceeds from no ~~officer~~ other ~~motive~~ than that of ~~being~~ having an opportunity of serving with the Grand Army, As we are equally desirous of obtaining Military Knowledge And as Opportunities daily offers for those Corps to distinguish themselves who have the Honor to serve with the Grand Army—And doubt ~~not~~ but we would in such case have an opportunity of serving our Country

[PG]

[Copy of a Letter Sent to his Excellency Govr Clinton]

On August 15, another court martial was underway; this time for five soldiers instead of one. Nicholas Hansen, John Calf, Christopher Tice, Nicholas Hartman, and Henry Whitmore had all been accused of desertion, and some of them had been accused of stealing a bateau in the process.[52] The bateau in mention was more than likely one belonging to the supply train from Henry Glen; this would certainly not be tolerated by Gansevoort or the rest of the men who had been holding out for these bateau's arrival for over a month. This feeling of vengeance was further confirmed in a petition made by the Third New York regimental officers on the same day as the trial. Within they insist on a speedy sentencing as the crime had "been frequent in the Regiment" and that still others under Gansevoort's command were suspected of similar intentions if given a chance.[53]

122—Petition from the Third New York Regiment

Fort Schuyler 15 August 1778

We the Officers of the third New York Regt beg leave to petition Colonel Gansevoort, representing the Necessity of speedily putting in execution the Sentence of a General Court Martial, held on the five prisoners who were tryed this day for Desertion, and taken on their Way to the Enemy, for the following Reasons vizt

1st Because this crime has been frequent in the Regiment

2dly Because we have never had the Sentence of a General Court Martial approved off whereby the Offenders have not received the punishment due to their Crimes

3dly Because we have reason to Suspect there are a number of Soldiers in this Regiment who are disaffected to the American Cause: and unless an immediate example be made it may encourage others to be guilty of the like Crimes

We are Sir with Respect Your most obedient & very humble Servants

Robt Cochran Major
Aaron Aorson Capt
Thos DeWitt Capt
Corns Jansen Capt
J Gregg Capt
Henry Tiebout Capt
George Sytez Capt Lt
John Welch Lieut
Philip Conine Lieut
William Tapp Lieut
Gerrit Staats Lieut
Benj Bogadus Lieut

Prentice Bowen Lieut
W Colbrath Lieut
Chrisr Hutton Crs
Peter Magee Ensign
Josiah Bagley Ensign
Saml Lewis Ensign
Eldert Ament Ensn
Benjamin Herring Ensign

123—General Courts Martial of Nicholas Hansen, John Calf, Christopher Tice, Nicholas Hartman and Henry Whitmozure

A General Court Martial held at Fort Schuyler 15th August 1778 for the Tryall of all such Prisoners as should be brought before them

Major Robert Cochran President

Members—Captains Aorson, DeWitt, Jansen, Gregg, Tiebout, Capt Lieut Sytez, Lieuts Welsh, Conine, Staats, Colbreath, Ensigns Magee, Herring

Lieut William Tapp Judge Advoe

The Court being duly sworn they Proceeded to the Tryall of Nicholas Hansen Private of Capt Thos DeWitt Company, John Calf Private of Collonel Gansevoorts Compy Christopher Tice and Nicholas Hartman Privates in Capt Tiebouts Company and Henry Whitmozure Private in Major Cochrans Company all of the 3rd New York Regt Commanded by Colonel Peter Gansevoort Confind by the said Colonel Gansevoort for Deserting to the Enemy and stealing a Batteaux belonging to the United States, they being seperately brought before the Court and the Charge read to them they Plead Guilty

The Court having duly Considerd the Nature of the Crime do (agreeable to the first Article of the Sixth section of the Rules and Articles for the better Government of the Forces raisd or to be raisd fot the service of the United States

Gansevoort sent Washington word of these frequencies of desertion, specifically stating that since late March his command had lost three sergeants, two corporals, and twenty privates.[54] Gansevoort had captured a few soldiers attempting to desert and had previously sent requests to Washington's camp for a court martial; Washington's camp had apparently never complied with these requests. Ultimately, Gansevoort had to make a quick decision: "...they were accordingly Shott at the Head of the Regiment on the 17th In doing of which altho, I could not find the Articles of war gave me the fullest Authority yet as Commanding Officer of a frontier Post & far distant from the Commander in Chief ... I hope your Excellency will be convinced of the Necessity."[55]

124—To George Washington

I have the unhappiness to inform your Excellency that desertion has lattely been very frequent from this Garrison since the 26 of last March we have had 3 Serjt 2 Corpls & 20 Privates desert from this Battn besides 1 bumdr 1 Gunr & 1 Mastr from the Artillery before the date above mentioned several Soldiers ~~who were~~ had been tryed by a General Court Martial at this Garrison for dertion but never received the Punishment due their Crimes, ~~by care of the Sentinee being not approved off~~ the Sentences of these different Court Martials ~~have been~~ were carefully Sent to Commanding General of this Department but no returns have been ever receivd Some time in June last Colonel Varick informed me a Recruit who had just joined ~~the~~ our Battn was Suspected of being a Confederate with Major Hammill I ordered his Conduct to be narrowly inspected—he was detected in the fact of corrupting & enticing the Soldiers to desert upon being apprehended, he confessed that he came upon Such desings, & was Sent by Lord Aid de Camp to Genl Sir Harry Clinton as a Spy—to endeavour to enlist what Irishmen he could from the American Army—there was every Appearance of his being a spy—he was immediately tryed by a General Court Martial the Sentence was directly Sent down for Approbation, but no answer has been received—& the Man Still lays confined in Irons—finding the Spirit of desertion to increase & the Men in General to be exceeding uneasy—probably arising from there being so long stationed on this Frontier Post—~~frequently~~ they have been frequently heard in their private Conversations to say that they woul'd Sooner die, that stay here the ensuing winter, My Officers as well as myself was Convinced that unless Some Example was made; we Should not be able to check this growing Evil—A party of five men deserted on the 10 of August they were taken by the Tuscarora Indians; on their way to Canada fifty Miles from this Fort—they were brought in on the 13th a General Court Martial was convened on the 15th they were Sentenced to die, the Officers in a body, desired their Immediate Execution, as the only way effectually to stop the increasing spirit of desertion—whilst these Men were under Sentence of death; a party returned from the German flatts, who been in Command to drive Cattle to this Garrison, they had lost Six Men by desertion, who were pursued, but without effect this together with the above Reasons & being apprehensive of Some design of the Enemy, & a Report that they had carefully Spread among the Savages of having upwards of ~~Eighty~~ Seventy Men enlisted in this Garrison, who woul'd rise upon their appearance—Convinced me of the necessity of a Rigid Example, & resolved me to take the advice of my Officers, by Ordering the prisoners to be Executed, & they were accordingly Shott at the Head of the Regiment on the 17th In doing of which altho, I could not find the Articles of war gave me the fullest Authority yet as Commanding Officer ~~yet I hope your Excellency will approve of it, Nothing but~~ of a frontier Post & far distant from the Commander in Chief In ~~fact~~ I having a Seperate Commission from Congress & ~~the highest regard for my country or Extreme Love for the Service woul'd have fraud me to an Action heretofore~~ unprecedented to me I hope your Excellency will be convinced of the Necessity, & approve of the Justness of the Execution—Inclosed your Excellency has a Copy of the Proceedings of the Court Martial as Commandant of this Post, I conceived, myself fully impowered in a Case of Such great Necessity

[Copy of Letter sent Genl Washington Ft Schuyler Augt 18th 1778]

This decision implied many things: Gansevoort's requests were frequently ignored by his superiors. Frustrated, Gansevoort had pointedly struck out and imposed his own authority without waiting for a response.

On the 29th, General Washington finally responded to Gansevoort's account of the five court martials earlier in the month. Washington announced that he was "respecting the court martial" Gansevoort had followed through with, and that his making examples of those found guilty was tolerable "altho' the proceeding was not strictly in the prescribed form."[56] In return for what appeared to have been a good move on Gansevoort's part, Washington pledged to take care of the officers in Gansevoort's camp applying for other positions in the army. Willett's letter on the same day confirmed that General Washington was "quite disposed to comply with the request of the Regiment," however the difficulties encountered in the Rhode Island campaign combined with the lack of supply and frequent desertion at the fort led Willett to believe the transfer would not be resolved until the end of the year.[57]

The same day Gansevoort received a letter from Captain Abraham Swartwout requesting compensation of eight yards of broad cloth. While surviving the British siege against Fort Schuyler, an American flag was constructed and flown over the fort. Swartwout gave his blue cloak which was used for flag. Gansevoort promised to place an order to the New York Commissary for Cloathing to replace his cloak.

125—From George Washington

Head Quarters White plains 29 August 1778

hi I have just received your favor of the 18th Instant

Inclosed is a copy of a letter sent you some time ago respecting the court martial you transmitted.

The spirit of desertion Which possessed your soldiers was certainly very alarming and required a serious check. I hope the intention of the example you have made will be fully answered; and altho' the proceeding was not strictly in the prescribed form, yet the necessity of the case may justify the measure.

I have spoken to Lieut Colonel Willet on the application of the officers of the garrison—It is impossible to comply at present with their request, things are so circumstanced—but I shall take steps to releive it before winter.

I am hi your Obt. hble sert.

Go Washington

Col. Gansevoort [Fort Schuyler]

126—From Abraham Swartwout

Dear Sir/ The great distance which Your duty calls us Appart obliges me at this time to give You this trouble which Otherwise I would not You may Remember Agreeable to Your promise; I was to have an Order for Eight Yards of Broad: Cloath, on the Commissary for Cloathing of this State In lieu of my Blue Cloak, which was Used for Coulours at Fort Schuyler—An Opportunity Now presenting itself—I beg You to Send me an Order inclosed to Mr Jeremiah Renseler pay Master at Albany or to Mr Henry Van Vaughter, Albany, where I will receive it, and You will Oblige me—who will Always Acknowledge the Same with true gratitude—

Please to make my Compts to the Other Officers of the Regimt

I am Dear Sir Your Hble Servt

Abraham Swartwout Capt

Poughkeepsie—29th Augt 1778

Colonel Peter Gansiworth Fort Schuyler

A break in the monotony finally occurred on September 8. According to a report from Robert Cochran, Benjamin Acker was ambushed and scalped by a band of Indians.[58] What was particularly strange was the other weapon involved in Acker's death. Apparently the Indians had developed something resembling a makeshift lance, which pierced his abdomen multiple times. According to Cochran the lance was then left by the fleeing Indians on purpose, "...there were several marks on it which is said to denote the number of prisoners & Schalps they had taken."[59]

127—From Robert Cochran

Fort Schuyler 8th September 1778

Dear Colonel I last Night received a Letter directed to you ~~and~~ by Nicholas Jordan and supposing to be about Garrison business took the liberty to open it found it was from Henry Glenn Esqr with intelligence that it was expected the Boats would arrive at Fort Dayton this day, and requesting I would send a Guard to convey them up, which I intend to do tomorrow morning.

This morning one Benjamin Acker of Capt DeWitts was out in Meadow near Brodacks House[60] *was kill'd and Scalpd by a party of Indinans, who were seen and fir'd at by the Centinal there, I heard the firing in my Room & ran to the Officer of the Guard to know what it was and was inform'd, that a party of Indians were seen firing at one of our Men who was gone to catch a Horse & that he was either kill'd or taken prisoner upon which I ordered Capt Bleecker to go out immediately with the new Guard (which was just paraded) to see if they could find him dead or alive on there coming to the spot they found Acker lying dead he was schalp'd and a Weapon about 2½ Feet long constructed something like this [image of the weapon drawn] lying near him The under part being steel in the shape of a lance had been stuck several times in his Body & is supposed to be left behind on purpose as there were several marks on it which is said to denote the number of prisoners & Schalps they had taken*

About 2 Hours ago Jacob Reed ~~an~~ the Indian[61] *that you sent to Osswego for Intelligence came in here, he informs that on the 5th Inst he with 4 other Onida's arrived at Oswego, He say that the place was Intirely*

[incomplete]

[Colonel Cochran]

[PG—Fort Schuyler]

Ten days later Cochran reported back to Gansevoort, having continued his investigation into the murder of Acker.[62] The Oneida and Tuscorara natives in the area were extremely

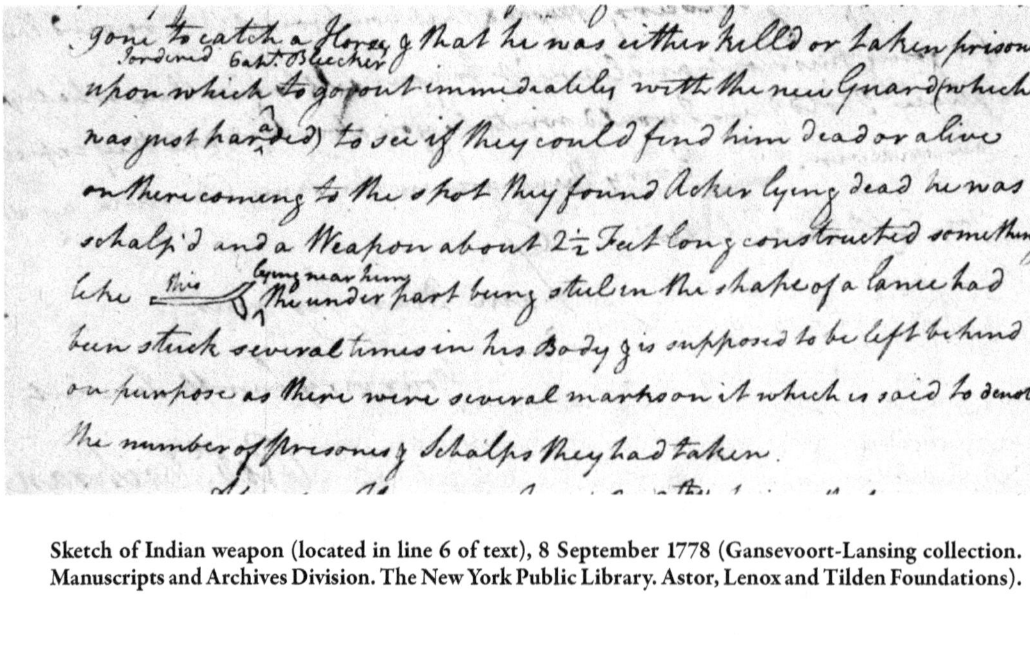
gone to catch a Horse & that he was either kill'd or taken prisoner I ordered Capt. Bleecker
upon which to go out immediately with the new Guard (which
was just paraded) to see if they could find him dead or alive
on there coming to the spot they found Acker lying dead he was
schalp'd and a Weapon about 2½ Feet long constructed something
like this lying near him the under part being steel in the shape of a lance had
been stuck several times in his Body & is supposed to be left behind
on purpose as there were several marks on it which is said to denote
the number of Prisoners & Schalps they had taken.

Sketch of Indian weapon (located in line 6 of text), 8 September 1778 (Gansevoort-Lansing collection. Manuscripts and Archives Division. The New York Public Library. Astor, Lenox and Tilden Foundations).

concerned upon hearing of the murder, especially since no one could determine the identity of the responsible party. They had however emphasized the continued nature of friendship between the two camps, and that "all Societys have their Bad people among them."[63] Whether or not the two tribes were directly involved, this one phrase implied that they may have had some knowledge of the individual or group responsible for the ambush.

128—From Robert Cochran

Fort Schuyler Sept 18th 1778

Dear Colonel Since my Last the Sachems and warriors of the Onyda and Tuscarroras Nations with Colo Lewee arrivd at this fort with a formal Speech from both nations—They Informed me of their great uneasyness in Regard to the matter of Scalping which had So Lately happened about this fort, and were Sorry any Suspecions Should be Entertaind that they had the least knowledge of any thing being Intended Against any Body here—That they had from the Beginning of the present dispute Declined acting against us, that they had been used well, at first by Colo Dayton then by Colo Elmor afterwards Colo Gansevoort Came to the fort, a native of Albany from whom we Expected much as the Commissioners of Indian affairs noticed him in particular—but we are Sorry—he has not noticed us much for Some time past, we are Sorry you Neglact us now, when your affairs were in a worse Situation you Courted us and our Interest—But now you are prosperous you Dont know us. you know we are one, that we have made an Agreement with Genl Schuyler and the other Commissioners that we would be friendly, and not Strike the ax at Each other—

The Nixt morning I Answered them as follows—that I was glad to See them here and that I had taken Particular notice of all they had Said, and further that we were Inclined to give them assurance of our friendly disposition to them, and were Sorry that any uneasyness Should arise in their minds, and in Regard to what Some Bad Soldiers might Say that they would Regnard it, as all Societys have their Bad people among them—to which they replied they would not Regnard what the Soldiers Should Say, but would apply to the head when occasion might require—I fed them plentifull, and gave them Drink also, which I thought was best at present for the public Service, and they went off greatly Satisfied—I think we are in Great want of Mr Deen at this post—

I am Sir your most obdt Humbl Servent
Robt Cochran
to Colonel Gansevoort [Albany]

Another piece of correspondence from Cochran on September 28 further embellished upon the murder of Acker and the tense relationship between the allied tribes. Over one hundred natives came to the fort representing the wishes of the Oneida and Tuscarora nations, proudly announcing that they had burnt a settlement known as "Unendells" and had taken prisoners from the areas, along with other ventures at Stillwater and Fall Hills. The phrase "We hope you are now Convinced of our Friendship" indicated that the raids were done in earnest to prove their noninvolvement in the murder earlier that year.[64] Along with the success of the previously mentioned raids, they had also passed along intelligence gained from Caughnawaga settlements with regards to the number of British troops along the immediate Canadian-New York border.[65]

129—From Robert Cochran

Fort Schuyler September 28, 1778

Dear Coll, On Fryday last arrived here, the Sachems & Warriors of the Oneida a Tuscarora Nations, their Number upwards of one hundred—After the usual Formalities, they Delivered themselves nearly as follows—

Brothers, We have now taken the Hatchet and Burnt Unendells & a place called the Butter Nutts we have brought five Prisoners from Each of the above Places—Our Warriors were Particular that no hurt should be done to Women & Children: we left four Old men Behind, who were no more able to go to War—We have Retaken William Dygart who was Taken about Nine weeks agoe by Brant, on the Fall Hills We now Deliver him to you so that he may return to his Friends—Last year we took up the Hatchet at Stillwater, and we will now Continue it in our hands—The Grass-Hopper,[66] *one of the Oneida Chiefs took to himself one of the Prisoners, to live with him in his own family, his name is William Lull and has adopted him as a Son—Brothers, We deliver you Six prisoners with whom you are to act as you Please—Brothers you had a man Scalped here, some time agoe—the Oneidas & Tuscaroras have now Taken revenges and have brot you some Slaves—We do not take Scalps—We hope you are now Convinced of our Friendship towards you and your great Causes—The Warriors Detain two of the Prisoners tilll To-morrow morning—*

The Canasaraugas have one more Prisoners in their Possession taken at the same time, they will bring him in To-morrow or next day—Then the Conference Ended—Accordingly next morning they delivered me the two Prisoners mentioned in their Speech the Evening before, I have them all in the Guard Houses here & allow them a pound of Beef & a pound of Bread per man per day, at the foot hereof you have their names—Richard McGinnis Inlisted amongst Butlers Rangers in January last and was at Wioming last Summer with Butler at the head—Capt Gilbert Tise came from Niagara a few days before the Party set out with Brant to Destroy the Germin Flatts, he had 33 Indians with him, Mostly Mohawks & Conajoharry Indians—Brants whole Party that Destroyed the Flatts was 300 Tories & 152 Indians—there were no regular Troops amongst them—The Indi that were here Behaved with the greatest Openness that I could have wished. I thanked them for their Services at this time—I fix them & gave them a hearty drink of rum—I promiss'd to Communicate this matter, to the General and to the Commissioners of Indian affairs at Albany—

With the above Indians arrived also Eight Principals Indians from Caughnawaga in Canada, they have Important Intelligence to Communicate to us, in regard to Canada affairs, which are in our favour by what I have yet Learn'd—But as I heard that Mr Dean is on his way from Schenectady to this place, I have Deferred Saying any thing Particular to the Caughnawagas

I have Victualled them for Six days, & they are returned to Oneida with the Sachems, & the moment Mr Deane arrives here, they know it the next day and Came Immediately—The intelligence they give will Doubtless be Communicated by Mr Deane without loss of Time—The 24th about sunsetting 7 of our men being out towards the [Sheire] were fired on by Indians, and returned the fire I sent off a party Immediately to Support them, who pursued the Indians over the [Sheire] and returned No harm was done—Last Evening one of Capt Jansen's Company was missing—we suppose he is taken by the Indians

I am Dear Sir with sincere respect Your Huml Servt

Robt Cochran

Prisoners Names William Lull—Richard McGinnis—John McGinnis—John Harrison—Michael Stopplepen—Barry Laythlin—Moses Thurston—Caleb Lull—Benjamin Lull—
To Colonel Gansevoort [Albany]

An October 5 letter from Cochran declared that "large Bodies of Indians" were amassing with designs to strike down the Susquehanna River; Cochran believed they were heading to Pennsylvania.[67]

130—From Robert Cochran

Fort Schuyler, October 5th 1778
Dear Coll I have received authentic intelligence that large Bodies of Indians are Collected upon the Susquehanna, at & Below Onohoguages—Their profess'd Design is to attack some part of the Frontiers of Pennsylvania or the Jersies—But from what has lately Transpired. I Strongly suspect they intend to Divide their Party, and attack Schohary or some part of Tryon County, while the remainder Proceeds Southward—I Believe it may be Depended on for Truth, that the whole force of the Six Nations and Delaware are Collected Except our Friends among the Oniedas & Tuscararas—
Capt Gregg is gone today to the Flatts with Sixty men to Guard up the Cattle & Boats—Our men are greatly in Want of Shoes, and every other Species of Clothing. 'Tis really Cruel to Order them on duty, as the weather is growing Colder, and we begin to have severe frosts; I am however so Solicitous for the safe Conveyance of thos articles, that I wish every necessary precaution may be used for their safety, which I doubt not will be done—
Mr Tucker is much Wanted here
I am Dear Colonel Your Sincere Friend & Humbl Servt
Robt Cochran
[PG—Albany]

Captain Gregg was informed and had sent a small force of sixty men to procure any bateaus and supplies in German Flatts that could be subject to an attack following the Indians' advance. On October 10, Cochran had received word that a Seneca chief known as "Great Tree" [68] had pledged his personal allegiance to the United States and had been running a recruitment of sorts.[69] Great Tree had been wildly successful at the first few villages he traveled through, yet a rumor of American invasion had spread through some of the bordering areas. In response to the news, the natives armed themselves with the ultimate goal to rendezvous off a branch on the Susquehanna River and strike into western Pennsylvania. The Oneidas had confirmed this intelligence was worth forwarding onto privy parties.

131—From Robert Cochran

Fort Schuyler 10th Octr 1778
Sir I have no material News to write to from this Garrison only the following important Intillegence which was communicated to Mr Dean at Oneida, which he has transmitted in one of the enclosed Letters a Copy of which is as follows,
"As the Seneca Chief called the Great Tree who was the summer past with General Washington,

returned through Onieda, he gave our Friends there the most Solemn assurances, that upon his arrival in his Country, he would exert his utmost influence to dispose his Tribe to peace & Friendship with the United States and that should his Attempts prove unsuccessful he would immediately have his Nation and join the Oneida's with his friends and Adherents—Along Time having elapsed without hearing from the great Tree, the Oneida's a few days since dispatched a runner to him desiring an account of his Success—The express returned Yesterday with the following Intelligence where the Sachems immediately forwarded to me by three of their Warriors, Namely, That upon his arrival into the Senokas Country he found that whole people in Arms and the two Villages Kanadasege & Jenesee where he was crouded with their Warriors who were all collected from their more remote Settlements; That upon the Great Tree's first arrival appearances seemed to promise him Success, but that a rumour being circulated that the Americans were about to Invade them, they had all flown to arms, the great Tree with the rest and determined to chastise the Enemy that dared presume to think of penetrating their Country; That they are to be joined by all the Indians as far as the Onandagas a small party of which Tribe has gone to meet them, and likewise by those of the Several Settlements upon the Branches of the Sisquehannah: That the Senokas were to march the eighth and the Quegoga's the ninth Instant, That the whole party were to rendevouz at Kanakalo a place Situation that Branch of the Sisquehannah called Tiyoga Branch, and from thence were to proceed against the Frontiers of Pennsylvania or the Jersies. Our Onida Friends rely on the authenticity of the above Intelligence and beg that it may not be neglected

I am Sir &ca

James Dean"

I have nothing further to inform you of only that all goes well at the Garrison in Same channel as when you left it and that you would much oblige me by sending by the Bearer the freshest intelligence you have in Albany

I am Sir most Obedient & Humble Servant

Robt Cochran

To Col Gansevoort [Albany]

No further intelligence was received until November 6, when Colonel Ichabod Alden of the Seventh Massachusetts Regiment warned Gansevoort that Oneidas had spotted a "Meeting of Indians & Tories" near the same spot Great Tree had predicted the forces would meet.[70]

132—To Ichabod Alden

Fort Schuyler 6th Novemr 1778

Sir We ware just now informed by an Onyda Indian, that yesterday an Onendago Indian Arrived at their Castle from one of the Branches of the Susquahana called the Tioga ~~Branch~~ that he was present at a great Meeting of Indians & Tories at that place and thus Result was to Attack Charevally and that young Buttler was to head the Tories I send you this information that you may be on your guard

no signature on this letter

At some point in mid–November Gansevoort had captured an Indian from the Cashnawaga tribe, and Gansevoort's uncle Volkert Douw had received a request from the Oneida chiefs to release him on the Oneida's claim that the man had peaceful intentions.[71]

On October 19 Colonel Goose Van Schaick received orders from Governor Clinton to prepare his regiment to march to Fort Schuyler to relieve Gansevoort. Two months after Gansevoort's petition, General Washington must have understood how important it was to sustain morale within the regiment by rotating them to other posts periodically. General orders issued to Colonel Goose Van Schaick from Fort Schuyler continued to place emphasis on word of a British or native coalition attack in the Susquehanna and New York tributaries. Van Schaick was constantly ordered to keep scouts in Oswego, as close as possible to Lake Ontario, and to fell trees to block Wood Creek in case of a British attempt to transport men.[72]

133—George Clinton to Goose Van Schaick

Head Quarters Octr 19th 1778

Dr Coll I received a Letter from his Excellency, on my way to this place dated the Day I left you, Informing me that he had determined to send your Regiment to Relieve Col Gansevoort, that I should signify you of it that you may be prepared for it as soon as the Cloathing expected in Camp arrives, you are to have a competent supply, and will then proceed, you are to mention the Matter to Coll Hay[73] *who will be—looking forward to provide Vessels to convey the Regt to Albany.*

The Troops of the Brigade at Norwalk are ordered to join those of the ligh[t] Troops are to remain for the present. All those of the Brigade on furlough are to be called in, and no Furloughs to be given till further Orders. The pay Masters of each Regiment are to attend with their Cloathing returns to draw the Cloathing for their respective Regiment as soon as it arrives.

Coll Courtland and myself are ordered this morning to Poughkeepsie on Business of importance I have Draw Some Money for Recruiting the Drafts.

[Copy of a Letter from Brigadier Genl Clinton to Colo G. V Schaick]

134—Extracts of Letters and General Orders Given to Goose Van Schaick

~~Extracts of Letter and orders from General Schuyler~~ Extracts of Letters and General Orders

Extract of a Letter July 18th

If you should get certain intelligence of the Approach of an Enemy thro' Lake Ontario, you Will then cause the Timber on the banks of Wood Creek to filled into it, in such a manner as to give the greatest obstruction to the Enemy—

Extract of Letter

In my letter of 18th Ultimo, I directed you upon the receipt of certain intelligence of the approach of an Enemy thro' Lake Ontario that you should cause the Cause the Timber on the banks of Wood Creek to be filled into it &c. You will please to observe that before you fall the Timber into the Creek I mean that your intelligence should be such as to give you the strongest reason to believe that an Enemy is Crossing Lake Ontario to come your way this will be best determined by their coming to Oswago or landing in some other part of the Lake in the vicinity of that place. In such case any Roads by which cannon could be conveyed, should also to rendered as impassible as possible should you at any time gain intelligence of the approach of an Enemy, you will not only dispatch an Express to the Commanding Officer at Albany, discribing this rout they take or you judge they may take but also send the same information to the Officers Commanding on any of the Posts on the Mohawk River—

Letter Augt 20th

Let me intreat you to keep Scouts constantly out towards Oswego & Oswegachie that you may have the earliest intelligence of the approach of any Enemy

Extract of a Letter Augt

You will distribute the Rum at such and in such proportions as you may think proper to Fatigue men not exceeding a gill pr day unless upon very extraordinary occasions, The pay to Carpenters and persons who Are good workman to be one fourth of a Dollar pr Day, other Artificers one Eight of a Dollar

From Letter 9th Septr

Do not forget to fill Wood Creek with Timber as that will Considerably retard thus progress, if they mean an attack upon your Post I do not by any means think you ought to comply with the Request of Indians not to send any white people to gain intelligence as in that case we must intirely depend on what accounts they are pleased to give, which may be attended with the most dangerous Consequences I would therefore have you by all means, mix some of your Officers and Men with any parties you may send and also send Small parties composed of your own Corps.

Extract from March the Sixth

It is a matter of Much Moment to the United States that no Officer or Soldier's should on any Account whatever Trade with any Indian or Indians, And you will therefore Publish this as my orders, that none presume to do it, on pain of being punished for disobedience of orders, should any however be so Austacious as to contravene the orders, you will if an Officer immediately put him ~~in~~ under Arrest, if a Non Commissioned Officer, or Soldier Confine him and report to me that proper ~~Steps~~ Measures may be taken to bring them to Punishment, if an Officer has Occasion for my thing immediately for his own use Mr Hansen will purchase it & deliver at first Cost

Extract of a Letter from the Commissioner of Indians Affair for Northern Depart

Whare as it is necessary that the Indians of the Six Nations & alliance with us should be furnished with provisions when wer they come to Fort Schuyler on public Business or on their way to or from the Commissioners of Indian affairs, you will therefore in such cases please to Issue your Orders to the Commissary of provisions for such Quantities as you may think necessary

Extract of Letter Albany July 9th 1778

You will keep up a Friendly Intercourse with our Indian Allies; and suffer no Speeches to be made to them, by any person, not employ'd in the Indian Department, and when you have occasion to Speak to them let your Speech be written and a Copy transmitted that the Commissioners may be informed of every transaction with those People

[Copy of Extracts of Letters & Genl Orders given to Colo Van Schaick Fort Schuyler Novemr 1778]

As before the Fort Schuyler siege and Burgoyne's defeat at Saratoga, the subterfuge and obstruction of the waterways nearly ensured that the invading parties would suffer from attrition, regardless of their scouting and reconnaissance capabilities.

These dealings with the Indians in the area further illuminated the nonsensical, perhaps even ethnically confused, American soldiers. They were often unable to differentiate allied tribe from hostiles, and usually found out after a confrontation. It was therefore understandable why the New York militia would later see fit to conduct a massive expedition into Indian country to make an example of those hostile tribes. Unfortunately, as seen in this year of Gansevoort's correspondence, the soldiers and officers of the American military had little time to determine which tribes were friend or foe, often resulting in atrocious and needless native casualties.

Chapter Five

1779: Expedition into Indian Country

Whereas the Battle of Saratoga secured the northern states, 1779 was far from the end of hostilities in the area. American intelligence, though impressive given its disparity between agents, had little to go on to acknowledge any cessation or retreat by the British armies into Canada. Tribes in the Hudson Valley, and along the western frontiers of New York, were still plotting revenge for the campaign against their tribes only a year earlier. Admiral Richard Howe's British navy was still maintaining dominance over the Atlantic coast. With no way to determine Howe's movements, the Americans could not be sure whether another British force was waiting on deck to land at any given moment.

Gansevoort's force and the rest of the regiments were also in a situation that might bereave them of their already meager ammunition, funding, and clothing. The close of 1778 accompanied the British capture Savannah in South Carolina and forces stationed there were reorganized to conduct further campaigns. Washington and the bulk of the Continental Army rerouted supply lines from the northern states into the southern campaign. Gansevoort and other New York officers would take the fight on the offensive before the supplies dwindled out; they would venture into Indian territory and engage in a scorched earth campaign.

On January 24, Gansevoort, now stationed in Albany, would receive more bad news from his subordinate officers. The notice from the "officers of the third New York regiment"[1] concerned Gansevoort's plan to bring back Lieutenant Moses Yeomans after dismissing him in 1778 due to the new arrangement of the Third New York Regiment. The officers expressed their opinion that although Yeomans was retaining the same rank, it was unfair for Yeomans to be entitled to a higher pension or "civil life" payment by gaining a position within Gansevoort's regiment that he had not earned, regardless of performance and promotion in his previous service. The officers cited the actual Congressional resolution on such matters made in November 1778, which contained provisions regarding payment of New York officers retired from service and engaged in what was termed as "Civil Life."[2] Yeomans must have not rejoined the regiment for at the end of March, as his name does not appear in the organizational list for the Third New York Regiment.

135—From the Officers of the Third New York Regiment

To Colonel Gansevoort

We the Subscribers Officers of the Third New York Regt under your command (being informed that you had sent orders to Lieut. Yeoman's to join your said Regt promising him that he shall have his Rank in the same manner as before he was left out as a Supernumerary Officer in consequence of a Resolve pass'd in Congress the 27th May 1778, beg leave to inform you, that we are unanimously of opinion as follows, first that his rejoining the Regiment in his former Rank and Station is contrary to the expressed intintion of a Resolve of Congress secondly that it is highly unjust & the precident prejudicial to the Rank of ~~all~~ most of the Officers who now serve in the Regiment, And thirdly that it very much tends to increase the many dissentions now Subsisting in the Army about the Rank of the Officers.

Our Opinion if founded on the following Reasons vizt

"In Congress the 24th November 1778, Resolved that the Congress gratefully acknowledge the faithful services of such Officers as have been or may be omitted in the new Arrangement as being Supernumerary who from their conduct and services are entituled to the honorable notice of Congress, and to a Suitable provision until they can return to civil Life with advantage: Resolved therefore that all Supernumerary Officers be entituled to one Year's pay of their Commission respectively to be computed from the Time such Officers had leave of absence from the Commander in chief on this account. And Congress do earnestly recommend to the Several States to which such Officers belong to make such farther provision for them as their respective circumstances and Merit entitle them to."

The above Resolve is so express to the purpose that it needs no comment, it plainly points out that the Supernumerary Officers are to be provided for by the State in "Civil Life" and not in their respective Regiments.

Secondly, ~~that~~ it is highly unjust and the Precedent prejudical to the Rank of ~~all~~ most of the Officers in the Regiment,

For by the same Rule the rest of the Supernumerary Officers (in case of a vacancy) might be recalled so that the Rank of most of the Officers would be uncertain, that it is clearly setled by another Resolve of Congress passed on the same Day as the former, in these words vizt. Resolved. "That whereas it will be for the benefit of the Service for promotions be established, they recommend to the several States to provide that in all future promotions, Officers Rise Regimentally to the Rank of Captain and thence in the Line of the state to the Rank of Colonel, except in Cases where preference may be given to distinguished Merit." And here give us leave to observe, that altho Congress are of Opinion that Merit should be rewarded. Yet we are of Opinion it is not the Case with any of those who were left out of the Regiment, if so they should have been continued and others less distinguished have been disbanded. And further, as Congress have resolved that all promotion shall rise Regimentally for the Benefit of the Service we cannot suppose the Supernumerary Officers, to have belonged to the Regiment, from and after the Date of the said Resolve of Congress wherein they are provided for. And therefore we think it not only unjust but that it will tend to increase the many dissentions in the Army, which at present we are Sorry to confess there is too much of, For what man of Spirit who after one or more Severe Campaigns, (having served faithfully and with Honor) returns home and justly expecting perferment if any Vacancies should happen, would not think himself injures to see one who has been inactive and not actually belonging to the Regiment profered above him, which we ~~are~~ think will be the Case if this present instance be admitted of.

We are Sir with respect Your very humble servants

Albany 24 Jany 1779

Aaron Aorson Capt, Leond Bleeker Capt, Ja Gregg Capt, Henry Tiebout Capt, George Sytez Capt Lt, Ph Conine Lieut, William Tapp Lieut, Thos McClelan Lieut, Prentice Bowen Lieut, Gerrit Staats Lieut, Chrisr Hutton Ens, Peter Magee Ens, J Bagley Ensign, Saml Lewis Ens, Geor J Denniston Ens

136—Arrangement of the Officers of the Third New York Regiment

Arrangement of the 3d N York Battn March 30 1779

Rank	***Names***	***Dateof Commission***
Colo	*Peter Gansevoort*	*21st Novr 1776*
Lieut Colo	*Marinus Willett*	
Major	*Robert Cochran*	
Captain	*1st Aaron Aorson*	
	2d Thomas DeWitt	
	3d Cornelius T. Janson	
	4th Leonard Bleeker	
	5th James Gregg	
	6th Henry Tiebout	
Capt Lieut	*George Sytez*	
Lieutenant	*1st Philip Conine*	
	2d William Tapp	
	3d Thomas McClelan	
	4th Prentice Bowen	
	5th Garrit Staats	
	6th Benjamin Bogardus	
	7th William Colbreath	
	8th Christopher Hutton	
Ensigns	*1st Peter Magee*	
	2d John Spoor	
	3d Jonah Bagley	
	4th Samuel Lewis	
	5th George Deniston	
	6th Jeremiah Van Rensselaer	
	7th Benjamin Herring[3]	
	8th Garrit G Lansing[4]	
	9th John Burhance[5]	
PayMaster	*Jeremiah Van Rensselaer*	
Adjutant	*Christopher Hutton*	
Q Master	*Prentice Bowen*	
Surgeon	*Hunloke Woodruff*	
Mate	*John Elliot*	

Still battling the difficulties of procuring clothing for the regiment, Peter's brother, Leonard Gansevoort, reported to the Colonel that on February 15 he had presented a request for £150 to the New York House of Assembly. Leonard believed it would receive the approval of the House soon, so that each commissioned officer would be able to purchase new sets of clothes.

137—From Leonard Gansevoort

My Dear Sir. *The Memorial from the Officers of the New York Brigade I had the Honor this Morning to lay before the House of Assembly, which was read and immediately committed to the Committee of the whole House, from the Temper of the House and the private opinions of the many of the Members, I imagine they will give you a Vote of Credit upon the Treasury of this State, for about £150 to each Commissioned Officer to enable them to purchase themselves a good Suit of Cloathes, I am persuaded you have the best wishes of the Legislature to grant you more but they conceive themselves not in a Capacity to do what they wish.*

My best love to Caty and Compliments to Mr Van Schaick's Family

Your's very Sincerely

Leonard Gansevoort

Pough: Feby 15.1779

Collo Gansevoort

February 22 saw a letter from General James Clinton[6] with orders for Gansevoort's men; they were to march towards Major Fundy's position at Cognawaga to await any intelligence that would require defensive maneuvers.[7] When and if the intelligence showed lack of enemy movement, Gansevoort was to send a detachment back to Albany with any spare ammunition; this would most likely either be distributed to other prioritized militia regiments or sent to support the Continental Army. A report from Pierre Regnier de Roussi[8] on the same day proved such a situation to be true. The end of de Roussi's report left his findings slightly bewildering as he mentioned that Gansevoort should not immediately march back as per his orders. Instead, de Regnier advised that his men stay in the area for a few days due to local concerns: "...Country people about here Insist upon that, the Ennemy must not be far off..."[9]

On February 24, de Roussi forwarded a report from Captain Copp[10] who had observed a small British force near Oswego Lake and had dispatched Indian scouts to watch their movements. These scouts were apparently sent over a week previous to the letter's writing and hoped for their quick return.[11]

James Clinton, published by Knapp, Peck and Thompson, 1887 (Gansevoort-Lansing collection. Manuscripts and Archives Division. The New York Public Library. Astor, Lenox and Tilden Foundations).

138—From James Clinton

[ca. February 22nd 1779]

Sir You are Desired to Proceed with Your Regiment as far as Majr Fundys where you will Halt them till you Receive further Intelligence About the Enemy If it should prove to be A false Alarm then you are to March Back to Albany Sending A Guard with the Amunition & to Coll Regnier takeing his Receipt for what you Deliver If you hear of the Enemy Advanceing then You are to Proceed to meet them Acquainting Coll Regnier and the Commanding Officer of the Militia of your Movement that they may Join You

I am Sir Yours &

James Clinton B Genl

To Coll Gansevort

139—From Pierre Regnier de Roussi

Sir Yours of yesterday; was Just handed to me By your Express &c

I have not received further Intelligence from the Enemy Since the 18th but I expect every minute an Express from Fort Schuyler by which we Shall be Informed of the truth as I have Sent him the day before Yesterday he cannot be longer time out, unless Some accident Should have appined to him under way—And as Soon as he arrive I will Send you the Contents—But; I would not advise you to march your Regiment Back before that time as by Several Circumstances the Country people about here Insist upon that, the Ennemy—must not be far off I have ordered a party of men to go and Escort the ammunition which you have for me and Expect they will arrive at Major Fonday by tomorrow noon

I am your Most obt

P Regnier Lt Col Comdt

Fort Plank[12] *Feby 22d 1779*

Col Ganseworth [at Cognawaga]

140—From Pierre Regnier de Roussi

Dear Colonel, At last the Express is arrived and hereafter is the Coppy of the Letter I received from Fort Schuyler and upon which I thought proper to Disband the Militia of which I was pretty tired already—

Coppy—Fort Schuyler Feb 21st 1779—

Dear Colonel I this moment Received yours of yesterday the Last Intelligence I have been able to receive was by a Letter from Captain Copp of the 19th Instant the Ennemy had then, taken the Gee on the Lake and their tracks were not Discernable the Indians are of opinion they have returned I Sent a Scout of four trusty Indians up Oswego Lake, the day before yesterday. They are to be out ten Days provided they make no Discoveries, our working parties go to the woods as usual &c.

John Grisham[13] *Captain Comdt*

—I beg you would Send the Inclosed to Genl Clinton as Soon as received as there is no other Express going to Albany

I Remain your obt Servt

P Regnier Lt Col Comdt

Fort Plank Feb 24th 1779—

Col Gansworth [at Cognawaga]

James Gregg had sent a letter to Colonel Gansevoort on March 12 describing the desertion of two men from Gregg's company.[14] The men had apparently complained about the condition of their clothing, specifically their shoes. They then marched off without notifying any officer of their intentions; ultimately they had eventually given themselves up to a nearby militia officer for fear of punishment. Normally this would then follow normal procedure, but the militia officer had noted that holding the men was taking up an unnecessary amount of manpower and resources, as well as restricting their movement. Gregg then asked Gansevoort as to whether they shall receive a pardon; Gregg believed based on their past character that they deserted out of fear but would not do it again. This was not to be an isolated incident for the 1779 winter; Aaron Aorson would note later in the month that an astonishing twenty-four men of his regiment had deserted Fort George for "wesels at the Seven Mile Island."[15]

141—From James Gregg

New Burgh 12th March 1779

Dear Col Tho' I am in great hurry as the Sloop is just going off I cant forbear relating to Some News which Col: Malcomb[16] *has just informed us off which he says he had from Genl Washinton himself vizt*

The Emperor of Russia has absolutely Refused to send any Men to fight against the Americans

The Kings of the two Sicily's has opened all the ports for the American Trade.

The Spanish Ambassador in the Court of England has declared, that unless Hostilities beare between France and England his Master will no longer be an Idle Spectator but will take an active part in Conjunction with France against England.

The Dutch have Sent to America for a description of the American Flag, that they may pay due respect to it. That they are determined to support their Trade to America with fifty Capital ships.

I conclude being in great hurry

Dear Col. Yours &

J Gregg

[Peter Gansevoort Albany]

142—From Aaron Aorson

Fort George March 14 1779

Dear Sir with Sorrow I must acquaint you that ~~this~~ Last Evinning betwen the ours of Eight and Nine Oclck twenty four of our men Deserted from this Post it was found out by the Sentenels Caling to the Serjeant of the Guard witch was Thomas Waiter when he was not to be found on witch he Caled for the Corparal and he was also mising on witch they Acquainted me that the Serjeant & Corparal and tow men moor of the Guard was mising I Emedintly had the men Paraded and the Rools Caled and found mising of my Company as follows Thomas Waiter; James Sutner, Thomas Willis Abraham Williams, Archl Smith, Culiph wise Christian Barwolf Sabens Burck Moses Brocket Joseph Slead Robard Mitchal Conradt Killian Thomas Foster, John

Flinn, Frances Everstin Moses Carpenter, John Cooper, Peter Buckstaf,[17] *and Stephen Barnes, and of the Major Company Corparal Barret Newbarugh Stimel Wasels and Rohall I Emedently Ordered Ensigns Bagly and Lewis with Thirty of our men in Porsute of them as we all toght they was gon acrose the Lake and they met wesels at the Seven Mile Island and Sade he Left them about Six mile a head they Continued ther march til they got to the narrows and then the most of the men Gave out on Account of the Snow being Deep and Crusty witch Cut ther Shoes and the men Complaning that thar feet was frost Bite on witch they Return to the Garrison I have Ondly forty Seven men with me at Present and I think ther are More Inclind to go of but I Shall have them all in the Garrison now I Shall not Rite to General Schuyler on Account I heard he was Gon to phiskills but Shold he be in Albany I wold be Ablight to you if you wold Acquaint him with this Curcumstance I wold be also Ever Glad you wold Order Mr Taap and Mr Staats up with the men we left in Albany and youil oblige your verry humble Servant*

Aaron Aorson

NB Lutner took his with him

Good news on American foreign relations was received by Gansevoort on March 12. Gregg announced that Russia would not participate in the war, the Kingdom of Two Sicilies had opened their ports for American trade, and the Spanish may possibly be inclined to enter the war against the British if the war was to drag on for too long.[18] The Spanish monarchy was certainly in support of a military venture that could secure its holdings in the Caribbean and Florida colonies, but was still dealing with inflation and a weak economy due to the massive influx of gold to Spanish markets.

On April 19, General Washington sent detailed orders to General Clinton, which were then passed along to Gansevoort on April 19. Washington began the letter expressing some annoyance at errors in the Third New York's officer rolls, and had submitted his own arrangement which was expected to become the default for the remaining campaign.[19] Whether or not this may have been connected to the officer protest earlier in the year is unknown. The rest of the letter concerned orders for Gansevoort's Third and other New York regiments to gather at the Canajoharie settlement on or before May 12.

Washington could not give exact orders for the men once assembled as he determined it to be "a most profound Secret,"[20] which would include forces to move north into "Indian Country" in the Mohawk River Valley. Washington may have also heard of the desertions by disgruntled men; he suggested that contracts requesting shoes be delivered to nearby supply lines prior to marching into the Mohawk valley.[21]

143—George Washington to James Clinton

Head Quarters, Middle Brook,[22] *April 19th: 1779:*

Sir I have been favd with yours of the 8th instant. I have furnished General Knox with the Return of deficiencies of Military Stores to the Northward and he will Send up a Supply.

In examining the Regimental Arrangements which you have transmitted to me, I observe that the dates of some Officers Commissions differ very much from those in the arrangement made by the Committee at White plains, and some Officers are introduced whose names were not in that arrangement. I have particularized them in the inclosed called "remarks upon the

Arrangement" and must desire you to inform me, before I transmit the Rolls to the Board of War to have Commissions issued, the reasons of such alteration.

The State arrangement of Colo Dubois's Regiment[23] *differs almost totally from that made by the Committee. But if the former has been acted under Since the Regiment was first commissioned, it ought to be preferred, more especially as the State had a right, upon raising the Regt, to the arrange the Officers as they pleased. Those who were discontented should not have accepted at the time. I have returned the Arrangement of that Regiment to you, that you may make the necessary enquiry and report to me upon it. Altho' Lt Colo Regnier was, in the arrangement transmitted to you, called Lt Colo Commandant of the Regt late Livingstons it was a mistake. Lieut Colo Weissenfeldts,*[24] *who appears to be the eldest of that Rank, will be appointed, and Lt Colo Regnier will take his place in Cortlands.*[25] *This cannot possibly give any disgust to Colo Regnier whose Rank in the line of the State was fully settled at Valley Forge—*

It is determined that Gansevoorts—late Livingstons—Dubois's—Aldens and Butlers Regiments Shall be held in every respect ready to assemble at Canojohare by the 12th: May. I have requested Govr Clinton to furnish immediately a Sufficient number of Militia to relieve any detachments from those Corps, which may be upon the North River, and the moment they are relieved, they are to join their respective Regiments—All Officers and Men upon furlough are to be called in. You Some time ago mentioned, that you had Sent 100 Men over to Haverhill[26] *at the request of General Bailey.*[27] *If they have not been already recalled, it may be done, as Hazens Regiment has been Sent up to Coos.*[28]

That you may the more fully comprehend me, I Shall inform you of the reason of the rendezvous at Canojohare, but I must depend upon your keeping it a most profound Secret. It has not been yet determined whether the Regiments before mentioned (Van Schaicks at all events will garrison Fort Schuyler) are to proceed up the Mohawk and enter the Indian Country by that Route—or whether they Shall cross suddenly over to the Waters of Susquehannah and falling down that River, form a junction with our main Body at Tioga—Owegy—or whatever place Shall be deemed most advisable: To be prepared to carry this into execution, a number of Batteaus of the lightest kind, Sufficient to transport the above mentioned Regiments, are to be, without loss of time, collected at Canojohare, and the Quarter Master General directed to take measures to have Carriages ready for the conveyance of them to the head of Susquehannah Should there be occasion.

You are to order the Quarter Master and Commissary immediately to lay in as large a Supply of provision as they possibly can at Fort Schuyler. This will be necessary, Should it be finally determined to move the Troops up the River in preference to Susquehannah—or it will at any rate form an ample Magazine for the Support of the Garrison—The collection of provision at that post will also hold up the appearance of operating from that quarter, altho' we may really have no Such intent.

The Batteaus may be immediately drawn together at Conojohare and a Suitable Magazine formed there. The troops which I have mentioned may all I Should Suppose, reach Canojohare from their present Cantonments in a few days. They need not therefore move untill you hear further from me: But as I have before directed, they are to be ready to march at a moments warning—

If you can contract for any number of Shoes to be delivered before you march, be pleased to do it, and carry them with you, as I fear we Shall fall Short in this Article.

The Council of Massachusetts have called for authenticated musters of their 15 Battalions that they may ascertain the deficiency of their Quota. You will therefore be pleased to direct the

Deputy Commissary of Musters to transmit a certified Muster Roll of Aldens Regiment to the president of the Council at Boston—

I have requested General Schuyler to favor you with his advice and assistance in carrying the matters recommended into execution, which I am persuaded he will do with the greatest cheerfulness—

Make me a Return of the light Cloathing that will be wanting for the Troops that I may endeavour to have it Sent up for them—

I am Sir Your most Obt Servt

Go Washington

P.S. I have directed Lt Colo Weissenfelds to take the command of the Regt late Livingstons as Lt Colonel Commandant. Be pleased to order Lt. Col Regnier to join Cortlands.

Brig Genl Clinton—

Initial stages of the campaign were met with disasters, reminiscent of Gansevoort's earlier river crossings in the failed Canadian invasion. First Lieutenant William Tapp noted that one of the men had drowned attempting to desert the nearby camp with preciously needed bateaus.[29] If the attempt had been successful, the marching force would have been seriously delayed. On April 26, Jelles Fonda reported that Colonel Van Schaick had burnt and destroyed the Onondaga Castle.[30] Van Schaick had also taken thirty-seven prisoners and killed twenty more.[31] Two weeks later, Colonel Van Schaick informed Gansevoort that the incursion onto Onondaga land spurred the tribe to offer men to scalp British in any nearby areas the armies had seen fit.[32]

144—From William Tapp

Fort George 25th April 1779

Dr Sir/ Three of Capt Aorsons Company & One of Capt Bleeckers A Servant to Doctor Elliot Deserted in two Canoes from us the night of the Seventeenth. next day I sent for a Batteau which arived the Ninteenth at Noon with which I sent Ensign Lewis and Eight Men after them who returned the twenty first with two. One being drowned the morning after they sett off One made his Escape and Lewis left two Men for three days to ambush him its imposible he can get away as His toes are frost Bitt. has no Arms and been without provisions four days, the Batteau went off after the two Men Yesterday who return'd ~~with the Other~~ without him this day. have sent ~~them~~ the two down. I have likewise sent Dennis Sulivan with them for particular refer you to Genl Clinton and am Sir your Hble Servant

Wm Tapp

[Peter Gansevoort Albany]

145—From Jelles Fonda

Kingsburgh 26 Apl 1779

Dear Jentelmen the Genral Just now Recd: a Letter from Coll Van Scaieck the he has Burnt and Distryed the Ondago Castel and Taken 37 Presines and Killed 20 od yung men got a fele of Plunder Indians Corn &

I am your &
Jelles Fonda
To Coll gansevert
Coll Visher & Coll wemp nere may field

146—From Goose Van Schaick

Fort Schuyler May 11 1779

Sir I am Sinsible that I neglected Writing After my Return from the Onandaga Expedition to afrind to Obliging as Mr Glen Brot So you will Consider that much fetuaged the Attention I was Obliged to pay to a person In High Rank and the who is placed Above me was the first work that Ingrozed that Attention I Judged from the Connextion at this place you Receved Early & perfact Account of our Success Which I Beliave Is almost forgott the people are not Sinseble what a good Affact It has had Among the Indians the Onandage Warriors offer to go to what post We Chuse to Direct them and Bring In what Number of prisoner and Scalp from the Enemy Brittish we may Desire

[PG]

A marching order issued on the May 24 from the Easton, Pennsylvania headquarters[33] goes into great detail about the military operation to be conducted.[34] Gansevoort and his men in the Third New York regiment were to march under the command of General Clinton.

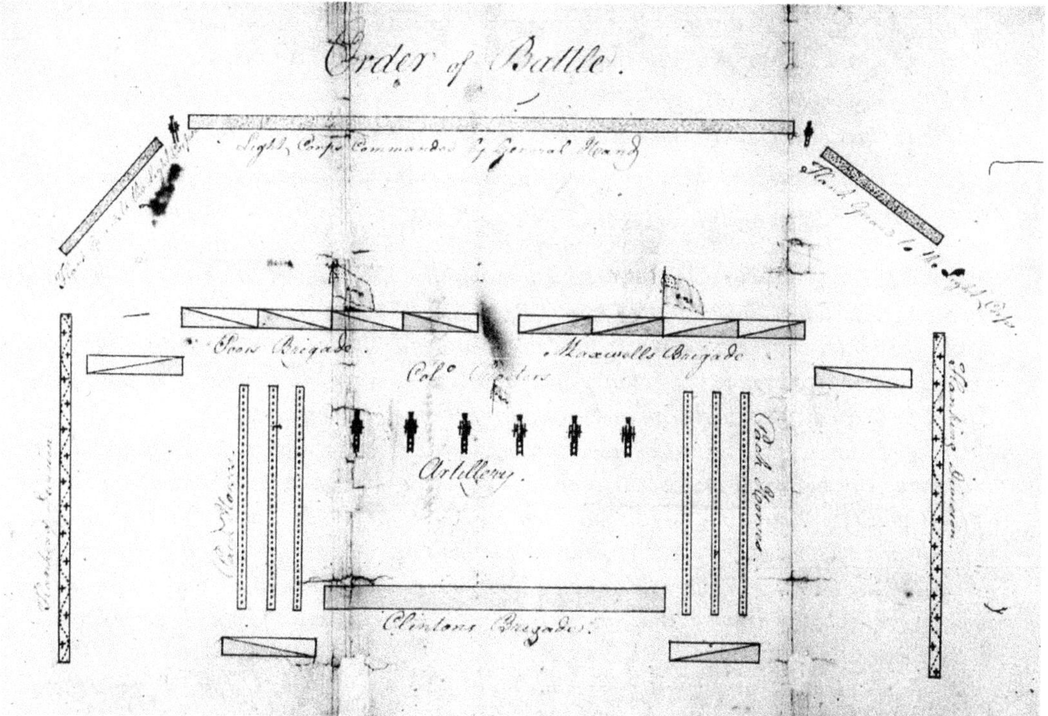

Order of battle during the Sullivan-Clinton campaign, 1779 (Gansevoort-Lansing collection. Manuscripts and Archives Division. The New York Public Library. Astor, Lenox and Tilden Foundations).

As the terrain would allow, Clinton's force was to flank the right side of a regiment under Colonel Maxwell[35]; the center forces would be largely made up of rangers, artillery batteries and horses carrying ammunition. If under attack while marching, Clinton was to direct his forces to outflank the sides and rear of any British threat and help relieve the first and second lines formed in the center. It would seem that Gansevoort's forces would not be in immediate danger for the length of the march; the orders anticipated a British attack on the batteries and supplies.

147—Order of March and Battle

Head Quarters Easton May the 24th 79
When the Army shall be fully assembled the following Arrangements is to take place
Viz
Light Corps to consist of and be commanded by Genl Hand[36]
Armandts[37]
Shotts[38]
6 Companies of Rangers
Wm Butler's Battalion[39]
Morgan's Corps and all Volunteers who may join the Army

Maxwell's Brigade to consist of
Dayton, Shreve[40] *Ogden*[41] *Spencers*[42]

Poor's Brigade to Consist of
Cilley,[43] *Reed,*[44] *Scammel,*[45] *Cortland and form the left of the 1st Line*

Clinton's Brigade to consist of
Late Livingston's, Dubois, Ganosworth, Olden, and form the second Line or Reserve

The right of the 1st Line to be cover'd by 100 Men draughted from Maxwell's Brigade. The left to be cover'd by 100 Men draughted from Poor's Brigade, Each flank of the 2d Line to be cover'd by 50 Men draughted from Clinton's Brigade. The flanking Divison on the right to consist of Hartley's Regt and Patten's with a Draught from the Line of 100 Men, The flanking Division on the left to consist of the German Battn and 150 Men from the Line. The Order of Battle and Order of March are represented in the annex'd Plan and are to be adher'd to at all times when the Situation of the Country will possibly admit and when a Deviation takes place, it must be carried on no further than the Necessity of that Time requires.

Order of March—The light Corps will advance by the right of Companies in files and keep at least one mile in front. Maxwells Brigade willl advance by its right in files. Sections or Platoons as the Country will admit. Poor Brigade from its left in the same manour. Clinton's Brigade will advance by the right of ~~the~~ Regiments in Platoons Sections or in files as the Country will admit. All the covering Parties and flanking Divisions on the right will advance by the left, ~~of~~ those on the left of the Army will advance by the right. The Artillery and Pack Horses will march in the Centre.

Shou'd the Army be attackd in front while on its March, The light Corps will immediately form to repulse the Enemy, The flanking Division will endeavour to gain the Flanks and rear of the Enemy. While the Line is forming the Pack Horses will in all Cases fall into the Position represented in the annexd Plan. Shou'd the Enemy attack be either Flank. The flanking Division attack'd will form a Front and sustain the Attack till reinforc'd in which case a Party of the light Corps is immedeately detach'd to gain the Enemy's Flanks and rear. The covering Flanks of the 2d Line will move to gain the other Flank. Shou'd the Enemy attack our rear, the 2d Line will face and form a front to the Enemy. The covering Parties of the 1st Line will move to Sustain it, while the flanking Divisions face about and endeavour to gain their Flanks and Rear Shou'd the light Troops be driven back they will pass through the Intervals of the main Army and form in the rear. Shou'd the Enemy in an Engagement with the Army when form'd, endeavour to gain either Flank. The covering Party will march up to lengthen the Line and so much as may be found necessary, from the flanking Division will display to prevent the Attempt from succeeding the Light Corps will have their Advance and flank Parties at a good distance from their main Body The flanking Divisions will furnish Flank Guards and the 2d Line a rear Guard, for the main Army.

When We find the light Troops engagd wth the Enemy in front—The front of the Pack Horses will halt and the rear close up; while the Columns in a small distance close and display which will bring the Horses in the position represented in the Plan for the Order of Battle. Shou'd the Attack be made either on flank or rear. The Horses must be kept in the Position they are in at the commencement of the Action, unless other Orders are given.

General Clinton updated General Washington on the campaign in a June 14 letter. Within, Clinton stated that the rough river passages and lack of sufficient transport demanded that he asked for another hundred boats to be delivered.[46]

148—James Clinton to George Washington

Sir, This Day I had the honour to receive your favour of the 10th instant, as also one from Genl Sullivan of the 11th containing Instructions for me to move ~~by the Head of~~ up to Connojoharie & transport my Boats &c across to Lake Otsego[47] *there to wait farther orders to ~~the Susquehanna and~~ join him*

I have ordered one hundred Batteaux ~~to be~~ loaded with Stores to be transported up the River to Connojoharie by the 3rd NY Regt & the Detachment under Col Butler the former ~~is to will~~ set off ~~this day~~ yesterday, the latter with set off ~~tomorrow~~ this day

When tryal I find the hundred Boats will be entirely inadequate to transport the Army ~~and~~ Stores & Provision—necessary for the Expedition, I have therefore ordered one hundred more to get ready immediately—

As the Road is difficult between the River and the Lake, it will require ~~near~~ a great Number of Waggons to transport the Boats &c across—I have ordered the QtrM to collect three or four Hundred, which I am in hopes will be effected—

The Genl advises me not to take Horses with me but to imbark all the Troop in Boats & take the Saddles ~~I shall take with me~~ if there is room for yr—he requires me to Store the Brigade Field Pieces & take the Grasshoppers from Fort Schuyler arming the Artillery men with Musquets, which I have ordered to be done—he also informs me that I can have a Supply of Miltary Stores when I join him, which will be much wanted as there destine for this place have not yet arrived

On Consulting Genl Schuyler & considering the Difficulties which arrive in this Place during my Absence for want of a proper Officer to command I have ordered Col V Schaick to take the

Command here, as he is the best Officer in the Department leaving Lt Col V Dep[48] *to command in the Fort, as ~~Major~~ Captain Graham is appointed Major—*

I enclose your Excellency a Certificate relative to Captain Graham and in the mean time shall appoint as Major in B. Orders—

Albany June 14th 1779

[James Clinton]

[George Washington]

The artillery men were also advised to be armed with extra muskets and that as Clinton may have to take leave to observe the handling of desperately needed supplies, Colonel Van Schaick was to be the temporary commander of the right flanking force.

Aside from sparse reports of British movement near Fort Dayton, correspondence became less about the campaign and instead focused on home life and supplying clothing to the soldiers. Jeremiah Van Rensselaer informed Gansevoort that his regiment will hopefully be fully fit with new clothing including overalls, breeches, hose, shirts, and especially "Good Shoes."[49]

149—From Jacob Klock[50]

Palatine July 28th 1779 at 9 OClock P.M.

Dr Sir Just as Lieut Bart was going to return I received a letter from the German Flatts informing that the Expected a large Body of the Enemy there tomorrow and warmly pressing me to march up the Militia. I shall therefore leave tomorrow morning very early to Consult with you

I am with due regard your hble Servt

Jacob Klock Col

Colo Peter Gansevoert [Fort Plank]

150—From Robert McKeen[51]

Fort Dayton July the 29th 1779

Sir Just as i arrived at a Fort ouer Pe Sentrys heard three Guns firing upwards the Canada Creek and no Peopel is there So it mus be the Enemies & as i supposed they Killed Cattel for provision as i am of opinion that they are insensibel of your being up here you will have the Pleasure of paying them a visit to morrow morning wheter the party is smal or strong is unknowen to me.

Sir i am your Hble Servt

Robt McKeen Capt

To Colo Peter Gansevort

151—From Jeremiah Van Rensselaer

Albany 29th July 1779

Dear Colonel the day before yesterday I returned from the High lands but without any Success in the Buiseness as was Intended it is true there was Some Cloathing designed for Officers.

the Quntity as Near as Can Recolect is as Viz. 300 Shirts at £10 Lawfull & no Cotton in Quality than Some Which I have frequently drawn for the Privates of the Regt 8 or 10 Rimnents of Diffr Cullerd Cloths Some hatts Abt 30 doz of different Kind hose 50 pieces of diaper and Some Smaller Articles the Whole in General by Substituting the one thing for Another it Might Compleat Abt 5 or 6 Regt all Which his Excellency Will not Suffer to have Issued but by the direction of the Board of War Which Said Orders had not then yet Arrived the prises Nearly Equal to the Retail Shops in this place

Regimatal Cloathing by the New orders is drawn by the Order of the Colonel from the State Cloathier there is one to be Appointed by Every State. Who is to draw from the Continatal Cloathier from time to time his proportion of Such Cloathing as is or may be provided & by him to be Issued on the Colo order to the Regiments Cloathier but as Good fortune Would have it—I have taken the Liberty to Sign your Name to a Return I made and have drawn before the Regulation takes place 175 Shirts 149 Overalls 379 frocks 415 pr Good Shoes 274 Pr White Breeches and 400 pr Hose all Which I have With me in Albany and Shall forward up to Anthony Van Veghtens 2 Hhls Containing 130 Overalls 360 frocks Which Will Compleat the Regt in them Articles if they have the Good fortune to Reach you before you leve your present Station they go up under Care of Capts Davis & Titus of the 4th Bato[52] to Mr Van Veghtens but if there Should be no Likilihood of your Getting them I Shall be glad to be Informed thereof So that I may Again have them Removed I am at present at A Stand Wor the Shirts I have drawn. they are not So Good as was Represented therefore belive Shall Send them back to Mr P Hanson to have them Exchanged: it was Hobsons Choice with me Respecting the Shirts, them, or none, they being the only ones in Store—

In a Short time I hope an oppertunity Will Offer to draw Shirts from Mr Cortonius Linnin for that purpose was provided Last Spring

I Could Wish that you would Send me one or two Blank Cloathing Returns Signed. that I may Always be Ready if an Oppertunity offers, to prevent me from being Gulty of Crimes ~~that I would~~ of fogery Which no Emergencey Can or Will Justefy Altho I must have the Impertince to ask your Sanction to my Eniquity in the Aforementioned Case—

I Must Also Sugest if it Would not be proper for the Officers of the Brigade to Request Genl Clinton to Represent to the Senate & Assembley (Who will be Setting in Abt 14 days, the propriaty of their furnishing thair Troops in Necessary's of Cloathing Agreable to A Resolve of Congress Authorising the different States to provide Such Necessarys as they Can for the Comfort of their troops and to Isue them at Such Moderate prises as their pay Will Admit of Chargeing the Loss to the United States

Now the Case Stands thus Every State Excepting ours has provided their officers With Cloathing at A Moderate Rate & Undoubtedly has thousands ~~More~~ of pounds More that Was Repar'd by their officers Which of Course is Charged to the United States Which by the Eoconomey of the State of NYork they will find to have made a Saving of the Annual Sum of Some 20 or 30 thousand pounds to be paid ~~for the~~ by our State towards furnishing the Officers of Other States Insted of their own

I am Just now Advised to Send the 2 Hhds to Henry Glen & to desire him to forward them if it Can be Safely done to Mr V Veghtens

I am Dr Sir with Respect yours &c

Jer V Rensselaer

Peter Gansevoort [Lake Otsego]

On August 6, Colonel Gansevoort wrote to his wife to reassure her that, although there were anticipations of some skirmishes with British soldiers, reinforcements would quickly arrive to solidify the position if necessary. He also mentioned that the force would soon be reinforced with another three to four hundred militiamen. One of the few times where Gansevoort seemed to convey emotion or opinion in the breadth of his correspondence is within the last two paragraphs. The first espoused his belief that he was to participate in the campaign to make peace with all hostile Indians; particular notice should be paid attention to his view that the peace would be made on "our own terms and thereby securing peace to our Distressed inhabitants on our Frontiers."[53] The last paragraph expresses love for his family and a yearning to hear details on their wellbeing. Apparently Gansevoort had expected a quick response, as another letter on the 6th relayed his "mortification" from not only receiving word on the family but any words from his friends as well.[54]

152—To His Wife, Catherine Van Schaick Gansevoort

Camp Otsego Lake 6th August 1779

My Dear Caty   Just after the Express left this yesterday with my last letter to you, The Genl called to gather the Field Officers of his Brigade, And shew'd them his last Letter from General Sullivan which was Dated the 30th day of last Month at Wyoming, and the purport of the letter is nearly as follows; That he with his Army woud leave that place the day following; And that we should leave this on the same day that he arrived at Tioga, which will be about the 9th Instant, The reason of his proceeding so far up the Suquahana before we leave this, is if there should be any danger that he might send up all his Light Infantry to our Assistance—The Governor writes to Genl Clinton that we shall be join'd by about 3, or 4 Hundred of the Militia at Oghquaga[55] *under the Command of Colo Pawling,*[56] *so that I cant conceive that we shall need the Assistance of General Sullivan, Even if there should be any Danger of an Attack.*

We shall leave this next Munday morning, And when we shall have the pleasure of hearing from each other again God only knows, As we shall for some time travel through the wild wilderness whare it is not probable an express will find us and as we shall constantly be marching from one place to another,

It however gives me some consolation when in my serious moments reflecting on my being absent from you at a time when I could most wish to be with you—That we shall this Campaign have it in our power to oblige the Crual and inhuman Savages to make peace with us on our own terms, and thereby securing peace to our Distressed inhabitants on our Frontiers, as well as many others

Let me intreat you my Dear Caty to make yourself as easy on Account of my absence as possible And let us trust, that God will be pleased to let the happy period soon arrive when we shall again meet in Love, and in Joy,

Remember me to our Parents and Families And believe me My Dear Caty to be yours with the Sincerest Sentiment of Love while

Peter Gansevoort

P.S. my last Letter to you I dated 7th instead of the 5th

[Mrs Catherine Gansevoort Albany]

Camp Otsego Lake 6th August 1779

My Dear Caty   An express arrived here yesterday evening, and to my great mortification not a single line did I receive from any of my friends, when in the greatest expectation of at least receiving one from her, in whom all my happiness in this World depends

what to compute this great disappointment to is at present a mistory ~~to me~~ whether to your not knowing of the opportunity, or to the neglect of Mr Glen at Schenectady in not forwarding your Letter; shall however suspend my opinion till you hear from you again—

Last Saturday evening I returned safe from an excurtion I had to the Mohawk River, the particulars of which I wrote you from Fort Harkimer[57]

Genl Clinton received letters this evening from Genl Sullivan the contents of which he has not as yet been pleased to communicate; only this that thare was no marching orders; The Genl did not at all appear to be Satisfied, after parusing the Letters, whether it arose from his not receiving marching orders, or from any other cause is hard to determine,

If by the latter end of this Month, or the beginning of the next, We should receive no orders to move from hence which will be about the time of your—shall then endeavour to obtain leave of absence to go down to pay you a Visit; And if on the contrary must in that case beg that you will make yourself as easy as the nature of your situation will admit of. As the express is waiting for this must conclude with my best respects to our Parents and Families

And Am Dr Caty with the Sincerest of Love yours while

Peter Gansevoort

[Mrs Catherine Gansevoort Albany]

Ironically, his brother and others from his hometown had often complained of Gansevoort's lack of timely response; perhaps this was a jab on Gansevoort's silence.

Colonel Gansevoort finally received marching orders from General John Sullivan on September 20. The orders were to send a party to the lower areas of Mohawk territory with the intention to capture posts of varying importance and to attempt to make some form of diplomatic treaty with the "Orheskes" in the upper Mohawk Castle[58] area; this was to convey "a continuance of their friendship ... give evidence of our pacific disposition towards them."[59]

153—From John Sullivan

Sir You are to take command of a chosen party draughted from the Army, & proceed by the shortest rout to the lower Mohawk Castle,[60] *destroy it & captivate, if possible, all the Indians that may be there. The upper Castle being Inhabited by the Orheske's you are to spare & treat them as Friends. Such necessary marks of*

John Sullivan, unknown artist (Gansevoort-Lansing collection. Manuscripts and Archives Division. The New York Public Library. Astor, Lenox and Tilden Foundations).

civility & attention you will shew them, as may engage a continuance of their friendship & give evidence of our pacific disposition towards them.

Whatever Prisoners may fall into your Hands, you are to proceed with to Albany, & collect the Baggage of the several Regiments from which your Party were draughted, & proceed with all possible expedition to Head Quarters. You are by no means to leave any of the Prisoners at Albany, unless particularly directed by General Washington or Congress.

As your rout will be through the Oneida Country, you are to take particular care that your Men do not offer the Inhabitants the least insult; &, it, by accident any damage should be done, you are to make reperation; for which I shall stand accountable.

From your Zeal, activity & prudence, I trust every precaution will be taken to execute these Orders to the advantage & honor of the united States.

Jno Sullivan MGenl
Colo Ganseworth
September 20th '79

The route taken into Mohawk territory involved crossing through an Oneida habitation; Gansevoort was under strict orders not to disturb or damage any part of it in an attempt to preserve their shaky alliance. However, General Schuyler wrote a few weeks later informing Gansevoort that Sullivan's intelligence was grossly misinformed and that the Mohawk tribes in the lower area had not acted violently or in a threatening behavior towards the Americans; he ultimately ordered that Gansevoort should then refrain from engaging the enemy.[61]

154—From Philip Schuyler

Albany Octr 7th 1779

Dear Sir Having perused Genl Sullivans orders to you respecting the Indians of the Lower Mohawk Castle and their Property I conceive they are Founded on Misinformation given to that Gentleman. Those Indians have Peaceably remained there under the Sanction of the Public faith repeatedly given them by the Commissioners of Indian Affairs on Condition of peaceable demeanor, this Contract they have not Violated to our Knowledge, It is therefore Incumbent on us as servents of the Public to Keep the Public faith Inviolate—And we therefore intreat you to Postpone the sending the Indians from hence untill the pleasure of his Excellency General Washington can be obtained, and a Letter is already dispatched to him on the Occasion and in which we have mentioned this application to you

I am Dear Sir you most Obedt Huml Servt
Ph: Schuyler
President of the board of Commission for Indian Affairs N: Depart:
Colo Gansevoort

Given the time span between Schuyler and Sullivan's letters, Gansevoort may have well been on his way to achieving Sullivan's request and had inadvertently disrupted the relations with the Oneida.

Gansevoort's report on his excursion into Mohawk territory unfortunately seemed to confirm that he had not received General Schuyler's warning, noting that while the Tuscarora and Oneida tribes greeted his army with hospitality, he had raided and "effectually Surprised" the lower Mohawk inhabitants, driving the majority of them out of the settlement and into the borderlands.[62] Instead of razing the village, it was instead taken over by members of the tribes loyal to the United States, resettling in the usurped homes of the Mohawk. Gansevoort seemed to have been afflicted by sickness while on this expedition; he finished the note with a statement from his surgeon claiming he had fallen ill to "Billious Fever"[63]

155—Recollection of the Lower Mohawk Castle Mission

Agreable to my Orders I proceeded by the shortest rout to the lower Mohawk Castle, passing thro' the Tuscarora & Oneida Castles where every Mark of Hospotality & Friendship was Shewn the party I had the pleasure to find that not the least damage nor insult was offered any of the Inhabitants, on the 25th Ultimo I arrived at Fort Schuyler, where refreshing my party. I proceeded down the River & on the 29th effectually Surprised the lower Mohawk Castle making prisoners of every Indian Inhabitants, they then occuppied but four Houses I was preparing agreable to my Orders to destroy them but was interupted by the Intercessions & Intreaties of Several Inhabitants of the frontiers, who have been lately driven from their Settlements by the Savages, praying that they might have Liberty to enter into the Mohawk's Houses, whilst they could procure other Habitations, & will knowing these persons to have lately lost their all Humanity tempted me in this particular to act in Some degree contrary to orders, altho' I ~~cannot~~ could not but be confident of your approbation ~~of this part of my Conduct —~~especially when you are informed that this Castle is in the Heart of our Settlements & abounding with every—Necessary So that it is remarked that these Indians live much better than most of the Mohawk River farmer their Houses where very well furnished with all necessary Household utensils, great plenty of Grain, Several Horses, Cows & Waggons, of all which I have an Inventory, ~~not allowing my party to plunder~~, leaving them in the care of Major Newkirk of that place who distribute the Refugees on the Several Houses Such being the Situation I did not allow the party to plunder at all

The prisoners arrived at Albany on the 2d Inst where closely Secured in the Fort ~~upon have arriving I informed them, that~~ Yesterday the 7th Inst. I received a Letter from General Schuyler (I have inclosed a Copy), respecting the prisoners, & desiring ~~they would be detained~~ the sending the prisoners down might be postponed until an Express arrived from his Excellency General Washington, ~~which I have inclosed~~ agreable to this request a Serjent & twelve we detained to keep charge of the prisoners untill his Excellency's pleasure is known—

If with the greatest Regret I mention my Indisposition being so great~~,~~ as to hinder my taking charge of the party to Head Quarters, I have been Several days confined, & my Surgeon informs my that my Complaint is the Billious fever—Capt. Sytez takes command of the detachment, & will proceed with all Expedition to Head Quarters with the Baggage of the Several Regiments, where I hope Shortly to join the Army remain &c &c

Peter Gansevoort

[October 8th 1779]

156—From George Washington

Head Quarters West point 25th: Octobr 1779

Dear Sir *General Schuyler has shewn me a letter from Mr Douw of Albany by which I perceive that you did not think my letter of the 12th to General Schuyler or in his absence to Mr*

Douw desiring the release of the Mohawks, a sufficient authority to you to give them up, as the order was not in positive terms, nor directed to you.

Upon referring to the letter, I find it was not a full order, tho' I meant it as Such. You will therefore be pleased on the receipt hereof to deliver the Indians to Mr. Douw, who will lay them under Such obligations for their future good behavior as he Shall think necessary.

I am Dear Sir Your Most H. Sert

Go: Washington

Colo Gansevoort [Albany]

157—From Marinus Willett

Camp near the Clove[64] *2d Novemr 79*

Dear Colonel, We arrived here yesterday the Regiment is in as good order as may be expected, the men have not yet received their Clothing which was left at Albany—but expect their arrival to day as I have sent Capt Tiebout to order them to this place—I have nothing New pattersen sets of with what Baggage their is of yours at this place to day—the principal part was forwarded to New Windsor by Major Cochran, where I hope Pattersen will find it in good order—I send you by this conveyance 5 yards Cordderoy—with two Skairs Silk & two Skairs Mohair—which I purchased at Philadelphia according to your directions, Omitting Purchasing the White & Blue Cloth as the former was not to be had & every thing much dearer then you can conceive 120£ Proik per yard I gave for blue Cloth to make a Coat for myself—and you may remember that Just before we parted at Conadosaga you told me If I found things dear beyond measure I should Omit buying any thing except the CordDeroy—

I am very sorry to hear of your Illness wish heartily that this letter may find you on the recovering hand—and that you may have a Speedy and perfect restoration of your health—

Please to present my Complyments to Mrs Gansevoort and receive my Congratulations for the Gift of a Son[65]*—May he live to be a very lasting Blessing his Parents—I am Dr Sir yours Affectionatly*

M. Willett

Coll Gansevoort Albany

November 1779 was the beginning of the end for the expedition into frontier territory as the winter was rapidly approaching and supplies were starting to dwindle. A November 13 letter from Gansevoort to Commissary General John Betty[66] describes the recent capture and stationing of a surgeon claiming to have been with one of the Hessian mercenary armies hired by the British.[67] The prisoner had been interred in Schenectady for some time, and the residents were becoming uneasy and wary of spies or any other unwelcome presence. Apparently some of the locals had claimed that deserters may have been collecting hard currency and trading goods with each other at an area referred to as the "Hellburgh."[68] Gansevoort then resolved to deliver the prisoner over to John Beatty's charge under the guise of a petition from disaffected Schenectady citizens. Gansevoort also noted that the same citizens accused deserting soldiers of committing several robberies in the area, though he personally emphasized that the robberies are "in general by the Foreigners."[69] The definition of "Foreigners" is never expounded upon; it is possible it is a reference either to Indians in neighboring settlements or traveling tradesmen.

158—To John Beatty

Albany 13th November 1779

Sir, This will be delivered you by Issac Sturgis a Sergeant of my Regiment commanding a Guard having Custody of Eberhart Unger one of the Convention Prisoners who says that he was a Surgeon to a Hessian Corps—He resided lately at Schenectady in this County and by a justice of the Peace was imprudently admitted to the Oath of Allegiance tho' this I presume will not deprive the States of the Benefit of his Exchange—The Inhabitants of Schenectady are particularly anxious for his Removal, they have the strongest Reasons to conclude, from his many Excursions to a Place called the Hellbergh (noted ~~Place of~~ as a Rendezevous for the disaffected Deserters, Robbers &c) at very late Hours of the Night his returning from thence with Quantities of hard Money, and from frequent Meetings of Strangers and suspected Persons at his House (particularly at Night) and from other concurring Circumstances, that he is deeply concerned in Practices dangerous to the Interests of the United States and of this State in particular—tho' no pointed Proof can be readily obtained against him—

Induced by these Reasons and in observances of a Resolution of Congress respecting Deserters from the Convention Troops—I have thought proper to deliver him over to your Care as coming within your Department—I transmit inclosed a short Petition or Memorial from the Inhabitants of Schenectady on this Subject as also Affidavits respects his Usage and Abuse of the Wife of Major Cochran of my Regiment during this Gentlemans Absence on the Western Expedition—

I would also mention to you that I am informed there are several other Deserters from the Convention Troops in the Neighbourhood of the above Town and that the Inhabitants only wait proper Directions for their Removal—I have only to add that we are all convinced that the greatest Part of the Robberies daily committed ~~by~~ in this State are perpotrated chiefly by Deserters from those Troops and in general by the Foreigners—

I am Sir with Respect Your most Obed Sert

[PG]

P.S. You will note that the Affidavits & Petition are agt John Kunger which Mistake was occasioned by the Prisoners true Name not being known (thro' his own Cunning) the Person being the same.

Colo Beatie Commy Prisoners for United States

[Copy of a Letter sent to the Commissary Prisoners Dated Albany 13th Novemr 1779]

Gansevoort was on leave for the rest of the year, most likely due to his sickness. A November 15 letter from Marinus Willett informed him that winter quarters were being constructed at their encampment at Pompton and that the clothing so eagerly sought earlier in the year found the men in comfortable spirits.[70]

159—From Marinus Willett

Camp at Pumpton 15th Novr 79

Dear Colonel/ We are still in the field but Im of opinion that the Georgeni Miss, will soon fix our Winter Quarters as we can have no farther Expection of the Count who has steered his course for the West India's—Nothing Material in the Regt The Army has not yet, received their Cloathing our Men however are tolerable Comfortable with the Stockings & Breches & Shoes.

Mr Ranselar had happily proveided for them. Mr Colbreath to whom I have given leave of absence will hand you this and can say everything you may desire to know respecting the Regt

My best Complyments to to Mrs Gansevoort and a Shake of the hand to Young Hanemanus

I am Sir yours Affectionatly

M. Willett

[Peter Gansevoort Albany]

Sickness continued for Gansevoort into December, requiring him to send a status report to General Washington. The contents and description of his sickness could lead one to believe Gansevoort was exaggerating his condition, as he was well enough to write yet "can only with Difficulty crawl about my Room" and requested that he be allowed to stay in Albany for the remainder of the winter.[71]

160—To George Washington

Sir Shortly after my Return from the Indian Country whence I had been detached ~~from~~ with a small Command to this place I was taken ill with a bilious Fever which has continued with a few short Intermissions till within about ten Days past ~~In Consequence and restored me so much~~ and has impaired my Strength so much that I can only with Difficulty crawl about my Room and as I shall in all probability be incapable of ~~attending to my duties~~ discharging and necessitated the Duties of my Station during the Winter I ~~must~~ beg your Excellency's Indulgence to permit me to remain here until my Health is perfectly re-established.

I have the Honor to be &

[PG]

[Copy of a Letter Sent his Excellency Genl Washington Dated Albany Decemr 18th 1779]

General Washington

Gansevoort's December 18 letter to Willett claimed that he encountered a relapse of the fever and was unable to read or write, making further communication sparse at best.[72]

161—To Marinus Willett

Albany Decr 18 1779

Dear Sir Believe me I should not so long have neglected answering your Letters if my indisposition had not prevented me I have not yet been able to venture abroad Since my relapse which attacked me so Severe that my Physicians inform me they for some Time despair'd of my recovery, and it has so weakened my sight that I am still incapable of reading or writing much I must however beg a continuation of your Correspendence and rely upon it Shall not omit writing when my Health permits—my State of Health I fear will prevent my joining the Regiment this Winter however disagreeable this reflection is it alleviates my Distress when I consider that the Command of the Regiment ~~is in~~ will be left with a person in whom I can confide—

I am Dr Sir Colo: Yours very Humble Servant Sincerely

[PG]

Lieut: Col: Willet

Despite this, Gansevoort requested that Willett continually update on the winter camp as it would alleviate the perceived severity of his situation.

Willett's December 19th report claimed that he had formally discharged twenty men and was preparing to further discharge another thirty in waiting.[73] Despite sickness and low supplies of clothing, Willett assures that the winter quarters are deemed comfortable by the rest of the men and that despite requests for leave of absence in light of weather, the command could be easily maintained.

162—From Marinus Willett

Morristown 19th Decr 1779

Dear Colonel, The business of disscharging three years men has taken place about twenty I have Already discharged, and there are upward of Thirty more whose times will expire before the opening of next Campaign—our regiment will notwithstanding continue respectable, if we meet with no accidents, as we have upwards of three hundred, who are engaged during the War: I heartily Wish however some means could be adopted for recruiting—but we cant expect to do much in this way without some Provesion to enable officers to go out on the recruiting Service is made by the Legislature of our State, to obtain such Provision I make no doubt you will employ all your Influence—It is undoubtedly a matter of very great Importance—

For two weeks we hace been very diligently employed in building our Hutts the weather has been rather against us—but we have got our buildings allmost finished and find em very Comfortable—so that barring accidents then The troops will have very ~~Comfortable~~ good Winter Quarters

Please to make my Complyments to Mrs Gansevoort—I hope this Will find you established in your health of which I should be glad to hear by a line from yourself—My respect to Major Cochran & his family &c

I am Sir Your very Humble Servt

M Willett

P.S. I suppose you have heard that absent officers are expected to Join there Corps by [yl] first of April

Colonel Gansevoort [Albany]

163—From Marinus Willett

Morristown 26th Decr 1779

Dear Colonel, A few days ago I wrote to you by Lieutenant Maghee, In which I hinted ~~to you~~ that all Absent Officers were ordered to Join there respective Corps by the first of April, I think it may not be amiss likewise to let you know, that there is an order for granting Furlongs with an express direction that no Regt is to be left without one Field officers, and that at least one officer with every Company is to keep contenually with the Regt This being the case and it being my Intention not to leave the Regt at all this Winter. It remains I conceive entirely at your own choise whether you Join the Regt during there continuence in Winter Quarters or not, But as most of the Captains & Subaulterns are desirous of leave of absence for some time during the Stay of the troops in there present Quarters I think It may not be amiss to Inform you that It is expected All the Officers who are at present absent will return to the Regiment as soon as the time for which they had leave of absence ~~is~~ expires, in order that the other officers may have an eaqual Chance with them—I mention this least from understanding that all absent officers ~~who~~ are ordered to Join there respective Corps by the the first of April, you might be Induced to long then the Furlongs of such of our officers who are In the quarter which would be a dissapointment to those officers now with the regt most of whome expect leave of absence on the return of such as are now abroad—

If Captain Gregg should be in your part of the World, I should be glad he might be made to remember that <u>his Company</u> wants <u>his presence</u>—

I enclose you a list of men belonging to the Regt who are by there officers returned ~~to~~ in Albany and whome I am by the Inspector directed to order to Join the Regt as you are upon the Spot you will know the best way to have em Collected and Ordered <u>on</u>—Some of them are in the Armory and otherways employed as Artificers such are much wanting with the Regt Esspecially the Armorours

It may not be amiss for absent officers to know that by a late resolve of Congress all officers who are absent from there regiments and ordered to Join are liable to be tryed by a Court Martial for noncomplyance during there absence and Cashered—I flatter myself however that our officers will be as punctual as possible in Complying with the terms of there Furlongs that no such dissagreable business may take place among us—

My Complyments to Mrs Gansevoort Please to remember me to Dr Woodruff—as the Legislature are to set at Albany you'll be handy to press them to make provisions for recruiting.

I am Sir yours Affectionally
M. Willett
Colonel Gansevoort [Albany]

Chapter Six

1780: Preparing for Imminent Attack

The beginning of 1780 found Colonel Peter Gansevoort struggling to recover from the fever that had set in almost four months earlier. However, the illness was not life-threatening nor severely affecting his ability to keep up correspondence with Lieutenant Colonel Marinus Willett, who had been in charge of the Third New York Regiment for winter quarters in Morristown, New Jersey.

Willett first responded on February 7, stating that "Nothing very particular present itself," though he noted clothing was starting to become scarce and that the men may become disgruntled quickly if the situation was not resolved.[1] The winter had iced over river crossings, significantly delaying any supply trains en route and requiring extra guards to ensure no spies were able to gain access to the camp. The letter ended with Willett wishing Gansevoort well and conveyed his happiness upon hearing that Gansevoort is slowly conquering his "dissorder."[2]

164—From Marinus Willett

Morristown 7 Feby 1780

Dear Colonel/ Nothing very particular present itself The regiment is quit as comfortable as our Situation will admit No Clothes have we received since Mr Rensaller left us so that you may be assured some of our men suffer on that scare—It has however been unavoidable on our part—But I have reason to hope we shall very soon be relieved from this disstresion a great measure and at present we labour under weather—Our duty is indeed hard owing princepally to the severity of the weather which has so closed the rivers with Ice as to cause a very easy communication between us and the enemy—and require much larger guards then Ussual as well to endeavour to protest the Country as the armey—

I am happy to hear from Doctr Woodruff that you are gaining uon your dissorder I wish to hear from yourself of the Intire reinstablishment of your health Mrs Willett Joins in Complyment to Mrs Gansevoort & yourself with Your Very Afft Humb Servt

M Willett

Please to send the Inclose to my Brother

Colonel Gansevoort [Albany]

A letter from General Clinton on the 12th was worded in a manner of suspicion, questioning the severity of Gansevoort's illness. Ostensibly General Washington himself had heard that certain soldiers were acting as "waiters" to Gansevoort and his long absence has encouraged other officers and even privates to ask permission for winter leave.[3] Clinton's letter ended with a request for Gansevoort to rejoin his men, health permitting.

165—From James Clinton

Camp Near Morris Town Febry 12th 1780

Dr Sir By the Last Reviewing Return of Your Regt Appears that you have four Men ~~of Your Regt~~ Returned with You as Waiters three of them being Absent fifteen Months And by A Letter which I Received this Day from ~~of~~ His Excellency Genl Washington he Requests to know the Reason of it and Likewise the Reason of Your being so Long Absent Yourself I Assure You he is much Displeased with officers staying from their Regt And keeping Soldiers As Waiters with them which is Now Contrary to Orders If Your Health Permits You to Return with these Men Pray Do it without Delay Otherwise Send ~~Al~~ the Men

I am Sir Yours &c

James Clinton BG

An unintentionally humorous letter from Gansevoort was created as a reply to Washington and Clinton's concerns in early March. Within his response to Washington he claimed he was still notably indisposed to residing over his command at the winter quarters, and that he did not bring four men with him as servants, but only two.[4]

166—To James Clinton

Albany

Dr Sir I have received your Favor of the 12th Ultimo ~~and are exceedingly Sorry that you~~ in Answer to which ~~can~~ I beg leave to inform you that I am totally ignorant of having ~~fou~~ one Waiter with me who has been absent from the Regt fifteen Months or who has not been on Duty on the Expedition into the Indian Country last Summer except one who was left at Canajohary nor can I conceive what Men can be meant by the Inspector in his return unless they are Smith & hickels whom you granted permission to remain with their Families last Spring and give me leave to add that as you must have known the Return to have been founded at least in Mistake I expected that you wanted rather [ ] have represented the Truth of the Matter to his—[ ] Excellency ~~that~~ than have ~~wrote the~~ reprehended me for Matters of which I am ignorant—

As I cannnot as certain when my Health will be so reestablished as to enable me to discharge the Duties of my ~~Der~~ Office it is impossible for me to determine when I Shall be ~~in~~ able to Join my Regiment which I cannot think of doing untill I Shall be so hearty as to take the field without the Danger of a relapse and I must fear that the ~~Time~~ period will not arrive before the First Day of May next—

Copy of a Letter Sent General Clinton Dated Albany 7th March 1780

167—To George Washington

It is with great Concern I inform you that Genl Clinton has intimated to me in a Letter your Excellency ~~was~~ is displeased with my long absence give me leave to assure your Excellency that nothing my indisposition has prevented ~~my~~ me from joining the Regiment which I have the

Honor to command Since my return from the Seneca Country whence I was Sent on Command by Genl Sullivan ~~and~~ the ~~enclosed~~ Certificate which I have the honor to enclose will manifest the assertions ~~to~~ which I beg to refer your Excellency, ~~the~~ General Clinton also informs me that by the last Return of the Brigade Inspector it appears that four Men of my Regiment are returned as Servants with me, this must be [ ] a Mistake as I never had more than two [ ] Servants either from or with the Regiment, there are two others of my Regimt in this City, but ~~neither~~ not with my permission, they were left here by ~~permission of the~~ General Clinton, but as Colo Willet informs me that he has demanded an Enquiry respecting that return and as I flatter myself that this Matter has been set in its true light I shall say no more on that Subject, ~~but~~ I beg leave however to add that I ~~have never yet absent~~ entered the Service in the Summer of 1775 ~~and~~ continued in it since and have never been charged with absenting myself from ~~the Regiment my Command~~ the Regiment to which I have belonged and ~~let~~ believe me Sir that I should not have been absent at this Time if I had been able to have discharged my Duty in the Field, permit me to beg your Excellency's Indulgence with leave of Absence untill my Health shall be so far re-established as that I may be capable of doing the Duty incident to my Office

I am with every Sentiment of Duty & respect Your Excellency's very Hum Servant

Copy of a Letter Sent his Excellency Genl Washington Dated Albany 7th March 1780

Surely Gansevoort must have misinterpreted the tone of Clinton and Washington's letters, as they seemed displeased with *any* soldiers being used as servants on a long leave. He ended the letter reminding them that he had been commissioned into service since 1775 and had not claimed a leave of absence until present. This would certainly not sit well with his commanding officers; Gansevoort had hoped to ameliorate the situation by sending a certificate of health from his physician to any officer questioning his condition.[5]

168—To Marinus Willett

Dear Willet I do myself the pleasure to acknowledge your Several favor's of the 7th & 19th Ultimo, and to thank you for the Attention you have evinced towards me by an Enquiry into the Inspector's Return wherein he returns four Waiters with me and that three of them had been absent from the Regiment for 15 Months, it is needless for me I presume to controvert the Facts as you are as sensible of the Mistake as I am myself, I have done myself the Honor of addressing a Letter to his Excellency on the Subject and transmitted him a Certificate from my Physicians ~~declaring~~ declaratory of the Reasons of my Absence, to wit ~~that of~~ my Indisposition of which [ ] I am now pretty well recovered but much [ ] doubt whether I Shall be enabled to join the Regiment till about the first of May as I cannot think of entering it before I Shall experience a perfect re-establishment of my Health—

As Capt DeWitt has resigned (ƒ (which I much regret) I conceive it will be but to let the Officers rise in their due Rank which I must by you to carry into execution, and could wish you to defer ~~the~~ filling up the Vacancies until I get down, you Will please to take Notice that the ~~promotion &~~ appointments be dated at the Time of the respective resignations—

Copy of a Letter Sent Col Willet Albany 7th March 1780

Sickness would not disable Gansevoort for much longer. Though there were no letters mentioning a complete recovery and return to service, a June 6 letter from General Clinton contained marching orders for Gansevoort's regiment to Fort Plank in order to secure supplies to be distributed to the Fort Schuyler garrison.[6] Clinton declared that enemy soldiers were spotted "in force on the Mohawk River."[7]

169—From James Clinton

Albany June 6th 1780

Sir You will proceed with your Regiment as soon as posible to Fort Plank, where you will find a Quantity of Provision destined for the Use of the Garison at Fort Schuyler which you will take into your Charge and escort to that Post

As the Enemy are said to be out in force on the Mohawk River, it is absolutely necessary that you shou'd pay the strictest Attention to prevent a Surprise and in Case of an Attack, to defend the Stores to the last Extreamity—the present Situation of the Garision points out the absolute necessity of this Caution—

You will receive a Supply of Provision before you March for the Use of your Troops to and that you may not make use of that destined for the Garisson—if you shoud fall short you must impress from the Inhabitants avoiding every degree of Irregularity—

The Troops both Officers and Soldiers will move as light and unencumbered as possible—Your heavy Baggage Sick and Women will be left under the Care of an Active Officer—

You will use you utmost Caution to prevent your People from Desertion and repair to this Place as soon as you have complyed with this Direction—

I am Sir with great respect Your very humbl Servt

James Clinton B.G.

Col Peter Gansevort

The end of June resulted in Gansevoort's men being recalled by General Clinton to West Point, though the reasons were not specified.[8]

170—From James Clinton

Sir/ You'll Please to hurry on Your Regiment to this place, Immediately after Your Arrival at fort Schuyler—they Being ordered to West Point

I am Sir Your Most Obedient Servant

James Clinton B.G.

Albany 13th June 1780

Colo Gansevoort

With the passing of winter, problems with supplies plagued Gansevoort's regiment and other armies stationed in New York. The first letter in Gansevoort's collection mentioning such problems involved one of the scarcest of resources: hard currency. Jeremiah Van Rensselaer sent word on July 27 that the men required an "Arrival of Cash," as "poverty Stares one in the face From Morning till night and Seens Never Ceasing."[9]

171—From Jeremiah Van Rensselaer

Albany 27 July 1780

Dr Colonel. I Could wish that before this Comes to hand. that it has been in your power to forward to me Inteligence of the Arrival of Cash to the army. poverty Stares one in the face. from Morning till night and Seens Never Ceasing perplexes me without End. At all Risque Sometimes I Resolve to Join Without any prospect but A Cool Moment Informes me that I Cannot better myself Admidt yet greater Want than I Experence here—

Whenever the distant prospect of Cash Reaches your Ear pray Communicate the Same by first Conveyance that I may at Least Share in the Gleening of A Slender harvests for a Scarce me the first will be I do Belive—my Respects to Mrs Gansevoort Mrs Woodruff & all frinds and are pr your Humb Serv

Jer V Rensselaer

The complaints of a lack of hard currency must have aroused suspicion as to whether the meager funds the regiments had were being distributed fairly.

Fever had affected Gansevoort's colleague and friend John Lansing, Jr.; the type of fever seems to be strikingly similar to the one that allegedly had Gansevoort bedridden for over half a year. Despite this, Lansing's August 16 letter relayed some information on the health and well-being of Gansevoort's own family, as well as the safety and security of the overall community.

172—From John Lansing, Jr.

Fish Kill Augt 16t: 1780

D Sir Inclosed I do myself the pleasure to transmit you a letter from Mrs Gansevoort which I flattered myself I should have had the pleasure of delivering to you personally but your remoteness from this place renders that impracticable as the Fever which I have been so long subject to renders me incapable of undertaking a Journey to Camp—I purpose to remain here a few Days and as I have promised Mrs Gansevoort to bring a Letter from you I hope you will put in my power to comply with My Promise

Your Boy is well and desires his Compliments to his papa

The Indians in large Bodies daily infest our Frontiers—They have destroyed 55 Houses at Canajoharie and last Thursday burnt twelve at Schohary and killed eight Men The Women & Children were in the Forts

I am D Sir with great Esteem & Regard Your most obedt Servant

J. Lansing Junr

[PG]

This letter interestingly enough sheds some light on the blowback from the expedition into Indian Country in late 1778 and 1779. Canajoharie was noted as a meeting place for most of the forces to assemble before proceeding; Gansevoort moved into the right flank under the command of General Clinton. Canajoharie must have become a target by vengeful natives seeking to disrupt the logistics of any future campaigns, or at the least to intimidate local citizens into protesting against future aggressions.

On September 30, John Post,[10] commissary of issues, issued a notice that Gansevoort was due 128 pounds of flour and 257 pounds of beef for the New York Brigade, which he was commanding.

173—From John Post

Camp Orange Town 30th Sep 1780

This Certifyes that their is due to Col. Gansevoort as Comdr of the Brigade for Augt & Sepr One hundred twenty eight pounds of Flour, and two hund Fifty seven pounds Beefs which he has drawn short of his allowance for the above months—

Jno Post A.Comy D

No further news of any military action was heard from or directly involving Gansevoort and his men until October 15th, where a letter from Nathaniel Greene to Cornelius Johnson ordered Johnson's troops to join with Gansevoort in Albany for a meeting with Governor Clinton. The subject of the meeting is not expressed, though Greene insisted that Johnson's rendezvous be completed swiftly and that his arrival was of the "utmost importance."[11]

174—Nathaniel Greene to Cornelius Johnson

Sir You will proceed with Colonel Gansvoort's regiment in the most expeditious manner for Albany to join the troops under His Excellency Governor—Clinton. Should not the Governor be at Albany on your Arrival you will immediately dispatch on an Express to him, with information of your arrival, and obtain his further directions. It is of the utmost importance that you proceed on your voyage in the most expeditious manner; and I rely upon your making your passage as short as possible.

I am Sir, your very huml Servt

West Point Octr 15th 1780

Nath Greene M General

Captain Johnson Comd 3d N. York regiment

Nathaniel Greene. Engraved by J. B. Longacre based on the painting by John Trumbull, 1833 (Gansevoort-Lansing collection. Manuscripts and Archives Division. The New York Public Library. Astor, Lenox and Tilden Foundations).

Word from Colonel Alexander Webster[12] on October 26 included mention of the sighting of over one thousand well-supplied troops crossing the Balwagge Bay with the intention to "Destroy the Frontier of Vermont & Threaten white Creek." It was also inferred that loyalists in the area would most likely join the force in completing such objectives.[13] This may have been connected to the capture and transport of multiple loyalist prisoners from the frontier to Albany, beginning in September. A prisoner exchange between the two forces was supposed to occur once safe arrival of the prisoners was confirmed; however a letter from William Monsel to Colonel Van Schaick noted that movement among local tribes were severely delaying the prisoner escorts.[14] The loyalists must have joined the British force after waiting for news of the prisoner's arrival. The next step was to join the British army in intimidating the Americans into an early release of the imprisoned.

In response Gansevoort ordered James Gregg and any under his command to immediately march towards Palmertown with the expectation of a conflict or to relay intelligence regarding the number of reinforcements required to defend the prisoners.[15] Colonel Lewis Van Woert[16] claimed that a substantial number of British ships and smaller vessels were transporting the force towards Castle Town at the end of October.[17] Apparently the Governor had left Albany in hopes that the meeting forces could be consolidated and then dispatched to support the defensive, though he seemed confident that for the time being Van Woert would be able to frustrate the movements of the enemy.[18]

175—From Abraham Ten Broeck

Albany 27th Oct 1780

Dr Colonel/ His Excellency the Governor left this Place this Morning for Poughkeepsie he approves of your Regiment being in the Quarter you are in and has directed Me to desire you to advise with Genl. Schuyler in posting your Men and that you will remain untill farther Orders—

The inclosed is Copy of a Letter I have just received from Collo Van Woert which I have communicated to his Excellency, he think that your Regiment together with the four Northern Regiments Vizt McCrea—Schonhoven[19]*—Van Woert and Yates are competent to oppose and frustrate any Attempts of the Enemy in that Quarter, and I do hereby desire you to take the Command of the Militia now at Fort Edward and its Vicinity and to call upon the above Regiments or such Parts of Them as you shall from Time to Time think necessary to Co-opperate with you advising Me of the Same—Should the Enemy really Advance into the Country you will immediately inform Me of it that I may order if necessary a greater Proportion of my Brigade to your Assistance—your own Prudence will direct you to send out good and faithfull Scouts with great Regard*

I remain Dr Colonel your most humble Servt

Abm Ten Broeck

Collo Gansevoort (Saraghtoga or Fort Edward)

Regardless of the enemy's announced or perceived intentions, the rest of October saw little to no action as far as Gansevoort's authority was concerned. The only particular correspondence involving action was issued by James Gregg on October 29, wherein he noted that the militia was to build and repair certain areas of the settlements in and around Block House Town and that scouts sent to determine the movements of the enemy resulted in nothing except the capture of one British deserter.[20] No intelligence seemed to have been procured from the deserter, as there is no further description or mention of his character. However, Marinus Willett does mention that North Carolina experienced a rough battle involving the British army led by Colonel Ferguson, resulting in a victory and eight hundred prisoners.[21]

As the New York militia and remnants of the Continental Army in the northern states prepared their winter quarters, the British threat against Vermont was claimed to have increased by six hundred men, yet their movements could not determined if any at all.[22]

176—From Alexander Webster

Head Quarters Granvill October 30th 1780

Dear Sir By a letter from Gennal Schuyler of yesterday's Date I am Inform'd you have the Direction of the Militia in this Quarter In consequence of which I imagine it necessary for you to be Inform'd of our Strength and Situation as well as that of the Enemy (from the Best Inteligence we can procure they are upwards of 1600 And Were Two days Since at or about Crown point and [ ] this way I imagine they Intend to try there Strength I was not at that time Inform'd of nor do I know as yett; for what Intention it came I beg you will Inform me; as Soon as Possible what Routs the Scouts take from Fort Edward For Notwithstanding my Scouts going to Fort Edward yesterday with a Letter for the Commander of that Post I was not favoured with an Answer and they mention it was with they greatest Deficualty that One days provision was procured for there return

I remain with the greatest respect and Esteem your Most Humble Servt

Alex Webster

N.B The Inhabitants of this place Informs me that In case a Strong Guard is not kep'd here they will all move off

Multiple scouting parties were sent in the beginning of November but turned up little in the way of discerning the British forces' intentions. Henry Watson Powell[23] sent an update on the status of the prisoner exchange on the second of November, noting that the American prisoners seemed to be in good spirits and were not subject to abuse.[24]

177—To Henry Watson Powell

Saratoga Novr 2d 1780

Sir Your letter of the 22nd Septr last directed to Colo Van Schaick It becomes my duty to Arrive as Commanding in this Department untill the Arrival of Genl McDougall who is daily expected, The Prisoners which you mentioned I am informed have taken the rout to Albany tho Bennington,

The Families specified In your list whom I believe to be all In the Vicinity of this place, were to have been sent to the British Shipping in lake Champlain. In the beginning of the last Month, Major Carltons incursions prevented ~~that~~ their being forwarded then, and as all the Batteaus In lake George non carried of by that Gentleman It may have been Impracticable to have sent them on since If it had been proper whilst he Remaind at Ticonderoga & Crown Point, I have written Major Carlton and requested him to send Batteaus to Fort Ann or Fort George If he can for their Conveyance, as soon as I am advisd of his Determination, the necessary measures will be taken—

The Accounts of Cash advancd to the Prisoners In Canada, I shall do myself the Honor to transmit to his Excellency Genl Washington

It affords me great satisfaction to learn that the British have at lenght found it prudent to follow the Germans examples exhibited them by the American, in the Mild treatment with which the Prisoners in the power of the latter have been Invaribly Indulg'd during the War.

It is however a Justice due to Genl Carlton and his Successors to declare that from all Accounts the Prisoners immediately in their power have been treated with much lenity. but you Sir suppose that British Subjects In our Possession have experienced executions the Horrors of a Dungeon loaded with Irons and the miseries of want, It is true some Spies have been executed and amongst these Major Andre Adjutant Genl to the British Army Under the Command of Sir Henry Clinton, and even his death Altho Justice required it and the laws of nations An Athorizd It, was and is lamented by us with a Generosity which does Honour to human nature, None have experiencd the Horrors of a Dungeon or been loaded with Irons excepting a few on whom it was thought proper to retaliate for the many the very many indeed of ours whom British cruelties could Intramanely suffer to Perish for want In Dungeons and Prisonships loaded with Iron & with Insults If you are Ignorant of these facts I can excuse your Observations. If not give me leave to tell you they are unworthy the Gentleman and the Officer, and wince a disengenuity unbecoming either—If Genl Halderman conceives the governing powers of these States, to have been guilty of a breach of faith with respect to the Carteel at the Cedars, he ought to apply to them on the Occasion, barely to mention it to a Subordinate Officer was Indelicate and improper, but as you have been pleased to Accuse, I will Venture to deny the Justice of the chargd and as far as my memory of that transaction serves I think I can do It with propriety—The News papers announce that a Genl ~~Carteel~~ exchange of Prisoners is settled below, wether it extends to Canada is not specified

I am Sir your most Obedient Humble Servant
Peter Gansevoort Col
3d N.Y. Regt
[A Letter to Genl Powell]

However, Gansevoort had noted that British spies within the multitude of prisoners had been executed; these actions would certainly affect British dispositions towards their own Continental prisoners. British officer Christopher Carleton claimed that an attempt to cross the Mile Bay was underway and expected to be ready for deployment in mid–November. Carleton also mentioned a particularly disturbing incident in which a dispute involving two separate native villages resulted in the death of a militiaman.[25]

178—From Christopher Carleton

Mile Bay Novr the 6th 1780

Sir By your Flag, I have this moment recd your letter of the 2d Inst with one directed to Brigr Genl Powell—respecting the Families intended to have been sent in, In answer to both being intirely ignorant of the purport of Brigr Powells letter to you on the subject, & having no Instructions from General Haldimand respecting that business—I was only say that such persons as are specified in the Brigadiers list will be recd provided the Number of Boats mentioned in my P: S: can contain them shou'd there be room to spare, the names contained in the enclosed lists as many as can be taken on Board will be recd—My Boats shall be at Skeensborough the 9th where they shall remain 'till the 14th at night & then return to me as I could not take upon me to riske their being froze up there

I should have expected Captn Chipman[26] *would have given a flat Contradiction to James Van Driesons Confession. no Prisr was Scalped or tortured alive—I saved the lives of several of the Prisrs the Prisrs were not stripp'd nor insulted in the smallest degree after the affair was over. I heard of one man being kill'd after He was taken during the firing, owing to a dispute betwen 2 Inds of different Vilages which took him & he wou'd not suffer himself to be Conducted to the British Guard by a Loyalist Officer, the Officer was obliged to attend to his men & after the Action I heard of the Man being kile'd—I believe he was a Negro, or a Hockbridge Ind.*

I am Sir your Most Obedient & most Humble servant

Chr Carleton Major 29th Regt

Col: Gansevoort

P: S: there being no Idea of this business the Shipping went down Some days ago. I find it will not be in my power to furnish More than 5 Boats could not the Boat I gave to Carry up the last families be Sent down with these.

Jansen's scouting parties had revealed nothing as to British movements in the area, though it was noted that a dry tree had been curiously set on fire, pressuring Jansen to send out another scouting party in an attempt to unveil the motive of the fire.[27]

179—From Cornelius T. Jansen

Fort Edward November 8th 1780

Sr Last Evening Lieut Bowen Came in from Lake George he was as far as the Landing and Stayed there for about three hours but Saw no Sign of an Enemy. The fiere he Saw Some Nights ago was a Dry tree which Serjr Hunter had Set on fier and was fallen Down and was on fier in Different places

I am resolved to Send a Scout to Fort Ann and perhaps as far as Sckeenesburgh this day—I hear flying reports from the Southward but know not whether it worth while paying attention to or not I hope you will Let me know in Your next what accounts you have from there

I am Dr Colo your Humbl Sert

Corns T. Jansen

P.S. when Bowen answer his return he met the Scout that was sent from Saratoga about three miles from the Lake

[PG]

Jeremiah Van Rensselaer relayed some bad news concerning the continued lack of money and clothing; due to some complications in Albany, the request for clothing shipments would be delayed. He suggested that there may be extra clothing at the Albany headquarters but that its discovery should not be relied upon.[28]

180—From Jeremiah Van Rensselaer

Albany 9th Novemr 1780

Dr Colonel By the Arrival of Dc: Woodruff I Learn that there is no hope of Money until Some time in January for paying the troops if so I belive it will be best for me to lay Close to Mr Tho Reed D P:[29] *Who Expects to Receive A Considerable from Connecticut & has promised me all he Can Spare Should that Arrive we Shall in All Likelihood have the fore hand of the Southern Troops*

About Cloathing Another Essential point I am Almost at a Loss About it Mr Black the State Cloathier[30] *has promised me the Earlyest Inteligence About it but have not heard A Word yet time & Cold Weather is drawing on & What Can be done I am at present Ignorant of Capt Tiebout & Others have Informed me that there is A Likelihood of a Sufficient Quantity of Cloathing to be at or About Head Quarters I Would therefore Sugest if it would not be proper to have Some person of the Regement in or about that Quarter With a proper Return & Order to take the first oppertunity in Accomplishing that desireable End. I do belive that the Captain Who is used to be on Command & having his famely in that Quarter would be verry fond of that Business if it will Meet your Approbation*

I Shall Tomorrow Make out a Return & forward it to the Adjutant to be filled up who will produce it to you for your Approbation

I am With Esteem Dr Sir Your Humb Servt

Jer V Rensselaer

[PG—Saratoga]

Captain James Rosekrans[31] of the Fourth New York Regiment announced his decision to leave the defenses at the Block Town settlement on November 20 due to lack of significant intelligence and his belief that the inhabitants were more than able to defend it themselves.[32]

181—From James Rosekrans

Saratoga 20th Novr 80

Dear Colo Yours by express of yesterdays date was delivered me last evening wherein you mention the determination of Majors Fish & Graham I cannot say that I have the least right to find any fault with their intention, But must say that I feel sorry for my bad fortune in being a supernumery, I have a full Idea of the resolve being for the welfare of the Public for which reason I feel more content then what I perhaps otherwise might do (altho it effects me) if you should Continue in the Service and affair turn as you mentioned shall think my self exceedingly happy to be under your Command; as also all the Officers of the Regiment who feel exceedingly Anxious to know the Commanders

I this day left Palmertown and think it needless to Continue Capt Gregg there any longer, as I am fully satisfied of their being no danger in that quarter for this season, There are Several Inhabitants in this Town who can in a few minutes take possession of the Block house and defend it against any number which in any Likelyhood may attempt it this time of the year as also that Country being full of Hunters both White people & Indians which Generally make it their Centure about that quarter Nights—it is also verry dificult on account of geting him provisions every two or three days must send to him on Acct of our geting so scanty a Supply never get more then three days at a time and that exhausted before we get more,—the road also exceedingly bad, & shall be glad of your Answer on the Subject—

The Shoe makers shall be sent down on soon as possible and believe to be with due respect

Your most Obt and verry Hum Servant

Jas Rosekrans

Colo Gansevoort

Have Inclos'd the determination of the Officers and Send it by Ensgn Fonda who returns immediately by whom I Shall be glad to hear from you in full I have Inclos'd Lt Bagley's & Lewis's—warrants, Bagley's has Lewis's date and Lewis's Bagley's, which Bagley desires may be rectified

The lull in action and the onset of winter had put Gansevoort and officers of a similar rank at ease; a letter of agreement between Gansevoort, Van Rensselaer and other parties to purchase land near the main street in Albany was issued during this time.[33]

182—Agreement Between Henry Osthoudt, Jacob G. Klock,[34] Jeremiah Van Rensselaer and Peter Gansevoort, Jr.

Memorandum of an Agreement Between Henry Osthoudt Jacob G Klock and Jeremiah Van Ranselear Commissioners of forfeitures for the Western District of the one part and Coll Peter Gansevoort of the City of Albany—of the other part The said Commissioners Do hereby Acknowledge to have sold to the said Peter Gansevoort a Certain House and Lot of ground Scituate Lying and being in the Colony of Ranselearwyck near the City of Albany Containing in Breadth in front on the Main Street Leading from the City to Water Vliet Sixty feet two Inches in the rear to the West on the Street Called --- Street Sixty feet and in Length five Hundred and fourty feet all By land Measure and Also a Lot of ground Adjoining the above Lot Containing in breadth on the said Main Street Thirty nine feet Ten Inches in the rear fourty feet and in Length five Hundred and fourty feet all By land Measure Subject to the Rent Reserved by Van Ranselear Patroon of the Manor of Ranselear to himself and Heirs on the said Lotts and also to the Arrearages of the Rent due on the said Two Lotts—And That the said Premisses Immediately before the forfeiture thereof were Deemed to Belong to Alexander Crookshanks now or late of the City of Albany Merchant—And the said Peter Gansevoort—Doble Hereby Agree that he will within one Month after he shall receive from the said Commissioners The Necessary Certificate Pay into the Treasury of of this State the sum of Twenty Seven Thousand and fifty pounds—Being the Amount of the Purchase Money for the said Premisses And the said Commissioners Do hereby Agree that they will forthwith after the said Peter Gansevoort—shall Deliver to them a Receipt from the Treasurer for the said sum Execute to the said Peter Gansevoort—a Good Conveyance in the Law for the Premisses aforesaid Dated the 24th—Day of November 1780—

Coms of forfs W District

Heny Osthoudt

Jer V Rensselaer

Jacob G Klock

Peter Gansevoort

Witness

Note an Interlineation Made of the Words [five Hundred and] between the Tenth and Eleventh line from the Top before the Execution hereof—

Benjr Egberts

Abrm Bloodgood

Colonel Gansevoort ended the year by relinquishing his command in the Continental Army on December 30. He offered his "sincerest thanks to the Officers and Soldiers whom he has had the Honor to command for the Alacrity, chearfulness and Zeal..."[35]

183—To the Officers of the Third New York Regiment

Saratoga 30th December 1780

R.O. The Colonel being by the new arrangement necessitated to quit the command of his Regiment and intending to have this post on the Morrow returns his sincerest thanks to the Officers and Soldiers whom he has had the Honor to command for the Alacrity, chearfulness and Zeal, which it affords him a peculiar satisfaction to declare they have so frequently winced in the execution of those Duties which their Stations required them to discharge and for their Attention to his orders, which as it ever merited always had his warmest Approbation,

Tho' he confesses it with some Degree of pain he reflects that the Relation in which they stood is desolved he will endeavour to submit without repining to a Circumstance which though it may have a Tendency to wound his feelings, his Fellow Citizens who form the ~~Counsels~~, Counsels of the States have declared would be promotive of the public Weal.

In whatever Situation of Life he may be placed he will always with pleasure cherish the remembrance of those deserving Men who have with him been Sharers of almost every Hardship incident to a Military Life. As he will now probably return to that Class of Citizens whence his Country's Service at an early period of the War drew him he cordially wishes the Day may not be very remote when a happy peace will put them in the full Enjoyment of those Blessings for the Attainment of which they have nobly endured every Inconveniency & braved many dangers

P Gansevoort

[Address to the late 3d New York Regt]

Gansevoort's men reciprocated similar feelings in a letter; a particularly interesting note was the other officer's acknowledgment of his "known and approved Abilities,"[36] suggesting that during the course of his service he had developed into a more than competent officer.

184—From the Officers of the Third New York Regiment

An Address to Colonel Peter Gansevoort by the Officers of his Regiment on his retiring from service in Consequence of the New Arrangement ordered by Congress.

Sir Permit us who are now with Reluctance seperated from your command, and deprived of the benefits which we frequently experienced therefrom to declare our sentiments with a warmth of Affection and Gratitude inspired by a consciousness of your unwearied attention to the Welfare, Honour and Prospurity of the Third New York Regiment, whilst it was honor'd by your Command.

We should have been Peculiarly happy in your continuance with us.—From our long experience of your invariable attatchment to the service of our Country. Your known and approved Abilities; and that Affable and Gentlemanlike deportment by which;—(Permit us to say) You have so endeared yourself to Officers and Soldiers, that we cannot but consider the seperation as a great Misfortune

Although your Return to the Class of Citizens from whence our Country's Cause, at an Early Period called you is not matter of Choice in you, nor by any means agreable to us, yet it cannot but be ~~Agreable~~ Releasing to know that you retire with the sincerest Affection and most cordial Esteem and Regard of the Officers and Men, you have commanded.

We are with the utmost respect Sir your most Humble Servants
Saratoga 31st Decemr 1780
[An Address from the Officers of the Late 3d New York Regt]
[PG Saratoga]

This was in stark contrast to many officers' opinions of him prior to the Fort Schuyler siege and Sullivan's expedition a year prior. Considering his absence of multiple months in the first half of the year and disappointment expressed by General Washington and others, his subordinates intensely respected his conduct as an officer. Though Gansevoort was stripped of his post and certainly felt it as a personal affront to some degree, he would nonetheless continue to attempt to return to the Continental Army, and would eventually serve as a brigadier general in the Albany militia for the remainder of the war.

Chapter Seven

1781: The Albany Militia Brigade

The year 1781 was an important one. The Continental Army would triumph over the British with help of the French navy at Yorktown, Virginia. This victory more or less secured American independence and marked the decline of fighting on the American continent. However, it is important to stress that events were occurring throughout the South: in the Carolinas, Georgia, and guerrilla skirmishes along the western borders. While the South became the focus of the British, the northern United States had long deflected the immediate threat of British General John Burgoyne's forces after the Battle of Saratoga.

Part of this victory could indirectly be attributed to Peter Gansevoort's impressive performance at the siege of Fort Schuyler. Burgoyne had sent St. Leger to capture the westernmost forts along the Hudson River route in order to gain free access to the river in support of supplies. By successfully defending Fort Schuyler, Gansevoort had recovered substantial supplies and armaments from the enemy and also ensured that the main Continental forces in New York need not divert precious manpower for the fort's recovery. Gansevoort's victory also settled most doubts over his ability to command; General Gates had engaged in particularly intense correspondence over Gansevoort's ability as a commander just before Gansevoort's victory.

Even though the British focus shifted to the southern states, the northern states were certainly not safe from British attack. Communication between the commanders in the Hudson Valley was often spotty and subject to disruption. The Hudson River also acted as a transportation system for spies and British diplomats sent to encourage Iroquois raids against the Americans. Indeed, even the slightest logistical disruptions in the north deeply affected local and national economies already heavily in debt.

On February 5, Gansevoort wrote to the New York State Assembly applying to purchase a plot of land with a house situated in the Colony of Rensselaerwyck that had "become forfieted to the People ... by the conviction of Alexander Crookshanks."[1] He purchased the estate for a third of its value. After Gansevoort's purchase of part of Crookshanks' former property, he then engaged in correspondence and conversation more applicable to the military realities of the present situation.

185—To the New York State Assembly

Albany 5th February 1781

Gentlemen; In pursuance of an Act of the Legislature of the State of New York intitled

"An Act to liquedate and settle the Accounts of the Troops of the State in the Service of the United States," I do hereby apply for the purchase of the House & Lotts of Ground situate in the Colony of Rensselaer Wyck near the City of Albany Together with the Buildings thereon, all which are deemed to have become forfieted to the People of this State by the conviction of Alexander Crookshanks now or late of the City of Albany Merchants And information that I am ready to deposit with you a Certificate what you shall deem to be one third of the Value of the said Estate, And as the said Act directs that one of the Said Appraizers be elected by me I do make choice of Mr Garret Groisbeck of this City Merchs I am Gentlemen Yours &c

Peter Gansevoort Late Colo 3d NY Regt

On February 9, George Washington wrote to Continental Congress president Samuel Huntington[2] commending Gansevoort's actions during the siege at Fort Schuyler and that Gansevoort receive a resolution of thanks rewarding him a special commission of Colonel Commandant.[3] Due to the army's new arrangement, Gansevoort was apparently encouraged to retire his command; Gansevoort remarked that "...a General regulation of this kind does not vacate a Commission ... [and] ... He therefore Still considers himself as an Officer in Service."

186—George Washington to Samuel Huntington

Head Quarters New Windsor Feby 9th 1781

Sir Colo Gansevoort has applied to me on a Subject, which I am under a necessity of reffering to Congress, ~~as they alone~~ as they alone are competents to decide upon it.

On the 4th of October 1777, Congress were pleased to pass a resolution of thanks to Colo Gansevoort and to the Officers & Men under his command for the bravery and perseverance displayed in the defence of Fort Schuyler appointing him; as a reward Colonel Commandt of ~~Fort Schuyler~~ the Same, He also received a Special Commission as Colonel Commandt of Fort Schuyler"

It happens that Colo Gansevoort bring Junr to Colonels Van Schaick & Cortlandt has been obliged to retire on the New Arrangement; but he conceives that a General regulation of this kind does not vacate a Commission granted by special authority for a particular reason—He therefore Still considers himself as an Officer in Service

I shall be happy to know the Sence of Congress on this point as soon as may be convenience, I have the honor

with perfect respect yr Excellency's Most Obt Servt
Go Washington
His Excellency
Samuel Huntington Esqr
President of Congress
Philadelphia

Gansevoort had cleverly used the appointment as defense for his continued employment in the Continental Army. This personal battle would be ongoing throughout most of the Revolutionary War, as Gansevoort refused to acknowledge his temporal career status as a local militia leader despite his increasingly renowned victory at the fort under his Continental command.

On April 3, Gansevoort began his new military assignment as commander of the New

York Militia Brigade in the County of Albany with a rank of Brigadier General. He was chosen as a replacement for Abraham Ten Broeck, who had wished to pursue political office. The brigade orders also mentioned the establishment of numerous court martials for delinquents throughout his brigade. Lieutenant Colonel Richard Varick, future private secretary to Washington, was assigned Major of Brigade.[4]

187—Brigade Orders

Head Quarters Albany April 3rd 1780
Brigadie~~r Genl Gansevoorts~~ Orders

His Excellency Governor Clinton having by & with the Advice of the Council of Appointments been pleased to confer on Colo Peter Gansevoort the Rank of Brigadier General & the Command of the first Brigade of Militia in the County of Albany in the room of the Honorable Abraham Ten Broeck Esqr resigned; Genl Gansevoort Orders ~~That~~ that the General Court Martial whereof Lieut Colo Wendell[5] is President convene immediately at such Places as the President shall appoint, for the Trial of all such Delinquents of Colonels Cuylers Philip P. Schuylers[6] & the late Colo Quackenboss's[7] Regiments as Still remain to be tried; the the Members Parties concerned & Witnesses to all & And the President accordingly on Notice from the President report the Proceedings to Genl Gansevoort without Delay.—

That the Genl Court Martial wherof Colo Vroman is President convene immediately, at such Place as the Presidt shall appoint & proved ~~without Delay~~ to the Trial of all such Delinquents of Colos Wemple's & Vroman's Regiments, as still remain to be tried.—The Members, Parties convened & Witnesses to attend on Notice from the Presidt the Presidt to report the Proceedings to the Genl without Delay That Lt. Colo Blair[8] be appointed Presidt of the Genl Court Martial whereof Colo Van Woert was lately Presidt & That The Court convene immediately at Such Place as the Presidt shall appoint, for the Trial of all such Delinquents of Colo Van Woerts & Colo Peter Yates's Regiments as Still remain to be tried

The Members Parties concerned & Witnesses to attend on Notice from the Presidt Who is to report ~~the Proceedings~~ to the Genl without Delay That Lt. Colo Van Veghten[9] be appointed Presidt of the Genl Court Martial whereof thair late Colo McCrea was ~~lately~~ Presidt & that the Court ~~will~~ convene immediately at Such Place as the Presidt Shall appoint, for the immediate Trial of All such Delinquents of the late Colo McCrea's now Lt. Colo Van Veghten's & the late Colo Van Schoenhaven's now Major Taylors Regts[10] who as yet remain to be tried.—The Members, Parties & Witnesses to attend on Notice from the Presidt.—Who is to report the Proceedings to the Genl without Delay—

That the Genl Court Martial of which Lt. Colo Henry K. Van Rensselaer is Presidt ~~to~~ convene immediately At such Place as the Presidt Shall appoint for the immediate Trial of All the Delinquents of Colo Killian Van Rensselaers & the Late Colo Stephen Schuylers[11] now Lt Colo Henry K. Van Rensselaers Regts ~~as Still~~ who as yet remain to be tried.—The Members, Parties concerned & Witnesses to Attend on Notice from the Presidt.—The Presidt. to Report the Proceedings to the Genl without Delay

Lt. Colo Richard Varick is appointed to Act As Major of Brigade, His to be Obeyed & respected as Such.—

The next day, a letter from Varick ordered reports on regimental manpower in the area, and that these regiments should be immediately relayed to Gansevoort. He also noted the devastation the court-martialed officers have created, noting that "The Officers commanding unregimented Companies of Exempts are to make immediate Returns of their respective Companies..."[12]

188—From Richard Varick

Richard Varick. Etched by H. B. Hall, 1873 (Gansevoort-Lansing collection. Manuscripts and Archives Division. The New York Public Library. Astor, Lenox and Tilden Foundations).

Head Qurtr Albany April 4th: 1781

B. Orders The Captains or Officers commandg Companies are to make immediate Returns to the Colonels or Officers commanding Regiments of the Strength of their repective Companies, agreeable to the Same were furnished them.—And the Colonels or Officers commandg Regiments are from these Returns to make ~~immediate~~ Returns of their respective Regts to ~~the~~ Genl Gansevoort without Delay.

The Officers commanding unregimented Companies of Exempts are to make immediate Returns of their respective Companies to the Colos or commanding Officers of Regiments in the Districts where such ~~Captains of commandg~~ Officers ~~of Compys~~ of Exempts respectively reside

The Companies of Exempts are to be inserted at the Bottom of the regimental Returns next after the enrolled Militia Comps as in the forms now furnishd, is prescribed.—

All Persons who were by Law priviledged to join the associated Exempts & have neglected so to do, are to do Duty & be returned with the enrolled Militia in the Companies & Regiments of the Regts & districts where they respectively reside until they shall properly join the Associated Exempts

The Persons who are between 50 & 60 Years of Ages whether serving in any Company of Exempts or with the enrolled Militia are to be returned in a Seperate Column in all future Returns.

The Genl expects that the most punctual Attention will be paid by all Ranks of Officers, to the Exactness of the Numbers in the Returns made by them

No Persons who are by the 32 Sections of their Milita Law exempted from ~~Military~~ Duty are to be included in the Returns above [?] to be made

By Orders of B. G. Gansevoort

R. V. Ma of Br

The next day Gansevoort wanted to take inventory of his brigade. His second order demanded all his captains to send him regimental returns. He assigned Varick to issue the order. A letter from Varick to Colonel Abraham Cuyler[13] on April 5 emphasized that these returns should remain in this structure for the known future so that "a Uniformity may take Place throughout the Regts."[14]

Major Varick was successful in his requests, as an April 10 letter from Cornelius Van Veghten had the enclosed return from his station in Saratoga, less than a week after Gansevoort issued the brigade orders.[15]

189—Richard Varick to Abraham Cuyler

Hd Qurs Albany April 5. 1781.

Sir I have it in Command from B. Genl Gansevoort to transmit to You the Orders of the 3rd & 4th instant & to request your immediate Compliance therewith. I do for that Reason inclose you a form of a Return of a Company with a Copy of Which You will please to furnish Such of your Captains on Receipt hereof, & require from them the most Speedy Returns of their respective Companies, precisely agreeable to the form.

I do also inclose You a Form of a Regimental Return agreeable to Which You will please to [?] Your future Returns, that a Uniformity may take Place throughout the Regts of the Brigade.—

Genl Gansevoort desires that all such Persons, who are under the Age of 50 Years, as have heretofore held civil or Military Offices & as by the 30th Sections of the Militia Law were privilidged to associate as Exempts & choose their own Officers & Who have neglected to unvail themselves of the privilidge or who have neglected to join any Company of Exempts in the districts proper Dristricts Shall Do Duty be enrolled with & comprized in the Next Returns of the enrolled Militia of that District.—And that such Persons in the District of your Regt as are above 50 & under 60 Years of Age have not joined any Exempt Company be inserted in the last Column but one of your Return.

The Associated Exempts of your District are to be included in your Returns immediately after the enrolled Militia Comps of your Regt, as in the form—

The Genl earnestly injoins the greatest Exactness & Attention as to the Numbers of the Returns, That of required, the Officers may [?] thereto without the least Hessitations.—

You will please to preserve the inclosed forms as a Directories on future Occasions.—

I am Sir Your Obed Servt

Richd Varick Major of Brigade

Colo. Cuyler.—

190—From Cornelius Van Veghten

Saratoga 10th April 1781

Sir I Inclose you return of the Regiment Exscept one Compine Which is Capt Winne from fort miller informed me That his Compine is most brook up & he him Self Doont Exspect to be there above afartsnot belose his Compine is more Above the out post of ower troops he informs me that Do are Soo Scatteret that Cannot macke aproper return of Them at present for the Sumer to be inclind to be from There in a few Days as for the Rest of the Compinies is Of All the men in the Ground at present beloning To the militia By the Return of the Captins

I am Sir your Obed Servt

Cornelius Van Veghten

To Brigadier General Gansevoert

Gansevoort sent George Clinton a letter on the 14th claiming that although Gansevoort's regiment received multiple barrels of gunpowder, he received no lead balls or lead itself; twine and flints were said to be in desperate need in order to construct cartridges.[16] Despite even state militia requiring the most basic of armaments, General Washington had placed a stop on "any Arms to the Militia in future ... he has ordered all those Arms which are already in the Hands of some of the Militia to be immediately collected & returned into the Store."[17]

191—To George Clinton

Albany April 14 1781.

Dr Sir A few Days since arrived at this Place eight Barrels of Powder from the Main Army for the Use of the Militia in this Quarter But not a Single Pound of Ball or Lead or any Cartridge Paper Thread ~~Flint~~ or Twine ~~or Flint~~ are to be had at this Place to make the same up into Cartridges, nor are we furnished with any Flints ~~for the Use of the Militia~~

I therefore find myself necessitated to apply to Your Excellency for Infirmation, from whence I am to be Supplied with these neccessary Articles,—

Many of the Militia in this Part of the Country are destitute of Arms & were ~~formerly~~ occasionally Supplied from the Continental ~~Mags~~ Armerery in this Place, But I find that Genl Clinton has by Order of his Excellency G. Washington directed Mr Rensselaer the ~~Storekeeper~~ D. C. G. of M. Stores ~~here~~ not to deliver out any Arms to the Militia in future & that he has ordered all those Arms which are already in the Hands of some of the Militia to be immediately collected & returned into the Store

~~Much of~~ The Men who were so furnished with Arms by the public are so poor as not to be able to purchase for themselves ~~them~~ & There is not a Shilling to my Knowledge, in the Hands of any Militia Officer here, which may be applied to the purchase of Arms ~~for~~ as the Law directs I shall be very happy if Your Excellency will be pleased to ~~appl able~~ apply to Genl Washington for his Orders to the ~~Storekeeper~~ D. C. G. M Stores here to deliver out Arms to the Militia in this Quarter for their Men who are destitude, Subject to be accounted Sir by such Officers, And that a Supply of Flints, Lead or Ball, Cartridge Paper, & Twine or Thread may be sent to this Place as soon as possible for the Use of the Militia

I have ordered ~~Returns~~ the Officers commandg Regts of my Brigade to make Returns to me without Delay, As soon as I receive them all, I will do myself the Honor of transmitting to Your Excellency a Genl Return.

I am with Sentiments of Respect & Esteem Dr Sir Your Excys Most Obed Servt

P. G.

His Excellency Govr Clinton

According to Gansevoort, the public were the only ones funding the militia with arms, which almost always came from their own houses always from their own houses. Gansevoort required that this be remedied by passing along by way of Clinton a request to overturn this order.

Although Gansevoort's perception of the armaments request was understandable, Washington must have transferred the armament priorities down towards the Southern states, as they were experiencing far more bloodshed at this course of the war than New York. The Southern states were also in the midst of its own miniature civil war, with loyalist neighbors brutally murdering rebel neighbors and vice-versa. To further increase regional confusion, British orders were issued declaring any runaway slaves free if they were to join the British army, threatening the entire slave-based economy of the southern states. Surely Washington saw the need for guns and munitions to be in part shipped from the northern states, as the course of the war dictated that even local Southern merchants and munitions depots were not guaranteed to be easily accessible: they could fall to any party at anytime.

Gansevoort passed along the announcement by Congress to "pay clothe and Subsist at the Genl Expence the two Regiments proposed to be raised for three Years, on Condition th[a]t this State Shall compleat to Quota of Troops for the Continental Army"[18] and pledged to use his "utmost Influence" to try to gain extra goods and munitions.

192—To Abraham Cuyler

Albany April 18. 1781

Sir I have this day recd a Letter from His Excellency Govr Clinton dated the 15th inst. informing Me that Congress have by their Act of the 2nd instant engaged to pay & Subsist the Levies of this State to Serve until the 1st Decr And also to pay clothe & Subsist at the Genl Expence the two Regiments proposed to be raised for three Years, on Condition tht this State Shall compleat to Quota of Troops for the Continental Army:—

I am therefore directed by the Governor to inform him whether & here fore this Business, is effected in my Brigade & if there is any Deficiency that I will se my utmost Influence & Authority to have it prefected that a Service so essentiably necessary as that if embodying the Corps designed for the immediate Defence of the State may not be delayed or Obstructed.—

It appears from the Genl Orders of Novr last that the Quota of orderd to be raised by your Regiment for the War is 18 Men—& Colo Philip P. Schuylers 12. You will therefore with the least possible Delay ~~inform~~ Make a Return to Me of the Number of Men actually raised by the Classes of Your Regts & by that Part of Colo Schuylers lately annexed to Your Regt Specifying the Names of the Men so raised, the Time when & the Continental Officers Name to whom scribe Men were delivered.—

In Case of any Deficiency you will take the most effective & Speedy Measures for procuring the Men.—& for punishing as the Laws direct such Classes a who remain Delinquent,

You will also without the least Delay or Excuse Send me the Return of your Regt as orderd in the 4. inst.

I am Sir Your Most Obedt Servt

P. G. BGenl

Colo Abm Cuyler

P.S. You will inform me what Nr of Men were to be raised by that Part of Colo Schuylers Regt which is annexed to Yours.

It should be noted that Congress had not agreed to supply munitions, weapons, or other forms of supplies needed to reequip the Continental Army in New York. It was also important to note that Congress mentioned sending aid to only two regiments; a letter from George Clinton confirmed this resolution offered little help overall, as "...every Part of the State are subject to the same Difficulties in Want of Ammunition and Arms."[19] Clinton also mentioned that means to gain ammunition were being employed east of New York from the other colonies. This may have been particularly dangerous, as British soldiers were still stationed in southeastern New York. Finally, the independent Vermont Republic was still in talks with both the British and United States armies, as well as territorial talks with the New York state government itself.

Gansevoort further expressed fears that his command was lacking magazines, something not even local families could supply. Gansevoort's fears of a raid appeared to be justified, as a letter from Colonel Anthony Van Bergen[20] of the New York militia declared that a small group of British soldiers captured one David Abeel and his son[21] along with multiple slaves, breaking much of the Abeel's possessions in the process.[22] The end of the letter also suggested that Washington's prevention of arms redistribution to the militia was a disastrous decision, as the militia would be in pursuit of the men responsible, but Van Bergen and others "think that the Militia Cannot Sufficiently Guard them."[23]

193—From Anthony Van Bergen

Hond Sir I have just Reced Intelligence from Lieut Col: DuBois "that David Abeel and his Son were taken last night and two of his Negros by about 15 or 16 of the Enemy the Express says that they have broke a Large Looking Glass and broke open the Chests and Robb'd him of ~~A Good~~ what they could take along so that I suppose it is a Party of Robbers Col DuBois has wrote me no particulars other than above he has sent A Party after them and I shall send A Party to Beesick as I suppose they are gone to the Westward—I must intreat the General to Order A Party of the New Levies to our ~~Frontiers~~ Assistance as our Frontiers are so Extensive; That the Inhabitants Whereon have made Application to me & will remove unless they can be immediately Assisted as they Apprehend themselves in Danger & think that the Militia cannot Sufficiently Guard them—I am

Sir Your Most Obedt Huml Servt

Anthony Van Bergen Col

Cockrackie Monday Noon

Apl: 23d 1781

PS David Abeel lives on the Caters kill abt 4 Miles South of Catts Kill

The Honble Brigd Genl Gansevoort [Albany]

PS I have just now Recived your Order of ~~the~~ April 18th: Respecting the Men to be raised in my Regt during the War—There is 4 Men raised in my Regt but I dont know their Names neither by whom Mustered but shall make Enquiry—Your Order of the 4th Inst I only received the 21st Inst and have sent Orders to have the Companies returned to me immediately which As Soon I receive shall make Return to the General

I am Your Obed Servt

Anthony Van Bergen Col

An April 28 letter from Major Varick addressed to the brigade officers requested a meeting at the house of a Mr. Hugh Denniston in Albany to discuss recent matters and the returns needed by the regimental officers.[24] According to Varick, "The Genl is Surprised to find that so little Attention is paid to the Orders of the 4 & 12th.—& 18th"[25] Judging from the tone of the letter, the initially successful attempt to create a new form of structure in manpower accounts still resulted in non-communication. It is possible that in the up -coming meeting Varick and Gansevoort would express the importance of these returns in regards to disbursement of munitions from Governor Clinton and other state authorities once received.

194—Brigade Orders

Albany April 28th 1781

Brigade Orders The Field Officers of General Gansevoorts Brigade are to meet at the House of Mr Hugh Denniston in this City on the Second Tuesday in June next agreeable to the Militia Law.

The Colonels or Officers commanding Regiments will make all the Returns what are directed to be made by the Genl Orders of His Excellency Govr Clinton of the 23 March last, Without the least Delay or Excuse whatsoever; to Genl Gansevoort the Genl Hopes he will not be under the Necessity of repeating this Order to the Gentlemen remained.

The Presidents of the several Genl Courts Martial are immediately & from Time to Time to repeat to the Genl their Proceedings of their respective Courts, that the Sentences may be carried into Execution without Delay.—

By Order of B Genl. Gansevoort

RV. M B

The Genl is Surprised to find that so little Attention is paid to the Orders of the 4 & 12th.—& 18th inst respecting the Regimental returns directed to be made to him.

The latter half of May's correspondence involved troop movements and further reorganization of Gansevoort's command. In a May 22 letter to George Washington, Brigadier General James Clinton confirmed that many of the officers in New York wished to abandon Fort Schuyler and redirect their troop concentrations to the German Flats area and at Fort Herkimer.[26] However, Clinton also stated that such a movement would leave the New York borders especially vulnerable to attack and was "confident the Enemy intend something serious against our Frontiers." He then requested that regiments stationed near West Point be diverted up to the area to guard against any British activity, but only if he "could see any Prospect of supplying them with Provisions."[27]

195—James Clinton to George Washington

Albany May 22d 1781

Sir I have been honored with your Excellency's favour of the 18th Inst agreeable to the Governors advice I consulted Generals Rensselaer & Gansevoort the Mayor ~~and~~ in Council and several other Gentlemen whome I could confide in respecting the abandoning of Fort Schuyler and establishing a Post at the German Flatts who were unanimous in opinion that under our present circumstances the Fort should be evacuated and the Garrison removed to Fort Herkermer [I have this day given orders accordingly as ~~Copy~~ will appear by a Copy of a Letter herewith enclosed to Colo Cochran—if we errect works at ~~fort Herkermer~~ the German Flatts an Engineer will be much wanted for that purpose—last night I received an Express from Genl Schuyler which Contains all the news I have at present from the Northward for the information of which I refer your Excellency to his Letter—I am confident the Enemy intend something serious against our Frontiers—we have but few men to the Northward as Colo Cortlandt's Regiment with Part of the new Levies will be for a Considerable time employed to assist in the evacuation of Fort Schuyler—I could wish to have the other six Companies of the Brigade which are at west point ~~if I~~ could see any Prospect of supplying them with Provisions—I have been able to procure a Quantity of Flour by impress the cheif of which appears to be purchased for the use of the French Army which is considerable amounting to near three thousand Barrels—I have not been able to procure one Barrel of Beef or Fish The Flour I have not yet removed but the purchasers have promised not to send it off without my notice or Consent

23d May

I will yesterday I have detained my Letter expecting to receive farther intelligence from the Northward—/ Last night Hagenbottom the Pretended deserter and Meaker of the first New York Regiment were brought to Town—they are both in Irons and Close confined / at the Same time a second Letter from Genl Schuyler for your Excellency was received which was Left open for my perusal & Contains all the news at present from that Quarter

I have &c

James Clinton

His Excellency Genl Washington (Copy)

On May 28, Major Richard Varick resigned his commission as major of brigade as he accepted a position of an "Office in the Service of the United State of America under His Excellency General Washington."[28] The brevity of this letter shone little light on the conclusion of his relationship with Gansevoort, though he does end the letter with the necessary "Sentiments of the Highest Respect and Regard."[29]

196—From Richard Varick

Albany May 28th 1781

Dear Sir Having accepted of an Office in the Service of the United State of America under His Excellency General Washington, I do hereby resign the Office of Major of Brigade to the first Brigade of Militia in the County of Albany & State of New York, which I have held under Law.—

I am, with Sentiments of the highest Respect & Regard Dear Sir Your Obedt & very Humble Servt

Richd Varick

The Honble B. Genl Gansevoort

[Albany]

With Varick's appointment, it had seemed through correspondence that Gansevoort had now lost an officer whom he greatly depended on to keep order within his ranks. This may explain the sudden increase in correspondence between Gansevoort and locals. Major Varick was probably the stopgap between multiple letters that Gansevoort would have found to be beneath his command.

Tensions in New York seemed to rapidly increase in the summer months of 1781. Peter Vrooman,[30] stationed at Schoharie Lower Fort,[31] informed Gansevoort that the inhabitants of the settlement had constructed two blockhouses and were building another one. Governor Clinton had ordered only one and the other ones were being erected by residents who "have not Excerted Themselves as they Should in the Cause of America Liberty."

197—From Peter Vrooman

Schohary Lower fort June 1st: 1781

Dear Genl/ This is to acquainth you that Some of the Inhabitants of this place have Erected two forts or Blokhouses in this Settlement and one more Erecting within Sight of this, which gives great uneassiness to the well affected here, as mostly of those that have and are Erecting as above have not Excerted Themselves as they Should in the Cause of america Liberty, But to the Contrary Some of them have Remained in their houses when Sir John Johnsons was here Last fall, and thru that means as we are of oppinion Savd their Buildings and others took the woods altho the had Timly notice to Repaire to the forts and assist to Defend it, I Refer you to the Bearer hereof Leut Johannes Deitz who will more particularly inform you thereof—I have been in albany a forthnight ago to speak to you for information Concerning the general Court martial whereof I am appointed presidant, and about Raising the men to Serve in the Continental Regiments During the war, as you was not in Town, have Communicated the Same to your Brother in law Mr Van Schaick and promisd me to Communicate the Same to you your answer upon the whole will be Received with the greatest Sadisfection Dear genl I Remain with Respect your most humble Servt

Peter Vroman

To the honorable B D General Gansevoort [Albany]

P.S. Genl Clinton Told me that they have his Leave to Build one fort where about we have not So much against as those inhabitants Live more Distantly

PV

A June 3 letter from Thomas Smith of Vermont declared that any persons under the authority of the state of New York were forbidden by the Vermont Republic to engage in any activities compromising Vermont's sovereignty.[32]

198—Thomas Smith to Mr. Van Buren

Copy Mr Van Buren these are to inform you that I have received Instructions from his Excellency Governor Chittenden[33] *which are as follow's Viz.*

I am sorry to hear that any Person living without the limits of the ~~State~~ late Union should expose himself by making Disturbances within the State of Vermont; I do therefore forbid any person residing without or within the Limits of the said Union to Execute any kind of Authority under the Goverment of New York within the Said Limits, While the Body of the people profess to be subjects of this State.

Thoms Smith

Saratoga East Hudsons River

June the 3d 1781. State of Vermont

A July 12 letter from Colonel Peter Vrooman declared that an engagement with British soldiers occurred at the "upper End of Turlack"[34] which may have been an attempt to clear the roads for a larger British force to stream down from Canada towards Albany. Indians were included in the opposing party and had killed a civilian couple a few hours after the initial attack; the woman was killed and the man killed and scalped "by the Treck."[35] The end of the letter requested badly needed reinforcements and that the enemy force could number anywhere between one to two hundred men. Judging by Vrooman's estimates and tone in the letter, the area was certainly caught by surprise with little to defend themselves.

199—From Peter Vrooman

Schohary Lower fort July 12th 1781

Dear Genl/ We are greatly alarmd here, yesterday two OClock P.M. I received an Express from Cobus kill with a Letter from hendrick Boret a Lieut of my Regt informing me, that he had information that Coll Willet had an Engagement with the Enemy at the uper End of Turlack how it went he had not heard, after I receive the Letter yesterday parties of the Enemy have been seen at three Diffrent places near to this post. Crossing the Roads that Leads from this to albany and Schonectady one place two an other four and at an other Six, perhaps gone to the beverdam recruiting Last night a man arrivd at this post and Calls himself william Soal and Says that he is a Sergeantt Quarter master in Coll willets Regt of Levies and marchd with Coll willet and a Detachment from fort Rensselaer[36] *to the first Settlement of Turlack and there fell in with the Enemy in the beginning of the Engagement he was unfourtunately taken prisoner and Carried back to a Swamp by two of the Enemies Indians where he made his Escape that the firing ~~Lasted~~ was kept up for half an hour, how it went he did not know this happened Last Tuesday ten OClock in the morning, in the afternoon of the Same day he came to a house in Turlack where ~~there~~ Some of the inhabitants had Colected, Soon after news Came there that a man and woman were killd at the next house from there ~~from~~ Immediately after Receiving the news he went with two of the inhabitants and found the man and woman killd and the man Sculpd by the treck it appeard to him the Enemy were about between hundred and two hundred Strong, it might be that they will fall on Some part of this Settlement and we are Distitute of troops as I wrote you the 7th of this Instant, wherefore a Reinforement is wanted with all possible Speed hoping nothing will be wanted on your part to forward the Same I Remain with great Respects—*

Dear Genl your most obedient humble Servt

Peter Vroman

The honorable B Genl Gansevoort [Albany]

Troubles in August contributed to Gansevoort's continued state of weariness. Lieutenant Colonel John Blair sent a letter to Gansevoort on August 7, claiming that he was unable to raise the quota of men in his area, and that the local regiment had officially joined the State of Vermont in defending their frontier, independent of the rest of the United States.[37] Blair finished the letter with an ominous resignation in light of his failure to adequately secure the manpower in his area, though according to his letter, it was due to his "age and Infirmity."[38]

200—From John Blair

Cambridge August 7th—1781

Honoured Sir I Recived your orders of the 12 of July on the 30 with his Excellency orders inclosed in yours; it is out of my power for to fullfil your orders were it to advencetage me a kingdom

I cannot Raise the men under the State of New york of wrote to your Hon Some time ago that this Regiment had joyned the State of Vermont and Chosen there officers under that State of am informed that they are Raising every tenth man in the Regiment to go to northward to gard the fronttires I also am informd that they are Raising a nomber of Rangers for three weeks to Range the northen wood still the levys are completed—I do Request that your Honr would Send no more orders to me for I can do nothing with them this Regiment has Chosen Joseph Calwell for there Colo; and John Mc Clong Majer Companys have Chosen there under officers &c I Requsted my Resignation by a letter To the Honble Brigadier General TenBrook Dated April ye 13–1781 for Resons then given which was my age and Infirmity I would therefore In treat your Honor to accept of my Resignation whilst I am with respect Your Honors most obedint Huml Savrt

John Blair

The Honble Bridgadier General Gansevoort Albany

In August, Gansevoort kept his brigade in "perfect Readiness" so they could take the field on the shortest notice, collecting accounts of the enemies in the northern and western frontiers. Another letter received on August 14 claimed that an enemy force of over three hundred men including loyalists were approaching the Ulster County area, Clinton then requested Gansevoort send a detachment to protect the nearby settlement of Schoharie.[39]

201—From George Clinton

Poughkeepsie Augt 9th 1781

Sir As the probable Operations of the Campaign and the present critical Situation of the North & Western Frontiers render it necessary that the Militia should be held in the most perfect Readiness, you will pay the strictest Attention to the several Regiments of your Brigade and see that they stand prepared to take the field on the shortest notice; and you will give express Orders to the commanding Officers that they cause the Classes of their respective Regts to be revised and carefully formed agreable to Law that if a part of the Militia only should be wanted they may be drawn out with ease and expectition. I have not yet been favored with the Returns, directed by Law, of the Levies raised by the Regimts of your Brigade pursuant to my Orders of the 22d of March last and for want of which I am ignorant how far those Orders have been complied with and it has been out of my Powers to put the Law in force against the Delinguents / if any there are / I have therefore to request that you will cause these Returns to be made immediately that Prosecutions may be commenced against those who have been deficient in their Duty. I shall also expect similar Returns of the present Levies which you will please to press your Officers to make without Delay.

I am with great Esteem Sir Your most Obedt Servt

Geo: Clinton

A Return of your Brigade is likewise requested as soon as possible—

Brigr Genl Gansevoort [Albany]

202—From George Clinton

Poughkeepsie 14th Augt 1781

Sir Last Sunday a Body of the Enemy to the amount of about 300 Indians & 90 Tories appeared on the frontiers of Ulster County.—They took a small Scout Colo Pawling had sent out & from them it is supposed obtained Information of the Disposition of the Levies posted in that Quarter whom they passed by and were first Discovered at the Settlement of Warsing.[40] *From the last accounts they had retired: but how far is not known.—the Militia are collected and marched to oppose or pursue them as circumstances as may render expedient—from their force it is not probable they will leave the Country without attempting further Mischief in that or some other Quarter. I conceive it necessary therefore to give you this Information that you may take proper Steps with your Militia in case this Party should take their Route towards the Frontier of your County.—and I would particularly recommend that a part of your Brigade be immediately marched to Schoharie for the Protection of that Settlement until this Party shall have entirely give off. The account of the Enemy's Strength is from one Vroman who deserted them; which is confirmed from their appearance to a small Party of Levies who saw them paraded at a house they attacked & which the Party defended*

By a more particular Account recd this Morning (& which was the first that demanded credit) they have burnt & destroyed about a dozen houses' with their Barns &c among which are those of Johans G Hardenbergh Esqr,[41]*—They killed only one of the Inhabitants. the rest having made a timely escape from their houses.—The Levies stationed there were by no Means sufficient to turn out and oppose them: but those who were in house defended them with Spirit agt the assaults of the Enemy by which Means several of the Enemy are said to have fallen & many houses were saved.*

Yesterday I recd whether from Colo Paine for ammunition for his Militia who he informs me are entirely destitute—the State Magazine has long since been entirely exhausted and the only resource we have to apply to is that forwarded by Genl Washington to Albany; out of which if it is not already all distributed, I must request you to deliver Colo Paine a proportion equal to the Strength of ~~your~~ his Regiment I have directed our Commissy of military Stores to forward you a couple Ton of Lead or as much as he can with Justice to the Militia in the other Parts of the State spare; out of which where it arrives I must request you to deliver Colo Paine a proportion likewise.—

I am with great Esteem Sir Your most Obdt Servt
Geo: Clinton
Brigr Genl Gansevoort

Included in the report was the statement that twelve civilian homes had been set aflame by the invaders and the death of one local. The locals were admonished by Clinton for their inability to defend themselves. However, even he admitted that they had little in the way of defenses as the "State magazine has long since been entirely exhausted."[42] The only recourse was to procure a loan of armaments by way of General Washington.

Gansevoort issued orders to Colonel Wempel[43] and Major Schermerhorn to round up all officers and privates to march as quickly as possible to Schoharie to join a brigade detachment under Lieutenant Colonel Henry Van Rensselaer.[44] Schermerhorn reported back on August 24 that no sign of the enemy was discovered within forty miles of Schoharie.

203—From Jacob C. Schermerhorn

Lower Fort Augt 24th 81
Sir *Arrived here the 20th Instant, since my arrival; several scouts have been sent no Dis-*

coveries have been made of any Enemy within forty miles of this place, I Shall this day send out another scout from this place, and another from the middle fort, the Men in General are very Uneasy about Staying as they think they have nothing to do, I Shall write you every oppurtunity but expect a few lines from you,

I Remain your very Hbble Servt

Jacob C: Schermerhorn

NB The Number of Men I have one the ground Consists of about one Hundred & forty Men Office Included

[PG Albany]

As contact with British and loyalist forces seemed increasingly inevitable, Gansevoort sent word to Colonel Philip P. Schuyler on September 12[45] to proceed to Beaver Dam where the news of the murder of Captain Dietz[46] and his family had quickly spread. The orders warned of numerous enemy scouting parties likely to be within the area, and that the purpose of the expedition was to make "every Exertion for surprizing and Destroying them (enemy scouting parties)."[47]

204—To Philip P. Schuyler

General Orders—Albany 12 Sept 1781

Colo. P. Schuyler will take the Command of the Troops ordered here by General Orders of the 9th Instant—And proceed without Delay—Agreeable to those orders to remove the Persons and Families of ~~those~~ the disaffected named in the List hereunto annexed & as it will to be impossible to have their Effects immediately removed (X) he will take such Measures respecting the same as he may esteem most proper

Colo Schuyler will make such from ~~under the~~ the Party under his command Detachments as he shall conceive ~~most expedient~~ necessary for carrying this Business into Execution with the greatest Expedition—possible—It is particularly recommended to Colo Schuyler ~~to send a Detachment~~ to go to the ~~Place when Capt Dietz the Family was~~ Neighborhood of the Beaver Dam where in the Family of Capt. Dietz were lately murdered &, to apprehend & bury off from them, the most notoriously disaffected in that vicinity and to ~~those~~ acquaint the other Residents there suspected of Disaffection that ~~if any similar Crimes~~ unless they immediately give notice to their proper Officers upon any future Incursion of Parties of the Enemy and turn out to offer there they ~~must expect to receive similar Treatment with those now under~~ also to be removed from their respective Habitations (X) as it is probable that small Parties of the Enemy may be lurking in the different Parts of the Country where this Party may have Occasion to go—particularly those under Command of Bettis & John Walter Meyer Colo Schuyler will ~~so dispose of It has Detachments at be~~ take every necessary Precaution to prevent the Disgrace of Surprize and in the Disposal of his Detachments make them sufficiently strong if they should meet those Parties to ensure Success and also ~~take~~ if he should gain Information ~~Colo Schuyler~~ and he ~~will~~ will act discretionally with Respect to the ~~Number~~ Persons he may think proper to remove ~~under their Orders & those of the 9th Instant~~ and also in every other Respect where ~~Events~~ Circumstances may dictate as to every other matter not particularized in those Orders.—of their being in the Country make us of every Exertion for surprizing and destroying them.—Colo Schuyler will also be careful that the Troops under his Command do not distress or injure the Persons or

Property of the well affected ~~of~~ Inhabitants of the respective Distants into which he may march or forward Detachments for the above Purposes ~~aforesaid~~—

[Copy of Orders Colo Ph: Schuyler]

205—From Henry K. Van Rensselaer

Sir I send you a return of the Levies raised in my Regiment, and likewise those for the Defence of the State. Those for the defence of the Frontiers I have delivered Twenty four: and six deficient who lay claim under the New State For the Defence of the State, I have deliver'd Eighteen, and twelve deficient, who Likewise lay claim under the New State. And agreeable to the Law and too Orders receiv'd from You, I have Order'd them to be Detach'd, and two of them have been Apprehended, and deliver'd to the receiving Officer in Albany, upon which I receiv'd a letter from Governor Chittenden wherein he Orders me, to Desist from exercising my authority over those People who belong to their State, and Desires me to return the two Men who are Detach'd by my Orders. I have sent him the following answer: That I had acted agreeable to the Law and to the orders I receiv'd from his Excellency the Governor. and from You. And was determin'd to have the Orders carried into Execution, and therefore should not return the two Men, unless I was order'd so to do by my superiors Therefore shall be glad to have Your sentiments on the Subject.

I am Sir Your most Obedient Humble Servant.
Henry K. Van Rensselaer
Green Bush
August 30th 1781
The Honble Peter Gansevoort, B Genl
Albany

206—To Abraham Wempel and Ezekiel Taylor

Albany Septemr 9th 1781

Sir Being determined to carry into execution a late Law of this State with Respect to the Hilleberg & Beaver Dam having for that purpose put in Motion a part of my Brigade also for the purpose of Defeating the Intentions of a Party of Torys thirty in Number headed by the well known Infamous Walton mire[48] *& Bettis*[49] *for that purpose include extract of Genl Orders of this Day*

(Copy of a Letter to Coll Wemple & Major Taylor which included Genl Orders with Respect to each of them)

A letter from Schuyler dated the 16th indicated some form of victory; with the nearby Beaver Dam area secured, General Schuyler declared that over one hundred prisoners had been taken in the area.[50] Subsequent letters from the Commissioners for Conspiracies [51] apparently gained some intelligence from this assortment of Beaver Dam prisoners; the most significant was that British soldiers under Sir John Johnson were planning to meet up with another party of "White Men and Savages" to conduct a series of attacks either at the

Mohawk or North River areas.[52] The letter also claimed that the ultimate goal of the party was to destroy Albany within the year and that they were expecting yet more reinforcements from the Niagara region. Certainly the Beaver Dam incident and the following interrogations were confirmation to Gansevoort and other officers of what they had feared for most of the year: that the British were slowly reorganizing their forces for a large attack into New York with the purpose of capturing Albany.

207—From Philip P. Schuyler

Bankers Normans hill 16 Sept 1781

Sir I Have a Number of Prisoner from the Bever Dam and will be In Albany with them This day and Request of the General where To Deliver them

To Wit 41 men
16 Women
69 Children
I am with Complyment
The Generals most Humble Servert
Phil. P. Schuyler
[PG Albany]

208—From the Commissioners for Conspiracies

Campbell Lefever,[53] Joseph Willson, John Angel,[54] John Duncan[55]—Inhabitants of Kanctucky County in the State of Virginia and James Dugan (son of Coll Dugan) being Examined say that they left Montreal the 26th of August that the Saturday before they came away between Two Hundred and Fifty or Three Hundred of Sir Johns Men crossed the River St. Lawrence on their way to St Johns where they were to be joined by some more White Men and Savages who were to come over the Lake and to make an Attack either on the Mohawk River or the North River—that previous to their leaving Montreal a large Quantity of hard Bread was baked that it is conjectured that they intended to fall upon some Place and draw the whole of the Militia that way and that a Party is then to fall upon that Part of the Country which is left destitute of Men that it was reported that the Fleet had arrived in Canada but that they do not beleive it as there have often before heard it Reported without foundation—That they have frequently heard Sir John's Men say that they intended to distroy Albany this Fall and that they have understood a Party is to come from Niagara who are to join with the Party that is to come over the Lake—

Albany 19th Sept 1781
Commissrs for Conspiracies
Saml Stringer
John M Beeckman
Isaac P Fondes
Stewart Dean

After discovering a sizable British force massing near Point au Fer, Brigadier General John Starks requested two hundred reinforcements and quickly relayed the message to Governor Clinton that Sir John Johnson was planning an attack on Saratoga and that there were reports of thirty British soldiers approaching the outskirts of Ballston. Gansevoort ordered the entirety of his available forces towards the aforementioned area and requested Clinton to give any assistance within his means.[56] The same day, Gansevoort had sent orders to all of his immediate subordinates and informed Stark of the coming reinforcement.

209—To George Clinton

Albany 9th Octr 1781

Dear Sir I transmit your Excellency enclosed the Copy of a Letter red I have just recd by Express from Genl Stark—As the Troops expected on the Northern Frontier are commanded by Genl Reidsill it is more than probable that an Attempt will also be made by Sir John Johnson to the Westward and this ~~Opinion~~ Conjecture is counter anced by Intelligence received ~~last~~ Yesterday Evening of the Appearance of about 30 British in the vicinity of Ballstown—

In Consequence of the Requisition & Accounts in Genl Starks Letter I have ordered Yates' Van Veghten's & Tayler's Regts to Saraghtoga ~~and I have just ordered ordered~~ Wemp's & Van Bergen's to hold themselves in Readiness for imprudent service the Remr of my Brigade ~~under~~ to march to this Place without ~~Marching Orders to be in Hand of to~~ Delay here to receive my farther Orders— ~~March at the Shortest Notice It is just probable at from the Enemy have in this Quarter have hitherto laid still that they have now collected their whole Force together & mean to make use of their utmost Efforts to destroy~~ I have also forwarded the Intelligence to Genl Van Renselaer ~~and mention~~ & informed him what I have done in Consequence of it—

I submit to your Excellency (who are doubtless acquainted with the force of Genl Heath[57] *& whether he is able to spare a Part of it) ~~for the Emergency~~ the Propently of requesting from him some Assistance in the presant Emergency and are &c*

[PG]

[Dr Letter to Gov. Clinton]

210—To Abraham Cuyler, Henry K. Van Rensselaer, Robert Van Rensselaer,[58] Philip P. Schuyler, Peter Yates, Cornelius Van Veghten and Ezekiel Taylor

Brigade Orders By information just now received from Brigadier Genl Stark commanding the Dept at Saratoga that the Enemy are in Force at point a fare on Lake Champlain under marching orders it is apprehended that they are seriously meditating an Attack on Some part of the Frontiers.

You are hereby ordered to march your Regiment ~~forthwith to this place including~~ and ~~order~~ the exempt Corps within the Dist of your ~~Compani~~ Regimt ~~also~~ forthwith to this place—

The General flatters himself that none will be so lost to their Duty and affection for their Country as to remain behind at this critical Juncture when by their Spirit & Exertions they will be enabled to cause the Enemy to repent of an Enterprize so often attempted by them ~~Enemy unsuccessful~~ and as often rendered unsuccessfull by the Bravery and intrepidily of the Militia

Seven Copies

[Copy Genl Orders to Colonels Cuyler H V. Rensselaer, R. V. Rensselaer. Ph: Schuyler. Yates. Van Veghten and Major Taylor—9 Octr 1781]

John Stark, unknown artist (Gansevoort-Lansing collection. Manuscripts and Archives Division. The New York Public Library. Astor, Lenox and Tilden Foundations).

211—To John Stark

Albany Octr 9 1781

Dear Sir I was this morning honoured with your favour of yesterday—In consequence of which have ordered the Regiments of Colonels Yates Van Vechten and Taylor to march to Saratoga the Regiments of Wemple of Schonectaday and Van Bergen of Coxsackie[59] *to collect and hold themselves in perfect readiness to march on the shortest Notice and the remainder of my Brigade have Orderd to march to this Place from thence I shall march them to Halfmoon where I shall wait your Orders I have communicated the Intelligence received from you to Governor Clinton and to Genl Renselaer who command the Lower Brigade in this County and I flatter myself that should the Enemy have the imprudence to attempt a Descent we shall have it in our power to make them repent their enterprise*

I am Sir very humble Servt

[PG]

To Genl Stark

Reports of the enemies' position changed in various letters almost daily, though they all confirmed the British troops were still within the Lake Champlain area. Gansevoort's letter to Brigadier General Van Rensselaer on the 11th described the inevitability of a confrontation:

"By information this moment Received I am informed that the Enemy are now in Raelity on this side Lake George—for Goods Sake hurry on with all the force you can collect as perhaps this may be Last information I can give you untill they are in Raelity here—I can give no information of their force but we must Be prepared for the worst..."[60]

The importance of recovering crucial intelligence of the British armies' movements in the New York region was noted by most of the state officials as well. Robert Benson wrote Gansevoort that the Governor was impressed with Gansevoort's decision to "apprehend the

Enemy's real Design ... in this case you will be the more ready & able to throw speedy succour into that Quarter."[61]

212—From Robert Benson

Poughkeepsie Octr 11th 1781—9 'OClock A: M:

Sir Your Letter of the 9th was just now delivered to his Excellency the Governor who is very indisposed with a fever—He therefore directs me to acknowledge the Receipt of it & to inform you that he approves of the Measures you have taken with respect to the Militia and that he has confidence that you will make the best use of the force under your command to oppose the common Enemy—Genl Rensselaer will be written to by the bearer to hold his Brigade in readiness and to march such part as shall be necessary to sustain Genl Stark or Colo Willet—the Governor presumes from the situation of Vromans Regiment you have not ordered it to Albany, tho' from your Letter it would appear you had.—

Genl Schuyler's letter will be forwarded His Excellency is not sufficiently acquainted with the force below to determine whether any part of it can be spared but he will write to Genl Heath also on the Subject.—

I am with great Respect Sir Your most Obedt Servt

Robt Benson ADC

P.S. His Excellency particularly approves of your ordering so considerable a part of your Brigade to rendezvous at Albany; as he apprehend the Enemy's real Design, notwithstanding present appearances, is against Tryon & the western part of Albany Counties and in this case you will be the more ready & able to throw speedy succour into that Quarter.—He thinks it advisable and it is his Desire that one Regt, exclusive of Wemples, should be immediately ordered to Schenectady—it will not take them much out of their Route if Saratoga is the object. I do myself the Pleasure of inclosing you an extract of a Letter giving a further acct of the matters mentioned in it which in some measure serves as a confirmation.—

Brigr Genl Gansevoort [Albany]

213—To George Clinton

Albany 12th October 1781

Dear Sir, I inclose your Excellency the Copy of a Letter I have this Instant received by Express from General Starks—I shall march this Evening for Saraghtoga with four Regiments of my Brigade—This may however probably so much weaker our Strength in this Quarter ~~Force and disenable us to~~ that if the Enemy should appear in Force on the Western Frontier ~~we show be~~ Colo Willett must defend ~~upon himself~~ solely upon the small Number of Troops he command as we should not be able to render him ~~the least~~ any effectual Assistance—The Intelligence now transmitted is ~~about as~~ so certain that not a Doubt remains of the Truth of it I am therefore to entreat your Excellency (as we have the best Reason to think the Enemy are in Force) if it is in your Power to grant or obtain for us such aids as you may conceive necessary in the present Emergency—I would ~~sent~~ also add that ~~It we the Militia~~ we are destitute both of Provisions nor Ammunition—I need not point out the Necessity of immediately Supplies of both particularly of the latter without a Sufficiency of which your Exy knows it will be as possible to oppose the Enemy—

I am &

[Copy of a Letter to Governor Clinton]

214—From Matthew Visscher[62]

City Hall—Albany 12th Octr 1781

At a Meeting of the Magistrates and Members of the Corporation, who have taken into Consideration the Eminent danger threatned this City, deem it highly expedient that the Inhabitants should remain in it during the present Alarm in order to protect the same, Whereupon it is unanimously resolved that General Gansevoort be requested to Countermand his orders of this day commanding the Militia of the Town to March to Half Moon—

By order

Mat Visscher Clk

An October 12 letter from Brigadier General Stark reaffirmed the intense need for ammunition and a supply line if a successful defense was to be made; those "without arms are altogether useless and those without ammunition must be also ... until then I can give you no interesting particulars."[63]

215—From John Stark

Head Quarters Saratoga 12th Oct 1781

Dear Sir It is with Sorrow that I must inform you that the militia of your Brigade have no ammunition, and great numbers of them without arms—and I have not a sufficient supply for their necessities, those without arms are altogether useless and those without ammunition must be so also, unless you can send a Supply from Albany—

I have no further Confirmation of the advance of the Enemy—my scouts are almost every where, and I expect several to return very soon—untill then I can give you no interesting particulars—

I am Dear Sir your assured Hum Servt

John Stark BG

BGenl Gansevoort

Some good news may have been inferred from Stark's letter a few days later to Gansevoort, in which Stark congratulated Gansevoort for having received the artillery unit. The letter also mentioned that according to Stark, "...friends to the North East wince a Disposition of Cooperateing with us."[64]

216—To John Stark

Albany October 14th 1781

Dear Sir I have the pleasure of Congratulating you upon the arrival of a Regiment of regular Troops from the Southward with a detachment of artilery, & yr alacrity with which the Militia in General manifest to turn out at this time to Repel the Expected invasion of the Enemy

It gives me ~~particular~~ peculiar Satisfaction to hear that our friends to the north East wince a Disposition of Co:operateing with us ~~in repelling the Enemy~~

It appears very probably to me that the Enemy are not Serious in makeing an Excursion from the north ward as they cannot have the least hope of success—and that while they amuse us in that Quarter they will strike a Blow to the westward I threrefore Submit to you whether it would not be Expedient that I should march the Militia who are now Collected at Half moon to Schenectady and its Vicinity if you should approve this measure and Can spare Colo Schuylers Regt. I Could wish they might be ordered to march to Half moon

Genl Rensselaers Brigade I have Ordered to march to Schenectady

I am &

[PG]

[Copy of a Letter to Genl Stark]

Gansevoort's October 15 letter to Governor Clinton informed of a prisoner captured by Van Rensselaer's detachment, and suggested that he might be of use in determining the position and objectives of the nearby British encampment.[65] Gansevoort also pledged that he would march his force up to Schenectady to await further news of the possible confrontation. Yet despite intelligence against a British attack, Gansevoort implored Clinton to forward any supplies of ammunition available.[66]

217—To George Clinton

Albany Octr 15 1781

Dear Sir, *I Yesterday went up to the New City for the Purpose of hastening on to Saraghtoga that Part of my Brigade ordered to reinforce Genl Starks—I returned in the Evening and this Morning received from Colo Van Renselaer—a Letter of which the inclosed is a Copy—The Affray it describes was occasioned by Colo Van Renselaers having made Prisoner on the Evening of the 12th Inst of a certain Fairbanks a Private of his Regt residing at the New City ~~who~~ who is commissioned as a Colo—& appointed as a Select Man under the New State (so called)—this Fellow by some Means effected his Escape & collected the Men mentioned in Colo Van Renselaers Letter.—*

As I conceive this Affair may be attended with some important Consequences—I have that proper—more especially as the Legislature are now probably convened—to write to your Exy by Express—and wod wish to have if possible particular Instructions for my ~~own~~ Conduct—in this Business

I last Night recd your Exy's Letter of the 13th by the Return of my Express—Vrooman's Regt have not been called from Schohary—and I mean to forward to that Place Colo Henry Van Renselaer with 300 of the Claverack Militia as soon as they come in—

I have ordered Genl Van Renselaer's Brigade to Schenectady—this has now become the more necessary as Genl Starks has drawn from Tryon County the two Companies of Levies under Major Logan's Command[67]*—I shall proceed to Schenectady to Morrow and issue Orders to the Officer commanding the Troops collecting there to hold them in Readiness to march whenever the movements of the Enemy may render it most necessary.—I must again mention to your Exy that our want of Ammunition & Provisions Still continues and that is of the utmost Moment we should be spedily supplied with both but particularly with ~~the first~~ Ammunition*

I am &

[Copy of a Letter to Governor Clinton 15th Octr 1781]

However, Clinton responded with not only vitriol against reliance on Vermont's defenses but that he had absolutely no ability to procure any extra supplies.[68] The same day Gansevoort wrote to Clinton, Colonel Henry Van Rensselaer reported a thwarted plot to capture Gansevoort. Mr. Tanckrey devised a plan to take Gansevoort prisoner at the ferry near Halfmoon. After gaining information from a prisoner, Van Rensselaer ordered Major Schermerhorn to proceed to the house of a Mr. Douglas where a gang was assembled. Schermerhorn attempted to surround the house but the gang opened fire and made their escape out of the back door.

218—From Henry K. Van Rensselaer

Half Moon Octor 15th 1781

Dr Genl/ Yours of the 14th I recd together with William Sander Prisoner, after receiving your Letter, I gain'd intelegence by a Prisoner that Mr Tanckrey with a party had weigh laid you at the Ferry in order to make you a prisoner; for which purpose and not knowing whither you intended to proceed I with the Advise of the field Officers detach'd a party under the command of Major Schermerhorn in order to apprehend him and his gang, the Major proceeded to the house of a Mr Douglas where they were Assembled, on his approatching and attempting to surround the House which he had compleetly effected in front but not in the rear of the House, they fir'd and made their escape out of the back doore excepting one who is a prisoner, two of our Militia Men are Wounded but I hope not mortelly, for farther perticulars I referr you to Major Schermerhorn

I could wish that you would imediately send me a Surgion

I am Sir Your Hble Servt
Henry Van Rensselaer
[PG Albany]

The attack so closely awaited by Gansevoort and his officers does not appear to happen, save for a slight instance near Balltown in which approximately one hundred British soldiers were spotted on the move.[69] However, an October 23 letter from Lord Stiring indicated that the British were in the process of moving a large force towards Crown Point[70] and Colonel Stark informed Gansevoort that multiple enemy ships had been sighted at Ticonderoga along with reports of enemy movements in the Eastbury area. Stark ended the correspondence with a wary insistence of having "no time to lose ... their stay in this quarter cannot be long."[71]

Lord Stirling, William Alexander. Engraved by G. B. Hall, c. 1860s (Gansevoort-Lansing collection. Manuscripts and Archives Division. The New York Public Library. Astor, Lenox and Tilden Foundations).

219—From Lord Stirling, William Alexander

Albany October 23d 1781

Dear Sir Yesterday evening I received Intilligence from General Stark, which he received from Lieut Colo Fletcher[72] *commanding at Fort Warner That friday last at 3 oClock PM a large body of the Enimy was landed & landing at Crown Point and that tis justly sapposed from private Intelligence the Enimy intend an excursion to the frontiers of this State &c*

The Marching of Militia without first having the object assertained is ever attended with pernicious consiquences: I desire you will therefore put your Brigade of Militia in perfect readiness to march on the first Intelligence of the Enimies advance.

The alertness with which they turned out on the late Alarm gives me a flattering prospect that should their assistance be necissary. it will be readily and chearfully offered,

I am Dear Sir with Esteem Your Most Obt Servt

Stirling MG

Brig Genl Gansewort [Albany]

220—From John Stark

Saratoga 24th Oct 1781

Dear Sir By my last information from the Northward I am told that the Enemy have six Ships at Ticonderoga, and that they had reconnoitred East bury—This Issurance to be a falacy to draw the force of the country to that quarter while their capital stroke is aimed at this place I must therefore request you to collect as many of your militia as can be immediately put in motion, and conduct or send them to this place under the care of some vegilint officer on whose despatch you can fully confide

If they have a design upon this post we have no time to lose and as their stay in this quarter cannot be long, I think they must appear as soon as tomorrow or next day at the farthest—Lose no time to fly to my assistance

I am Dear Sir your most Hum & very Obt Sert

John Stark BG

B Gnl Gansevoort [Albany]

According to Gansevoort's relay of intelligence, the British were going to mount a considerably fierce attack on northwestern New York within three days of October 25.[73] On the day of Gansevoort's orders, Colonel Wempel witnessed over 350 British soldiers in full march only fourteen miles from Schenectady.[74] The British advance, though relatively small in comparison to offensives conducted in the early phase of the war, nonetheless caught many American officers off guard, as Colonel Willett had retreated from his position (most likely due to being outnumbered).[75]

221—To Philip P. Schuyler, Henry K. Van Rensselaer and John Bleeker[76]

Albany 25th October 1781

Brigade Orders This moment I recieved ~~an~~ a Letter from General Stark at Saratoga who informs me that the Enemy are advancing in force and expects to be attacked within three days—You will therefore without delay give orders for your Regt to collect as soon possiable at ~~the~~ Half Moon with three days of provisions whare you will receive farther Orders—And send from thence Waggons to this place for such necessaries as you may stand in need of with proper returns for the Same—The Associated Exempts within the distreet of your Regt you will give the same Orders—

[Copy of Orders to Colonels Ph: Schuyler Henry K Van Rensselaer & John Bleecker]

222—From Abraham Wempel

Schonectady Octr 25th 1781

Sir Just now an other Express is Arrived who brings the Disagreable news that the Enemy are in great force and were this afternoon at 3 OClock engaged at fort Hunter[77] *A body of 350 Red Coats have been seen marching along the Road about 14 miles above this place*

We have ocasons to believe that the Enemy are strong we Expect to be Attacked this night if possible Send us some reinforcement soon—

I am Sir Yours in haste

Abm Wempel

NB the enclosed is just Come to hand for God Sake Send Some Ammunition

A W

[PG Albany]

223—James Winney to Henry Glen

Sir The Enemy are in Johnstown the last Account we have from there was that ~~our~~ Colonel Willett had lost his field Piece and that he had Retreated into the fort at that Place.[78] *I was on my way to Join him but Received the [?] Intellegance on my way which made me Retreat to this Place. I have met a Good many of this County Militia here severel of whom will go with me to Johnstown this night*

I am Sir Your Hum Servt

Jas Winney

Vidois Mills 25th Octr [1781] 8 OClock PM

There has been a Severe Ingagement

[Henry Glen Schenectady]

John Van Rensselaer's letter to Gansevoort in the first week of December expounds upon yet another situation the militia may have to soon deal with. Van Rensselaer was taken prisoner by soldiers loyal to Vermont who specifically denounced their connection with the state of New York. Rensselaer's party was claimed to have been treated "in the most Scandalous manner and abused when we arrived at Bennington where they Expected aid and assistance, They ware treated with Contempt."[79]

224—From John Van Rensselaer

St Coick Decemr 4th 1781

Dear General These are a short Narative to inform you of the Deplorable situation we are in and Redused to, Caused by the opperation and Userpation of tyrannical Ruffiens who have Disavowed alegience to the state of New York, and say they are subjects to the state of Vermont, a few Days ago I was taken prisoner by them with Colls Bratt Mr Fonda and other Gentlemen who where Carried to Bennington treated in the most Scandilus manner and abused when we arived at Bennington where they Expected aid and assistance they ware treated with Contempt by the Authority of Vermont, We Ware treated by them like Gentlemen Ware Discharged and told We Could go home about our Buisiness—yeasterday Mr Rouse of Tomhanick was taken by an armed force was Rescued on his way to this plase by a Number of faithfull true Subjects to the State of New York—I have Collected an armed force but Very Inconsiderable and mean to support our persons and property under the authority of New York at the Expence of my life against all assalts and userpation—therefore I beg leave to Intreat you sir as a Dear frind Engaged in the same Couse to give me all the Assistence with the Greatest Dispatch possable Least I shall be Redused to the Necessity of Subjecting my self to a Superior force of Ruffiens—

I am Dear Sir With Respect your Very sincere frind and Humble Servent

Jno Van Rensselaer L Col

PS you will be pleased to send to Coll Henry V Rensselaer to march with his Regiment ~~through~~ by the way of little Hosick in order to sease upon the Randells and other Villens

I should be Very Desirus of you for an answer upon the subject

General Peter Gansevorth

Albany

It is ironic that he claimed having suffered abuse at the hands of the Vermont militia, yet would, immediately following the accusation, describe them as "Gentlemen" and that most of Van Rensselaer's company were released and allowed to return to New York. He ended the correspondence by requesting additional aid from the New York militia, lest he be subject to another capture by Vermont.

Gansevoort seemed to have responded in kind; a December 6 letter to Governor Clinton requested that additional brigades be sent to support Van Rensselaer to quell an "Insurrection."[80]

225—To George Clinton

Albany 6th Decemr 1781—

Sir On the 5th Instant I received a Letter from Lt Col: John Van Rensselaer of which the inclosed is a copy in consequence where of I instantly dispatched orders to Colonels Yates & Henry K. Van Rensselaer to march their Regiments to the relief of Lt Col Van Rensselaer & for quelling the Insurrection mentioned in his Letter, copies of the Orders I also do myself the Honor of inclosing

This morning about Two OClock Mr Rouse called upon me—he left Lt Col John Van Rensselaer at 7 yesterday Evening, And sent by him expressly for the purpose of requesting farther Assistance, As it is impossible to say what consequences may result from the present disturbances and as I have not received from your Excellency any directions on this subject since the rising of the Legislature at their last meeting who I am informed have passed some resolution respecting this controversy I have thought proper to defer calling out any other part of my Brigade untill I shall hear from your

Excellency farther on this Business Mr Rouse who goes Express will deliver your Excellency this Letter to him I beg leave to refer for the particulars of his capture and proceedings of the Insurgents
I am &c
P Gansevoort
[To Governor Clinton]

Samuel Safford,[81] a major in the Vermont Green Mountain Boys, sent a letter to Gansevoort a few days after the capture of Van Rensselaer to express that all parties involved return to their origins and not pursue this incident further, "in hopes that the Contest may be settled between the two states in a Different manor."[82]

226—From Samuel Safford

Nosick Decemr 8th 1781
Gentlemen it is agreed by the People under arms at this Place that Hostilities shall cease on their part on the Condition that we have agreed on viz, that when you shall Receive orders to Return home or Disperse your men, they do likewise and that Each party Return to his Respective Place of abode and ~~Return~~ Remain unmolested for the Present in hopes that the Contest may be settled between the two states in a Different manor
I am Gentlemen your Humble Servents
Saml Safford
a True Copy
[No 2 proposal]

Judging by this response, it would appear that the Vermont Republic staged the capture of Gansevoort's men as a ploy to hurry the United States Congress into diplomatic talks guaranteeing its sovereignty over the area. The ploy had apparently worked; Colonel Peter Yates declared that his forces would withdraw from the Bennington area until Congress reached a conclusion over the existence of Vermont.[83]

227—From Peter Yates

St Coick 8th Decemr 1781
Memorandum of Proposells made by Moses Robertson General Safford and Coll Wallbrige from Bennington—that is withdraw ~~for~~ the men now under arms on their Part if We will with draw ours on our side untill a finell determination of Congress is finelly known—they Ingage as far as lays in their Power to stop taxes and Laws in the Western union—In answer to the above Proposell We thought it Necessary to Come to articals of Sessation of arms still we Recevd, an answer from General Gansavort on the subject—as We expect Coll Henry Van Rensselaer by the way of Little Nosick, we Could not answer for his conduit ill he has word from us by Exprass—
[No 1 proposal]

From Poughskeepie, Governor Clinton sent an extended letter to Gansevoort on December 11 describing the situation with Vermont.[84] He acknowledged as a militia leader that Gansevoort's securing of the New York frontier far superseded any orders that he could issue himself. In regards to the incident involving the capture of Van Rensselaer, Clinton believed that the incident was not "countenanced by the Authority of the usurped Government of Vermont."[85]

228—From George Clinton

Poughkeepsie Decr 11th 1781

Sir Your Letter of the 6th Instant with its enclosures was handed to me, by Mr Rous, on Sunday last. The Legislature at their late Meeting entered into certain Resolutions respecting the Conduct and Usurpations of the Inhabitants of the Grants and declarative of their Sense on the Proceedings of Congress with respect to that Part of this State; but no Measures were adopted which can influence your Conduct relative to the Insurrection which has taken Place within the limits of your Brigade.

Your Duty on this Occasion is so clearly pointed out by the Militia Law as to supercede the necessity of any particular Order from me. I perfectly approve of your Conduct and have only to add that should the force already detached prove insufficient to quell the Insurrection, you will make such addition to it as to render it effectual. I have transmitted to Genl Rensselaer the Information contained in Lt Col Rensselaers Letter and have directed him in case it should be necessary on your application to give assistance from ~~your~~ his Brigade.

Altho' it would appear from Colo Rensselaers Letter that the Insurgents were not countenanced by the Authority of the usurped Government of Vermont, yet I think it my Duty, lest you should be deceived by a false confidence in their Conduct, to apprize you that the Legislature of that pretended State did on the 19th of October last by an Act which appears to be unanimous reject the Resolution of Congress of the 20th of Augt last respecting the extension of their assumed Jurisdiction "as destructive of their universal Harmony & agreement and a violation of the solemn Compact entered into by Articles of Union & Confederation; and recommended to the Authority in every Part of the State to remain firm in the support of Government and the faithful execution of the Laws notwithstanding the various Measures taken to create Divisions and Discord among them"

I am Sir With great Respect Your Most Obedt Servt
Geo: Clinton
Brigr Genl Gansevoort [Albany]

In spite of the shaky truce the soldiers initiated upon release of Van Rensselaer, Vermont had gone forward and rejected the New York Congress's August 20 resolution regarding the borders and sovereignty of the state of New York. Clinton further interpreted this as a direct violation of the Articles of Confederation and deemed Vermont to be an illegitimate country and in direct conflict with the United States itself.

It was from this juncture that Gansevoort was forced to act upon the situation; Colonel Yates noted that the Vermont soldiers in New York territory outnumbered the local New York garrison almost two to one[86] and Vermont Governor Thomas Chittenden informed Major Stark to suspend his operations in the western theater.[87]

229—From Peter Yates

St. Coick 12th December 1781—

Dear General— In your last you left me at Liberty to enter into an agreement I thought best subject to His Excellency's Will, as nothing of that is likely to be done, they being fill with Deceit as you will see by the enclosed Affidavit and as by my Orders I was sent here for the Purpose of quelling the Insurrection, I beg to have the Troops forwarded with all Speed as I am weak, only about 80 Men, and the Insurrectors about 146, as to the People of the Grants I cannot from every Information I can get, believe that they will do any more than make a great Show and encourage the others on—as the Rioters are secured in a Block House, I beg you will send me a Field Piece with some Artillerymen, for we cannot think of leaving the Ground, [?] the Matter can be brought to a Decision arrive shall all be taken immediately by the other Party and be obliged to comply to their Will—General Stark has offered if Occasion should require he would march his whole Camp. I make no Doubt Sir, as you have ordered our the most of your Brigade that you will take the Command—If not Sir, I beg that some particular Gentleman would come up immediately and assist in Council on particular Circumstance—as the Season of the Year is troublesome, the Men is very uneasy wanting either to go home or to fight them. I expected some Answer as to Provision mentioned in my Last as to farther Particulars I refer you to the Bearers Messr Bratt & Van Ransalear

I am Sir &c

Peter Yates Coll—

Genl Gansevoort

Copy

[available from the Papers of the Continental Congress]

230—Thomas Chittenden to John Stark

Arlington Decbr 15th 1781

Dear Sir/ I have consulted my Council on the perplexed Situation of this State, and have resolved to call the Legislature thereof to meet at Bennington as soon as maybe at which Time they will doubless consult such Measures as may tend for the Peace and Tranquility of this and the united States

In the mean Time I earnestly request that you write to the Officers of N.York that are daily making Depredations to the West to Suspend any further Operations of that kind until the Assembly meet and that if they do not comply; you will not interfere with your Troops—And I do assure you that, if they comply with said Request, and liberate the Prisoners they have taken, I will suspend the Exercise of Jurisdiction or Law over any Person or Persons who profess themselves Subjects of New York during that Time

I am Sir with Sentiments of Esteem Your most Obedt and most humble Servant

Thoms Chittenden

Honble Brigr General Stark

Late December saw hostilities increase between Vermont and New York, with Vermont artillery units moving to support the 140 men already in Central New York.[88] Ebenezer Walbridge[89] sent a flurry of correspondence to Van Renesslaer and other New York militia officers in the area demanding a cessation of hostilities towards Vermont, release of any prisoners captured, compensation for any damages caused by New York militia in the Vermont claimed boundaries, and influence in United States Congress to approve the inclusion of Vermont as a sovereign part of the confederacy.[90]

Walbridge also informed Gansevoort that the citizens pledging allegiance to Vermont's cause were building fortifications in the event that a conflict was to escalate. For the time being, it seemed appropriate to release the Vermont prisoners in respects to the republic's demands, in order to stall for time and prevent any immediate or unnecessary bloodshed.

231—Ebenezer Walbridge to Henry K. Van Rensselaer

Maple Town 17th Decr 1781

Sir Yours of this Day to Genl Safford has been duly Considered, and as you are pleased to Say, that you are not authorised to Treat with any but Subjects to the State of New York It is Immagined there is no such opposed to you—Those in Opposition to the Authority of New York, now in Arms, Inhabitants of this Territory Claimed by your State, who profess to one Allegiance to Vermont, now propose for your Consideration, and request your immediate answer viz.

1t That you release all the prisoners which is in your Custody, belonging to the Claims in dispute,

2d That you make good all Damages sustained by Individuals by the Troops under your Command.

3d That all those Inhabiting said Territory respectively professing to one Allegiance to New York & Vermont, shall rest Quiet and Unmolested in their Persons and properties, until the dispute shall be finally Adjusted by Congress, or such other Tribunal as shall be mutually agreed on by the Contending Power.

I am Sir Your most obt Huml Servant.

E Walbridge Collonel Commandt

Col. Henry Van Ransellear

Gansevoort's correspondence closing 1781 was of a less hopeful tone. He announced that various garrisons were ready to march against the dissenters, and that a specific "Blockhouse" had been cleared of insurgents in what appeared to be a quick skirmish.[91] A review of the following few days is given: Colonel Yates had issued an order of retreat from the frontier, General Starks claimed illness and was unable to bring his troops to the front lines, and that the majority of the forces had as of the date of writing holed up in the town of Schacktehoke to wait out the approaching winter weather.[92] The last few days of the year ended in somewhat of a stalemate; the militia was more or less unable to conduct normal operations due to need of supplies and the onset of harsh weather—the towns bordering on high insurgent activity were unable to properly defend themselves due to similar reasons.

232—To George Clinton

21 decr 1781

Sir Your Excellency's Letter of the 11th Inst. ~~I did~~ sent by Mr Rous I did not receive until the 15th in the Evening. on the 16th I sat off for Saratoga and applied to Genl Starks for a field piece and some of his Troops in order to assist those of my Brigade at Schacktehoke and Hoseck detached there for the purpose of suppressing the Insurrection—I was induced to make this Application in Consequence of a Letter from Genl Starks to Coll Yates dated the 8th Inst. wherein he ~~voluntarily~~ declares his Readiness to march his whole Garrison (in order to suppress the Insurrection) where occasion might require and of which he desired Coll Yates to give him the earliest Intelligence ~~Copy of which Letter is inclosed.~~

With a Field Piece & a few Troops from Genl Starks added to the Militia then on the ground I flattered myself I should have been able to dislodge the Insurgents from the Blockhouse in which they were posted & to have dispersed ~~them~~ or captivated them—

But Gen. Starks informed me that the he was disposed to give me did yet he did not think it justifiable with an order of Genl Heath, and at the same Time declared that ~~most of~~ his Men were almost naked— ~~and therefore~~ Whether these were the true Reasons of his Refusal or on Account of the Letter he received from Chittenden dated the 15th Inst. ~~(of which a Copy is inclosed) your Excellency will Con is inclosed) your Excellency will be~~ requesting him not to interfere with his Troops, your Excellency will be able to determine—

Upon this I ~~repaired~~ went from Saratoga in order to take the Command of the Militia at Schacktehoke and Hoseck— ~~On~~ shortly after my Arrival at the House of Charles Toll at Schacktehoke the Sheriff of Albany (with a Magjstiate & some private gentlemen) came there ~~and~~ with a Warrant granted by Mr Justice Yates ~~ag~~ in order to apprehend a Number of the Insurgents. We had not been above half an Hour in the House before the Militia on their Retreat from the House of Coll John V. Renseler from the White House consisting of about 80 Men, arrived at Mr Tolls. This Retreat was ~~in Consequence of Intellig~~ ordered by Coll Yates ~~who~~ in Consequence of Orders I had given him not to risk an Action unless he had a Prospect of Success and not to ingage if the ~~was too much over powered by Numb~~ disparity of Numbers against him was too great ~~which~~ This appeared to be the Case from the Intelligence he received previous to the Retreat, which was that the Militia of the pretended State of Vermont ~~were~~ consisting of at least 500 Men with a field piece had joined the Insurgents and were on their March and within a few Miles of Coll John Renselars House & the White House where our Troops were stationed—And Coll Henry Van Rensselar informs me that the Vermonters ~~were~~ appeared in Sight of the White House within one Mile when he left it

In this Situation of Matters I deemed it advisable to retire 5 Miles farther to the Town of Schacktehoke where the Men might be housed from the Inclemency of the cold Weather and to prevent the Interception of our Retreat ~~as this were Enemy Vermonter &~~ in Case the Insurgents ~~were divided~~ (who had divided their Force) ~~and from~~ should advance which from their Superior Numbers I had reason to expect ~~they march rapidly~~

On my Arrival at the Town of Schacktehoke

Alderman P Yates made out Process agt. 4 Insurgents whom we had taken and sent them to goal.

I then wrote a Letter to the Officer commanding the ~~Vermonters~~ Insurgents dated the 18 decemr requesting him to inform me by what Authority they came with such a military into the interior Parts of this State and the Design of it. Altho I was well satisfied as to both in my own

Mind, yet if I could ~~have~~ obtain~~ed~~ an Answer, I supposed it might ~~have~~ answer~~ed~~ some good Purposes at a Future day before the Legislature or ~~and~~ Congress I waited for an Answer until the next day the 19th Inst. ~~until~~ near Sun Sett, but receiving none and the Messengers ~~of~~ who carried my Letter not returning I ordered the Militia to be discharged. To which I was induced from ~~a Number of various~~ Considerations.

With ~~Wilt~~ Only 80 Militia who had already been a considerable Time from Home unsupplied with Provisions I could not expect to ~~oppose~~ engage the Insurgents with the lest Prospect of Success. To augment our Number in due Season to answer any salutary Purposes I deemed impossible. Out of the Regiments of Coll Yates, Henry Van Renselaer Major Taylor & Van Vechten only [ ] Men appeared on the ground—From ~~out of~~ That of Coll Van Vechten were only himself & few Officers and one private. ~~and~~ Add to this that had my whole Brigade with that of Coll Genl Rensselar been called out on the Occasion I am confident that they would not have been sufficient to suppress the Insurrection as the People from the Grants were all ordered out ~~against us~~ to aid the Insurgents and a large Body of them in Force already on their March ~~towards us~~ with a field Piece towards us.—

I was induced to believe that ~~the pretended State of~~ Vermont did not mean to interfere or assist the Insurgents but from the Letters of Chittenden & the Officers under him ~~Copies~~ which are inclosed (and some which are in Possession of Coll. Yates which will be transmitted to your Excellency as soon as I obtain them) and the actual Movement of their Troops against us even on this Side of the 20 Mile Line I ~~am now fully~~ was at Length ~~fully conceived~~ undeceived. This being the Case I thought it ~~exped~~ most expedient upon the whole to discharge the Militia and advise your Excellency of every Thing relative to the Matter in order that your Excellency, the Legislature, or Congress ~~might~~ may adopt some speedy and effectual Measures in Consequence thereof.

The Inhabitants residing in the districts of Hoseck & Schacktehoke (and especially those who have taken an active Part against the Insurgents) are in a very precarious Situation—Numbers of their complained to me on the Subject—~~and~~ they say that they ~~expect~~ daily expect to be taken by the people of the grants & that they will be ~~obleged~~ reduced to the Alternative of either to ~~suff~~ swear Allegiance to Vermont or being obleged to abandon their ~~Homes~~ Habitations—

& that several of them had been already reduced to that dilemma.

I promised to State their Cases to your Excellency ~~&~~ assuring them that this Government or Congress would undoubtedly ~~without the least Delay~~ adopt some speedy vigorous & effectual Measures for their Relief. Alderman Yates ~~who was with me at Schacktehoke~~ has taken two Depositions which are inclosed & is ~~expects some~~ to take more from ~~some~~ Persons whom he expects shortly in Town for the Purpose. These he informs me will Seem to prove that the ~~People of the Grants are~~ pretended State of Vermont is in actual Alliance with the Enemy. ~~As soon as these depositions are taken they will be transmitted to your Excellency.~~ I have ordered ~~Major Taylor &~~ the ~~other~~ officers who did not turn out on this Occasion to be put in Arrest—

I am your Excellencys most obed & very Hum Servt

[PG Albany]

[George Clinton]

P.S. I this Moment received Coll Wallbridges Answer ~~of the~~ dated the 19 to mine of the 18th Inst which I have also the Honor to inclose—

Though this must have seemed incredibly troubling to the New York militia, word would spread throughout the United States and reach General Washington himself. The beginning of the next year would see Washington personally intervening via correspondence with Vermont leaders to ensure security in the disputed territories. If not, Vermont may well have been inclined to hold out for another year or two against the New York militia, while the Western areas of the state could still be threatened by the large British forces seen organizing only a few months ago.

CHAPTER EIGHT

1782: Protecting New York State

The year 1782 was a watershed moment for the American Revolution. Following the defeat of Cornwallis's army at Yorktown, Virginia, in October 1781, the British Parliament was beginning to turn against King George III's wishes to continue financing the war. The British treasury was in dire straits, and the American rebellion inspired other discontented British colonials around the world to protest and rebel. The success of the American army and the French navy ensured that the alliance would hold strong and that the French were craving British territories of their own. The individual state governments were finally confident to negotiate over the structure of the independent American States and offical British recognition of their sovereignty.

However, 1782 did not mark the end of the war, especially for the American garrisons and state militias in New England. British soldiers still held spotty tracts of territory in New England, and were still making minor incursions into the southern colonies with mixed success. British diplomacy with certain Indian tribes along the 1763 Proclamation borders ensured their continued loyalty against the Americans, temporarily halting colonial expansion west of the Hudson. In the years after the American's disastrous invasions of British Canada in the winter of 1775, the British had solidified a front and had been sending small forces of raiders to ransack American villages and coerce loyalists in the area to enlist in the British army.

Beyond the threat of the British, the very territorial integrity of the colonies was under attack. The area of Vermont had been declared an independent republic in 1777 with the support of Ethan Allen and his Green Mountain Boys. Though Allen and his cohorts despised the British in the open, the Vermont government had good reason to bide time and conduct diplomacy with both the Continental Congress and the British Empire. Vermont's original claimants had declared that parts of New York belonged to the new republic, yet the great influence of New York gentry and involvement in the Continental Congress led to the refusal to recognize Vermont as an independent entity unto itself, instead standing by the boundaries dictated in the ambiguous New Hampshire Grants. In a state of desperation and stubborn need for recognition among the other colonies, brief clashes with New York and Vermont militias were an increasingly common occurrence. Certain members of the Vermont Republic even entertained the idea of being reabsorbed into the British Empire, with the possibility of acquiring their New York land claims at the end of the war.

George Washington's firm yet cautious letter to Thomas Chittenden, the governor of the Vermont Republic, confirmed how delicate this diplomatic situation was. He began by stating that he would like nothing better than to see the citizens of the Vermont Republic incorporated, with "the just rights of the people of every part fully established."[1] However,

Washington through a thin veil of gracious language questioned the validity of the Vermont claims on New York by stating that although the Continental Congress were willing to confirm Vermont as a part of the union of independent American states, the new state would be "confined to certain described boundaries,"[2] referring to the New Hampshire land grant of 1777. This would mean that Vermont's acceptance of the New York land claims would be a primary requirement of Vermont for confederate incorporation. Washington (and perhaps most members of Congress) assumed the claims outside of the New Hampshire land grants to be a "more political Manoeuvre, than one in which you conceived yourselves justifiable."[3] Regardless of the motivations, Vermont's acceptance of the New Hampshire Grant boundaries could not be justified if it was to incorporate itself into the Confederacy. Vermont's accession to New York's boundaries would be seen as a landmark in the fledgling nation, as Vermont would become the first state recognized in the Confederacy that was not founded prior to the conflict with Britain. By doing so, it would clearly show not only that the government was powerful enough to restrict an independent entity's challenge to land and thereby dispel any citizens concern of territorial integrity; the incorporation of Vermont would show that the fledging government was willing to acquiesce to certain demands from discontented autonomous areas provided they had a historically legal claim to those demands.

233—George Washington to Thomas Chittenden

Philadelphia, January 1, 1782.

Sir I received your favor of the 14th November by Mr. Brownson. You cannot be at a loss to know why I have not heretofore, and why I cannot now, address you in your public Character, or answer you in mine. But the confidence which you have been pleased to repose in me, gives me an opportunity of offering you my sentiments, as an individual wishing most ardently to see the peace and Union of this Country preserved, and the just rights of the people of every part fully established.

It is not my business, neither do I think it necessary, now to discuss the origin of the right of a number of Inhabitants, to that tract of Country formerly distinguished by the name of the New Hampshire Grants, and now known by that of Vermont. I will take it for granted that their right was good, because Congress by their resolve of the 7th August imply it, and by that of the 21st. are willing fully to confirm it: provided the new state is confined to certain described boundaries. It appears therefore to me, that the dispute of boundary is the only one that exists and that that being removed, all further difficulties would be removed also, and the matter terminated to the satisfaction of all parties. Now I would ask you candidly, whether the Claim of the people of Vermont, was not for a long time confined solely, or very nearly, to that tract of Country which is described in the Resolve of Congress of the 21st. of August last, and whether agreable to the tenor of your own letter to me, the late extension of your Claim upon New Hampshire and New York, was not a more political Manoeuvre, than one in which you conceived yourselves justifiable. If my first question be answered in the affirmative, it certainly bars your new Claim, and if my Second be well founded, your end is answered, and you have nothing to do but withdraw your Jurisdiction to the confines of your old limits, and obtain an acknowledgement of Independance and Sovereignty, under the Resolve of the 21st. of August for so much Territory as does not interfere with the ancient established Bounds of New York New Hampshire and

Massachusetts. I persuade myself you will see and acquiesce in the reason, the Justice and indeed the necessity of such a decision.

You must consider, sir, that the point now in dispute, is of the utmost political importance to the future Union and peace of this great Country. The state of Vermont, if acknowledged, will be the first new one admitted into the Confederacy, and if sufferd to encroach upon the Ancient established Boundaries of the adjacent ones, will serve as a precedent for others, which it may hereafter be expedient to set off, to make the same unjustifiable demands. Thus, in my private Opinion, while it behoves the Delegates of the states now confederated, to do ample justice to a Body of people, sufficiently respectable by their numbers, and entitled by other Claims to be admitted into that Confederation, it becomes them also to attend to the interests of their Constituents, and see, that under the appearance of Justice to one, they do not materially injure the rights of others. I am apt to think this is the prevailing opinion of Congress, and that your late extension of Claim, has, upon the principles I have above mentioned, rather diminished than increased your Friends; and that if such extension should be persisted in, it will be made a common cause, and not considered as only affecting the rights of those States immediately interested in the loss of Territory, a loss of too serious a nature not to claim the attention of any people.

There is no calamity within the compass of my foresight, which is more to be dreaded, than a necessity of coercion on the part of Congress, and consequently every endeavour should be used to prevent the execution of so disagreeable a measure. It must involve the ruin of that State against which the resentment of the others is pointed.

I will only add a few Words, upon the subject of the negociations which have been carried on between you and the Enemy in Canada and in New York. I will take it for granted, as you assert it, that they were so far innocent that there never was any serious intention of joining Great Britain in their attempts to subjugate your Country; but it has had this certain bad tendency, it has served to give some ground to that delusive opinion of the Enemy, and upon which they in great measure found their hopes of success, that they have numerous Friends among us, who only want a proper opportunity to shew themselves openly, and that internal disputes and Feuds will soon break us in pieces; at the same time the seeds of distrust and Jealousy are scattered among ourselves by a conduct of this kind. If you are sincere in your professions, these will be additional motives for accepting the terms which have been offered (and which appear to me equitable) and thereby convincing the common Enemy, that all their expectations of disunion are vain, and that they have been worsted at their Weapon, deception.

As you unbosomed yourself to me, I thought I had the greater right of speaking my sentiments openly and candidly to you, I have done so, and if they should produce the effects which I most sincerely wish, that of an honorable and amicable adjustment of a matter which if carried to hostile lengths may destroy the future happiness of my Country, I shall have attained my end, while the Enemy will be defeated of theirs. Believe me to be with great respect

Sir Your Most Obt Hum Servt

GWashington

[appears in the George Washington Papers at the Library of Congress 1741–1799—memory.loc.gov]

Washington was apparently willing to overlook Vermont's negotiations with Great Britain as part of the "political Manoeuvre," the very premise that Vermont was engaging in such negotiations was encouraging British hopes that loyalists in New England could be roused to fight against the Continental Army. Such negotiations might continue at a more beneficial pace by Continental Congress but only as further evidence that Vermont drop their claims against New York in good faith.

Washington's style of writing on this matter was intentionally in a diplomatic tone as he hoped to prevent an unnecessary spread of the theater of war. As the British lost their main force in the south, the idea was to focus on strengthening Canadian defenses and conducting border raids. As the year progressed, Gansevoort's letters confirmed the necessity not for a major engagement against the British-Indian forces, but instead a defensive policy of raid prevention.

By securing Vermont, Washington hoped that the consensus of the British generals was to abandon their ideas of impressing or securing border settlements perceived to be British, or of wavering loyalties. With the end of negotiations between the Vermont Republic and the British army, the British would have to spread their forces to ensure the stability of the Vermont-Canadian border. By doing so, the raids on the Hudson River Valley and Western New York settlements could dwindle in both frequency and ferocity.

Brigadier General Peter Gansevoort, while having secured his name among both the ranks of the Revolutionary Army and the New York gentry following the siege at Fort Schuyler in 1777, was still finding great difficulty in securing the Hudson River Valley. With the Continental government running on little other than French and Dutch loans, the state seemed in favor of downsizing the Continental Army in favor of the New York militia. Gansevoort would find his responsibility in the militia significantly more pronounced than when he was an officer in the Continental Army.

On March 1, Gansevoort communicated with Governor George Clinton urging that court-martials and disciplinary actions within Gansevoort's camp be dealt with as soon as possible.[4] While Gansevoort petitioned for an extension of the Regimental Court's rights to discipline unruly soldiers, the likelihood of such an authority existing for the remainder of the year would be under considerable stress. Many officers stationed in the area were looking forward to payment and release from their military obligations; the lack of funds reaching the militia no doubt made them all the more eager to avoid normal duties. Gansevoort seemed to share these suspicions as he stated he was "...convinced that many weighty objections be against this measure but the consideration of the Difference of expence ought I conceive to outweigh them all especially when it is next to an impossibility for the Officers to attend..."[5] Gansevoort also expressed concern over the inability of the Continental Army to issue orders or request supplies from the local militia. Requests made between Continental and state forces occasionally resulted in unnecessary paperwork and the coordination of both hierarchies to confirm such orders. This unnecessarily bureaucratic process robbed both entities of time and money.

234—To George Clinton

Albany 1st March 1782

Copy) *I lately ordered a General Court Martial for the Trial of Delinquents in my Brigade to convene at this place but have prolonged the time upon a representation from the Gentlemen who ware to form it & a number of other Officers sitting forth that they are not able from the reduced circumstances to be at the expences necessarily incurred in the attendance on General Court Martial occasioned by their being called & obliged to remain for long Periods of Time at a considarable distance from their places of residance—I would therefore submit to your Excellency the Propriety of requesting the Legislature to make provision for extending the powers of Regimental Courts Martial & if they conceive it right leave a discretion some where of appointing Regimental or General Courts Martial as may be most expedient I am convinced that many weighty objections be agt this measure but the consideration of the Difference of expence ought I conceive to outwiegh them all especially when it is next to an impossibility for the Officers to attend as the Law stands at present at the same time I would wish to be understood that this provision should have a Limitation Just be suffered to exist longer then necessaty requires it*

I would also submit to your Excellency the propriety of requesting the Legislation to make some alteration in the Militia Law respecting the Corps of Exempts many inconvinînces arise from their not being subject to the orders ~~to~~ of the Officers Commandg Regiments one in particular

By the United States in Congress assembled

March 6. 1782

Resolved

That Col. Gansevoort be informed that although Congress have a high sense of his military abilities and courage particularly displayed in the defence of Fort Schuyler in 1777. yet it is impracticable with the present arrangement of the Army to reinstate him therein, without manifest injury to other Officers he having been deranged as a Junior Colonel of that line and his Regiment incorporated agreeably to the principles prescribed in the Resolutions of Congress of the 3d. and 21st. of October 1780—

Chas. Thomson Secy

A true Copy from the Record in the War Office

Charles Thomson to Peter Gansevoort, Jr., 6 March 1782 (Gansevoort-Lansing collection. Manuscripts and Archives Division. The New York Public Library. Astor, Lenox and Tilden Foundations).

is that Brigadiers when they Issue Genl Orders in which the Exempts are included to transmit Copies to every Captain the unnessary expence attending this Business might be spared to the State and ~~also~~ almost every other objection now existing against the Institution removed by making them subject to the Officer Commandg the Regt

[Copy to His Excellency Governour Clinton]

The end of the winter season still had Gansevoort seeking reinstatement into the army. Unfortunately the Secretary of Congressman Charles Thomson[6] informed Gansevoort that even with Gansevoort's well-documented "military abilities and courage," that Congress still could not reinstate him "without manifest injury to other Officers."[7]

235—From Charles Thomson

By the United States in Congress assembled

March 6. 1782

Resolved That Col. Gansevoort be informed that although Congress have a high Sense of his military abilities and courage particularly displayed in the defence of Fort Schuyler in 1777 yet it is impracticable with the present arrangement of the Army to reinstate him—therein, without manifest injury to other Officers he having been deranged as a Junior Colonel of that line and his Regiment incorporated agreeably to the principle prescribed in the Resolution of Congress of the 3d and 21st of October 1780—

Chas Thomson Secy

A true Copy from the Record in the War Office

As Gansevoort watched over his command at Albany, he received news from his outpost possible British activities in the Hudson River Valley. On April 20 Gansevoort received word from Schenectady indicating that the American-allied Oneida were coerced into meeting local British officers for diplomatic talks.[8] Upon suspecting a possible ambush, the Oneida fled towards American encampments, losing one of their own in the chase. The Oneida believed the British detachment of two hundred men would move either one of two ways, that "...their intention is the westine Ballton or Thanistegayone...."[9] Gansevoort's response to the information was to prepare his men for a skirmish.

236—From Abraham Wempel

Schenectady April 20th—1782

Dear General Some of the Onida Indians who where going on the Hunt fell in with three Enemy Indians at the Sacondago River about 16 Miles North of Ballton who Spoke to Each other a Cross the River, the Enemy desired our Indians to go down the river where their Main body was to Speake with them which ours consanted to do but instead of going to them they made for this placee with all Spead. there was Six of our Indians one of which fell Back by reason of not being able to keep up with the others, which Indian (to wit, the one that fell back Saw about 200 of the Enemy about 8 Miles North of Ballton Mostly with Green Cloaths on the indian says he cannot Judge whether their intention is the westine Ballton or Thanistegayone. these indians are Just arived the three Indians at Sacondago river they saw yesterday Morning, the 200 where seen this Morning—

I have given orders for all my men to be in parfect readyness with their arms and aCoutrements if I can find the Enemies intention I shall March part of them there shall give you all the inteligenes I Get of the Enemies movements
I am Dr General your Obiedt: H: Servt
Abm: Wempel
To B General Gansevoort [Albany]

The Oneida reports appeared to have been accurate. The next day a British raid had captured civilian Jacob Smith and his son from a neighboring community of Freehold. Along with the Smiths, the British also confiscated the family's horses and bedding. Gansevoort was further advised to keep arms ready and ears open. The raid was said to be of an unknown number, though it is possible it was part of the British body discovered by the Oneidas a few days earlier.

One particularly interesting mention in this ordeal was the brief story of Thomas Barker. Barker was also apprehended by the British during the same series of raids. However, unlike the Smiths, he was marched about twelve miles out into the frontier and then released. Barker claimed that "...there must have been More of the Enemy which have kept themselves in the Woods as he heard Wistling and Calls."[10] This may have been an attempt by the British to feign dwindling numbers in the areas, and relied on Barker's release and subsequent testimony to intimidate American troups nearby.

237—From Anthony Van Bergen

Coxtractry 21th: Aprill 1782
Sir I have received a Letter from Lt: Coll Dubois Informing me that Yesterday the Enemy had taken Jacob Smith and his son from Freehold, their Numbers and other particulars not known. He farther Informs me that he had ordered the three Lower Companies of my Regt to be Warned to March Early this Morning. I have Since the receipt of the Letter of Coll Dubois been Informed the Enemy had taken 2 More to wit Thomas Barber and Casper Clarius the Latter of which it is said they have Suffered to return Just now received Information that Coll Dubois with 40 Men was in pursuit—I have sent a Party to Make Discoveries to the West of us and ordered 2 of the Companies to be ready upon a Miniuts Warning
I am Sir your Humble Ser
Anthony Van Bergen
To Genl: Gansevort
22d Aprill
PS This Morning one of the party sent yesterday returned and brings the following Account, that Jacob Smith and his son are taken and Carried off with two of his horses and all his Bedding Then Thomas Barker is returned whom they had taken along about 12 Mile to the place Called Eycken Bergh and then Dismissed him. Then said Barker says he was taken about 4 Mile above freehold by one White Man and 2 Indians the white man was Dressed Gentely and had a Gold Lace Hat Examined him Concerning one Cole and others. He farther says there Must have been More of the Enemy which have keept themselves in the Woods as he heard Wistling and Calls
AVB
[PG Albany]

Spring continued to test Gansevoort's leadership skills. General orders were issued on April 23 announcing a general court martial over which Gansevoort would preside, and that it ultimately found three men guilty of British espionage. With the approval from Governor Clinton, Gansevoort condemned the three men to death.[11]

238—From Robert Benson

General Orders Poughkeepsie 23d April 1782

Peter FitzPatrick,[12] *Joseph Beatty and John Parker, charged with being Spies, for having adhered to the Enemy, coming from them and secretly lurking in this State, having been severally tried by a General Court Martial, consisting of Officers of the Militia of this State, whereof Brigadier General Gansevoort was President, convicted of the Crime aforesaid and sentenced to suffer Death.—His Excellency the Governor approves of the proceedings of the Court confirms the Sentences and directs that the Sherif of the County of Albany*[13] *do cause the same to be carried into execution, at the usual Place, on the thirtieth Day of April Instant between the Hours of nine and twelve in the forenoon, by hanging the said several Culprits by the Neck until they shall be dead;—for which purpose a Copy of these Orders shall be his Warrant.*

A true Copy compared with the original in his Excellency's the Governors orderly Book.

Robt Benson ADC.

This would continue over the course of the 1780s; Ezekiel Taylor's reports in July indicate that about seven civilians within the area were well known "Good Whigs very Dangerous persons for harbouring and assisting our enemies."[14]

Four months after the New Hampshire grants insurrection, many experienced officers formerly under Gansevoort had defected to the state of Vermont and were currently waging their own operations independent of the Continental command.[15] Gansevoort was certainly aware of the lack of officers for quite some time, as a letter received from Major James Ashton[16] proclaimed that Gansevoort had allowed him to take up command over a regiment which had lost the previous field officer to Vermont.[17]

239—From James Ashton

Cambridge 27th April 1782

Sr Yours of the 18th I Receiv'd 20th with the Acts of the Legislature, and as their is no acting Field officer in the Ridgmt. but mySelf (and as their was no orders to the Contrary) I called on they former Capt to assist me in Executing them, would be glad to know whether those who Excepted under Vermount is to be Continued or no.

Dr Sr I am greatly oblighed to you for the Honour you confered on me in giving me the Command of the Ridgt. and am Sorry my Infermityes Interupts me in Continuing in my Commition, the Bearer Col: Vanwoert Can inform your Honour I am Much Afflicted with the Palsy; and Rhumetism, and would take it as a Great favour if you would Except of my Resignation

this from Dr Sr Your very Humbl Sert to Commd

Jams Ashton—Major

[PG B Genl in the City of Albany]

May 1782 finally showed progression in Gansevoort's efforts back into the higher officer ranks of the new Continental Army. As Gansevoort planned to travel to Philadelphia to visit Congress of the Confederation, William Duer, a member of the Board of War, had released a flood of letters of introduction personally appealing to state congressmen and other officers such as Major General Benjamin Lincoln. The letters defended Gansevoort's position by again stating his gallantry in the defense of Fort Schuyler, and that because of these actions he should rightfully be declared Colonel and Commander of the fort. Duer's letter to New Jersey Congressman Elias Boudinot[18] even stated that Gansevoort deserved to be put "...on a Similar Footing with the Military Governours of Forts in Europe," and that his ability as an officer "...gave a decisive Turn to the affair of this Country."[19]

240—William Duer to Elias Boudinot

Albany 31t May 1782

Sir General Gansevoort, who sustained with so much Firmness and Address the Siege of Ft Schuyler when Genl Burgoines Army penitrated into this Country will have the Honor of delivering to you this Letter

He wishes to have the sence of Congress fully Exprest on their resolution appointing him Col: Commdt of Fort Schuyler with the Rank of Col: in the Army of the United States—As I was both a Member of the Board of War when this resolution was agreed to there, and in Congress when it was Acted upon, I can with Truth Assure that their Intention was to give a Substantial as well as Honorable Tistomony of the Sence they Entertained of this Services and to make such a provision for this Officer as he might feel the Effects of even in time of Peace, by putting him on a Similar Footing with the Military Governours of Forts in Europe—I therefore trust that that the Original Disign of this appointment will not be forgot and that we may still retain him in the Line of the Army as an Officer whose firmness in holding out a Garrison against a powerful Force first gave a decisive Turn to the affair of this Country where they ware the most unpromising aspect

I have the Honor to be with much Esteem Sir Your most Obl Hum Servt

Wm Duer

Honble Elias Boudinot Esqr

Member of Congress for the State of Jersey

241—William Duer to Samuel Huntington

Albany 31th May 1782

Sir This Letter will be delivered to you by General Gansevoort, the Gallant Defender of Fort Schuyler, at the time Genl Burgoine Army was penetrating this Country, he goes to Congress, in order to have their sence fully Exprest on their Resolution, appointing him to the Command of that Garrison—As I was a member of the Board of War at the time the Resolution in his favor was past. And in Congress when they concurred with it, he wishes me to declare in what Light I Considered it. I think it a duty I owe to the public, and an Act of Justice to General Gansevoort to Assure you, that the intention of the Board when they reported to Congress the Resolution appointing that Officer to the Command of Ft Schuyler was to give a Substantial, as well as

Honorable mark of the Approbation of Congress, and that the Honorable Body Concurred in the Sentiments & Views of their Committee so far as I could Judge, by those who spoke on this Subject—I therefore trust that General Gansevoort will not find any Difficulty, in having a memorial which he purposes presenting to Congress on this Subject, decided upon in such a manner, as will give retain him in the Service of his Country, in the Line of the Army, for which he feels that Enthusisms which Characterises a Good Officer

I have the Honor to be with great respect your Obt Servt

Wm Duer

Honble Sam Huntington

242—William Duer to Benjamin Lincoln

Albany 31th May 1782

Sir General Gansevoort who Sustained with so much firmness the Siege of Fort Schuyler, when Genl Burgoines Army penitrated the Country will have the Honor of delivering you this Letter

He wishes to have the sence of Congress Exprest on their resolution in appointing him Colo Commandt of Fort Schuyler with the Rank of Colonel in the Army of the United States. As I was both a member of the Board of War, When the Resolution was agreed to there; and in Congress when it was Acted upon, I can with Truth Assure you that their intention was to give a Substantial as well as Honorable Testimony of the Sence they Entertained of his Services and to make such a Provision for this Officer as he might feel the Efferts of Even in time of Peace, by putting him on a Similiar Footing with the Military Governours of Forts in Europe; I therefore Trust that the Original Design of this Appointment will not be forgot, and that General Gansevoort (though unavoidably thrown out of the (Line of the State) will still be retained in the Line of the Army, in which he was appointed a Colonel by the Express resolution of Congress

I have Honor to be Sir Your Obt Hum Servt

Wm Duer

Honble Major Genl Lincoln Secratory at War

In retrospect, it is easy to imagine why Gansevoort's position was of such a precarious nature in spite of his actions against the British. Financial difficulties must have taken priority in the nature of the confrontation over his post, but it must have also reflected the Confederate hierarchies' view of Gansevoort's performance in contrast to other officers involved in more spectacular activities. Indeed, the testament to this was the collective American reflection on Saratoga as the turning point in the American Revolution, without considering the skirmishes that led to such a victory.

Perhaps it was that a dependence of the Confederate states on the decisions of a select few such as Washington and Greene meant all eyes were diverted from any other portion of the struggle. Though Gansevoort had made strong political allies, enemies remained; General Horatio Gates was still bitter over Gansevoort's sudden success in 1777, and his removal from command of the Northern Territories prior to the siege of Fort Schuyler. Perhaps Gates had continued to lobby against Gansevoort in favor of an officer more loyal to Gates' ambitions.

June 21 marked another report of a British detachment numbering two hundred men wandering around "Balls town."[20] This was more than likely the same band of men that were in roughly the same position near the town a few months earlier, and could have been the raiders that had captured members of the Smith family. Colonel Abraham Wempel had requested extra ammunition and flint and had sent out a scouting party to determine the nature of the British movements near Balltown.

243—From Abraham Wempel

Schonectady 21st June 1782

Dear Genl A Scout of my Regiment is Come in this Morning on who I can depind Leut: Swart was one of them who reports that last night the Sun about one hour high they Discovered a tract of about 200 men 12 Miles north from Balls Town—I have sent an other Scout—when ever any thing further is Discovered Shall give you the Earliest Intelligence

I have wrote to Philip Van Renselaar for some powder Ball Catrid paper & flints I have wrote him that I shall be Answerable to him for it; If your Order is necessary pleas to give your Order and I Shall Comply with any requisitie you shall see necessary

I am Sir Your Humble Servt

Abm Wempel

To Genl Gansevoort or next Commandg Officer at Albany

A letter from July 7 confirmed that the British raiding parties were making aggressive movements in parts neighboring the Susquehanna River. An escapee named Henry Richard had given testimony that an Indian party loyal to the British camps placed him under captivity for approximately two months. Richard claimed the Indian party, consisting of approximately five hundred natives, captured three hundred prisoners over the course of their operations.[21] With "orders from Niagaria by Captain John Johnson," the raid parties sent vessels to and from Oswego and other parts of the Niagara tributaries.

The Richard affidavit led to Governor Clinton ordering Gansevoort and other officers in the region to relay this intelligence to other nearby posts. Future letters to Gansevoort continued to place emphasis on keeping the scouts vigiliant.[22]

244—Affidavit of Henry Richard

Henry Richard of lawful Age testifies and says that on the 5th: Day of last May he was taken by a Party of Indians from the West Branch of Susquahana and carried to some Indian Settlements on the Waters of Genesee that the greater Part of the six Nations have their Residence there and that they are able to raise about 500 Men capable of bearing Arms—That there is about 300 Prisoners including Men Women and Children among them: That himself and Adam Groninger made their Escape from Captivity yl 25 of June; and further some Days before they made their Escape a Party of 50 Indians set out to make an Attack upon one of the Branches of Susquah: on the Delaware & had marched two Days but were called back in Consequence of some Deserters or Tory's who came from the Mohawk River or some Parts adjacent & informed that there were large Numbers of Cattle at those Parts & the German Flats: which Object turned their Attention all the Warriors and even Children were called upon to go on the Expedition, that in case they obtained any Cattle the young Ones were to drive them while the Warriors were to harrass our People should they pursue; that this last Party marched from these Towns two Days before they made their Escape & marched down the Genesee near to the Mouth where it falls into the Lake there they were to stop and make Canoes & were to be reinforced from Niagaria and some Vessels were to go in Company to old Oswego—That they had these Orders from Niagaria by Captain John Johnson & upon Jos Brants receiving the Message the Indians were called back and ordered as above

Henry Richard—

Westmoreland on Susqueaa July 7th 1782

This Day Henry Richard came to this Garrison from Captivity personally appeared & made solemn Oath to the Truth of the within Deposition before me.

Nathan Denison[23] *Justice of Peace*

There are a Number of Gentlemen here that have had a long Acquaintance with Mr Richard & recommended him to be an honest penetrating Gentleman & a Friend to his Country and by my own observation I think him a very intelligible Person

Copy

Nathan Denison Colo:

245—From Robert Benson

Poughkeepsie July 23d 1782

Sir His Excellency the Governor is informed that there are sundry disaffected and dangerous Persons residing on the Frontiers in Cambridge District who hold a continual Correspondence and intercourse with the Enemy in Canada and who by their Conduct endanger the Safety of the well affected Inhabitants.

His Excellency directs me to inform you of this and to suggest to you the Propriety of having them removed into the interior Part of the State in pursuance of the Act for removing disaffected Persons from the frontiers—Their Names you will be enabled readily to collect from the well affected Inhabitants there; but it ought to be done in a secret manner lest the Revenge of the Disaffected & the Enemy from Canada might in consequence be practised against the Informers.—

I am with great Respect & Esteem Sir Your most Obedt Serv

Robt: Benson

Brigr Genl Gansevoort [Albany]

Gansevoort's correspondence in the latter part of 1782 once again illustrated that despite Continental troop movement to meet the British and Indian scouting parties, no major engagement or new positioning had yielded any results. Governor Clinton and Robert Benson's letters from early October and November respectively indicated an overall increase in readiness; Gansevoort in particular issued brigade orders on October 11 to his men stating that his brigade was to be ready to take the field "on the shortest notice."[24]

246—From George Clinton

Pokeepsie 8th October 1782

Sir In Consequence of Intelligence which I have this Day received from Canada by a Prisoner who lately is made his Escape from thence & through other Channels is and which I have by the present Conveyance communicated to Major Genl Lord Stirling commanding in the Northern Department I have to request that you will hold your Brigade in perfect Readiness to take the Field on the shortest Notice

I have the Honor to be with great Respect Sir Your Most Obed Servt

Geo Clinton

Brigr Genl Gansevoort [Albany]

247—Brigade Orders

Albany 11th October 1782

B.O. In consequence of Intelligene which his Excellency the Governour has Received from Canada by a person who lately made his Escape from thence, And through other channels, has Ordered my Brigade to hold itself in the most perfect readiness to take the Field on the shortest notice—You will without loss of time take such steps as will enable you to move with your Regt at moments warning—

His Excellency the Governor has ordered to me to hold my Brigade in readiness to take the Field on the shortest notice—You will therefor without loss of time take such steps as will enable you to move ~~on the shortest~~ with your Regt at moments warning

After I

The Exempt Corps within the District of your Readiness you are here also Ordered to Order them to Hold themselves in the same Readiness with your Regt

In Consequence of Orders received from his Excellency the Governor your are hereby Ordered to keep your Regt in the most Perfect readiness to take the field at the shortest Notice

[PG Albany]

248—From Robert Benson

General Orders

Poughkeepsie, 1st November, 1782.

His Excellency the Governor thinks it proper to remind the commanding Officers of Regiments, that by the Act passed the 10th of September, 1781, and the subsequent Laws for embodying Levies for the Defence of the State, they are directed to return to the Person administering the Government, the Amount of the several Bounties paid by the respective Classes within their Regiments respectively; and to repeat his Orders to the Gentlemen concerned, that they complete and deliver in their Returns by the 10th of January next, as in Case of Failure or farther Delay, he will be reduced to the disagreeable Necessity of ordering Prosecutions to be instituted, against the Delinquents, for the Penalties imposed upon them by Law, for Disobedience of Orders in this Respect.

It is particularly essential to the public Service, that his Excellency should at this Time, be furnished with correct Returns of the Militia: The commanding Officers of Brigades, and of unbrigaded Regiments, are therefore enjoined, to transmit Returns of their respective Corps to the Governor's Office, by the above Day.

By his Excellency's Command,

Robert Benson, A. D. C.

Chapter Nine

1783: Organization After the War

Although the Americans had won two devastating victories against the British, natives, and Hessian mercenaries at both Saratoga in 1777 and Yorktown in 1781, the inclusion of France into the Revolutionary War seemed to ensure a prolonged conflict with the possibility of spanning across multiple continents in yet another bloody and costly war for colonial domination. Whereas the British treasury had been greatly diminished in the pursuit of quelling the revolution in North America, the strained confederacy of the thirteen former colonies had not established an organized economic system to determine the exact amount of debts, and how they should be appropriately paid. Many frontier posts and coastal areas in the colonies were still subject to British and Indian raids; many troops in the Continental Army had reached both their mental breaking points as well as the end of their terms of enlistment. State militia were forced to compensate for this increasing burden with younger and more inexperienced men filling the vacancies, often equipped with sub-par rifles, ammunition, and other supplies.

Brigadier General Peter Gansevoort still remained at the heart of these inconsistencies in Western New York. It had been almost six years since he successfully routed a British detachment at Fort Schuyler, thereby guaranteeing a full strength Continental detachment to meet Burgoyne's main army in Saratoga. The victory also seemingly solidified Gansevoort's rank and post, which had been under scrutiny from a few of his doubtful superior officers. However, this illusory security also faded in light of the Continental Armies' success in the late stages of the war. 1782 saw his post fall under question due to the economic hardships suffered by the states and the confederate government. Even prestige and victory would not guarantee officers a sustained place in American history alongside the long-term veterans such as Washington, Greene, or Schuyler.

The year 1782 shattered any illusion among the soldiers and the countryside of complete and guaranteed victory over the British troops. The British and their Indian allies had continued to wage a guerrilla war along the Canadian border and Hudson River Valley areas for many years, with considerable success. With the defeat of Cornwallis's army in Virginia, the British attempted to emulate the same guerrilla tactics that the Americans employed in preventing a successful British invasion of the southern colonies. Under the orders of Governor Clinton and with Gansevoort's own resolve, one hundred men were ordered to take up defensive positions in Albany in anticipation of a decisive confrontation with the British raiding parties appearing around Balltown and the Susquehanna River settlements. According to Gansevoort's correspondence, his ability to enact such a movement required almost half a year to put into action; by the time the detachments were moved to their appropriate locations, the British raiding parties had ceased hostile activities.

Brigadier General Gansevoort was in particularly poor spirits as 1783 began. Much of his disposition could have been attributed to his and fellow officers' failure to apprehend the enemy in defensive or scouting skirmishes. The winter season had had severed normal forms of communication and forced his subordinates to act independently without any updates on military objectives. Their independence could have occurred due to the ever-changing nature of guerrilla tactics in the Hudson Valley. Gansevoort wrote to George Clinton on January 4 concerning the constant lack of written orders due to poor road conditions and harsh weather. Gansevoort wrote that Clinton's general orders issued on November 6 had not been carried out, save for a single return and confirmation of said orders on November 14.[1] Another letter issued from Gansevoort to Henry Van Rensselaer, Philip Schuyler, and John Beekman[2] expressed his apparent anger over these officers not responding to issued orders. Given the letter was written almost two months after the January letter from George Clinton,[3] Gansevoort was obviously running out of patience and was probably experiencing a large amount of pressure put upon him by his superiors. Another piece of evidence for this was a rather long letter addressed to George Clinton on February 27.[4] Apparently Gansevoort was becoming so desperate for acknowledgment of orders that when Major James Ashton was one of the first officers to relay information back to Gansevoort's camp, Gansevoort recommended Ashton for a promotion to command Colonel Van Woerdt's regiment. Gansevoort commended Ashton's character, one of "universal satisfaction and Justice."[5]

249—To George Clinton

Albany Jany 4. 1783

Sir I do myself the Honor to acknowledge the Receipt of your Excellency's favor of the 6th Novr last enclosing the General Orders of the 1st of the Same Month, ~~in~~ which came to hand some time about the 20th this Current—in ~~wh~~ Answer to which am Sorry to inform you that only one Return has yet been made (to Wit) ~~from~~ by Colo Van Bergen altho' I Issued ~~mine~~ my Orders on the 26th of the Same Month, but must add that Some of the Letters covering the Order laid by me a considerable Time owing to the want of Opportunities to forward them and being destitute of Cash to ~~furnish of~~ employ ~~few~~ Expresses and have yesterday been appriz'd that my Orders to Cols Van Veghten Yates and Major Ashton ha~~d~~ve been lost on the Road, in consequence whereof have this Day renew'd them, the little intercourse between the City and the Country for Some time past occasioned by the Want of Snow and the Small Pox—being in Town ~~has meant~~ will I hope in Some Measure ~~I hope~~ apologize for the ~~Letters~~ Orders lying a few Days with me before they could be Sent—have only to add on this Subject that I wish to be furnished with a little Money to enable me employ public Messengers on just Occasions—

Your Excellency I will observe that my Orders to the Regiment lately commanded by Colo Van Woerdt are directed to Major Ashton, which was occasioned by Colo Blair's being in Arrest at the request of many principal Inhabitants of Cambridge District should be happy to know whether your Excellency determines to institute a Court for his Trial or whether it is your pleasure that I Should do it and I fear that the Confusion which now exists in that Regiment by Reason of their opposition to Colo Blair and many others of their Officers will prevent a compliance with the Orders above mentioned

I enclose your Excellency Copy of a Letter from Major Ashton ~~in which your~~ from which your Excellency will see the Necessity of new Arranging that Regiment

[Copy of a Letter to His Excellency Governor Clinton dated 4th Jany 1783]

250—To Henry K. Van Rensselaer, Philip P. Schuyler and John Beekman

Albany 24th Feby 1783

Sir I am at a loss how to Account for the long delay of your Regimental return Agreeable to my orders of the 26th Novr last— ~~If I sho request again~~ You will without fail Transmit me your return within seven days from the date hereof, or shall be under the ~~disgreeable~~ Necessaty of taken such steps as will be very Disagreeable

I am Sir Your hum Servt

Peter Gansevoort

[Copy of order to Colonels Henry K. Van Rensselaer Ph: P Schuyler & John Beekman or his Commanding Officer]

251—To George Clinton

Albany Feby 27th 1783

Sir I do myself the Honor to ~~transmit~~ enclose you Sundry Papers received from Major Ashton, by which your Excellency will perceive that it is the Wish of the Officers of the late Colo Van Woerdts Regiment that Major Ashton should be appointed to the Command of the Said Regiment and I cannot help Second their wishes~~ing~~ from the Character given me of that Gentleman, it is very probable from the Information I have received that Some designing and ambitious Men will ~~attempt to~~ endeavour to get another Person appointed to that Command, but I must by leave to suggest that I believe no other Person in the District will give Such universal satisfaction and in Justice to Major Ashton I am constrained to declare that ~~I have not~~ my Orders to ~~Major~~ him have always been executed with all the dispatch ~~and~~ I could reasonably expect, and he has been indefatigable in procuring the returns last required and are now among the papers above alluded to—

The Return from Colo Yates's Regiment is also enclosed your Excellency will please to observe that the Captains who have not made their returns to him agreeable to the~~ir~~ Orders, Colo Yates informs me have refused doing it from a spirit of disaffection to the State, ~~as Colo Yates informs me~~

In consequence of my Orders to the Officers commanding Regiments in my Brigade I have received all the Returns except three necessary to enable me to ~~comply with~~ make a return of my Brigade ~~except from Colonels Beekman Schuyler & Van Rensselaer~~ and as Soon as I receive them will ~~comply with the~~ make it out and transmit ~~the Same~~ it, I cannot Account for the remissness of these Officers who have neglected and have now written them that unless they make the returns requested by the 3d Day of Feby next I shall be under the Necessity of arresting them—

I am apprehensive that you will consider me ~~Some~~ remiss in the Duties of my Officers and a regard for my reputation with you, obliges me to declare to you candidly, that where your Orders have not been punctually observed it is to ascribed ~~not~~ to a want of the Means necessary to have them executed & that ~~I am so bare of Cash that I have not been able to advance it~~ if some Cash is not advanced me for the purpose of employing Messengers occasionally, I ~~am fear it will be the Case~~ hope that no delay or remissness will be imputed to me as it will arise entirely from that Cause

The Bearer hereof is Capt Elisha Benedict,[6] *who goes down to the Legislature with a Petition ~~the~~ which he will Shuw your Excellency I have perused it and beleive the ~~purport~~ Substance of it to be true, Capt Benedict & his Sons*[7] *have uniformly conducted themselves as good Whigs and have been Witness to their exertions, he has requested this Testimonie of himself and one of his Sons from me ~~and~~ which I considered my Duty to grant*

[Letter to His Excellency Geo Clinton]

[PG]

However, the break in communication had not relented from straining Gansevoort's reputation and command. He informed Clinton that even as of the writing of the letter he was still waiting for confirmation from three officers. Gansevoort was therefore able to make a return of the majority of his regiments to send to the central command, but also reassured Clinton that if these three officers do not comply quickly, he "shall be under the Necessity of arresting them."[8]

A lapse in Gansevoort's correspondence occurred through the remainder of February and most of March. However, on March 26, Gansevoort received a letter from George Clinton that though the United States has not yet achieved a "General Peace,"[9] British hostilities were to cease that month. General Clinton notified Gansevoort that the set date for the cessation was March 20, but also noted in the letter that it was sent through communication channels on the 23rd. Therefore by the time Gansevoort had received the letter, hostilities had officially ceased six days prior to Gansevoort's knowledge of the announcement. It was not clear through the correspondence as to whether Gansevoort's men were still engaged in skirmishes in this weeklong period. It was possible that Gansevoort's men were still hunting out the British and Indian raiding parties that had terrorized the Hudson Valley area for the past two years.

252—From George Clinton

Cosopus March 26th 1783

Dear Sir I have this minute received an Account that may be relied on, tho' not officially of a General Peace being concluded and Hostilities in consequence thereof, were to cease in America the 20th of March[10]*—This important Intelligence I communicate by a Special Express to prevent Impositions which the Citizens of this State might be liable to for want of knowledge thereof—You will therefore make it as generally known to the People as can conveniently be done but not in Such a Manner as to occasion any public demonstrations which could not be Justified upon the private Account I have received My Letter is dated Philadelphia the 23d Instant was dispatched by Express and mentions the Packet with the Dispatches, was arrived in the Delaware a few Miles below the Town; but the Dispatches were not then received by Congress—*

I am with respect and Esteem Your obedient Servant

Geo: Clinton

Brigadier General Gansevoort [Albany]

A second letter was sent by Clinton on April 12 informing Gansevoort that a raiding party (possibly the same one Gansevoort was desperately seeking out) had been razed by "Savages."[11] It is interesting to note that Clinton only described the "Savages" having been involved with the raid; it could be considered possible that although the British formally ordered cessation of hostilities against the Americans, they nonetheless encouraged Indians to continue guerrilla warfare and disrupt the incredibly vulnerable Western New York settlements. Gansevoort sent out brigade orders immediately after receiving the letter. These orders were somewhat optimistic in that only half a brigade was necessary to confront the raiders and that such a confrontation would be "...in All Probability be of Short Duration and principally from Parties already out."[12]

253—From George Clinton

Poughkeepsie April 12th 1783

Dear Sir I am this Moment informed that the Settlement at Wioming has lately been destroyed by the Savages[13] *and lest they may extend their Ravages to your County I would recommend that such Detachment from your Brigade as you may judge necessary be ordered to the frontier Settlements for their Protection. Dispatches are forwarded by Sir Guy Carlton across the Country to Genl Haldiman in Canada informing him of a Peace and directing Hostilities to cease; which I have taken Measures to expedite as much as possible The Danger we have to apprehend will in all probability be of short Duration and principally from Parties already out and it is therefore to be hoped that the Militia will cheerfully acquiese in this short and last Service.—I will endeavor to induce Sir Guy Carlton to send Dispatches across the Country to Niagara & other Western Posts as I am apprehensive that those gone to Genl Haldiman may be attended with too much delay.*

I am Dear Sir with great Esteem Your most Obedt Servt

Geo Clinton

Brigr Genl Gansevoort [Albany]

Colonel Peter Vrooman sent a letter to Gansevoort after the Wyoming settlement incident delivering the "...Blessed news of peace,"[14] and that in order to celebrate, Gansevoort could expend a barrel of gunpowder. There must have been some irony inferred by this letter, as Gansevoort had been under heavy criticism in earlier years for wasteful expenditures in gunpowder. Everyone involved in the operations seemed to be incredibly relaxed in comparison to the previous years.

254—From Peter Vrooman

Schohary april 30th 1783

Dear Sir/ have Received the proclamation of governor Clinton Concerning the Blessed news of peace to me Directed By you, am informed that you will allow a Quantity of powder to keep Rejoycing on Said news if imployed to you therefore, you will therefore Sent By the Bearer thereof Lieut Peter Snyder[15] *Such a Quantity of powder to keep Said Rejoycing with my Regiment as you Shall think Sufficient*

I am with Esteem Sir your most obedient humble Servt
Peter Vroman Colo
To B. Genl Peter Gansevoort [Albany]

Gansevoort continued the celebrations within his own camp evidenced by brigade orders issued in sometime in late June-early July for proper distribution of rum rations.[16] However it was most likely that the rum was far more important in alleviating the masses of disgruntled soldiers eager to return home; the placation of soldiers with the rum distributions was so important to Gansevoort that he specified that if any officer in charge of distributing failed in his orders, he would be personally responsible and "Shall forfitt Eight times the Value for Every Such offence."[17]

255—Brigade Orders

Orders for delivering the State Rum to the Regts

A Sergeant of Each Company to Make Returns to the Officer Commanding Said Company of Every Non Commissioned Officer & private present fitt for duty

Officers Commanding Companies to Examine and Sine the Same & Return ~~Said It~~ them to the Qurr: Mastr Sergeant: Who Shall Issue under the Inspection of an Officer the Quantity Specified by Each Return Not Exceeding the Quantity of [ ]for Each Non Commissioned & private pr Week taken a Receipt from the Sergeant to whom it is deliverd which Said Return & Receipt Shall be Lodged with the ~~Commanding~~ officer Commanding of Companies Who is hereby Ordered to be Accountable to the paymaster for Said Returns at the Next time of payment and assist the paymaster in Makeing Stoppage for the Amount of Such Issues

If any Sergeant Shall be found Guilty in Not delivering the Rum drawn to Such men as are by him Returned be the Sd Sergeant So Offending Shall forfitt Eight times the Value for Every Such offence

In the first days of July General George Washington visited Albany, accompanied by Governor Clinton. The *Salem Gazette* on July 2nd described the much-anticipated event. As one of the many "gentlemen of distinction" along with General Schuyler and the Governor,[18] Gansevoort personally escorted Washington to Saratoga, which was termed by the newspaper, "the theatre of the glorious campaign of 1777," and the other northern battlefields of the Mohawk Valley.[19] Acting as Washington's personal chaperone would have solidified Gansevoort's position of respect amongst the men of New York.

256—Extract of a Letter in the *Salem Gazette*

[From Salem Gazette]
Fish-kill, July 17. [1783]
Extract of a letter from Albany, dated July 2.

"We have been very unexpectedly honoured with a visit from the Commander in Chief—His Excellency Governor Clinton accompanied him. They were received with uncommon marks of joy and congratulation. The Mayor and Corporation presented a congratulatory address to his Excellency General Washington, with the freedom of the city in a gold box. All the principal cit-

izens waited upon the General with the most cordial gratulations on his arrival. On Saturday he set out to visit the troops, with the Governor, Gen. Schuyler and many other gentlemen of distinction. Brigadier-General Gansevort, with forty volunteers, escorted him to Saratoga, where, after surveying the theatre of the glorious campaign of 1777, he reviewed the field regiment of New-Hampshire, and examined the block-houses at that place. From thence he went, the next day, to Schenectady, five miles from which he was received by sixty of the principal inhabitants on horseback, who attended him into the town, amidst the ringing of bells, firing the cannon, and every other possible demonstration of felicity. About one hundred warriors, of the Oneidas and Tuscaroras, compleatly armed and painted for war, met him without the [gates?]. The magistrates, military officers and respectable citizens, who had caused a public dinner to be provided, seemed anxious to give the most incontestable proofs of their gratitude and feasibility for the honour of the visit. The General viewed the town and fortifications, and returned to Albany the same evening. Yesterday morning he went on board his barge, on his way to the [army?] amidst the benedictions of the multitude, leaving the citizens of this country strongly impressed with the ideas of a great character, in which are combined every public and private virtue."

Letters received in August primarily discussed distribution of funds amongst the military. Edward Dunscomb[20] informed Gansevoort that there were some bureaucratic mishaps in financial accommodation toward the enlisted men and official government acknowledgment of the American army. According to Dunscomb, the Congress did not completely understand the makeup, strength, and money required to support the new army and what government agency (Congress or state) would provide such funding.[21] Within this argument, it was not yet decided as to whether the debts incurred by financing the army would be considered as "general Debt ... unless counteracted by the States for the Discharge of it."[22] The overall sense of the dispute remaining unresolved ultimately meant, according to Dunscomb, that "every Person receiving public Money is made Debtor for it & must consequently account for the Disposition of it."[23] This would certainly not sit well with officers like Gansevoort who were in charge of entire brigades, as collections for anything deemed a public debt would have to be organized by him. At the same time, soldiers had been constantly complaining over payments for their service in the war and they certainly had little means to pay public debts.

257—From Edward Dunscomb

New-Windsor, August 4th 1783

Dear General, *Since my last Letter to you, I have been informed the Pay-Master General has received the Orders of Congress to make a complete & final Settlement with the Army, comprehending ~ Commutation & every other Claim against the States. The Moment I had notice of his Instructions, I repaired to this Place & am show fully employed in settling with him You have been, I believe, apprised by my Brother of Charges against you in the Books of the Pay Office, amounting to several Thousand Dollars. Tho' this Money was evidently received for public Purposes being had for recruiting your Regimt & is indeed so charged yet still it is necessary & 'tis required by the Pay Mr Genl that your account for the application. It my Wish, Sir, to close every Acct to the Satisfaction of the Persons interested; but this cannot be done unless sufficient Vouchers to enable me to make a Settlement are put into my Hands. as these are Charges of some*

Magnitude, I should imagine, it would be most satisfactory to you to attend to it yourself; but should you, however, think that I can do it as well, you may prevent yourself the Trouble of freely command my Services.

Will you be so kind, Sir, as to acquaint the following Gentlemen of the Sums agt them. Colo Willet 1400½ Dollrs recd in 1776 as Pay per his Compy

Colo Livingston very large Sums for recruiting Service

Immense Sums agt them as Paymasters—

Abraham Ten Eyck

John D P Ten Eyck

Captn Finck[24] *2381 4/8 9 recd of Mr Trumbull as Pay per his Compy*

The Gentlemen may perhaps be startled at these Charges; but the Principle is simply this, that every Person receiving public Money is made Debtor for it, & must consequently account for the Disposition of it.—I hope, Sir, you will excess this horrid Scrawl, I am really very much engaged, & cannot copy.—

I am, Sir, With much Respect Your Most Obt Servt

E. Dunscomb

Compts to the Gentn

General Gansevoort [Albany]

Even in the closing months of 1783, gaps in security were disrupting the celebratory period of the new nation. Many of these disruptions were of a violent nature, in sharp contrast to the talks over recent financial disputes. Gansevoort issued a general order throughout the Albany area on the ninth of September, claiming that many citizens of Western New York had been neglecting internal security and must be reminded that border protection cannot be solely enforced by military forces. The orders even explicitly stated that militarily active citizens who had once participated in the militias were "...unmindful of the Duty they owe their County regardless of its Safety and notwithstanding the Protection they receive from its Laws harbour and comfort lurking Parties of the enemy."[25] He then declared that the men they harbor and may believe to be sympathetic to preservation of American frontier life do in fact wish to raze and pillage villages, "savagely murdering the well affected their defence of wives and Children ... burning their Houses and other Property."[26]

258—General Orders

Heavy Sept the 9 1783

General Orders

~~The~~ It being represented to the General that the disaffected Inhabitants ~~of the County of Albany~~ residing ~~between~~ on the Western & South Western Parts of this County ~~this City of Albany & Schohary the Hellbergh~~ do unmindful of the Duty they owe their County regardless of its Safety and notwithstanding the Protection they receive from its Laws harbour and comfort lurking Parties of the Enemy sent from Canada for the Purposes of taking off such of the Inhabitants as they conceive most active in the Cause of the Country, ~~and of more particularly of Distressing the Country by~~ of cruelly and savagely murdering the well affected their defence of wives and Children and burning their Houses and other Property It is therefore ordered that the ~~Regiments & disaffected~~ Inhabitants residing within the above Bound must notoriously disaffected

be immediately removed with their Families & Effects from their respective Habitation to the City of Albany to be Subject to the farther Disposition of the General—And that for this Purpose ~~two these be detached for Companies with 4 days provision be ordered for the Regiments of Militia commanded by~~ Colonells William van Renselear—Philip P. Schuyler ~~&~~ Henry van Renselar and Coll Anthony V Bergen do immediately cause two Companies residing nearest this ~~City~~ Place of their respective Regments with four Days Provisions to parade here on Tuesday the 11th Instant at 10 OClock in the Forenoon properly armed & equipped where a Field Officer will be appointed to command them and they will receive these further Orders—It is expected this Order will be immediately complied with as the ~~Safety~~ Security of the well affected in a great Measure depends upon the Execute of it.

His Excellency the Govr having upon requested the immediate Returns of the Levies raised for the Defence of the State and the General not having it in his Power thro' the Neglect or Delinquency of some of the Officers commanding Regiments to perfect this same ~~Return~~—He therefore ~~for express~~ Orders in the most express Manner that ~~the~~ such the commanding Officers of Regiments as not yet furnished him with those Return of those Levies that they forthwith do the same ~~as he cannot or had we~~ as he cannot longer consistent with his Duty ~~prevent the Law from being~~ suspend the Execution of the Law against them

[PG Albany]

259—To George Clinton

Albany 13th September 1783

Sir As the day on which the Annual appointment of Sheriff of this County is to be made approaches, I beg leave to recommend to your Excellency's Attention for Nomination to that Office Mr John Ten Broeck[27] *who formerly held it a Short time And was then Superceeded*

If however it be thought improper to re-appoint that Gentleman and I should be supposed not unqualified to discharge its Duties by nominating me[28] *your Excellency will confer a particular Favor on Sir*

Your most respectful and very Humble Servt

Peter Gansevoort

Your Excellency will be pleased to deliver the Inclosed Letters to the Gentlemen of the Counsil when they meet—

[Governor Clinton—Poughkeepsie]

CHAPTER TEN

1784–1812: Service After the War

Gansevoort's role in the new nation seemed to change little from 1783 to the first years after the Paris treaty was signed. The New York militia was still concerned with the distribution of war debts to itself, the Continental Army, and the militias of the other states. As New York contained a large swath of frontier lands ripe for further future settlements, debt created problems. Many New Yorkers were still concerned with protection from the local tribes. Those who served on the Sullivan expedition were all too well aware of the damages inflicted upon those who had allied (or were even suspected) with the British. It was only logical to expect word of these damages to spread amongst an already cautious Indian population, who feared an outpouring of land-hungry colonists over the 1763 Proclamation line.

By the time the Treaty of Paris has been signed, Gansevoort's military career was a strange mixture of sweeping success and intrigue within the military systems of the Revolution. Gansevoort almost certainly saw his placement within the New York militia as a demotion from the Continental Army and sought to regain his position within its ranks. The last correspondence directly involving the brigadier general of the Albany militia was addressed to the United States Congress in 1785 as "The Memorial of Peter Gansevoort late Colonel Commandant of Fort Schuyler." Within this document, Gansevoort reviewed his performance during the war with particular attention paid to his victory at the Siege of Fort Schuyler in 1777.

Gansevoort continually repeated and placed emphasis on receiving an honorable title from the Continental Congress and that due to such an honorable performance in service to the United States, he might reap the benefits "intended him by said Act of Congress." The particular wording of his letter shed light on Gansevoort's personal trials in preserving his reputation as a decent and well-deserved officer. Certainly the skepticism from General Horatio Gates had left him under constant distress regarding his validity as a high ranking officer within the new army. Given the enormous response and positive reception of his deeds in 1777 among other actions, he had rightfully earned his place in the military annals as an officer befitting his aims. Gansevoort would certainly continue to reap these "Benefits" throughout his later life.

260—To the United States Congress

To the United States of America in Congress Assembled
The Memorial of Peter Gansevoort late Colonel Commandant of Fort Schuyler—

Sheweth—That your Memorialist in the year 1777 commanded one of the Regiments of Infantry of the State of New York in the Service of the United States and in the Spring of that year was ordered with his Regiment to Fort Schuyler the Command of which was entrusted to your Memorialist.

That on the 4th Day of October 1777 Your Memorialist was honored with The Approbation of the United States of his Conduct during his Conduct during his Successful Defence of Fort Schuyler and a Commission appointing your Memorialist Colonel Commandant of that Fort. That your Memorialist has never derived any Emolument from that Appointment, his powers not being extended or any Compensation allowed him for his Services as Commandt.

That your Memorialist when the United States did him the Honor to appoint him Commandant conceived And he is informed That such was the Sentiment of the Honble Congress, That, The Appointment was intended as both An honorable and Substantial Mark of the Approbation of the great Council of the United States If should not have been the Case the Act of Congress which appointed him Commandant must necessarily have been emopesative Your Memorialist being already Commandant of Fort Schuyler tho' not sanctioned by a Resolve of Congress

Your Memorialist submits These Facts to the Consideration of the United States in a Reliance that they will reconsider the Act of the 4th of October 1777 And Determine whither Your Memorialist was in Consequence thereof intitled to any and What Advantages—And if was the Intention of ~~Congress~~ the Honble Congress to Annex any Emolument to that Appointment Your Memorialist prays the United States to make Provision that your Memorialist may receive the Benifits intended him by said Act of Congress

And your Memorialist will ever gratefully Acknowledge the Attention ~~of Congress~~ of the United States

PG

10th September 1785

By 1788, Gansevoort had been appointed an Indian Commissioner by the Confederation Congress and was tasked with other respected gentlemen to negotiate treaties with the native tribes in western New York determining future territorial boundaries and legitimate means of colonial settlement. He was chosen for this duty due to his extensive experiences in dealing with the Indians throughout western New York. One of the most important treaties during Gansevoort's time in the western militia was the Fort Schuyler (formerly Fort Stanwix) Indian Treaty in 1788. Diplomatic business between New York and the Six Nations was temporarily settled with a peace treaty in 1784 but the treaty essentially dictated the end of the last major native-controlled polities within the boundaries of New York. In exchange for French coin, clothing, and provisions, the Oneida and Onondaga nations were to cede "all lands to the people of the State of New York forever" and that, while land leasing options would be available to the Oneida for twenty to twenty-one year periods, the state of New York had ultimate law and authority.[1] The treaty was meant by both sides, certainly by New York, to end several disputes over fishing and hunting rights and to officially break the sovereignty of the two tribes.[2] For a small sum of money, New York believed it had unquestionable privileges to expand into the western frontier. Along with treaties conducted separately with the Cayuga and the Onondaga in 1790, Gansevoort proved instrumental in opening the frontier for future settlement. Whereas he had participated in a military venture to pacify native resistance during the war against the British, his post-war life revolved around political means of pacification.

Many of the Oneida and Onondaga chieftains would quickly react to the treaty with protest. They declared the agreement illegitimate, as they were never present nor consulted. The vague language in this and many other treaties would haunt the descendants of the Six Nations. By 1795 the Six Nations were limited to arbitrary reservations all of which would be subjected to further annexation by the state of New York.

Gansevoort's efforts were widely appreciated by future settlers. Alice Kenney noted in her book, *The Gansevoorts of Albany*, that in 1790 "one unanticipated result of this trip—or perhaps of some similar but unrecorded one—was the establishment among the Seneca Indians of a family named 'Gansworth' who claim to this day to be descended from him."[3]

While participating in the treaty negotiation, Gansevoort continued to seek out opportunities in the public arena. He was appointed Sheriff of Albany, serving from September 29, 1790, to September 28, 1792. In 1788, Gansevoort was selected as a delegate for Albany County to the New York State Convention to consider ratifying the Federal Constitution. As a Federalist, he supported the Constitution.[4]

It was not surprising that Gansevoort had played a major role in these treaties for economic reasons as well. Gansevoort, like many other New Yorkers, was entranced by the potential for new land other settlers had shared. Indeed, many men had considered purchasing lands that they had marched through on campaign, to return later after payments for service had been issued. Gansevoort in this respect was at an advantage: whereas many of the lower officers in the Continental Army and state militias received pay far delayed from its original promised date (some pay was not received until generations later), the family brewery had generated enough surplus capital before the war to engage in land speculation.

In 1779, while on the Sullivan expedition, Gansevoort had purchased a small tract of land east of Cayuga in modern-day Aurelius, New York.[5] It is unclear how much Gansevoort had initially paid for the land, but the sale of the tract in 1805 to Samuel Smith earned him a hefty four thousand dollars.[6] In his next venture, his entrepreneurial spirit would lead to the establishment of a mill community which would later bear his name. During the close of the Revolution, Gansevoort discovered the irons of an old mill near Snook Kill Falls. The land was formerly owned by Hugh Munro, a Tory who fled to Canada during the war. Gansevoort purchased the 1,500 acres and erected a new sawmill and added a grist mill. An independent New York meant new expansion and settlements westward, which would always require a healthy supply of lumber. Likewise, his purchases would provide his family a sustainable future income by selling agricultural commodities to new farmers and merchants.[7]

Gansevoort seemed to have had a keen awareness of his ability to stake out the territorial and economic future for post-war New York, but his military and political legacy was still unclear. As the militia slowly demobilized, he naturally turned towards state government. In late 1798, Gansevoort was made aware that the New York State Treasurer Robert McClellan planned to resign, and he sought to pounce on the opportunity. It is understandable why Gansevoort would have thought himself qualified. His family name was well established within the New York economic strata, and expansion of his industries would seem to prove his abilities in financial management. He had served closely under Philip Schuyler, who in July 1789 was elected as a United Staes senator. Finally, his participation with George Clinton in negotiating Indian treaties no doubt convinced him that he had made very powerful political connections within New York, and the respect of the new nation at large.

Gansevoort also courted an old acquaintance to curry favor for his election as treasurer. From December 1789 to January 1790, he engaged in a vigorous correspondence with Marinus Willett, who had himself been maneuvering into New York's political spotlight. After serving as a member of the state assembly, he helped quell Shay's Rebellion in 1787. During the ratification process for the U.S. Constitution, he joined the ranks of the anti–Federalists, along with George Clinton, Robert Yates, and other New York contemporaries.[8] Willett's anti–Federalist leanings may have been an advantage on their own terms; whereas much of the Anti-Federalist leaders of New York were from Albany and western settlements, Treasurer McClellan was a Federalist, and thus represented the interests of New York City. Willett and others might have been swayed to advocate for a Treasurer with similar economic interests at stake.

The language used by both men in their correspondence was subtle but masked very clear positions. Building on the "Friendship which as Always subsisted between us," Gansevoort made it known he wished to offer himself as the next Treasurer, should the current Treasurer resign.[9] Willett responded to Gansevoort's initial letter with vague, but overall positive language. He avoided specifically mentioning whether, in fact, the treasurer might vacate his office, but if Gansevoort was able to further "ascertain" the validity of said statements, Willett would send recommendations for the new appointment when possible.

Gansevoort's response was sent only a few days later, and showed his skill for picking up the subtleties of Willett's language. Both men appeared to be hesitant about stating support for a new official in any respect; to do so and be discovered might severely harm their reputations and current standings within political circles. In contrast with the openness of his first letter, Gansevoort claimed to have no authorization that "...the present Treasurer will abandon that Office," but that applications to that office have already started elsewhere.[10] Despite being aware of this, he does not divulge any specific knowledge. The request for "...the Influence of your friends upon the Same Ground" highly suggests that Gansevoort was nervous about falling behind in political maneuvers. Despite all of the conversation focusing on the possible appointment of a new treasurer, Gansevoort firmly claimed in a short statement that the request that his name be heard by certain circles was not designed to remove McClellan from power, the "...application not being directed to divert him of the Office."[11]

Ultimately, Gansevoort was not selected for the position, and McClellan would remain treasurer until 1803.[12] Gansevoort would also fail in a bid for the U.S. Senate, losing out to the far more politically established Gouverneur Morris during a special election in 1800 to fill James Watson's former seat.[13] Despite these setbacks, Gansevoort would eventually find that many important positions would come to him via reputation, rather than through campaigns of correspondence.

Having now established a solid economic base, new land grants, and a booming agricultural business, Gansevoort seemed to retire from public life. The new nation would continue to undergo a turbulent period of transformation, creation and destruction.

The Election of 1800 and the new presidential administration started to shift political dialogue away from stringent post-war Revolutionary rhetoric. Many would claim that John Adams lost the Election of 1800 due to an emphasis on nation-building and his monarchist tendencies, whereas his victorious opponent Thomas Jefferson was portrayed as a real revolutionary, who upheld the ideals of the common yeoman against the Federalists and the centralized systems proposed by Alexander Hamilton. Jefferson's election and subsequent presidency turned out to replicate the former administration in many unexpected ways. Fears of another war breaking out were common and frequent. The French Revolution continued to stir up common resentment towards the federal government for refusing to help their ideological brothers-in-arms overseas. Territorial claims and trading disputes along the Mississippi River threatened to engulf the new nation in a war against the Spanish Empire. The immense British navy and dominion in Canada still threatened northern American borders both on land and water, and a lack of a modern navy meant the States would be increasingly subject to acts of piracy from Spanish Florida.

These problems forced the Jefferson administration, much like the preceding administrations of Washington and Adams, to reorganize and reinvigorate the U.S. military. It was within this paradigm that Peter Gansevoort once again found himself a military man. On April 29, 1802, Gansevoort was appointed a military agent for the Northern Department of the United States. The duties of the military agents included the purchasing, receiving and forwarding to their destination all military stores and other articles for the troops in their respective departments, and all goods and annuities for the Indians. The forts under Gansevoort's responsibility included Forts Niagara, Detroit, Wayne, Dearborn and Michilimackinac.[14] Gansevoort seemed to be a natural choice: he had some of the most intimate experience with logistical organization and the western fort systems over the course of the Revolutionary War.

Over the following years due to his efforts within and outside of the Northern Department, Gansevoort again raised his public profile. He was appointed to the Board of Directors for the New York State National Bank of Albany in 1803, and was appointed a regent to the University of the State of New York in 1808. He would continue to hold both positions until his death in 1812. In 1807, he was elected a director of the Cohoes Bridge Company which he held stock in since 1792. Perhaps the greatest achievement in Gansevoort's later life was his appointment to high rank in the United States Army.[15]

For seven years, Gansevoort served his country well and because of that he was rewarded. On February 11, 1809, President Thomas Jefferson nominated Gansevoort to be a Brigadier General "in the troops raised by virtue of an act, entitled 'An act to raise, for a limited time, an additional military force.'" Five days later, Congress conferred the appointment. He would be put in command of the Northern Department of the United States Army, which was comprised of the Fourth, Fifth and Sixth Regiments. Stationed at Carlisle, Pennsylvania, his responsibilities included the coast defenses of New England and New York, and the border defenses of the Great Lakes and the St. Lawrence Valley. Upon accepting his new position, Gansevoort submitted his resignation as major general of the New York Fourth Division of Infantry to New York Governor Daniel Tompkins, a position he held for nearly twenty years. His son, Leonard H. replaced Peter as the military agent for the Northern Department.[16]

His appointment to his new post must have finally confirmed to him and perhaps more importantly, his fellow countrymen, his invaluable service to the new republic. But Gansevoort would have one more service to render his nation before his death in 1812. Since 1804 there was suspicion that General James Wilkinson, commander of the armed forces under Jefferson and governor of the Louisiana Territory had conspired in a plot with then vice president Aaron Burr to create an independent state with the help of the Spanish. Burr, already notorious in Washington political circles for being opportunistic, was accused of having plotted "to sever the western from the eastern states" and to create his own empire in the west.[17] Burr was immediately branded a traitor by Jefferson and ordered arrested. After giving chase, Burr was finally apprehended and tried in 1807. Burr was, to the dismay of many, acquitted of all charges of treason, as there were no witnesses willing to give testimony of his ambitious plot. Dishonored and humiliated, the ambitious Burr fled the United States for Europe until 1812.

The extent of Burr's involvement in the Louisiana Purchase treason has never been firmly established. But it was determined in 1807 upon discovering a particularly damning letter, that charges be arranged against General Wilkinson. Wilkinson was long supposed by many Burr supporters to have been the real mastermind behind the conspiracy put upon the former vice president. Edmund Randolph, elder Virginia statesman and one of the defense attorneys for the Burr conspiracy trial, had engaged in a quarrel with General Wilkinson. Refusing to see General Wilkinson on any matter, Randolph "...refused to meet ... on the principle that Wilkinson had degraded himself and that he (Randolph) would not descend to Wilkinson's level."[18] Over the following months, Randolph was determined to muddy Wilkinson's reputation and brought the attention of the House of Congress to documents implicating Wilkinson in the Burr conspiracy. The piece of evidence with the most potential to condemn Wilkinson was a loan of over nine thousand pounds allocated to him by the Baron de Carondelet, the former governor of Spanish Louisiana.[19] Though Randolph submitted the accusation that Wilkinson used this money to further his efforts in seizing land and allying himself with the Spanish, Wilkinson retorted that the letters were forgeries, and that the money was used for "Tobacco speculations."[20] In response, Randolph and members of the House requested that shipment invoices detailing the alleged tobacco transactions be submitted for perusal. Failure to submit the invoices seemed to imply that Wilkinson had indeed planned to use the money to set up his own personal fiefdom in Louisiana.

261—Daniel Clark[21] to Thomas Power[22]

"Washington 2 January 1808

"My dear Friend

"The die is cast and Wilkinson is accused before the house of Representatives, or rather, Randolph has brought forward a resolution to have an enquiry made into his Conduct which must end in disgrace and Shame. The business originated thus—Wilkinson after a considerable lapse of time challenged Randolph on the 29th of last month—Randolph refused to meet him on the principle that Wilkinson had degraded himself and that he (Randolph) would not descend to Wilkinsons level—Wilkinson immediately posted Randolph and the whole party in Congress which has constantly appoved the Presidential measures seemed to glory on the occasion and could not contain their triumph—Things had now come to a Crisis—Randolph or Wilkinson must fall, and if the former, every thing and everyone would have been born down by the latter, and his Patriotism even would have been blazoned in Letters of Gold. It would ever after have been in vain to have entertained a thought of self defence against such a Giant—There was I thought but one remedy and that was a desparate one—I had hitherto retained in my possession your address to the Public respecting the General which it became, as you know yourself, incumbent to publish for your own Justification & I put it into Randolph's hands with two other Papers of those you had committed to me, neither of which however appears by anything on the face of them ever to have been in your Possession—they are first a Copy of Wilkinson's cyphered Letter to Governor Gayoso and secondly a Copy of a Letter from the Baron de Carondelet to Portell respecting the transmission of the 9640$ to him for Wilkinson's ac[coun]t. These two Papers

became absolutely and assentially necessary to support your own Statement and with this view only did I put them in Randolph's hands. He then brought them forward and stated to the house that a Member of it could give more damning information—I was named—I rose, but conscious that anything I should then say would pass marely as a speech and would be subject to the same cavilling as any other I refused to give any information unless compelled by the house stating as a reason that all former attempts to inform the President of certain transactions in Kentucky had been disregarded. This implied a knowledge of facts and I shall if an Equiry be made, be compelled to give testimony on oath which is what I desire, when its effect will be greater by its appearing not to be offered voluntarily, and God knows I never would wish to come forward voluntarily and accuse him—

Wilkinson I am informed declares all the Papers forgeries and intends resting his defence on Tobacco speculations. He has various forged documents for this purpose, or rather false Certificates from Gilbert and Folch and others—his Confidence will betray him his his ruin, and you can easily effect it—

When his Papers and Documents are presented I shall have it suggested that it would be well that he should furnish his Invoices of the Shipments with the names of the Patrons Boats by which they were made and the time when they were made with the time of the Sale—this must embarrass him and as all he can allege on this score must be false, he can have no other scape hole than a pretence that his Books & Papers are lost—

In this case as he will have no proof to bring we shall be allowed to bring what may be called negative Proof to contradict his assertions—

It is a well known fact that Wilkinson has made no Tobacco Shipments since the Year 1791 and I even believe since the Year 1790, as at the end of 1791 Nolan his confidential Friend left his service and went to San Antonio—to prove with certainty that these shipments were not made or if made that they never sold to the Spanish Government you have only to call upon Dn Matias Alfuente the Inspector of Tobacco who has been in Office as I believe since 1792 and he will give you a certified copy from his Books or an Affidavit that no Tobacco was purchased or inspected by him or entered the King's Store from Wilkinson or any of his Agents during the time he has been in Office—this time he must clearly state, and from his Books or other Vouchers he must give you a Copy of all the Quantities of hhd or Kentucky Tobacco bought by the King in his time—I have reason to believe that a parcel which I myself sold in the beginning of 1794 was the last parcel ever delivered of Kentucky Tobacco in the Ware houses and this parcel Alfuente himself inspected by particular order of the Baron de Carondelet—Whatever Papers or Vouchers you may procure from Alfuente must be afterwards sworn to and duly authenticated by the Governor—

Request Relf to assist you, who can be of material service, and write to Minor for such further intelligence as he can give—it is all important to us, for you and I and every one else who knows any thing of Wilkinson's nefarious transactions will be sacrificed, if we do not now effectually prove his Guilt—

For heaven's sake my dear Friend lost not a moment, time is pressing and let what you do be well done—

If Bradford or the Browns can be of any Service now is the time to come forward, he has accused them all and self defence will render a disclosure of all his Villainies justifiable—

I shall expect to hear from you without delay on this subject & remain Dear Sir very sincerely Your friend

Daniel Clark

Thomas Power Esqr

It would not be until 1811 that Gansevoort found himself involved in Wilkinson's trial. A June 10 letter from Secretary of War William Eustis summoned Gansevoort for what was termed "A general court martial," of which Gansevoort would serve as president. He was ordered to Fredericktown, Maryland, as soon as possible to oversee the proceedings.[23] His duties as president of the court martial were numerous: he opened the court and called it to order; he announced it adjourned at the close of the session; he preserved order during the session; he checked disorder or indecorum by members of the court, the judge advocate, the accused, the counsel, the witnesses, and the audience; saw to it that the rights of every one entitled to consideration are respected in the routine conduct of each day, calling for or announcing the proper proceedings in turn, and finally to take care that the regular forms of business were duly observed.[24]

262—From William Eustis

June 10th 1811.
Sir
A general court martial, of which you will be President, will be held early in July, probably at Fredericktown in Maryland, of which I have thought it proper to give you this informal notice, in order that your arrangements may be such as to meet the official communication, which you will receive in a few days.
I am with respect your obedt Servt
W Eustis
General Gansevoort
Albany

263—List of Clothing

List of clothing belonging to Peter Gansevoort Junr
16 August 1811
& taken to Fredericktown
8 shirts with ruffels except 1 being No form 1 to 8
4 " 4 to 8 } fine
4 " plain for traveling 1 " 4
16 in all (Shirts)
12 Cambrick neck Hkfs.
12—Pocket do—
6 pair of fine cotton Hose 1 pr of Cotton Socks
6—linnen &—(for boots)
2 pair of linnen drawers
2 " of Canton Crape Breeches & 1 Vest
4 white Vest.
1 full trimed Uniform Coat do. Vest & Breeches
2 Undress Coats. 1 pair of Gaitors—Cherry Valise
2 pr of nankeen Breeches & 1 pr of do panteloons

2 " Cassemere " & 1 Casemere Vest
1 frock Coat—1 silk Morning gown & 1 Callico do—
2 Bandawa Pocket Hkf—1 Silk Military sash
2 Blk silk & 1 leather stock 1 Blue cloth Breeches &
1 Buff cassmere Vest 1 pair Eapuletts 1 Sword & Belt
1 Military Hat—2 Razors strap & shaving box &
Ink stand. Books. 1 Clothes Brush & 1 pr Spurs
Notes Hr Lr C G

Gansevoort arrived in Fredericktown within months and began the Court Martial proceedings on September 2. Many of the details regarding Wilkinson's trial are known, but of significance here was Gansevoort's correspondence during the trial. Curiously enough, the majority of the found correspondence was with his wife Catherine. Barring a few notable exceptions, Catherine was largely absent from the correspondence of Peter Gansevoort's Revolutionary War days.

There may be several explanations for this sudden flurry of letter writing. The most obvious may be boredom; Gansevoort never seemed particularly suited to governing over military court tribunals even during his days in the Revolution and it was very likely that any interest in the matter may have evaporated after a few sessions of legal repartee. He was also surrounded by his political patrons and friends, negating the need for correspondence between New York and the seasoned politicians from Washington. Finally, copious evidence in his correspondence with his wife showed a keen interest in the affairs of his children. No longer the adventurer he was decades ago, left in a political arena of which he seemed to have little experience or interest in, Gansevoort continued to gather information on the workings of his burgeoning family businesses near home.

Gansevoort first corresponded with his wife on October 9. In an ironic parallel with his brother's requests for letters during the Revolution, Peter informed his wife that, despite her promises, their daughter Maria had neglected to "answer every letter I should write her."[25] This would remain a constant source of complaints throughout his stay in Fredערickstown. There were some instances of humor. In a December 15 letter addressed to his wife, Gansevoort had received a notification that his son Peter had received a letter from his father, but with no accompanying reply. The elder Gansevoort took it in good stride, noting "the Short was welcome because it says that you are all well."[26] Towards the end of the proceedings he almost appeared to have concedingly accepted his isolation from family affairs, stating in a later letter "My servant again as usual Announces nothing for you Sir."[27]

264—To His Wife, Catherine Gansevoort

Frederick town 9th Octr 1811

My Dear Caty I am hourly looking out for the arrival of the mail when I flatter myself to receive a letter from home, My daughter promised to answer every letter I should write her, this she has not done, the cause for this must be best known to herself, I am sorry that it si not in power to tell you, how long we shall be detained on the Court, Genl Wilkenson appears Anxious to ficelite the proceedings, but much is yet to be done (as the old saying is misery likes company) I find that members of our Court are as eager to push the business, as myself, having their families at a great distance from them, I shall now wait untill the arrival of the mail before I close this Hart just returned from the post Office to me great astonishment not a word from home. If Maria nor any other of my Children will write request my daughter to send the news papers, both Register and Garrett; from which I shall be able to collect the news of the day, I merely write to find a little fault & to let your know that I am well my respects attend our Children Aunt Polly & all Other friends

I remain Dr Caty Yours

P. Gansevoort

Though he could not inform his wife of the inner workings of the court testimony, he does mention the anxiety amongst the members of the court, as they were "...eager to push the business ... having their families at a great distance from them."[28] In concluding the letter, Peter complained of "a little fault": not having been sent the latest New York newspapers, a task he seemed to have assigned to his children.

Letters written throughout October and late November showed that Gansevoort remained concerned with matters at home, sending money to his sons[29] and continually requesting the latest issues of the New York newspapers. Some of the letters mentioned Catherine collecting rent payments from tenants and forwarding payments for Gansevoort's financial ventures. Gansevoort's many financial "partners" were very familiar names: fuel was purchased from Colonel Anthony Lamb, the military agent stationed in Albany, and bills sent to a "Mr. Yates the Cashier."[30] One letter dated November 20 concerned missing financial papers which apparently contained a record of the Gansevoort household debts. Luckily his memory had served him well; he claimed to have had sent a particular payment to his Brother-in-Law in advance of the due date.[31]

265—From James Wilkinson

To the Hon Brigadier General Gansevoort President and the members of the General Court Martial, before whom I have plead to Specific charges, Set forth under the Authority of the President of the United States.

Gentlemen.

I have seriously refleceted on the communication of the Judge Advocate, made to me yesterday in open Court, indicative of a disposition on your part to abandon that branch of the Enquiry into my conduct, which bears relation to the treasonable dessigns of Aaron Burr: In a case of just vital importance to my character, I trust I shall be exused for submiting, most respectfully to your consideration, the reasons which incline me to hope, that you may determine to investigate all the charges which have been exhibited against me.

I will not presume to say how far it may be proper for this court, to receive evidence to prove that an overt act of Treason was commited by Aaron Burr or any other person; nor would the decision of the Court on this point be of any consequence, to me; For whether treason according to the legal definition of the Crime, was commited or not; yet if I am found guilty of having combined with conspirators, in any unlawfull enterprize, or having countenance or aided the conspiracy directly or indirectly—my Honour as an Officer would be forfeited—and the permission to drag out a life of disgrace, would be a heavier inflication than prompt millitary execution.

In the charges exhibited against me to this Court. I am accused of many and horrible crimes, but in the whole black catalodgue I feel that most sensably which imputes to me a participation in a conspiracy against the Pence and Interist of that Country, to which my life has been devoted. It may and probably will be infered that the grounds, on which those charges rest, are supposed by the Government to be at least Sufficiently Strong, to warrant Suspicion and justify investigation. The weight of formal and solemn accusation has thus been added to the floating slanders, by which my life has been assailed for more than four years. It has given to them a Body and a form.—Two witnesses have already been examined, on the points under consideration, before a crowded audience, for the purpose of inculpating me on those very points: and I cannot forget that one of those witness's (William Simmons) who holds a public Office of considerable respectability, manifested clearly throughout his whole examination, the disposition to add to his testimony the weight of his opinion, if indeed the one or the other could ballance a straw

I acknowledge that should the Court be of opinion that those charges are not cognizable before a Millitary tribunal, nothing could justify them in proceeding with the trial, on the Points to which they have refference.

But I hope I shall not be deemed obtrusive or presumptious, when I represent that altho the crimes charges may be cognizable in the civil Courts, it does not follow that they may not also be millitary offences. For if I am guilty of them, I am unworthy to wear the Garb of Honour, and yet the decision of a civil court could not strip me of it—nor can the refusal of a Grand Jury to indict me be considered as an requital, so as to take away the Jurisdiction of this Court, it being the right of a Grand Jury to accuse and not to try. And even, if an accusation had been made, and a trial and acquital had taken place, it rests with the prisoner to plead it:—but I disdain to make Just plea. And I will reiterate for the hundredth time my earnest desire that I may meet my accusers and be judged by my peers: I beg leave to add that Conl Burr was not finally acquited, on the charge of having committed a high misdemeanor; he was recognized to answer for just offense and forfeited his recognizence by fleeing his Country:

A Sense of justice to myself int he delicate and painfull Situation to which I am reduced, for the most meritorious conduct of my life, has induced me to Submit these remarks to the Court—and I am certain I shall find in their bosoms a ready pardon, for yealding to those [?] which a soldier cannot stifle when the dearest object of his addections,—his honour is jeopardized by ruthless persecution, and relentless malignity.

(Signed) Ja: Wilkinson
Geneneral Court Martial
Frederick Town Md
Octr 10th 1811

266—To His Wife, Catherine Gansevoort

Fredericktown 20 Octr 1811

Dear Caty The day previous to my leaving home Mr Yates the Cashier of our Bank furnished me with a memorandum of the amount of my note's due to the Bank & the time they would become due. this paper has been mislaid or lost, knowing a note indorsed by your Brother to fall due the latter part of this month induces me to send you the inclosed for him to indorse, The Other not becoming due untill the latter part of the insuing month shall be attended to in season—Genl Wilkinson & the Judge Advocate have agreed to examine the remaining Witnesses by depositions to be attested to before a Majestrate, by way of interrogation. To be first submitted to the Judge Advocate and his consent thereto will go to the Court a proper testimony. This measure is adopted in order to acceliorate the business. Mr Jones & Genl Council will soon have to attend the Circuit Court at the City of Washington which is to set sometime in the beginning of next month

My respects as usual
I am Dr Caty yours
P Gansevoort

267—To His Wife, Catherine Gansevoort

Frederick Town 30th Octr 1811

My Dear Caty Your letter of 19 Inst I have just recd by the mail I have but just time to write you a Short letter before the Mail Closes, you did will to sell dine, The daring Villen Prince has meet with his desert, your arrangement with Judge Van Ness for his transportation was a very judicious one, I expect in about 3 days after this that Genl will finish & says that it will take him about 8 days to prepare his defence, when the business or proceedings will be forwarded to the President of the U.S. how long it will take him to deliborate before he approves is uncertain we flatter ourselves that he will soon determine on the sentence & dissolve the Court. As Congress are about meeting & having Other important business before him will induce him soon after to order us to our different stations when it is evident that members are much wanted at their posts I shall in my next inclose a Return for Wood, My respects to our Children Aunt Polly and all inquiring friends I must close by saying that I do not despair of being home in all next month— I wrote Peter a few days since & inclosed him One hundred dollars, he wrote for a larger sum but had it not in my power to Send him more soon after my arrival he wrote for fifty which he has acknowledged to have recd

I am Dr Caty Yours
P. Gansevoort

Maria must continue to send the papers the expense is trifling You will collect the rent after the 1 of Novr

Putnam at—$130 pr an
Legrange—400
J Marius—at Cl
and Baker at $180

Other letters relayed the closing statements of the prosecution, with Gansevoort awaiting General Wilkinson's defense and subsequent dissolution of the Court. These letters also revealed Gansevoort's distaste for General Wilkinson, noting upon conclusion of the prosecution's case that "...The daring Villen Prince has meet with his desert."[32] It was also alleged before the trial that Wilkinson had prepared to engage in a lengthy defense, either under the premise of defending his honor and disproving the charges, or to test the patience of the court and its members. It was certainly possible that Gansevoort did not find Wilkinson's conduct, including a staggering five-day defense dressed in full military regalia during its entirety, very appealing.[33] Language reflecting anxiety to return home was used often; in one particular letter written on November 8, Gansevoort became far more meticulous in listing dates for the General's defense (which he noted "will be a very lengthy one"), the

Judge Advocate's response, the deliberation of the jury, and the courts' dissolution at the behest of President Madison.[34]

268—To His Wife, Catherine Gansevoort

Fredericktown 3d Novr 1811

My Dear Caty I have again returned disappointed from the Post Office, not a letter from home. It is expected that the prosecution & the defendent will finish tomorrow when the Genl will require about five days for his defence, after which the Court will adjourn to the City of Washington to receive their orders. It is expected that the President of the U.S. will not deliberate long on whatever the sentence may be, and Dessolve the court as a number of Officers are wanted at their different Posts. Thro' the blessing of God my health is as yet preserved and hope that yours our family & all friends may experience the same. My best respects to our Children Aunt Polly, and enquiring friends—A Short letter is better then none—Send me the papers respecting Prince—

I am yours Sincerely

P. Gansevoort

269—To His Wife, Catherine Gansevoort

Fredericktown 8th Novr 1811

My Dear Caty On the 6th Inst the Court having heard all the testimony that was Offered by both parties adjourned until next week Thursday the 14th when the Genl will enter or his defence which will take it supposed until Saturday 17th to sum up all the testimony that has been adreced, and to deliver his defence which will be a very lengthy one, when the Judge Advocate will review all the proceedings and make his reply on Munday the 19th which he say s will not take him long as the whole of the business must be fresh in the minds of the members, when the Court will be in conclave it is supposed to the remainder of the week to make up their oppinion on the guilt or innocense of the accused, on all the different Charges and their specifications which are very numerous, when the Court will Adjourn to the City of Washington whare all the members have some business to transact, and receive our orders after the Court shall have been dessolved, which we calculate will take up the last week in the present month, about the begining of the month it is expected we shall set our faces toward home, I wish you to send to New York by some safe conveyance to the care of Dr Boyd my Great Coat leather mittons two pair of white woolen stockings & cloggs, in the absence of all our sons Mr Graham I trust will take the trouble of forwarding them, when I left New York I left my saddle & bridle with the Doctor. I inclose a note for $2.420 which will fall due about the 20 Inst. which was indorsed by Gansevoort and Legrange if sent to Mr Yates the Cashier it will be attended to, you will find inclosed returns for Fuel for the Months of July & August which you will send to Colo Anthony Lamb. The Papers respecting Prince you will send to me as soon as possable, when I leave this place the Post Master will be directed whare to send my letters & papers I shall wait the arrival of the mail before this letter is closed when one hour is left to acknowledge the receipt of some letters I may receive, My servant just now brought me two letters brought by the northern mail the one from my daughter Maria in which she mentioned the health of the Family which you *may naturaly suppose must have given much pleasure I shall answer her by the next mail—The other letter is from Capt Bebie in which he inform me that he has recd from yourself the papers for the transportation of Prince I shall write him on that subject. I must conclude with my best wishes for your health & that of our Family & friends, and all inquiring after my wellfare, tel Aunt Polly that I often think of her and all her Concerns*

I must conclude by subscribing myself yours Sincerely

P. Gansevoort

P.S. Bebee informs me that you have sent him the papers respecting Prince—I have no time left to correct this letter

270—To His Wife, Catherine Gansevoort

Fredericktown 15 Novr 1811

My Dear Caty The Court Martial Adjounred on the 6th Inst. to meet on this day to give the Genl the imtermediate time to prepare his defence, This morning we expected that the defence would have commenced when behold at the opening of the Court the Judge advocate introduced two Witnesses who had just arrived from New Orleans what time will be required to hear their testimony cannot be conjectured by the Court. I expected before this to have started for home by the beginning of next month, I hope soon to be able to give you a more pleasing detail, not a line from home by this day mail—I injoy good health and wish to be remembered as usual

I am sincerely Yours

P. Gansevoort

In a letter issued only a week later, he mentioned new witnesses arriving from Louisiana to testify. As "what time will be required to hear their testimony cannot be conjectured by the Court," Gansevoort delayed his plans to set out for New York once again, concluding the letter with hopes that he might send Catherine a "more pleasing detail" in the coming days.[35] Gansevoort defended remaining in town to see the trial to its completion, claiming that Catherine would "be abashed & Ashamed did I direct my duty & return home without being directed so to do by the proper Authority, my experiences As a soldier has taught me to Obay the orders of my superior without a murmer."[36] It also revealed a level of maturity in the Brigadier General; previous letters during his service in the Revolutionary War indicated numerous and extensive unannounced absences of service.

A letter dated November 29 bore mixed news for Catherine and the family. While the court of the Wilkinson Trial "again exhausted all the evidence" brought by the two men from the Mississippi Valley, acting Judge Advocate Walter F. Jones, Jr.[37] had unexpectedly left to argue before the Supreme Court, delaying the proceedings. In a comprehensive letter addressed to James Madison on the same day, Gansevoort urged the president to appoint a replacement; one "over whom the Court can have a proper control."[38] It is interesting to note that behind the formalities, Gansevoort revealed his consistent frustration with the proceedings, claiming the constant adjournments of the court to be "a waste of time and expense alike injurious to the public service and the public purse." With so many adjournments, Gansevoort found time to pay his respects to President Madison, Vice President George Clinton and General Samuel Smith, a senator from Maryland. In high spirits, he expected to arrive back home within the month.[39]

271—To James Madison

To the President of the United States

Sir, At a meeting of the members of the General Court Martial constituted for the trial of Brigadier General Wilkinson, it was decided that you should be informed of the difficulties the Court has to strugle with.

On the 6th Instant, being apprised by the Judge Advocate as well as the accused that they had no more evidence to produce, the Court adjourned to afford an Opportunity for the accused to prepare his defence. In the mean time two witnesses arrived from the lower Mississippi whose testimony has been duly taken and recorded.

The Court exhausted all the evidence on the 23d Instant the accused has declared that he is now ready to deliver his defence; but the Court cannot regularly proceed owing to the absence of the Citizen who had been apppointed its Judge Advocate.

The Officers composing the Court feel assured Sir that you will cause a successor to be appointed, and particularly one over whom the Court can have a proper controul, or signify your pleasure that I may exersise the power given by the 21st Section of the Act fixing the Military peace establishment of the United States.

The want of a Judge Advocate has already more than once arrested our proceedings thereby occasioning a waste of time and expense alike injurious to the public service and the public purse; to say nothing of our own pessissiary recourses and the Dignity of the Court.

The great Interest that a long train of circumstances appears to have excited in the public mind; the repeated examination of these before the Representative Council of the Nation; the reference of the whole of them to this General Court Martial for a final, full and equitable decision must justify the most solemn and regular proceeding as well as the most accurate and independant Judgement, in the case, and I trust Sir this sentiment will serve as an ample apology for the Liberty taken in thus addressing you.—In hopes of bring honored by an answer on or before Wenesday the 4th of Decr. I have adjourned the Court to Thursday the 5th.

With Sentiments of profound respect I have the honor to be, Sir Your most obt

Fredericktown Maryland

November 29th 1811

[PG]

[James Madison]

272—To His Wife, Catherine Gansevoort

Frederick Town 29 Novr 1811

My Dear Caty On the 6th Inst. the Court being apprised by the Judge Advocate, as well as by the accused, that they had no further evidence to produce, The Court adjourned to offerd an opportunity for the accused to prepare his defence in the mean time two witnesses arrived from the lower Mississippi, whose testimony was of course taken, The Court again exhausted all the evidence and again adjourned on the 23d Inst. to meet on the 28th The accused says that he is now ready to deliver his defence but for the want of the Judge Advocate the Court cannot legally proceed to business, he is at present engaged in his private business as a lawyer attending the supreme Court in the district of Columbia, During the last adjournment Colo McComb & myself took a hack from this place for Washington City whare we passed all Munday & Tuesday,

This I was induced to do because the secretary of War told some of the Gentlemen of the Court meet, & that I might proceed home immediately after our business is closed, the secretary did me the honor of to accompany me when I called on the President of the U.S. to pay my respects to him and have now the pleasure of informing you that I was politely recd by them The Vice President and General Smith from Baltimore, did me the honor of returning my Call on Tuesday morning, before I conclude this letter I must inform you that the Court have this day addressed a letter to the President of the United States praying that a successor may be appointed in the place of Mr Jones, I am still in hopes to leave this place by the 26th of next month we may possiably git thro' a few days sooner, can you inform me of the reason why none of my Children write me—I have the pleasure to tell you that my health is as yet preserved which I must earnestly wish may be the Case with yourself & family & all friends please to present my respects to all particularly to Aunt Polly

I am Dr Caty Yours Affectionately

P. Gansevoort

P.S. if an Opportunity Offers send to N. York my Sherry Valize

The last few letters to Catherine in December rarely deviate from the previous themes. Still an "impossibality to say when we shall see the end of this long investigation," the General again criticized his part in what seems to be wasteful bureaucratic practices.[40] Regarding the recording of all testimony and proceedings of the court, he noted that they have taken "such amasing mass." The Wilkinson trial papers numbered more than six hundred pages, all of which were eventually forwarded to President Madison for analysis.[41] Madison would not be able to issue a verdict of "Not Guilty" on the trial until February 14, 1812. Nonetheless, Gansevoort's job seemed to have been fulfilled by late December; Madison congratulated Gansevoort and the members of the court for a successful proceeding, "which tho' interesting, and important to the Country & Government, The accused and ourselves, has from variety of circumstances, been both painful and tedious."[42] One of the last letters to Catherine, written on Christmas Day found Gansevoort in reflection, and a mood more dour than anxious for return. The lack of correspondence from his family had left him to equate "this total silence to some bad Oman ... I shall yet flatter myself that I have drawn too near me the dark side of the picture."[43] Gansevoort hired a carriage and set off to Philadelphia, where he hoped to arrive in four or five days and continue to "progress towards home as expeditiously as the season will admit—paint to your imagination what must be my feelings while progressing towards home."[44]

273—To His Wife, Catherine Gansevoort

Fredericktown 15 Decem 1811

My Dr Caty *I again take the pleasure of writing you, altho shoret letter I trust will be acceptable I cannot account for neglect are in attention of our Children towards me Mail after mail arrives not a line from home I am obliged to write my letters before the arrival of the mail because is Closes very soon after its arrival, Gennal Wilkinson concluded his defence on friday last he was five days engaged in reading it, what time the Judge advocate will require in his reply is uncertain, we do however expect that by the last of the ensuing week we shall nearly draw to a Close—The mail has just arrived & acknowledge the receipt of Peter's letter the Short was wel-*

come because it says that you are all well—Capt Bebee has by my directions sent the Wine & Gin fearful that the navigation might be obstructed by Ice. When I return induced me to trouble him with it—My return home will be as Speedely as possiable—If I may judge of your correct mind You would be abashed & Ashamed did I direct my duty & return home without being directed so to do by the proper Authority, my experiences As a soldier has taught me to Obay the orders of my superior without a murmer—I had wrote part of this letter before the arrival of the mail that brought Peter's letters which Caused me to make an addition to this, remember me to our Children Aunt Polly, & all our relations & friends before I conclude I must tell you that I have hopes of being home by the first day of the New Year Maria Wrote me some time since that Hammer was going to New York & would write me from thence—not a scrap has been recd from him

I am sincerely yours

P Gansevoort

274—To His Wife, Catherine Gansevoort

Frederick Town 18 Decemr 1811

My Dr Caty Inclination as well as duty again prompts me to write to you, & inform you of my health, Owing to same casualties has prevented the Judge advocate from commencing his defence untill this morning, It is impossiable to say with any degree of precetion from the immencity of oral tistimony, and the documents heretofere taken by the different Commitees of Congress and the Court of inquiry, all of which proceedings are to be recinced by our Court as legal tistimony—I say the whole taken together forms such amasing mass, that it is all most next to an impossibality to say when we shall see the end of this long investigation—As the old adage say that there is no end to whare there is no begining and as the latter is made—I have some reason to hope before the Close of the ensuing week to give you a more satisfactory detail of our probable [?] here, I consequence of the incessant rains the roads have become so intorable cut up that none of stages with their mails have yet arrived, it is now 6 OClock, when they generally arrive between the hours of 3 & 4 OClock, five in number, to wit from Baltimore, Winchester, Washington City, Lancaster, & Hagerstown, their Arrivals are on Sundays, Wednesday & fridays, This moment my servant tells me that the Baltimore mail has just arrived shall defer writing until his return from the Post Office, in hopes of the pleasure of receiving a letter from home & the satisfaction of acknowledging the receipt of it half an hour is allowed from its arrival untill it Closes, My servant again as usual Announces nothing for you Sir—My respects to all not forgetting neighbour Tways family

I am Dr Caty yours

P. Gansevoort

275—To His Wife, Catherine Gansevoort

Frederick Town 22d Decemr 1811 Sunday Afternoon

My Dr Caty The Northern mail is again arrived and as usual nothing for me. I take pleasure of addressing a few lines, our long & tedious attendence at this Court is drawing to a Close, We meet tomorrow to set in judgement, in all probably we shall terminate our business by the middle of the week. Mr Jones must be at Washington by the last to prepare himself for the Court Which meets the next week . remember me to all my friends

I am Dr Caty Yours sincerely

P. Gansevoort

276—To Members of Wilkinson General Court Martial

Gentlemen The time has at length arrived when I am able to congratulate you on the termination of a trial, which tho' interesting, and important to the Country & Government, The accused and ourselves, has from variety of circumstances, been both painful and tedious—But Gentlemen I cannot part with you without expressing how sensible I am, of the respectfull attention shewn to me, on all occasions, by every member of the Court, Believe me. it has made a lasting impression on my mind, And Altho I am able to congratulate you on the prospect of once more returning to your Posts & families, Still a Melancholly sensation creeps in, at the Idea of our separation—But rest assured Gentlemen, that wheresoever you go—you carry with you my best wishes for your health & happiness

277—To His Wife, Catherine Gansevoort

Frederick town 25th Decemr 1811

My Dr Caty The northern mail has again arrived, not a letter or scrap from home, I now begin to [?] but this total silence to some bad Oman, whatever the Cause may be I hope to be able to breast my self to bear the shock with Christian firmness—I shall yet flatter myself, that I have drawn too near me the dark side of the picture, which I have drawn to my view—On this Memorable day called Christmas I have signed the proceedings of Genl Court Martial & Adjourned the Court sinae Die numbers of the members were of within one hour, of such as had their Horses—Colo Williams and myself have hired a Hack to take us to Philadelphia which place, wind & weather permitting, we shall reach in about four or five days, from which place I shall progress towards home as expedesiously as the season will admit—paint to your imagination what must be my feelings while progressing towards home, & not the least prospect of meeting with any communication by Letter or otherwise to eleviate a mind so distrustful as mine &c

remember me to all

I am Dr Caty yours sincerely

P Gansevoort

278—From Walter Jones, Jr.

This is to certify that Brigadier Genl Gansevoort President of the General Court Martial convened at Frederick Town by order of the President of the United States for the trial of Brigadier General James wilkinson attended the Court from the 2d of September 1811 the first day of its session until the 25 day of December 1811 inclusive being the day the Court adjourned sine die.

Given at at Fredericktown in the Genl Court Martial this 25 day of Decemeber 1811.

W: Jones Jr Off: as Judge Adv:

On February 18, 1812, Military Agent of the Northern Department Anthony Lamb issued a payment of $179.60 to Gansevoort for twenty days travelling from Albany to Fredericktown and for the 115 days presiding over the general court martial.

279—From Anthony Lamb

The United States

To Brig Genl P. Gansevoort Ds

To twenty days travelling from Albany N.Y. To Frederick Town M.d. to attend a General Court Martial agreeable to an Order from the War Department, at 1 doll pr Day is—$20—

To Same time returning—$20—

To the allowance three dollar for every hundred miles—Distance—820 miles—is—$24,,60

To 115 days attendance, as per the accompanying Certificate of Walter Jones Esqr at 1 dollar pr Day is—$115—

[total] $179,,60

I Certify on honor that the foregoing account is accurate and just

P Gansevoort Brigr Genl

Received Albany February 18th 1812 of Anthony Lamb Military Agent

The Sum of one hundred and Seventy nine dollars and Sixty Cents in full of the above account Signed Duplicate—

$179,,60

P. Gansevoort Brigr Gen

At sixty-two years of age, Peter Gansevoort, Jr., had fought in the war for American independence, had risen through the military ranks, and had proved himself to be a foundation of early New York institutions. His legacy secured, the aging general had become ill on his journey from Maryland to his home in New York, where he would eventually die on July 2, 1812. Gansevoort's death could not have come at a more inopportune time; a second war against Great Britain had begun less than a month prior. Gansevoort's personal experiences in the first Canadian invasion in the Revolution may have helped deter the two failed invasions of upper and lower Canada in 1812–1813. His knowledge of supply, the natives, and the New York borderlands would have been of immense benefit to his subordinates.

Gansevoort's legacy continues in New York and the nation. A hamlet in Northumberland County, New York, is named Gansevoort. He was the maternal grandfather of Herman Melville, regarded as one of America's greatest authors. Gansevoort's portrait, painted by the famed Gilbert Stuart, reveals a stark resemblance to other portraits of George Washington, the patriarch of the republican experiment in North America. His letters and correspondence as historical artifacts can provide to historians and aficionados alike a nuanced and personal portrait of an individual lost to the national historical narrative of the American Revolution.[45]

Appendix

On August 22, 1777, after a morning of enemy bombardment, seven British deserters entered Fort Schuyler and informed the commander of the fort, Colonel Peter Gansevoort, Jr., that Colonel Barry St. Leger with his army had "retreated with the utmost precipitation." After hearing this, Gansevoort fired his cannon towards the enemy encampment. Partially convinced when the enemy did not answer, he ordered some parties under the command of Major Robert Cochran and Captain Cornelius T. Jansen to investigate the accounts more thoroughly.

Upon their return, they discussed their discovery. After twenty-one days laying siege on Fort Schuyler, the British invaders under the command of Colonel St. Leger abandoned their blockade and fled to Canada. Not foreseeing the gallant resistance of the fort's inhabitants and the volatile relationship with the Indians accompanying him, St. Leger retreated northward with such haste that he left a huge supply of clothing, ammunition, artillery and engineer's stores behind.

After all the bounty was collected, a return was made on August 24 listing all the military stores taken. In the month of September, another return was made and signed by Joseph Savage, Captain Lieutenant of the Artillery.

A Return of Ammunition and Artillery Stores Taken at Fort Schuyler from the Enemy, August 24, 1777

Ammunition and Artillery	*six pounder*	*three pounder*	*total*
Royal 4 2/5	0	0	4
Shells	0	0	128
Damaged Travelling Carriages	1	1	0
Damagd Limber	1	1	0
Round Shot	20	135	0
Round Shot fixd with flanil Cartriges	15	72	0
Tube Boxes	2	2	0
Tubes	30	0	0
Cannisters	11	0	0
Setts of horse Harniss	1	0	0
Set of Mens Herniss	1	0	0
Springes	1	2	0
Ladles	1	1	0
Wad Hooks	1	1	0
Box M. Balls	0	0	8

Ammunition and Artillery	*six pounder*	*three pounder*	*total*
Powder Horns	0	2	0
Lanthorns	0	2	0
Tompkins	1	0	0
Handspikes	0	4	0
Aprons	0	1	0
Haver Sacks	0	3	0
Oyl Cloths	0	27	0
Hare Cloths	0	2	0
Coils of Rope	0	1	0
Musket Cartriges	0	2160	0
Copper Hoops	0	30	0
Boxes Damagd Cartriges	0	17	0
Tanned Hides	0	2	0
A Large Quantity of Damagd M.	0	0	0

A Return of Clothing and Baggage Taken at Fort Schuyler from the Enemy, August 24, 1777

Clothing and Baggage	*total*	*Clothing and Baggage*	*total*	*Clothing and Baggage*	*total*
Blankets	36	White Breeches	2	Frying Pans	4
Tents	54	White Vests	2	Brass Kettles	1
Bell Tents	5	Stocks	5	Indian Shoes	6
White Shirts	20	Sheets	6	Veileeses	2
Speckled Shirts	49	Set of Curtains	1	Saddle Bags	1
Coats	40	Table Cloth	1	Dearskins	5
Breeches	34	Matresses	6	Case of Soap	1
Stockings	54	Pillows	1	Yds of Strowds	4
Shoes	2	Bolsters	1	Tea Pot	1
Boots	1	Camp Stools	5	Brass Candle Sticks	4
Half Boots	1	Camp Kettles	24	Bed Cases	18
Nap Sacks	10	Blanket Coats	36	Pewter Plates	12
Hankerchiefs	20	Canteens	40	Tent Poles	100

A Return of Engineers Stores Taken in the Enemy's Camp at Fort Schuyler, August 24, 1777

Engineers Store	*total*	*Engineers Store*	*total*	*Engineers Store*	*total*
Wt of Iron	250	Grind Stones	3	Hand Saws	2
Wt of Steel	128	Sett of Blacksmith Tools	1	Tarr Barrrels	2
Spades	106	Sett of Mine Harness	10	Pitch Barrels	1
Picks	100	Cash of Nails	2	Batteaus	15
Falling Axes	80	Whip Saws	2	Hand Cuffs	10
Fathom of Rope	300	Cross Cut Saws	3	Bell Hooks	50
Waggons	19				

A Return of Ammunition and Artillery Stores Taken from the Enemy, Fort Schuyler, September 1777

Ammunition and Artillery total	*six pounder*	*three pounder*	
Royal Cohs: 4 2/5 In Dr:	0	0	4
Shels 4 2/5 In Diameter	0	0	129
Brass Cannon	0	2	0
Prov:s Carriages Good	0	2	0
Damaged T: Carriages	2	0	0
Good Lumber	2	0	0
Damaged Lumber	0	1	0
Round Shaft	20	135	155
Round Shaft fixt with flanil Cartridges	15	72	87
Tubes	30	30	60
Tube Boxes	2	2	0
Cannister Shaft	11	1	0
Sets Horse Harnets	0	0	1
Sets Mine Harnets	0	0	1
Springs	1	4	0
Ladles	1	2	0
Wad Hook	1	2	0
Box M Ball	0	0	18
Powder Horns	0	0	2
Lantherns	0	0	2
Tompkins	1	2	0
Hand Spikes	0	8	0
Aprons	1	2	0
Haversacks	0	0	3
Druging Boxes	0	0	1
Lind Stocks	0	0	2
Oyl Cloaths	0	0	27
Musqt Cartridge	0	0	3000
Damg'd Amn: Boxes	0	0	17
Good A Boxes	0	0	4
Coils of N Rope	0	0	1
Copper Hoops	0	0	30
Store Cloaths	0	0	2

NB A large Quantity of Musqint Cartridge Damaged
Numbers Not Known
Errors Excepted A Quantity of Junk
—also a Quantity of [Wollen Yarn]
Joseph Savage Capt Liut Artilly

Chapter Notes

Chapter One

1. Benedict Arnold (1741–1801) began his military service as a captain in the Lexington Alarm in Apr 1775. After the capture of Fort Ticonderoga and Crown Point, he was appointed by General Washington the rank of colonel in the Continental Army on 1 Sep 1775. He was wounded at Quebec on 31 Dec 1775 and assigned to the Twentieth Continental Infantry on 1 Jan 1776. On 10 Jan 1776, he was promoted to brigadier general and major general on 17 Feb 1777. He participated in the battles of Danbury and Ridgefield in Connecticut and the Battle of Saratoga in New York but regardless of his successes, he was passed over for promotion. Heavily indebted and opposed to the alliance with France, he deserted to the enemy on 25 Sep 1780. Involved with a British plot to capture West Point, it was thwarted and Arnold escaped. After the war, he lived in Canada and Britain, dying poor and obscure in 1801. Francis Bernard Heitman, *Historical Register of Officers of the Continental Army during the War of the Revolution, April 1775, to December, 1783* (Washington D.C.: The Rare Book Shop Publishing Company, Inc., 1914), 75–76; Mark Mayo Boatner, *Encyclopedia of the American Revolution* (New York: David McKay Co, Inc., 1966), 25.

2. Ticonderoga was situated on the western shore of Lake Champlain. Ethan Allen and the Green Mountain Boys, along with Benedict Arnold, captured the fort on May 10, 1775. The capture stalled a planned British invasion from Canada and also enabled American troops to invade Canada themselves. The British recaptured the fort in 1777 but abandoned it in 1780. Boatner, *Encyclopedia of the American Revolution*, 1100–1108; David Ranzan, "'Thus a war has begun': the capture of Fort Ticonderoga and its influence on the American Revolution." MA thesis, East Stroudsburg University, 2002, 27.

3. Harme Gansevoort (1712–1801) was the first child born to brewer Leendert Gansevoort and his wife, Catharina De Wandelaer Gansevoort. Through his hard work, the Gansevoort family became Albany's commercial elite and in May 1740, with his marriage to Magdalena Douw, united two influential families in the region. Father of Peter and Leonard Gansevoort, he served on the city council for more than ten years, elected assistant alderman and then alderman, and constable for the third ward. Stefan Bielinski, "Harme Gansevoort," *Colonial Albany Social History Project*, http://www.nysm.nysed.gov/albany/bios/g/hagansevoort4662.html.

4. Alice P. Kenney, *The Gansevoorts of Albany: Dutch Patricians in the Upper Hudson Valley* (Syracuse, New York: Syracuse University Press, 1969), "Principal Members of the Gansevoort Family" chart, 9, 24–25.

5. Volkert Petrus Douw (1720–1801) was Peter Gansevoort's uncle. During the American Revolutionary War, he served as a Rensselaerswyck member of the Albany Committee of Correspondence, delegate to the Provincial Congress, and as a commissioner and commissary to the Indians. In 1786, he was elected to the New York State Senate and served until 1793 when he retired. Stefan Bielinski, "Volkert P. Douw," *Colonial Albany Social History Project*, http://www.nysm.nysed.gov/albany/bios/d/vopdouw2234.html.

6. Kenney, *The Gansevoorts of Albany*, 89.

7. Kenney, *The Gansevoorts of Albany*, 89.

8. On 4 May 1775, Peter Gansevoort, Jr. was commissioned with the rank of lieutenant in Albany's Third Ward militia. After Philip Lansingh resigned his commission, the Committee of Arrangement appointed Peter Gansevoort, Jr. the rank of major in the Second Regiment on 19 Jul 1775. James Sullivan, ed. *Minutes of the Albany Committee of Correspondence 1775–1778* (Albany: The University of the State of New York, 1923), I: 26, 270. Goose Van Schaick (1736–1789) first served in the French and Indian War, rising to the rank of lieutenant colonel of the First New York Regiment. During the Revolutionary War, he was commissioned colonel of the Second New York Regiment on 28 Jun 1775. On 8 Mar 1776, he was given the command of the First New York Regiment and served until 6 Jul 1777. On 10 Oct 1783, he became brevet brigadier general, serving until Nov 1783. He was wounded at Ticonderoga on 6 Jul 1777. Heitman, *Historical Register*, 557; Boatner, *Encyclopedia of the American Revolution*, 1141.

9. Kenney, *The Gansevoorts of Albany*, 30.

10. *Ibid*, 40.

11. *Ibid*.

12. *Ibid*, "Principal Members of the Gansevoort Family" Chart.

13. *Ibid*, 34.

14. Philip John Schuyler (1733–1804) was elected to the Continental Congress in 1775, and served until he

was appointed a major general of the Continental Army in Jun. General Schuyler took command of the Northern Department, and planned the Invasion of Canada (1775). His poor health required him to place Richard Montgomery in command of the invasion. When Fort Ticonderoga fell to the British in 1777, Congress replaced Schuyler with General Horatio Gates and resigned from the army in 1779. He was a member of the New York State Senate from 1780 to 1784, and at the same time New York State Surveyor General from 1781 to 1784. Afterwards he returned to the State Senate from 1786 to 1790, where he actively supported the adoption of the United States Constitution. He was elected a United States Senator to the First United States Congress, serving from Jul 16, 1789 to Mar 3, 1791. Losing his bid for reelection, he returned to the State Senate from 1792 to 1797. He was elected again to the U.S. Senate and served in the 5 United States Congress from Mar 4, 1797 until his resignation because of health problems on Jan 3, 1798. Heitman, *Historical Register*, 485; Boatner, *Encyclopedia of the American Revolution*, 991.

15. Letter 2.

16. Sir Guy Carleton (1724–1808) served as Governor of the Province of Quebec from 1768 to 1778, concurrently serving as Governor General of British North America. He was recalled to England in 1778 but returned in 1782 to replace Sir Henry Clinton as a military commander-in-chief of the war effort. Boatner, *Encyclopedia of the American Revolution*, 182–183; Charles Henry Jones. *History of the Campaign for the Conquest of Canada in 1776. (*Philadelphia: Porter & Coates, 1970), 16.

17. Halfmoon is in the southeast part of Saratoga County and north of Albany. The town is named for the crescent shape of the land between the Hudson River and Mohawk River. John H. French, *Gazetteer of the State of New York: Embracing a Comprehensive View of the Geography, Geology, and General History of the State, and a Complete History and Description Every County, City, Town, Village, and Locality* (Syracuse, NY: R. Pearsall Smith, 1860), 589.

18. A half-mile southeast of Fort William Henry, Fort George was situated at the head of Lake George. Robert B. Roberts, *New York's Forts in the Revolution* (Rutherford: Fairleigh Dickinson University Press, 1980), 208.

19. Whitehall was incorporated by patent in 1765 as Skenesborough. Its name was changed in 1786. It lies at the southern extremity of Lake Champlain, situated near the mouth of Wood Creek. Named after Major Philip Skene, around 1770, he built a massive stone house and barn, a forge and two sawmills. French, *Gazetteer of the State of New York*, 686.

20. Called the Great Carrying Place, Fort Edward was the closest point on the Hudson River that allowed armies to cross over land to the southern end of Lake Champlain. Roberts, *New York's Forts in the Revolution*, 194.

21. Richard Montgomery (1738–1775) was appointed Brigadier General of the Continental Army on 22 June 1775 and promoted to Major General on 9 December 1775. When General Philip Schuyler became ill, Montgomery took over to lead the invasion of Canada. He was killed in the assault on Quebec on 31 December 1775. Heitman, *Historical Register*, 397; Roberts, *New York's Forts in the Revolution*, 244.

22. Fort Chambly was located at the foot of the Chambly rapids on the Richelieu River in Quebec, Canada. Roberts, *New York's Forts in the Revolution*, 25.

23. Brother of Peter Gansevoort, Leonard Gansevoort (1751–1810) served as a New York delegate to the Continental Congress in 1788. He represented Albany County in New York's revolutionary assembly in 1778 and 1779 and served in the militia, eventually becoming a colonel. He served in the State Assembly from 1787–1788 and in the State Senate from 1790–1793 and 1796–1802. Jerry Kail, ed., *Who Was Who During the American Revolution* (New York: The Bobbs-Merrill Co., 1976), 232.

24. Letter 3.

25. James Van Rensselaer (1747–1827) was assigned aide-de-camp to General Montgomery from Aug to 31 Dec 1775. In Apr 1776, he was commissioned as a captain in the Second NY Regiment in Apr 1776 and later served as aide-de-camp to General Schuyler from Jun to Aug 1776. Heitman, *Historical Register*, 557, Cuyler Reynolds, *Genealogical and Family History of Southern New York and the Hudson River Valley: A Record of the Achievements of Her People in the Making of a Commonwealth and the Building of a Nation* (New York: Lewis Historical Pub. Co, 1914), III: 1164.

26. Timothy Bedel (ca.1740–1787) received a commission as captain of the New Hampshire Rangers in Jun 1775. In the same month, he was promoted to colonel of the New Hampshire Rangers and served in this position until Aug 1776 when he cashiered. From 1777 to 1781, he served in the Vermont Militia, ending with the rank of Brig Genl. Heitman, *Historical Register*, 95; Samuel Carroll Derby, *A List of the Revolutionary Soldiers of Dublin, N.H.* (Columbus, OH: Spahr and Glenn, 1901), 20.

27. Philip Van Rensselaer (1747–1798) was in charge of the military stores of the Northern Department. Cuyler Reynolds, *Hudson-Mohawk Genealogical and Family Memoirs: A Record of Achievements of the People of the Hudson and Mohawk Valleys in New York State, Included Within the Present Counties of Albany, Rensselaer, Washington, Saratoga, Montgomery, Fulton, Schenectady, Columbia and Greene* (New York: Lewis Historical Pub. Co, 1911), 180–181.

28. Harrison Bird, *Attack on Quebec: The American Invasion of Canada, 1775* (New York: Oxford University Press, 1968), 91.

29. Jones, *Conquest of Canada*, 82.

30. Letter 4.

31. John R. Livingston (1750–1822) was an aide-de-camp to George Clinton. Reynolds, *Genealogical and Family History of Southern New York and the Hudson River Valley*, 1324.

32. Letter 5.

33. Bird, *Attack on Quebec*, 108.

34. Cornelius Van Slyck and Andrew Finck, Jr. to Peter Gansevoort, Jr. December 7, 1775. Military Papers of Brigadier Peter Gansevoort, Jr., Gansevoort-Lansing Collection, Humanities-Manuscripts & Archives, New York Public Library.

35. Henry Beekman Livingston (1750–1831) was commissioned captain of the Fourth NY Regiment on 28 Jun 1775. He was promoted to major on 2 Aug 17775 and transferred to the Third New York Regiment in Dec 1775. He served as an aide-de-camp to General Schuyler from Feb to Nov 1776 and was promoted colonel of the Fourth New York Regiment on 21 Nov 1776. He resigned his commission on 13 Jan 1779. Heitman, *Historical Register*, 354; William R. Denslow, *10,000 Famous Freemasons from K to Z* (Trenton, MO: Missouri Lodge of Research, 1957), III: 93.

36. Montreal surrendered 13 Nov Boatner, *Encyclopedia of the American Revolution*, 729.

37. Captain Effingham Lawrence (1734–1806) was a merchant and a member of the Corporation of Trinity House, 1796–1806. Reynolds, *Genealogical and Family History of Southern New York and the Hudson River Valley*, III: 1423.

38. John Gerritse Van Schaick (1748–1813), brother-in-law of Peter Gansevoort, Jr., was a financial supporter of the patriots in Albany. Stefan Bielinski, "Johannes G. Van Schaick," *Colonial Albany Social History Project*, http://www.nysm.nysed.gov/albany/bios/vs/jogvschaick3963.html.

39. Annatie Van Schaick married John Gerritse Van Schaick on Aug 2, 1775. Joel Munsell, ed., *Collections on the History of Albany: From Its Discovery to the Present Time* (Albany: J. Munsell, 1871), IV: 184.

40. Bird, *Attack on Quebec*, 165.

41. Bird, *Attack on Quebec*, 204.

Chapter Two

1. Letter 7.

2. The Siege of Fort St. Jean lasted from Sep 17 to Nov 3, 1775. Michael P. Gabriel, ed., *Quebec During the American Invasion, 1775–1776: The Journal of Francois Baby, Gabriel Taschereau, & Jenkin Williams* (East Lansing, MI: Michigan State University Press, 2005), 129.

3. Jarvis Mudge (1724–1810) served as first lieutenant in the Second NY Regiment from 28 Jun 1775 to Oct 1775. Heitman, *Historical Register*, 406; Alfred Mudge, *Memorials: Being a Genealogical, Biographical and Historical Account of the Name of Mudge in America, from 1638 to 1868* (Boston: Alfred Mudge & Son, 1868), 72.

4. Charles Lee (1731–1782) was appointed second ranking major general of Continental Army. Lee severely criticized Washington and while a prisoner, submitted plans to British General Howe for defeating Americans; After the Battle of Monmouth, he was court-martialed, found guilty of disobedience, of misbehavior before the enemy and of disrespect to the commander in chief. Dismissed from the army in 1780. *Webster Biographical Dictionary*, 875.

5. Letter 8.

6. Leonard Gansevoort to Peter Gansevoort, Jr., August 2, 1776. Military Papers of Brigadier General Peter Gansevoort, Jr.

7. Nathaniel Woodhull (1722–1776) was a member of the New York Provincial Assembly for Suffolk County from 1769 to 1775, a delegate to the First Continental Congress, a brigadier general of the New York Militia during the American Revolution. He was taken prisoner at Jamaica on 28 Aug 1776 and while in captivation, he was wounded. He died of his wounds at New Utrecht. Heitman, *Historical Register*, 604; Edna L. Jacobsen, "Nathaniel Woodhull." *Dictionary of American Biography, s.v.*

8. Letter 9.

9. Esopus is on the west bank of the Hudson River south of Kingston. *Merriam-Webster Geographical Dictionary*, 367.

10. Letter 10.

11. George Washington (1732–1799) was the general and Commander-in-Chief of all the forces raised or to be raised on 15 Jun 1775. He also was the first President of the United States, serving from 30 Apr 1789 to 4 Mar 1797. He was given the rank of lieutenant general and Commander of the United States Army on 2 Jul 1798 until he died at Mount Vernon, Virginia. Heitman, *Historical Register*, 571–573, Kail, *Who Was Who During the American Revolution*, 487–488; Lincoln Diamant. *Chaining the Hudson: The Fight for the River in the American Revolution.* (New York: Fordham University Press, 2004), 93.

12. Philip Van Rensselaer to Peter Gansevoort, Jr., June 21, 1776. Military Papers of Brigadier Gansevoort Peter Gansevoort, Jr.

13. Cornelius D. Wynkoop (1734–1792) was appointed major of the Third New York Regiment on 30 Jun 30 1775. He was promoted lieutenant colonel on 2 Aug 1775 and colonel on 11 Apr 1776. Heitman, *Historical Register*, 609; Richard Wynkoop, *Wynkoop Genealogy in the United States of America* (New York: Knickerbocker Press, 1904), 45.

14. Letter 11.

15. Located halfway between Whitehall and Fort Edward, Fort Anne was situated at the confluence of Wood Creek and Halfway Brook or Cheshire's Brook. Roberts, *New York's Forts in the Revolution*, 83–84.

16. Richard Varick to Peter Gansevoort, Jr., June 12, 1776. Military Papers of Brigadier General Peter Gansevoort, Jr.

17. Philip Conine to Peter Gansevoort, Jr., June 11, 1776. Military Papers of Brigadier General Peter Gansevoort, Jr.

18. Letter 12.

John Sullivan (1740–1795) was commissioned Brigadier General of the Continental Army on 22 June 1775. He was promoted to Major General on 9 August 1776. On 27 August 1776, he was taken prisoner at Long Island. He was exchanged in time to fight at Trenton and Princeton and later at Brandywine and Germantown. He led a scorched earth campaign against the Iroquois towns in 1779 and resigned his commission on

30 November 1779. He was elected Governor of New Hampshire in 1786, 1787 and 1789. Heitman, *Historical Register*, 527; Kail, *Who Was Who During the American Revolution*, 186–187.

19. John Lansing, Jr. (1754–1829) was appointed Second Lieutenant in the First New York Regiment on 21 November 1776. He resigned his commission on 8 December 1776 and served subsequently as Adjutant in the New York Militia Regiment and as Military Secretary to General Schuyler. Heitman, *Historical Register*, 340; Kail, *Who Was Who During the American Revolution*, 243.

20. Fort Crown Point was erected by the French in 1731 and called Fort St. Frederick. In 1759, it surrendered to the British troops under General Amherst. On 14 May 1775, it fell into the hands of the Americans but was evacuated in 1776 and again fell into the hands of the British. Horatio Gates Spafford, ed., *A Gazetteer of the State of New York* (Albany: B.D. Packard, 1824), 137.

21. Located at the confluence of Popolopen Creek and the Hudson River near Bear Mountain in Orange County, NY, Fort Montgomery, along with Fort Clinton, were known as the "Twin Forts of the Popolopen." Planned in 1775 and built during 1776, it was constructed on the north side of the creek five miles below West Point. General George Clinton commanded the fort. Robert B. Roberts, *Encyclopedia of Historic Forts: The Military, Pioneer, and Trading Posts of the United States* (New York: Macmillan, 1988), 542–543.

22. Across Lake Champlain, a chain fence or boom was positioned to protect the bridge that connected Fort Ticonderoga and Fort Independence. The purpose of the boom, which was anchored upon a series of rafts and sizable logs, was to halt any watercraft so cannon fire from Forts Ticonderoga and Independence would shatter the halted vessels. Michael O. Logusz, *The Saratoga Campaign and the Wilderness War of 1777* (Havertown, PA: Casemate Publishers, 2010), 74; Diamant, *Chaining the Hudson*, 94.

23. Letter 13.

24. John H. Wendell (1744–1832) was appointed captain in Wynkoop's New York Regiment on 1 Mar 1776. He received a commission of captain in the First New York Regiment on 21 Nov 1776 and resigned on 5 Apr 1781. Heitman, *Historical Register*, 582; John Schuyler, *Institution of the Society of the Cincinnati, Formed by the Officers of the American Army of the Revolution, 1783, With Extracts, from the Proceedings of its General Meetings and from the Transactions of the New York State Society* (New York: Printed for the Society by D. Taylor, 1886), 343.

25. Point au Fer was a tongue of land bending southeast from the New York shore of Lake Champlain about a mile south of Rouses Point. Roberts, *New York's Forts in the Revolution*, 87.

26. Letter 14.

27. Letter 15.

28. Ile aux Noix is an island on the Richelieu River in Quebec, close to Lake Champlain. Boatner, *Encyclopedia of the American Revolution*, 538.

29. The Oneidas were known as the "granite people" or O-na-yote-ka-o-no. In 1715, Tuscaroras were expelled from North Carolina and headed north to seek a home with the Iroquois. Known as the "shirt wearing people" or Dus-ga-o-weh-o-no, a portion of the Oneida territory was assigned to them. Lewis Henry Morgan, *League of the Iroquois* (Secaucus, NJ: The Citadel Press, 1975), vii, 24; Colin G. Calloway, *The American Revolution in Indian Country: Crisis and Diversity in Native American Communities* (New York: Cambridge University Press, 2009), 121.

30. Joseph T. Glatthaar and James Kirby Martin, *Forgotten Allies: The Oneida Indians and the American Revolution* (New York: Hill and Wang, 2006), 98.

31. Sir John Johnson (1742–1830), the son of British colonial official Sir William Johnson, was a Loyalist leader, who marched with St. Leger against Fort Schuyler in 1777. Later, Johnson became Indian superintendent and participated in Indian affairs and led a series of raids into the Mohawk Valley. Boatner, *Encyclopedia of the American Revolution*, 561–562.

32. *Ibid*, 101.

33. James Van Rensselaer to Peter Gansevoort, Jr., July 7, 1776. Military Papers of Brigadier General Peter Gansevoort, Jr.

34. Horatio Lloyd Gates (ca. 1727–1806) was a major in British Army during the French and Indian War. He was appointed a brigadier general and adjutant-general in the Continental Army on 17 Jun 1775. On 16 May 1776, he was promoted to major general and was given command of the Canadian Department. In 1777, he replaced General Schuyler as commander of the Northern Department. After the success at Saratoga, he was appointed President of the Board of War. After the unsuccessful Conway Cabal, which would have made Gates Commander in Chief, he was sent down to command in the Carolinas. He suffered a disgraceful defeat at Camden. He served to the close of the war. Boatner, *Encyclopedia of the American Revolution*, 412–416; Heitman, *Historical Register*, 244.

35. Letter 16.

36. Jonathan Trumbull, Jr. to Peter Gansevoort, Jr., July 24, 1776. Military Papers of Brigadier General Peter Gansevoort, Jr.

37. Elias Dayton (1737–1807) was commissioned colonel of the Third New Jersey Regiment on 18 Jan 1776. In the spring of 1776 he was put in charge of constructing fortifications to protect the colonists in the Mohawk Valley. These fortifications included Fort Dayton and Fort Schuyler. He was transferred to the Second New Jersey Regiment on 1 Jan 1781. On 7 Jan 1783, he was appointed brigadier general of the Continental Army and served until the close of the war. Heitman, *Historical Register*, 190; Kail, *Who Was Who During the American Revolution*, 198–199.

38. Letter 17.

39. John Burgoyne (1722–1792) was a British army officer, politician and dramatist. During the Saratoga campaign he surrendered his army of approximately 5,000 men to the American troops on October 17, 1777. *Dictionary of American Biography*, VII: 340–342.

40. German Flats was a ten-mile stretch of Palatine

villages on both sides of the Mohawk River. Roberts, *New York's Forts in the Revolution*, 188.

41. Situated a few miles north of the lower Mohawlk castle, Johnstown or Ka-la-ne-ka by the Iroquois was the residence of Sir William Johnson (1715–1774). Morgan, *League of the Iroquois*, 418.

42. Oswegatchie is a town in northern part of St. Lawrence County, NY. French, *Gazetteer of the State of New York*, 580.

43. Thomas Spencer (ca. 1749–1777) was a half-breed Oneida blacksmith, scout and spy who had resided among the Cayugas and Oneidas. His father, Elihu Spencer, was a devout Anglo-American Presbyterian who settled two miles east of Cherry Valley. Also known as Ahnyero, he died at the Battle of Oriskany. A. J. Berry, *A Time of Terror* (Victoria, B.C.: Trafford, 2005), 107; Glatthaar and Martin, *Forgotten Allies*, 89–90, 166; Augustus C. Buell, *Sir William Johnson* (New York: D. Appleton and Company, 1903), 54; J. Norman Heard, *Handbook of the American Frontier: Four Centuries of Indian-White Relationships* (Metuchen, NJ: The Scarecrow Press, 1990), II: 342.

44. Samuel Elmore (1720–1805) was appointed to the rank of major in the Fourth Connecticut Regiment and served from 1 May to 20 Dec 1775. On 15 Apr 1776, he was promoted to colonel in the Connecticut State Regiment and served to Apr 1777. In Oct 1776, Elmore's Connecticut regiment replaced Colonel Elias Dayton's Third New Jersey Regiment at Fort Schuyler and by May 1777, Gansevoort's Third New York Regiment replaced Elmore. Heitman, *Historical Register*, 215; Daughters of the American Revolution, *Lineage Book* (Washington DC: National Society of the Daughters of the American Revolution, 1908), XXVI: 141.

45. Stephen McCrea to Peter Gansevoort, Jr., August 29, 1776. Military Papers of Brigadier General Peter Gansevoort, Jr.

46. John McCrea to Peter Gansevoort, Jr., August 28, 1776. Military Papers of Brigadier General Peter Gansevoort, Jr.

47. Letter 18.

48. Commandant of Fort Niagara, Lieutenant Colonel John Caldwell (d. 1776) commanded the Eighth Regiment of Foot. Calloway, *The American Revolution in Indian Country*, 134; John R. Brodhead, *Documents relative to the Colonial History of the State of New-York; Procured in Holland, England and France*, ed. E. B. O'Callaghan (Albany: Weed, Parsons and Company, 1857), VIII: 509.

49. John Butler was a deputy agent for Indian Affairs. Barbara Graymont, *The Iroquois in the American Revolution* (Syracuse, NY: Syracuse University Press, 1972), 81; Isabel Thompson Kelsay, *Joseph Brant, 1743–1807, Man of Two Worlds* (Syracuse: Syracuse University Press, 1984), 179.

50. Letter 19.

51. Israel Spencer (1732–1813) received a commission as a second lieutenant in the Second NY Regiment on 28 Jun 1775. He was transferred as a captain of Burrall's Continental Regiment from 19 Jan 1776 to Jan 1777. He served subsequently as major in the NY Levies. Heitman, *Historical Register*, 511, Daughters of the American Revolution, *Lineage Book*, XX: 244.

52. Jonathan Potts (d. 1781) was appointed surgeon for the troops on the Canadian Expedition on 6 June 1776. On 11 April 1777, he was promoted to Deputy Director-General of Hospital for the Northern Department and transferred to the Middle Department on 22 January 1778. He retired on 6 October 1780. Heitman, *Historical Register*, 449.

53. Jonathan Trumbull, Jr. (1756–1843) accepted a commission as adjutant of the Second Connecticut on 28 May 1775. He was promoted to lieutenant colonel and became Aide-de-Camp to General Washington on 27 July 1775. He accepted the position of Brigade Major to General Joseph Spencer on 15 August 1775 and Deputy Adjutant-General of the Northern Department on 28 June 1776. He resigned on 19 April 1777. Heitman, *Historical Register*, 550; Kail, *Who Was Who During the American Revolution*, 30.

54. Horatio Gates to Peter Gansevoort, Jr. Military Papers of Brigadier General Peter Gansevoort, Jr.

55. Letter 23.

56. Jonathan Trumbull, Jr. to Peter Gansevoort, Jr., August 6, 1776. Military Papers of Brigadier General Peter Gansevoort, Jr.

57. John Visscher (ca. 1739–1821) was appointed Captain in the Second New York Regiment on 1 July 1775. He was promoted to Major in October 1775 and assigned to the Fourth New York Regiment on 8 March 1776. On 26 June 1776, he was promoted to Lieutenant-Colonel of Nicholson's Continental Regiment and was wounded at Johnstown on 22 May 1780. Heitman, *Historical Register*, 561; Daughters of the American Revolution, *DAR Patriot Index* (Baltimore, MD: Gateway Press, 2003), 2807.

58. *Ibid.*

59. Horatio Gates to Peter Gansevoort, Jr., August 14, 1776. Military Papers of Brigadier General Peter Gansevoort, Jr.

60. Letter 24.

61. Abraham Cuyler Gansevoort was born on Jul 23, 1775. Munsell, *Collections on the History of Albany*, 124.

62. Benjamin Egberts, born between 1739 and 1743, was a lieutenant in the Albany militia company. By 1776, he was promoted to captain and appointed storekeeper at Fort George, replacing Mr. Shephard. In 1778, he was exempted from militia duty because he was a clerk at the hospital, serving for more than two years. Stefan Bielinski, "Benjamin Egberts," *Colonial Albany Social History Project*, http://www.nysm.nysed.gov/albany/bios/e/beegberts4510.html.

63. Letter 25.

64. Letter 27.

65. Jacob Cuyler (1741–1802) was Deputy Commissary-General of Purchases from 18 Jun 1777 to Jul 1782. Heitman, *Historical Register*, 183; *DAR Patriot Index*, 679.

66. Robert Yates (1738–1801) was a member of the Albany Committee of Correspondence and as secretary of the Board of Indian Commissioners. Yates was appointed to the New York State Supreme Court in 1777.

From 1790 to 1798, he served as Chief Justice of the New York State Supreme Court. Kail, *Who Was Who During the American Revolution*, 277; Stefan Bielinski, "Robert Yates," *Colonial Albany Social History Project*, http://www.nysm.nysed.gov/albany/bios/y/ryates.html.

67. Letter 29.

68. Letter 30.

69. Cornelius Van Dyck (1740–1792), the second-in-command of Van Schaick's First NY Regiment. Heitman, *Historical Register*, 43; Willis T. Hanson, Jr., *A History of Schenectady During the Revolution to which is appended a contribution to the individual records of the inhabitants of the Schenectady District during that period* (Brattleboro, VT: E. L. Hildreth & Co., 1916), 234–235.

70. Enoch Poor (1736–1780) served as colonel of the Second New Hamphire Register from May to Nov 1776. He was promoted to brigadier general of the Continental Army on 21 Feb 1777. Heitman, *Historical Register*, 446; John C. Fredriksen, *Revolutionary War Almanac* (New York: Facts on File, 2006), 575–576.

71. John Stark (1728–1822) was Colonel of the First New Hampshire Regiment from 23 April to December 1775. He was reassigned to the Fifth Continental Infantry and served from 1 January to 31 December 1776. He was reassigned to the First New Hampshire on 8 November 1776 and resigned his commission on 23 March 1777. He was promoted to Brigadier-General of the New Hampshire Militia in 1777 and Brigadier General of the Continental Army on 4 October 1777 and served to close of war. Later he was promoted to Brevet Major-General on 30 September 1783. Heitman, *Historical Register*, 515; Kail, *Who Was Who During the American Revolution*, 186.

72. Marinus Willett (1740–1830) was a leader of the Sons of Liberty in New York City. He accepted a commission of captain of the First New York Regiment, serving from 28 Jun 1775 to 9 May 1776. On 21 Nov 1776, he was commissioned lieutenant colonel of the Third New York Regiment. On 1 Jul 1780, he was promoted to lieutenant colonel Commandant of the Fifth New York Regiment and colonel in Nov 1780. He retired on 1 Jan 1781 and subsequently served as colonel in the New York Levies and Militia. Heitman, *Historical Register*, 593; Kail, *Who Was Who During the American Revolution*, 273–274.

73. Robert Cochran (d. 1802) was appointed captain of a Connecticut Company under General Arnold at Crown Point in May 1775. He was reassigned as captain of Elmore's Continental Regiment on 15 Apr 1776 and promoted to major on 25 Jul 1776. He was reassigned again to the Third New York Regiment on 21 Nov 1776. On 30 Mar 1780, he was reassigned to the Second New York Regiment with the rank of lieutenant colonel and served to close of war. Heitman, *Historical Register*, 163; W. T. R. Saffell, *Records of the Revolutionary War*, Third Edition (Baltimore: Charles C. Saffell, 1894), 545.

74. Jeremiah Van Rensselaer (1738–1810) was commissioned ensign in the Third New York Regiment on 21 Nov 1776. He was assigned the regimental paymaster, serving from 28 May 1778 to Jun 1783. He was transferred to the First New York Regiment on 1 Jan 1781 and was promoted to lieutenant on 5 Apr 1781, serving to the close of the war. Heitman, *Historical Register*, 557; David C. Whitney and Kay Lovelace Smith, *The Colonial Spirit of '76: The People of the Revolution: The Lives of Members of the Continental Congresses and Other Prominent Men and Women of the Period* (Chicago: J.G. Ferguson Pub. Co., 1974), 395.

75. Letter 31; Letter 33; Letter 34; Letter 35.

76. Aaron Aorson (b. 1741) was appointed to the rank of first lieutenant in the First New York Continental Regiment under the command of Colonel Alexander McDougall. From 28 Jun 1775 to 15 Apr 1776, he was campaigning at Quebec. On 26 Jun 1776, he was appointed to Colonel Lewis DuBois's regiment, resigning on 8 Jul 1776. On 21 Nov 1776, he was promoted to the rank of captain in the Third New York Regiment under the command of Colonel Peter Gansevoort and served in that regiment until he was transferred to the First New York Regiment under the command of Colonel Goose Van Schaick on 1 Jan 1783. He was promoted to a brevet major on 30 Sep 1783 and served to close of war. Heitman, *Historical Register*, 72–73, 694.

Chapter Three

1. Letter 36.

2. Bernard Maussac de La Marquisie was a French engineer, employed by General Schuyler to repair Fort Schuyler in 1777. Due to the incompetence, he was sent back to Albany and replaced by Major Hubbel to superintend the works. Boatner, *Encyclopedia of the American Revolution*, 686.

3. William Colbreath, *Days of Siege: A Journal of the Siege of Fort Stanwix in 1777*, ed. Larry Lowenthal (New York: Eastern Acorn Press, 1983), 11.

4. Charles Neilson, *An original, compiled and corrected account of Burgoyne's campaign, and the memorable battles of Bemis's Heights, Sept. 19, and Oct. 7, 1777, from the most authentic sources of information; including many interesting incidents connected with the same* (Port Washington, NY: Kennikat Press, 1970), 36.

5. Nelson Greene, *The Old Mohawk Turnpike Book* (Fort Plain, NY: Nelson Greene, 1924), 284–287.

6. Abraham Ten Broeck (1734–1810) served as Colonel of the Albany County Militia from 1775 to 1778 and Brigadier General from 25 June 1778 to 26 March 1781. He served as chairman of the Committee of Safety and president of the New York Provincial Congress in 1777. In 1779, he was appointed mayor of Albany on the death of John Barclay, serving until 1783 and again, following the death of Abraham Yates, Jr., from 1796 to 1798. From 1780–1783, he served in the New York State Senate. Heitman, *Historical Register*, 536; Kail, *Who Was Who During the American Revolution*, 266; Franklin B. Hough, *The New York Civil List, Containing the Names and Origin of the Civil Divisions and the Names and Dates of Election or Appointment of the Principal State and County Officers, from the Revolution to the Present Time* (Albany: Weed, Parsons & Co., 1858), 49.

7. Letter 37.
8. *Ibid.*
9. Letter 38.
10. *Ibid.*
11. Marie Joseph Paul Yves Roch Gilbert du Motier, Marquis de Lafayette (1757–1834), came to North America in 1777 where he was appointed major general in the Continental Army. He was wounded on 11 Sep 1777 at the battle of Brandywine. He was appointed Commander of a body of troops to operate against Canada and in Rhode Island. In 1779, he was assigned to the staff of the army in Normandy but returned to America in Mar 1780. He was in command of a force of 10,000 men in Virginia and returned to France in Nov 1781 with news of the capture of Yorktown. He did not return to America but performed the duties of major general of the combined armies of France and Spain against Jamaica. Heitman, *Historical Register*, 337–338; Kail, *Who Was Who During the American Revolution*, 502.
12. Jean Baptiste de Gouvion (1747–1792) served in the French Engineers Corps since 1769. In 1777, he was sent to America as one of the four French military engineers in response to a special request of the U.S. Congress. He rose to the rank of colonel during the American Revolution. Heitman, *Historical Register*, 656; Paul K. Walker, *Engineers of Independence: A Documentary History of the Army Engineers in the American Revolution, 1775–1783* (Honolulu, Hawaii: University Press of the Pacific, 1981), 328.
13. *Ibid.*
14. William Colbreath served as second lieutenant of Nicholson's New York Regiment from Mar to Nov 1776. He received a commission of ensign of the Third New York Regiment on 21 Nov 1776, promoted to lieutenant a year later. He was appointed regimental quartermaster in Jul 1780 and transferred to the Second New York Regiment in 1781 and served to Jun 1783. Heitman, *Historical Register*, 163.
15. Kripplebush is a hamlet near the south town line of Marbletown, NY in Ulster County, southwest of Kingston. French, *Gazetteer of the State of New York*, 664.
16. John Nicholson accepted a commission in the Third New York Regiment with a rank of captain and served from 28 June to November 1775. He was promoted to colonel in the Continental Regiment and served from 8 March to November 1776. Heitman, *Historical Register*, 414.
17. Letter 40.
18. Letter 41.
19. Letter 43.
20. John Roof was a German, who was the first man along with his family, located at Fort Stanwix as a permanent settler; subduing the soil and becoming actively engaged in the transport of merchandise over the Carrying Place, between the Mohawk and Wood creek. He located there in 1760. Jeptha Root Simms, *The Frontiersmen of New York: Showing Customs of the Indians, Vicissitudes of the Pioneer White Settlers and Border Strife in Two Wars* (Albany: Geo. C. Riggs, 1883), II: 90.
21. Major Henry Glen (ca. 1840–1814) of Schenectady, NY was an assistant deputy-quartermaster general and an agent for the commissioners of Indian affairs in New York. Kail, *Who Was Who During the American Revolution*, 233; Leonard Bleeker, *The Order Book of Capt. Leonard Bleeker, Major of Brigade in the Early Part of the Expedition under Gen. James Clinton, against the Indian Settlements of Western New York, in the Campaign of 1779* (New York: Joseph Sabin, 1865), 25.
22. Myndert R. Wemple (b. 1742) served as an ensign in the Second Albany County Militia in 1777–1778 transporting provisions and stores on the Hudson and Mohawk Rivers. Heitman, *Historical Register*, 581; Hanson, *A History of Schenectady During the Revolution*, 271.
23. After a successful defense of the town of Peekskill, General Arthur McDougal with Lieutenant Colonel Marinus Willett pursued British General William Tryon who had been raiding western Connecticut towns along the Hudson River. The town of Danbury would be raided, and homes, warehouses and provisions destroyed. William M. Willett, *A Narrative of the Military Actions of Colonel Marinus Willett: Taken Chiefly From His Own Manuscript* (New York: G. & C. & H. Carvill, 1831), 40–42.
24. Jean Arthur de Vermonet received the rank of Brevet Captain in the Continental Army on 29 Jul 1776 and Brevet Major, 18 Sept 1776. Heitman, *Historical Register*, 560.
25. Horatio Gates to Peter Gansevoort, Jr., May 8, 1777. Military Papers of Brigadier Peter Gansevoort, Jr.
26. Letter 45.
27. Fishkill, formed as a town in 1788, lies upon the Hudson River, in the southwest corner of the Dutchess County. It is eighty-nine miles south of Albany. French, *Gazetteer of the State of New York*, 271; Spafford, *A Gazetteer of the State of New York*, 172.
28. Edward S Willet (1750–1810) served as forage master and transporter. He carried prisoners for exchange, cargoes, and intelligence on his sloop. Governor Clinton called him "a gentleman of undoubted loyalty." Stefan Bielinski, "Edward S. Willett," *Colonial Albany Social History Project*, http://www.nysm.nysed.gov/albany/bios/w/edwillett6905.html.
29. Gerrit Staats received his commission as second lieutenant in the Third New York Regiment inon 10 Aug 1776. He was promoted to first lieutenant on 23 Nov 1776 and resigned his commission on 1 March 1780. Heitman, *Historical Register*, 513.
30. Fort Constitution was built on Constitution Island or Martlaer's Rock in the Hudson River opposite West Point and six miles above Fort Montgomery. Roberts, *New York's Forts in the Revolution*, 123, 126.
31. Schenectady is derived from an Iroquois word Ska-neh-ta-de meaning beyond the openings. Morgan, *League of the Iroquois*, 415.
32. Colbreath, *Days of Siege*, 11; Neilson, *Burgoyne's Campaign*, 36; John Robert Elting, *The battles of Saratoga* (Monmouth Beach, NJ: Philip Freneau Press, 1977), 37.
33. Letter 46.
34. *Ibid*
35. *Ibid.*

36. Derived from the Iroquoian word meaning "place of the rapids," referring to the rapids of the Mohawk River, Caughnawaga was located on a rise of ground, known as the Sand Flats on the west side of Fonda. William Bright, *Native American Placenames of the United States* (Norman: University of Oklahoma Press, 2004), 84; Ellen Hardin Walworth, *The Life and Times of Kateri Tekakwitha: The Lily of the Mohawks, 1656–1680* (Buffalo: Peter Paul & Brother, 1893), 2.

37. Letter 47.

38. Leonard Gansevoort to Peter Gansevoort, Jr., June 2, 1777. Military Papers of Brigadier Peter Gansevoort, Jr.

39. Arthur Lee (1740–1792) was unsuccessful in gaining Spain's support for the rebel cause. In 1778, he helped negotiate the Treaty of Alliance with France with Silas Deane and Benjamin Franklin. *Webster Biographical Dictionary*, 872.

40. As the principal negotiator, Benjamin Franklin (1706–1790) urged France to sign a treaty of alliance with America in 1778. *Webster Biographical Dictionary*, 551.

41. The effort of Silas Deane (1737–1789) at The Hague led to Holland to enter the "League of Armed Neutrality" with Sweden, Russia, Denmark and Portugal. *Webster Biographical Dictionary*, 398.

42. On 15 Dec 1780, Congress appointed Francis Dana, minister to the court of the Russian Empress, Catherine II with two objects "to favor and support the sovereignty and independence of the United States," and to secure "the admission of the United States as a party to the convention for maintaining the freedom of the seas." Washington Chauncey Ford, *The Journals of the Continental Congress* (Washington D.C.: Government Printing Office, 1904–1937), XVIII: 1168–1173.

43. Samuel Holden Parsons (1737–1789) was appointed colonel of the Sixth Connecticut militia in 1775. He was transferred to the Tenth Continental Infantry in Jan 1776, promoted to the rank of brigadier general in Aug 1776 and major general in Oct 1780. He retired his commission in Jul 1782. In 1787, he was appointed as the first judge of the Northwest Territory. Heitman, *Historical Register*, 428; Fredriksen, *Revolutionary War Almanac*, 559–560.

44. Return Jonathan Meigs (1740–1823) crossed Long Island Sound from Connecticut to Long Island to attack the British fleet at Sag Harbor. Heitman, *Historical Register*, 388; George Bancroft, *History of the United States of America, From the Discovery of the Continent* (New York: D. Appleton and Company, 1885), V: 152.

45. George Clinton (1739–1812) served as brigadier general in the Continental Army from 25 Mar 1777 to 3 Nov 1783. He commanded the forces in the actions at Forts Clinton and Montgomery on 6 Oct 1777 and was promoted to brevet major general on 30 Sep 1783. He was elected the first governor of New York, serving from 1777 to 1795 and then served another term from 1801 to 1804. From 1805 to 1813, he was vice president under two presidents, Jefferson and Madison. Heitman, *Historical Register*, 161; Kail, *Who Was Who During the American Revolution*, 225–226.

46. Israel Putnam (1718–1790) accepted a commission of Lieutenant Colonel in the Lexington Alarm in April 1775. He was promoted to Colonel of the Third Connecticut Regiment on 1 May 1775 and to Major General of the Continental Army on 19 June 1775. He served in this capacity until his retirement on 3 June 1783. Heitman, *Historical Register*, 455.

Henry Knox (1750–1806) began his military career as a volunteer at Bunker Hill in Jun 1775 and was appointed colonel of the Continental Regiment of Artillery in Nov 1775. He was promoted to brigadier-general and chief of artillery in the Continental Army in Dec 1776. In 1782, he was promoted to major general and in Dec 1783, was appointed Commander-in-Chief of the Army, serving until Jun 1784. He later served as Secretary of War from 1785 to 1794. Heitman, *Historical Register*, 336; Kail, *Who Was Who During the American Revolution*, 123.

47. Peekskill is a city in Westchester County, New York, situated on a bay along the east side of the Hudson River, across from Jones Point. *Merriam-Webster Geographical Dictionary*, 913.

48. The 28-gun frigate USS *Congress*, commanded to Captain Thomas Grennell, and USS *Montgomery*, a 24-gun frigate, commanded to Captain John Hodge, were never completed and burnt in the Hudson River. They were built by Lancaster Burling under authority of an act of the Second Continental Congress. James L. Mooney, *Dictionary of American Naval Fighting Ships* (Washington: Navy Dept., Office of the Chief of Naval Operations, Naval History Division, 1959–1981), II: 163, IV: 428.

49. Rynier Mynderse served as a Commissioner of Conspiracies for the County of Albany from 1778–1782. He was on the Council of Appointment and a member of the New York Senate. New York. The Office of the State Comptroller. *New York in the Revolution as Colony and State* (Albany: J. B. Lyon Company, 1904), II: 172; Victor Hugo Paltsits, ed., *Minutes of the Commissioners for Detecting and Defeating Conspiracies in the State of New York: Albany County Sessions, 1778–1781* (Albany: J. B. Lyon Company, 1909), 826.

50. Nicholas Herckheimer or Herkimer (1728–1777) was a Brigadier-General of the Tryon County Militia, who tried to relief Fort Schuyler. His militia was ambushed and he was wounded at Oriskany on 6 August 1777 and died of his wounds on 16 August 1777. Heitman, *Historical Register*, 286; Boatner, *Encyclopedia of the American Revolution*, 501.

51. Jacob Cuyler served from 1777 to 1778. William B. Whiting served from 1777 to1780. Walter Livingston served from 1777 to 1779 and 1784 to 1785. Stephen J. Schuyler served from 1777 to 1779. Robert Van Rensselaer served from 1777 to 1781. Peter B. Vrooman served from 1777 to 1779 and 1786 to 1787. John Taylor served from 1777 to 1781 and 1786 to 1787. George Rogers Howell and Jonathan Tenney, eds., *Bi-Centennial History of Albany: History of the County of Albany, N.Y., from 1609 to 1886* (New York: W. W. Munsell & Co., 1886), IV: 354–355.

52. Jonathan Lawrence (1737–1812), along with

William Harper and Matthew Cantine, were appointed commissioners on May 9, 1777. In the course of his duties, he visited the Oneida Indians, procured the holding of a council of their chiefs, made satisfactory experiments on the waters of some of the salt springs in the western part of the state and contracted with the Indians for such salt as they might be able to produce. He was a member of the 1st, 3rd and 4th New York Provincial Congresses, of the New York State Senate (Southern District) from 1777 to 1783 and of the Council of Appointment in 1778–79 and 1782–83.Thompson, 423–425.

53. Letter 48.

54. Letter 49; Receipt from William Giles, undated. Military Papers of Brigadier Peter Gansevoort, Jr.

55. Robert Benson (1739–1823) was Lieutenant Colonel and an aide-de-camp to Governor Clinton of New York from 1777 to 1783. After the war, he was a clerk of the New York State Senate. Heitman, *Historical Register*, 100; Reynolds, *Genealogical and Family History of Southern New York and the Hudson River Valley*, 1445.

56. Letter 51.

57. *Ibid.*

58. Philip Schuyler was President of the Board of Commissioners of Indian Affairs since its inception in 1775. Benson Lossing, *The Life and Times of Philip Schuyler* (New York: Sheldon & Company, 1873), II: 395.

59. Letter 51.

60. Philip Schuyler to Peter Gansevoort, Jr., June 10, 1777. Military Papers of Brigadier Peter Gansevoort, Jr.

61. *Ibid.*

62. Bedford Williams (d. 1790) served as the Surgeon's Mate to the Second NY Regiment from 28 June 1775 to Jan 1776. He then was assigned to the Hospital Department from 1779 to 1781. Heitman, *Historical Register*, 593–94.

63. Letter 53.

64. *Ibid.*

65. Letter 54.

66. Major Nathaniel Hubbell (ca. 1734–1802) was Colonel Dayton's senior captain and Continental Army engineer. Gavin K. Watt, *Rebellion in the Mohawk Valley: The St. Leger Expedition of 1777* (Toronto: Dundurn Press, 2002), 34; *DAR Patriot Index*, 1393.

67. Also known as the Upper Castle of the Mohawks, Canajoharie was situated on the south side of Mohawk River, near the mouth of Nowadaga Creek. Kelsay, *Joseph Brant*, 46.

68. Fort Dayton was located on the North side of the Mohawk River at West Canada Creek in what is now Herkimer, New York. A fort had previously been built on the same site during the French and Indian War. Roberts, *New York's Forts in the Revolution*, 188.

69. Willett, *A Narrative of the Military Actions of Colonel Marinus Willett*, 50.

70. Letter 56.

71. James Gregg was commissioned a Second Lieutenant in the Third New York Regiment Third NY from 28 June 1775 to 26 June 1776 when he was promoted to First Lieutenant of DuBois's New York Regiment. On 21 November 1776, he was promoted to the rank of Captain of the Third New York. He was wounded and scalped by Indians near Kingston, NY on 13 October 1777. On 1 January 1783, he was transferred to the First New York Regiment and served to 3 June 1783. Heitman, *Historical Register*, 262.

72. Located on the western end of the Oneida Carrying Place, Fort Bull was built in 1755 by Captain Marcus Petri as a star-shaped stockade. Named for its commander, a Lt Bull, the fort was destroyed by Lt. Gaspard Joseph Chaussegros de Lery in 1756, after the fall of Oswego. Situated a half-mile from Fort Bull, Fort Newport, named for its commander, a Captain Newport, was built in 1756 to guard the upper Wood Creek Landing. Roberts, *Encyclopedia of Historic Forts*, 540, 568.

73. Hunloke Woodruff (1754–1811) was the Surgeon's Mate of the First New York Regiment from 21 July 1775 to March 1776. He was promoted to Surgeon of the Third New York Regiment on 21 November 1776, serving until his retirement on 1 January 1781. Heitman, *Historical Register*, 604; Ceylon Newton Woodruff and Maurine R. Herod, *Woodruff Chronicles; A Genealogy: The Long Island-New Jersey Family of John Woodruffe, the Immigrant Ancestor to America* (Glendale, Calif: A.H. Clark Co, 1967), I: 81.

74. Colbreath, *Days of Siege*, 16; Willett, *A Narrative of the Military Actions of Colonel Marinus Willett*, 46–47.

75. Letter 57.

76. Letter 58.

77. Letter 59.

78. *Ibid.*

79. The British offered monetary compensation to the Indians for their involvement in stopping the rebellion: eight dollars for ordinary farmer's scalps and ten to twenty dollars for militia officers and members of the patriot committee of safety's scalps. Codman Hislop, *The Mohawk* (Syracuse, NY: Syracuse University Press, 1989), 171.

80. Leonard Gansevoort to Peter Gansevoort, Jr., July 2, 1777. Military Papers of Brigadier Peter Gansevoort, Jr.

81. Letter 60.

82. *Ibid.*

83. *Ibid.*

84. Letter 61.

85. Joseph Savage (1756–1814) from Massachusetts held a rank of Sergeant in Gridley's Regiment, Massachusetts Artillery from April to December 1776. On 10 December 1775, he was promoted to Second Lieutenant of Knox's Regiment Continental Artillery; Captain-Lieutenant of the Second Continental Artillery on 1 January 1777; Captain, 20 September 1779 and served to 17 June 1783. After the war he was given the rank of Captain in the United States Artillery Battalion on 20 October 1786; Captain of Artillery Battalion United States Army on 29 September 1789; resigned on 15 October 1791. He removed to Berwick, ME and was the postmaster at Doughty's Falls, ME from 1796 to 1808. Heitman, *Historical Register*, 482; Lawrence Park, *Major Thomas Savage of Boston and His Descendants* (Boston: Press of David Clapp & Son, 1914), 39.

86. Jelles Fonda (1727–1791) was a captain in the New York Militia from 1777 to 1780. He was known as one of the best traders in the Mohawk Valley. During the French and Indian War, he served as a captain in the Provincial forces during the French and Indian War. He was at the Battle of Oriskany and was unharmed. He represented the Western District in the State Senate, 1777–1781 and 1788–1791. Heitman, *Historical Register*, 231; Gordon DenBoer, ed., *The Documentary History of the First Federal Elections, 1788–1790* (Madison: The University of Wisconsin Press, 1986), III: 241; Samuel Ludlow Frey, ed., *The Minute Book of the Committee of Safety of Tryon County: The Old New York Frontier, Now Printed Verbatim for the First Time* (New York: Dodd, Mead, 1905), 141–142.

87. John Spoor (b. ca. 1750) was commissioned an ensign in Captain Thomas DeWitt's Company in the Third New York Regiment on 21 Nov 1776. On 3 Jul 1777, he was taken prisoner while on a sod party and rejoined the regiment on 3 January 1778. He was dismissed on 31 Mar 1780. Heitman, *Historical Register*, 512; Franklin Henry Chase, *Revolutionary Soldiers resident or dying in Onondaga County, N.Y.: With Supplementary List of Possible Veterans*, ed. Rev. W. M. Beauchamp (Syracuse: The McDonnell Co., 1913), 195.

88. Letter 62.

89. Letter 61.

90. Letter 63.

91. Letter 64.

92. Situated in Monmouth County, Sandy Hook is a barrier spit, approximately six miles long along the Atlantic Ocean coast of eastern New Jersey, which encloses the southern entrance of Lower New York Bay south of New York City. Saul B. Cohen, *The Columbia Gazetteer of the World* (New York: Columbia University Press, 1998), 2732.

93. Richard Varick (1753–1831) was served as Captain in the First New York Regiment from 28 June 1775 to 24 September 1776. He was appointed an aide-de-camp and Secretary to General Schuyler in June 1776; Deputy Mustermaster General of the Northern Army on 25 September 1776; Lieutenant Colonel and Deputy Commissary-General of Musters on 10 April 1777 and served to June 1780. He served subsequently as an aide-de-camp to General Arnold from Aug 1780 until the treason of that officer was known and then joined General Washington's Staff and served as his private and confidential Secretary from 25 May 1781 to 14 December 1799. Heitman, *Historical Register*, 559; Kail, *Who Was Who During the American Revolution*, 271.

94. After hearing about the disgraceful evacuation and retreat of Fort Ticonderoga by St. Clair, John Adams, president of the Board of War, wrote to his wife, Abigail on August 21, 1777: "I think we shall never defend a post until we shoot a General." A month later on September 2, 1777, he wrote again to his wife: "Gansevoort has proven that it is possible to hold a fort." Kenney, *The Gansevoorts of Albany*, 105; Richard M. Ketchum, *Saratoga: Turning Point of America's Revolutionary War* (New York: Henry Holt, 1997), 219.

95. Letter 65.

96. St. Clair abandoned Fort Ticonderoga on 6 Jul 1777. The British took it over the next day. Henry B. Carrington, *Battles of the American Revolution*, 1775–1781 (New York: Promontory Press, 1877), 313.

97. Located in Berkshire County, Massachusetts, Great Barrington lies twenty miles southwest from Pittsfield. John Hayward, *A Gazetteer of Massachusetts: Containing Descriptions of All the Counties, Towns and Districts in the Commonwealth; Also, of Its Principal Mountains, Rivers, Capes, Bays, Harbors, Islands, and Fashionable Resorts. To which are Added, Statistical Accounts of Its Agriculture, Commerce and Manufactures; with a Great Variety of Other Useful Information* (Boston: J. Hayward, 1846), 160.

98. Leonard Gansevoort's wife, Hester Cuyler Gansevoort, was eight-months pregnant with their daughter, Magdalena, who would be born on August 17, 1777. Bielinski, Stefan, "Magdalena Gansevoort Ten Eyck," Colonial Albany Social History Project, http://www.nysm.nysed.gov/albany/bios/g/maggans4668.html.

99. John Nixon (1725–1815) was a captain commanded a company of minutemen at Lexington. He was promoted colonel of a Massachusetts Regiment, serving from 24 Apr to Dec 1775. He was wounded at Bunker Hill and assigned to command the Fourth Continental Infantry in 1776. He was promoted brigadier general on 9 Aug 1776 and resigned his commission in 1780. Heitman, *Historical Register*, 414; *Appletons' Cyclopaedia of American Biography*, IV: 525.

100. Letter 67.

101. Goose Van Schaick to Peter Gansevoort, Jr., July 21, 1777. Military Papers of Brigadier Peter Gansevoort, Jr.

102. Letter 68.

103. Lieutenant Henry Bird served in the advance guard of St. Leger's expeditionary force against Fort Schuyler in 1777. Mary Beacock Fryer, *King's Men: The Soldier Founders of Ontario* (Toronto: Dundurn Press, 1980), 77.

104. Letter 70.

105. For more information about St. Leger's approach to Fort Schuyler, see Sir John Johnson's Orderly Book.

106. Daughter of a Presbyterian clergyman of Paulis Hook (Jersey City), Jenny McCrea (ca. 1752–1777) was visiting her friend Mrs. Sarah McNeil at Fort Edward. Betrothed to David Jones, a loyalist serving as lieutenant in Burgoyne's army, Miss McCrea was pierced with three bullet wounds and scalped.when a party of Indians led by a sachem known as the Wyandot Panther attacked the house and took the two women. John Fiske, *The American Revolution* (Boston and New York: Houghton, Mifflin and Company, 1891), I: 277; Fredriksen, *Revolutionary War Almanac*, 503–504; Letter 71.

107. The town of Claverack, centrally located in Columbia County, was formed in 1778 from the older "District of Claverack." In 1782, the town lost some of its land to the new town of Hillsdale. The town was reduced again in 1785 to form the city of Hudson. French, *Gazetteer of the State of New York*, 244.

108. Tobias Van Veghten (d. 1777) accepted a commission as a second lieutenant in Second New York on May 1776. He was promoted to first lieutenant in the First New York Regiment on 21 Nov 1776. He was killed near Fort Edward on 27 Jul. Heitman, *Historical Register*, 558.

109. John Glover (1732–1797) served as a colonel of a Massachusetts Regiment from May to Dec 1775. He was assigned to the Fourteenth Continental Infantry in 1776 and promoted to brigadier general on 21 Feb 1777, serving until his resignation in 1782. Heitman, *Historical Register*, 250; William R. Denslow, *10,000 Famous Freemasons from A to J* (Trenton, MO: Missouri Lodge of Research, 1957), I: 120.

110. Benjamin Lincoln (1733–1810) was appointed major general of the Continental Army on 19 Feb 1777. On 7 Oct 1777, he was wounded at Saratoga. He was surrendered at Charleston, SC on 12 May 1780 and was a prisoner of war until exchanged on Nov 1780. He was appointed Secretary of War from 30 Oct 1781 to 17 Nov 1783. Heitman, *Historical Register*, 351; Boatner, *Encyclopedia of the American Revolution*, 635–637.

111. Brigadier General Cortlandt Skinner (1728–1799) served for many years as attorney-general. When the war began, he raised a brigade of loyalist known as Skinner's Greens or the Tory Brigade of New Jersey with his headquarters at Staten Island. Lady Maria Skinner Nugent, *Lady Nugent's Journal: Jamaica One Hundred Years Ago*, ed. Frank Cundall (Soho Square, London: Adam & Charles Black for the Institute of Jamaica, 1907), xlvii-li.

112. In February 1776, Admiral Richard Howe (1726–1799) was given the naval command in America. In 1777, he provided support to his brother's operation to capture Philadelphia, ferrying General William Howe's army to a landing point from which they successfully marched and took the city. Admiral Howe spent much of the remainder of the year concentrating on capturing the forts that controlled entry to the Delaware River without which ships could not reach Philadelphia. Boatner, *Encyclopedia of the American Revolution*, 520–521.

113. Letter 72.

114. Joseph Brant or Thayendanegea (1742–1807) was a Mohawk Indian chief, commissioned captain in British army, and a war leader of the pro–British Iroquois. He led Mohawk and Loyalist followers in Lt. Col. Barry St. Leger's expedition to besiege Fort Schuyler. He also ambushed General Herkimer's Militia at the Battle of Oriskany. Between 1778 and 1780, Brant led his Indian troops on raids in the Mohawk Valley, southern New York, and northern Pennsylvania. After the war, he obtained the Six Nations Reserve for the resettlement of Mohawk and others of the Six Nations on the Grand River near Brantford, Ontario. Kail, *Who Was Who During the American Revolution*, 493–494.

115. Letter 73.

116. Letter 74.

117. Brother-in-law of Peter Gansevoort, Gerrit W. Van Schaick (1758–1816) marched with the militia to defend Saratoga in 1777 and served as an ensign in Captain John Price's militia company in 1779. Heitman, *Historical Register*, 482; Reynolds, *Hudson-Mohawk Genealogical and Family Memoirs*, 993.

118. Stillwater, a Post-Township of Saratoga County, 10 miles SE. of Ballston Spa, and 22 miles N. of Albany; bounded N. by Saratoga, E. by the Hudson or the County of Washington, S. by Halfmoon, W. by Malta. Spafford, *A Gazetteer of the State of New York*, 505.

119. Barrimore Matthew St. Leger (1737–1789), Colonel of the 34 Regiment of Foot, was chosen to lead the western offensive of the Saratoga Campaign. His objective was to march down from Oswego, move along the Mohawk Valley, capturing Fort Schuyler, and rendezvousing with General Burgoyne and General Howe at Albany. He ambushed Nicholas Herkimer's Tryon County militia attempting to break the siege in the Battle of Oriskany of 1777. Unfortunately the battle weaken the alliance with the Indians and the rumors of a relief force under Benedict Arnold reaching Fort Schuyler him forced St. Leger to withdraw back to Canada. He continued guerrilla warfare from his Montreal headquarters and in the summer of 1781, failed to capture General Schuyler. That fall, he ascended with a strong force to Ticonderoga to persuade Vermont to ally with the British but did not accomplish his mission. At the end of the war, he was commandant of the royal forces in Canada in the autumn of 1784. Boatner, *Encyclopedia of the American Revolution*, 960–961; Letter 76.

120. Letter 77.

121. John Albert Scott, *Fort Stanwix and Oriskany: The Romantic Story of the Repulse of St. Leger's British Invasion of 1777 Told for the First Time, in Chronological Order and in Detail—Mainly from Contemporary Reports, Letters and Diaries, with all Sources Indicated* (Rome, NY: Rome Sentinel Company, 1927), 179.

122. *Ibid*, 180.

123. Captain James Wilson. Watt, *Rebellion in the Mohawk Valley*, 102.

124. William Max Reid, *The Story of Old Fort Johnson* (New York and London: G. P. Putnam's Sons, 1906), 88.

125. James Wesson (d. 1809) accepted a commission as a major of Gerrish's Massachusetts Regiment, serving from 19 May to December 1775. He was promoted to lieutenant colonel of the Twenty-sixth Continental Infantry on 1 January 1776 and colonel of the Ninth Massachusetts Regiment on 1 November 1776. He was wounded at the battle of Monmouth on 28 June 1778 and retired on 1 January 1781. Heitman, *Historical Register*, 582.

Ezra Badlam (1746–1788) was a lieutenant in the Lexington Alarm in April 1775. He accepted a commission as captain of Gridley's Regiment Massachusetts Artillery, serving from 25 June to December 1775. He was promoted to captain of the Twenty-sixth Continental Infantry on 1 January 1776; major of the Ninth Massachusetts Regiment on 1 November 1776; lieutenant colonel of the Second Massachusetts Regiment on 7 July 1777. He was transferred to the Eighth Massachusetts Regiment on 1 January 1781 and retired on 1 August 1782. Heitman, *Historical Register*, 80, *DAR Patriot Index*, 103.

126. James Mellen (d. 1812) was a private in the Lexington Alarm in April 1775. He accepted a commission as captain of Ward's Massachusetts Regiment, serving from April to December 1775. He was promoted to captain of the Twenty-first Continental Infantry on 1 January 1776; major on 15 August 1776 and lieutenant colonel of the Ninth Massachusetts Regiment on 1 November 1776.He was transferred to the Fourth Massachusetts Regiment on 1 January 1781 and promoted to lieutenant colonel commandant of the Third Massachusetts Regiment on 7 January 1783, serving to 3 June 1783. Heitman, *Historical Register*, 388.

127. Elias Van Bunschoten, Jr. (1749–after 1805) was appointed First Lieutenant in the Third New York Regiment on 28 June 1775. He was promoted to Captain on 25 November 1775. He resigned his commission on 15 December 1777 and in September 1778 was appointed a Captain of Associated Exempts. On 22 April 1779, he received a commission as Major in the New York Levies. Heitman, *Historical Register*, 132; William Henry Van Benschoten, *Concerning the Van Bunschoten or Van Benschoten Family in America: A Genealogy and Brief History* (West Park-on-Hudson, NY: William Henry Van Benschoten, 1907), 75, 87.

128. Cornelius T. Jansen was appointed as a first lieutenant in the Third New York Regiment on 28 June 1775. He was promoted to captain on 26 June 1776. He was transferred to the First New York Regiment on 1 January 1781 and served to June 1783. Heitman, *Historical Register*, 317.

129. Thomas DeWitt (1741–1809) was appointed as First Lieutenant to the Third New York Regiment on 28 June 1775. He was promoted to Captain on 25 November 1775 and served in this capacity until January 1776. He was reassigned on 26 June 1776 as Captain of the Third New York Regiment and resigned on 7 January 1780. He served subsequently as Major in the New York Levies. Heitman, *Historical Register*, 196; Sons of the Revolution, *Decennial Register of the Pennsylvania Society of Sons of the Revolution, 1888–1898* (Philadelphia: F.B. Lippincott, 1898), 290.

Abraham Swartwout (ca. 1742–1799) was appointed with the rank of Captain in Clinton's New York Militia Regiment on 27 April 1776. He was later commissioned to the Third New York Regiment on 21 November 1776 but was omitted in May 1778. He then served as a captain in Colonel Zephaniah Platt's Dutchess County Regiment of Associated Exempts. Heitman, *Historical Register*, 529; Daughters of the American Revolution, *Ancestral Register of the General Society of the Daughters of the Revolution, 1896* (Philadelphia: The Bailey, Banks & Biddle Co., 1897), 266.

Leonard Bleeker (1755–1844) was appointed with a rank of second lieutenant to the First New York Regiment on 28 Jun 1775. He was promoted to first lieutenant on 14 May 1776. He was reassigned to the Third New York Regiment on 21 Nov 1776 with a rank of captain. He served as brigadier major to General Clinton from 19 Jun to 22 Aug 1779 and brigadier major under Lafayette from May to Oct 1781. He was transferred to First New York Regiment on 1 Jan 1783 and later promoted to brevet major on 30 Sep 1783, serving to 3 Nov 1783. Heitman, *Historical Register*, 107; Bleeker, *The Order Book of Capt. Leonard Bleeker*, 38–39.

130. Henry Tiebout (d. 1826) received a commission as Second Lieutenant in the First NY Regiment on 24 February 1776. He was promoted to Captain in the Third NY Regiment on 21 November 1776 and then on 1 Jan 1783, he was transferred back to the First NY Regiment and served to 3 June 1783. He was given the rank of Brevet Major on 30 September 1783. Heitman, *Historical Register*, 543; Schuyler, *Institution of the Society of the Cincinnati*, 311.

131. Gilbert Tice (b. ca. 1739) was a veteran of the French and Indian War. In 1775, he was made a captain in the British Indian Department, conducting Indian raids throughout the war. Jack Harpster and Ken Stalter, *Captive!: The Story of David Odgen and the Iroquois* (Santa Barbara, CA: Praeger, 2010), 73–74.

132. Christopher Hutton was appointed the Regimental Adjutant in Meade's New York Militia Regiment on 23 September 1776. He was reassigned as an Ensign in the Third New York on 21 November 1776. On 28 May 1778, was appointed as the Regimental Adjutant and promoted to Lieutenant on 6 February 1779. He was transferred to the Second New York Regiment on 1 January 1783 and served until he retired on 3 June 1783. Heitman, *Historical Register*, 312.

133. Earlier, the Ninth Massachusetts Regiment brought news to the garrison that on 14 Jun 1777, the Second Continental Congress passed the Flag Resolution which stated: "Resolved, That the flag of the United States be thirteen stripes, alternate red and white; that the union be thirteen stars, white in a blue field, representing a new Constellation." On 3 Aug 1777, Gansevoort ordered a flag to be made by any means necessary. The white stripes were made from strips cut from army shirts, the red from bits of scarlet cloth from petticoats, either from the garrison or from a captured British cloak and the blue ground for the stars, from either a cloak belonging to Captain Abraham Swartwout of Dutchess County, NY Regiment, from the camlet cloak taken from the enemy at Peekskill, or from the petticoat of Anna Roff. History has it this could have been the first flag hoisted over a fort in the United States. William Max Reid, *The Mohawk Valley, Its Legends and Its History* (New York and London: G. P. Putnam's sons, 1901), 415–416; Willett, *A Narrative of the Military Actions of Colonel Marinus Willett*, 50.

134. Colbreath, *Days of Siege*, 26; Reid, *The Mohawk Valley*, 415–416; Willett, *A Narrative of the Military Actions of Colonel Marinus Willett*, 50.

135. Scott, *Fort Stanwix and Oriskany*, 181; Reid, *The Story of Old Fort Johnson*, 90.

136. Lieutenant John Adam F. Helmer (ca. 1754–1830) was one of three messengers sent to Gansevoort informing of Herkimer's advancement to Fort Schuyler to lift the siege. The other two men were First Lieutenant Hans Marcus Demuth and Private Hon Jost Folts, all from the 4 Deerfield Company of Colonel Bellinger's regiment. Watt, *Rebellion in the Mohawk Valley*, 152.

137. Reid, *The Mohawk Valley*, 417, Hislop, *The Mohawk*, 174.

138. Scott, *Fort Stanwix and Oriskany*, 181.

139. Scott, *Fort Stanwix and Oriskany*, 181; Willett, *A Narrative of the Military Actions of Colonel Marinus Willett*, 53–55; Reid, *The Story of Old Fort Johnson*, 91–92.

140. Letter 79.

141. *Ibid.*

142. Willett led a sortie against the surrounding enemy camps. Reid, *The Story of Old Fort Johnson*, 91.

143. Frederick Bellinger was a lieutenant colonel in the New York Militia who was taken prisoner at the battle of Oriskany on 6 August 1777. Heitman, *Historical Register*, 98.

John Frey (d. 1833) was appointed captain in the Second New York Regiment on 28 June 1775.He was promoted to Brigade-Major, serving from 15 July 1775 to January 1776 and served subsequently as Brigade-Major to General Herkimer's New York Militia. He was taken prisoner at the battle of Oriskany on 6 August 1777 and exchanged on 28 October 1778. Heitman, *Historical Register*, 236.

144. Reid, *The Story of Old Fort Johnson*, 93.

145. Letter 80.

146. *Ibid.*

147. *Ibid.*

148. Lieutenant William Osborne Hamilton was a military secretary of St. Leger. Watt, *Rebellion in the Mohawk Valley*, 75.

149. The Adjutant General was Captain William Ancrum, who was described having the odd mixture of a violent temper and great generosity. Watt, *Rebellion in the Mohawk Valley*, 353.

150. William W. Campbell, *Annals of Tryon County, or, The Border Warfare of New York, during the Revolution* (Cherry Valley, NY: Cherry Valley Gazette Print, 1880), 85.

151. Levi Stockwell (1740–1812) was appointed with the rank of second lieutenant to the Fourth New York Regiment in Apr 1776. He was reassigned to the Third New York Regiment with the rank of first lieutenant on 21 Nov 1776 but was omitted in May 1778. He served subsequently as captain in the New York Militia. Heitman, *Historical Register*, 522.

152. Neilson, *Burgoyne's Campaign*, 43, 51; Reid, *The Story of Old Fort Johnson*, 92–93.

153. Marinus Willett to Peter Gansevoort, Jr., August 11, 1777. Military Papers of Brigadier Peter Gansevoort, Jr.

154. Burgoyne occupied Fort Edward on July 30, 1777. Carrington, *Battles of the American Revolution*, 319.

155. General William Howe (1729–1814) was a British army officer who rose to become Commander-in-Chief of British forces during the American War of Independence. Howe was sent to North America in March 1775, arriving in May after the Revolutionary War broke out. He resigned his post as Commander in Chief, North America in 1778. Howe's record in North America was marked by the successful capture of both New York City and Philadelphia. Boatner, *Encyclopedia of the American Revolution*, 523–525.

156. *Ibid.*

157. Reid, *The Story of Old Fort Johnson*, 94–95.

158. *Ibid.*, 95–97.

159. Letter 83.

160. Captain Jacob Allen (1737–1777) of Bailey's regiment was killed 19 Sep 1777 at Freeman's Farm fighting Burgoyne. He was a sergeant in Lexington Alarm in Apr 1775. On 1 Jan 1777, he received his commission as captain in the Second Massachusetts Regiment. Watt, *Rebellion in the Mohawk Valley*, 383; Heitman, *Historical Register*, 67.

161. Henry Defendorff accepted a commission of second lieutenant in the Second New York Regiment in November 1775 and promoted to first lieutenant in July 1776. On 21 November 1776, he was transferred to the Third New York Regiment. He resigned his commission in November 1777. Heitman, *Historical Register*, 197.

162. Ensign Joshua Chase (b. 1756), who was a private in Lexington Alarm in Apr 1775, received his rank in the Ninth Massachusetts Regiment on 1 Jan 1777. Watt, *Rebellion in the Mohawk Valley*, 383; Heitman, *Historical Register*, 152; *DAR Patriot Index*, 497.

163. Thomas Ostrander was a second lieutenant in Swartwout's New York Militia Regiment in July 1776. He received a commission in the Third New York Regiment on 21 November 1776 and was omitted in May 1778. He served subsequently as lieutenant in the New York Levies. Heitman, *Historical Register*, 421.

Josiah Bagley was appointed as an ensign to the Third New York Regiment on 21 November 1776. He was promoted to lieutenant on 7 January 1781 and transferred to the First New York Regiment on 1 January 1783, serving to close of war. Heitman, *Historical Register*, 80.

164. George J. Denniston was the adjutant for the Third New York Regiment from 28 June to November 1775. He was promoted to ensign in 21 November 1776, second lieutenant on 20 May 1780. He retired on 1 January 1781. Heitman, *Historical Register*, 194.

Lieutenant John Ball (1756–1838) was first commissioned as a second lieutenant in Captain Samuel Van Vechten's Company of the Fourth New York Regiment on 2 Mar 1776. In Oct of 1777 he was promoted to first lieutenant and transferred to Captain Aaron Austin's Company of the Third New York Regiment and served therein until Jul of 1778. Heitman, *Historical Register*, 84; Revolutionary War Pension Application of John Ball (W5767); Bounty-Land Warrant Application of John Ball (1197–200).

165. Peter Magee received a commission of ensign in the Third New York Regiment on 21 November 1776. He was promoted to second lieutenant on 23 May 1779, transferred to First New York Regiment on 1 January 1781 and served to close of war. Heitman, *Historical Register*, 376.

Eldert Ament was appointed the rank of Ensign in the Third New York on 21 November 1776 and resigned on 23 December 1778. Heitman, *Historical Register*, 70.

166. Major Bedlow was actually Major Ezra Badlam

(1746–1788) of Massachusetts. Heitman, *Historical Register*, 80; *DAR Patriot Index*, 103.

167. George Singleton was taken during the sortie. Scott, *Fort Stanwix and Oriskany*, 196.

168. Dr. Charles Austin. Watt, *Rebellion in the Mohawk Valley*, 195.

169. Gansevoort detached two hundred men and one field piece under Willett with orders to rendezvous with General Herkimer's Tryon County Militia but Willett came upon an encampment of Sir John Johnson's regiment and the Indians. He plundered the camp and took four colours, hoisting them as symbols of his victory. Willett, *A Narrative of the Military Actions of Colonel Marinus Willett*, 53–55.

170. Jonas Fay to the Militia near Bennington, August 16, 1777. Military Papers of Brigadier Peter Gansevoort, Jr.

171. After the failed siege on Fort Schuyler, St. Leger marched back to Oswego and then to Montreal. An alternate plan was designed for St. Leger to proceed with his men down Lake Champlain to Fort Ticonderoga to join up with Burgoyne but he did not. Instead he stayed at Ticonderoga until Nov and then returned to Canada. William L. Stone, ed. *Orderly Book of Sir John Johnson during the Oriskany Campaign, 1776–1777* (Albany: Joel Munsell's Sons, 1882), 47, 96–98.

172. Hanjost Schuyler (1744–1818), nephew of General Herkimer, was arrested by Arnold near Schuyler Lake and sent to St. Leger with an exaggerated account of the arm marching to Gansevoort's relief. Arnold promised his fortune would be secured but held his young brother Nicholas as hostage. Lorenzo Sabine, *Biographical Sketches of Loyalists of the American Revolution with an Historical Essay* (Boston: Little, Brown and Company, 1864), II: 266–267; Phoebe Strong Cowen, *The Herkimers and Schuylers: An Historical Sketch of the Two Families with Genealogies of the Descendants of George Herkimer, the Palantine, Who Settled in the Mohawk Valley, N.Y., in 1721* (Albany: Joel Munsell's Sons, 1903), 48–50, 95–96.

173. Willett, *A Narrative of the Military Actions of Colonel Marinus Willett*, 61–62.

174. Letter 85.

175. Letter 86.

176. Lieutenant Governor Philip Skene died in England in 1810. Sabine, *Biographical Sketches of Loyalists of the American Revolution*, II: 304.

177. Letter 87.

178. *Ibid.*, 89–99.

179. Reid, *The Story of Old Fort Johnson*, 97–99.

180. *Ibid.*

181. Letter 89.

182. Named after the principal river, Pawlet is a southwestern town in Rutland County, Vermont. Zadock Thompson, *History of Vermont, Natural, Civil and Statistical, in Three Parts, with a New Map of the State, and 200 Engravings* (Burlington, VT: Chauncey Goodrich, 1842), III: 135–135.

183. Also known as Fort Constitution, Fort Lee was located on the New Jersey side opposite of Fort Washington. Roberts, *New York's Forts in the Revolution*, 330.

184. Marinus Willett married Mary Pearsee in 1760 and had one son, Marinus, Jr. She died in 1793. Ralph J. Caliendo, *New York City Mayors, Part I: The Mayors of New York Before 1898* (Bloomington, IN: Xlibris Corporation, 2010), 186.

185. Letter 91.

186. Horatio Gates to Peter Gansevoort, Jr., October 10, 1777. Military Papers of Brigadier Peter Gansevoort, Jr.

187. Letter 93.

188. Elting, 37.

189. Philip Conine (1752–1831) was appointed to First Lieutenant in the Third New York Regiment on 21 November 1776. He was later promoted to Captain Lieutenant on 7 January 1780 and retired on 1 January 1781. Heitman, *Historical Register*, 167; John L. Bronk Family Bible, Rossi Records, Volume 34, p. 25 at the Durham Center Museum. http://www.rootsweb.ancestry.com/~nygreen2/john_l__bronk_family_bible.htm.

John Welch was a second lieutenant of Wynkoop's New York Regiment in June 1776. He received a new assignment in the Third New York Regiment with a rank of first lieutenant on 21 November 1776. He was cashiered on 9 January 1779 and joined the enemy. Heitman, *Historical Register*, 580.

Nanning Vanderheyden accepted a commission as second lieutenant in the Second New York Regiment in May 1776. On 21 November 1776, he was promoted to first lieutenant of the Third New York Regiment and served into May 1778. Heitman, *Historical Register*, 555

190. Isaac Bogart (1741–1818) served as second lieutenant of the Fourth New York Register from May to November 1776. He was promoted to first lieutenant of the Third New York on 21 Nov 1776. He resigned his commission on 10 Feb 1778 and served subsequently as captain in the New York Militia. Heitman, *Historical Register*, 109; Munsell, *Collections on the history of Albany*, 100.

William Tapp was regimental quartermaster of the First New York Regiment from 5 July to November 1775. He was promoted to second lieutenant of Nicholson's Continental Regiment on 26th March 1776 and first lieutenant to the Third New York Regiment on 21 November 1776. He resigned on 20 March 1780. Heitman, *Historical Register*, 532.

George Sytez was appointed adjutant to the Third New York Regiment on 21 November 1776 and served in that capacity to 28 May 1778. He was promoted to captain lieutenant on 28 May 1778 and to captain on 7 January 1780. On 1 January 1781, he was transferred to the First New York Regiment and served to June 1783. Heitman, *Historical Register*, 530.

Prentice Bowen was commissioned to the Third New York Regiment with the rank of second lieutenant on 21 November 1776. He was appointed Regimental Quartermaster, serving from 28 May 1778 to 14 July 1780. He retired his commission on 1 January 1781. He then served subsequently as captain of the New York Levies. Heitman, *Historical Register*, 112.

191. John Elliot (d. 1809) was assigned the surgeon's mate in Third NY Regiment on 21 Nov 1776. He was

transferred to the First NY Regiment in 1781 and served to Nov 1783. In 1785, he was assigned surgeon's mate in the United States Infantry and in 1789 assigned to the First United States Infantry. He was promoted to surgeon in the Second United States Infantry in 1791. Assigned to the Fourth Sub Legion in 1792 and back to the First United States Infantry in 1896. In 1802, he was honorably discharged. Heitman, *Historical Register*, 214; Augustus W. Drury, *History of the City of Dayton and Montgomery County, Ohio* (Chicago and Dayton: S.J. Clarke Publishing Co, 1909), I: 245.

192. Thomas Warner accepted a commission of second lieutenant of Lasher's Regiment in the New York Militia in June 1776. He was assigned to the Third New York Regiment on 21 November 1776 and served to April 1778. Heitman, *Historical Register*, 418.

Benjamin Bogardus (d. 1812) was a Second Lieutenant of Graham's Regiment in the NY Militia from July to November 1776. He received a commission of a First Lieutenant in the Third NY Regiment on 21 November 1776. He resigned his commission on 26 May 1782. Heitman, *Historical Register*, 109.

Thomas Ostrander was appointed to Second Lieutenant in Swartwout's NY Militia Regiment in July 1776. He was transferred to the Third NY Regiment on 21 November 1776. He was omitted when the regiment was rearranged in May 1778. He served subsequently as Lieutenant in the NY Levies. Heitman, *Historical Register*, 421.

Thomas Williams, Jr. (d. 1828) was appointed as Regimental Quartermaster of Wynkoop's New York Regiment in July 1776. He was reassigned to the Third New York Regiment on 21 November 1776. In May 1778 he was omitted. Heitman, *Historical Register*, 597.

193. Josiah Bagley was appointed as an ensign to the Third New York Regiment on 21 Nov 1776. He was promoted to lieutenant on 7 Jan 1781 and transferred to the First New York Regiment on 1 Jan 1783, serving to close of war. Heitman, *Historical Register*, 80.

Samuel Lewis (1752–1822) was appointed ensign to the Third New York Regiment on 21 Nov 1776. He was promoted lieutenant in Jan 1780 and transferred to the First New York Regiment in 1781 and served to Jun 1783. Heitman, *Historical Register*, 349; Keith G. Harrison, *The Ancestry of Nathan Lewis Harrison, Revisited Nineteen Years Later* (Holt, MI: KGH Environmental PLC, 2008), 240.

194. Henry Glen to Peter Gansevoort, Jr., December 5, 1777. Military Papers of Brigadier Peter Gansevoort, Jr.

Chapter Four

1. On January 12, 1778, Gansevoort married Catherine Van Schaick, daughter of Wessel and Maria (Gerritse) Van Schaick at the Van Schaick Mansion located on Van Schaick Island at the junction of the Hudson and Mohawk Rivers in Cohoes, New York. Kenney, *The Gansevoorts of Albany*, 116.

2. Letter 96.

3. *Ibid.*

4. *Ibid.*

5. *Ibid.*

6. *Ibid.*

7. William Duer (1747–1799) was elected in 1775 to the New York Provincial Congress and served in the State Constitutional Convention. He also participated on the Committee of Public Safety and was a delegate to the Continental Congress from 1777 to 1779. Kail, *Who Was Who During the American Revolution*, 230.

8. Gouverneur Morris (1752–1816) served in the New York Provincial Congress from 1775 to 1777 and the Continental Congress from 1778 to 1779. Boatner, *Encyclopedia of the American Revolution*, 737–739; Kail, *Who Was Who During the American Revolution*, 251–252.

9. Henry Laurens (1724–1792) was a South Carolina delegate to the Continental Congress and the third President of the Second Continental Congress, serving from 1 Nov 1777 to Dec 9, 1778. In the fall of 1779, he was the minister to Holland and was taken prisoner by the British when he was travel home in early 1780. He was imprisoned in the Tower of London until his release in exchange of General Lord Cornwallis on 31 Dec 1781. Boatner, *Encyclopedia of the American Revolution*, 599–601.

10. Letter 99; Robert Cochran to Peter Gansevoort, Jr., February 21, 1778. Military Papers of Brigadier Peter Gansevoort, Jr.

11. Letter 100.

12. *Ibid.*

13. Moses Yeomans was the Sergeant-Major of the Third New York Regiment from July to November 1775. He was promoted to second lieutenant on 21 Nov 1776, serving until May 1778. He served subsequently as Captain in the New York Militia. Heitman, *Historical Register*, 610.

14. Matthew Potan served as ensign in the Third New York Register from June 1777 to May 1778. Heitman, *Historical Register*, 448.

15. Letter 101.

16. Colonel Christopher Carleton (1749–1787), nephew of Guy Carleton, spent the entire war leading raids along the shores of Lake Champlain, upper Hudson Valley and Mohawk Valley. Gavin K. Watt, *The Burning of the Valleys: Daring Raids from Canada Against the New York Frontier in the Fall of 1780* (Toronto and Tonawanda, NY: Dundurn Press, 1997), 274.

17. *Ibid.*

18. Letter 103; Letter 104.

19. Letter 105.

20. Thomas Conway (1735-ca.1800) was an Irish-born colonel in the French First Brigade, who volunteered his services to the American Cause. On May 13 1777, he was commissioned a brigadier general by Congress and served alongside General Washington. He was promoted to major general in Dec 1777. He resigned his commission in Mar 1778 after a plot to remove Washington as commander of the Continental Army was discovered. Boatner, *Encyclopedia of the American Revolution*, 276–277.

21. Ebenezer Stevens (1751–1823) received a commission of first lieutenant in the Company of Rhode Island Artillery on 8 May 1775. He was promoted captain of Knox's Regiment of Continental Artillery on 10 Dec 1775, major of Independent Battalion of Artillery on 9 Nov 1776 and lieutenant colonel of the Second Continental Artillery on 30 Apr 1778. He resigned his commission in Jun 1783. Heitman, *Historical Register*, 519; Saffell, *Records of the Revolutionary War*, 155.

22. Letter 106.

23. Letter 107.

24. Letter 108.

25. Letter 110.

26. On 2 Jun 1778, a raiding party consisting of one hundred Indians and Loyalist under Lieutenant John Ross destroyed the gristmill at Mayfield and invaded the settlements of Fish House and Fonda's Bush. James F. Morrison, *A History of Fulton County in the Revolution* (Gloversville, NY: Fulton County Bicentennial History Committee, 1977), 3.

27. Abraham I. Van Alstyn (ca. 1738–1808) was a colonel in the New York Militia in 1777–1780. Heitman, *Historical Register*, 554; *DAR Patriot Index*, 2769.

28. On 2 Jun 1778, Lieutenant Matthew Warmuth was ambushed by Joseph Brant, a personal friend before the war, two miles north of Cherry Valley, shot and tomahawked. He belonged to Captain William P. Fox's Company in Colonel Klock's Regiment. Warmuth was accompanied by Lieutenant Peter Sitz who was taken prisoner by Brant. Campbell, *Annals of Tryon County*, 109–110; Francis W. Halsey, *The Old New York Frontier: Its Wars with Indians and Tories, Its Missionary Schools, Pioneers, and Land Titles, 1614–1800* (New York: C. Scribner's Sons, 1901), 208.

29. Letter 114.

30. Letter 115.

31. *Ibid.*

32. John Lamb (1735–1800) accepted a commission of captain in the Independent Company of New York Artillery on 30 June 1775. He was wounded, lost an eye, and taken prisoner at Quebec on 31 December 1775. He was promoted to Major-Commandant of Artillery of the Northern Department on 9 January 1776 to rank from 1 January 1776; colonel of the Second Continental Artillery on 1 January 1777. He was wounded again at Compo Hill on 28 April 1777 and served to June 1783. Heitman, *Historical Register*, 338, Kail, *Who Was Who During the American Revolution*, 243.

33. Letter 116.

34. Before the war, Daniel Hammill was an Irishman who served in the British militia of Dutchess County, NY. When the war began, he was forced to join the American rebel militia claiming his family would be in harm's way if he did not. He was taken prisoner at Fort Montgomery and immediately flipped sides. He became the brigade major of British General Henry Clinton in Oct 1777. He was given the task to recruit for a British regiment of Irish-Americans, which would be commanded by Lord Rawdon. During this task, he was arrested and incarcerated in the Poughkeepsie jail, which he escaped in Aug 1779 before any trial was convened. He supported his family on six shillings a day as a clerk in the British fuel office. After the war, he resided in Nova Scotia until Aug 1784 when he went to London to be awarded with seventy-nine British pounds and sixteen shillings for his services to the crown. Harry Thayer Mahoney and Marjorie Locke Mahoney, *Gallantry In Action: Dictionary of Espionage in the American Revolutionary War* (Lanham, MD: University Press of America, 1999), 179–180.

35. Samuel Geake was an Irishman who was a private in the Continental Army but began corrupted and induced to act as a spy for the British when he was captured at the same time as Hammill in Oct 1777. After rejoining the Continental Army, he was caught as a spy and sentenced to be hanged. Washington postponed his execution so he could be a prosecution witness and testify against Hamill. Mahoney and Mahoney, *Gallantry in Action*, 160, 179–180.

36. George Augus Francis Rawdon (1754–1826) served as British General Henry Clinton's adjutant general. DNB, IX: 117; Mahoney and Mahoney, *Gallantry in Action*, 180.

37. *Ibid.*

38. *Ibid.*

39. Letter 117.

40. Thomas McClelan was appointed to the rank of Second Lieutenant of Nicholson's Continental Regiment in June 1776. He was promoted to First Lieutenant of the Third New York Regiment on 21 November 1776. He was cashiered in 1779 and joined the enemy. Heitman, *Historical Register*, 365.

41. Located in south-central Westchester County, White Plains was burned by Major John Austin on 5 Nov 1776. The battle of White Plains was fought on Chatterton Hill in Greenburgh, opposite of the town. French, *Gazetteer of the State of New York*, 707.

42. Peter Gansevoort, Jr. to Philip Schuyler and John Stark, July 10, 1778. Military Papers of Brigadier Peter Gansevoort, Jr.

43. Peter Bellinger (1726–1813) was a colonel of the Fourth Regiment of Tryon County militia from 1776 to 1783. Heitman, *Historical Register*, 98; Philander D. Chase, ed., *The Papers of George Washington: 15 September–31 October 1778, Volume 17* (Charlottesville: University Press of Virginia, 2008), 115.

44. Andrustown (presently Jordanville, NY) was a small settlement of seven families a few miles northwest of the lake. Eight men were killed and fourteen settlers were taken prisoners. Daniel P. Barr, *Unconquered: The Iroquois League at War in Colonial America* (Westport, CT: Praeger, 2006), 151; Letter 118.

45. Caleb Stark (1759–1838), the eldest son of General John Stark, received a commission of ensign in his father's New Hampshire Regiment, serving from May to Dec 1775. He was transferred to the Fifth Continental Infantry on 1 Jan 1776. He was promoted to second lieutenant on 14 Aug 1776 and regimental adjutant of the First New Hampshire on 8 Nov 1776. He retired on 1 Sep 1778. Heitman, *Historical Register*, 515; Boatner, *Encyclopedia of the American Revolution*, 1053.

46. Letter 119.

47. Letter 120.

48. Springfield was a small settlement at the northern tip of Otsego Lake. Barr, *Unconquered,* 151.

49. Ichabod Alden (1739–1778) was lieutenant-colonel of Cotton's Massachusetts Regiment from 23 Apr to Dec 1775. He was reassigned to the Twenty-fifth Continental Infantry on 1 Jan 1776. On 1 Nov 1776, he was promoted to colonel of the Seventh Massachusetts. He was killed at Cherry Valley on 10 Nov, 1778. Heitman, *Historical Register,* 65; Kail, *Who Was Who During the American Revolution,* 92–93.

50. Situated in the northeast portion of the Otsego County, Cherry Valley was the scene of two massacres by Indians in 1778 and 1780. French, *Gazetteer of the State of New York,* 532.

51. A xebec was a Mediterranean sailing ship that was used mostly for trading. It would have a long overhanging bowsprit and protruding mizzen mast. Dean King, John B. Hattendorf, and J. Worth Estes, *A Sea of Words: A Lexicon and Companion for Patrick O'Brian's Seafaring Tales* (New York: Henry Holt, 1995), 476.

52. Letter 123.

53. Letter 122.

54. Letter 124.

55. *Ibid.*

56. George Washington to Peter Gansevoort, Jr., August 29, 1778. Military Papers of Brigadier Peter Gansevoort, Jr.

57. Marinus Willett to Peter Gansevoort, Jr., August 29, 1778. Military Papers of Brigadier Peter Gansevoort, Jr.

58. Letter 127.

59. *Ibid.*

60. Mr. Brodock, neighbor of John Roof, resided at the "Traw Plat," south of Fort Schuyler. Pomroy Jones, *Annuals and Recollections of Oneida County* (Rome, NY: Pomroy Jones, 1851), 326.

61. Jacob Reed was the Oneida interpreter and schoolmaster at Old Oneida. Graymont, *The Iroquois in the American Revolution,* 235; Samuel Kirkland Lothrop, *Life of Samuel Kirkland, missionary to the Indians* (Boston: Charles C. Little and James Brown, 1848), 340.

62. Letter 128.

63. *Ibid.*

64. Letter 129.

65. *Ibid.*

66. The Grass-Hopper (Oneida Chief) was the first sachem of the nation and one of the most influential Oneida friends of the patriot cause. Glatthaar and Martin, *Forgotten Allies,* 126.

67. Letter 130.

68. The Great Tree or Ka-ran-dua-an was a Seneca Chief who spent a summer of 1778 with Washington. Graymont, *The Iroquois in the American Revolution,* 180.

69. Letter 131.

70. Letter 132.

71. Volkert P. Douw to Peter Gansevoort, Jr., November 13, 1778. Military Papers of Brigadier Peter Gansevoort, Jr.

72. Letter 134.

73. Ann Hawkes Hay (1745–1785) served from 1778–1780 as a colonel in the New York Militia. Heitman, *Historical Register,* 281; Charles J. Colcock, *Family of Hay: A History of the Progenitors and Some South Carolina Descendants of Col. Ann Hawkes Hay, with Collateral Genealogies, A.D. 500–1908* (New Orleans: Pelican Pub. Co., 1959), 125–126.

Chapter Five

1. Letter 135.

2. *Ibid.*

3. Benjamin Herring accepted his commission as sergeant of the Third New York Regiment on 7 January 1777. He was promoted to ensign on 18 May 1778 and transferred to the First New York Regiment on 1 January 1781 and served to 3 June 1783. Heitman, *Historical Register,* 287.

4. Garrett G. Lansing (d. 1831) became an ensign in the Third New York Regiment on 6 February 1779, transferred to First New York Regiment on 1 January 1781 and served to 3 June 1783. Heitman, *Historical Register,* 340.

5. John Burhance received a commission as sergeant in the Third New York Regiment in May 1777. He was promoted to ensign in Feb 1779 and resigned his commission in December the same year. Heitman, *Historical Register,* 134.

6. Brother of Governor George Clinton, James Clinton (1733–1812) was appointed on 30 June 1775 to the rank of Colonel in the Third New York regiment and served to January 1776. He then was transferred to the Second New York regiment on 8 March 1776. He was promoted to Brigadier-General in the Continental Army on 9 August 1776. On 6 October 1777 he was wounded at Fort Montgomery. In the summer and fall of 1779, he led a joint incursion through the Indian Country with General Sullivan. He was promoted to Brevet Major-General on 30 September 1783 and served until close of war. Heitman, *Historical Register,* 161; Boatner, *Encyclopedia of the American Revolution,* 241.

7. James Clinton to Peter Gansevoort, Jr., circa February 22, 1779. Military Papers of Brigadier Peter Gansevoort, Jr.

8. Pierre Regnier de Roussi (d. 1810) was appointed lieutenant colonel in the First Canadian Regiment on 11 Nov 1775. On 21 Nov 1776, he was transferred to the Fourth New York and served in this regiment until 26 Mar 1777. He was transferred to the Second New York Regiment on 28 Jun 1779 and served until his resignation of 29 Mar 1780. Heitman, *Historical Register,* 195.

9. Letter 139.

10. John Copp served in the First NY Regiment with a rank of First Lieutenant from 28 June 1775 to Jan 1776. He was then a Captain in Nicholson's NY Militia Regiment in 1776 until he received a commission as a Captain in the First NY Regiment. He resigned his commission in 14 July 1779. Heitman, *Historical Register,* 171.

11. Letter 140.

12. Constructed by Frederick Plank in 1777, Fort Plank was located two and a half miles to the southwest of Fort Rensselaer. He enclosed his house in a square of palisades with blockhouses at the angles. Roberts, *New York's Forts in the Revolution*, 387.

13. John Graham (1756–1832) began his military service as captain in the Second New York Regiment on 30 Jun 1775. He was transferred to Nicholson's Continental Regiment in Feb1776 and to the First New York Regiment on 21 Nov 1776. He was promoted to major in 1779 and served to close of war. Heitman, *Historical Register*, 255; *DAR Patriot Index*, 1104.

14. Letter 141.

15. Letter 142.

16. A native of Scotland, Colonel Malcomb settled in America where he has served with distinction in the Continental Army. When he retired, he served as a colonel in the militia. Francois J. De Chastellux, *Travels in North-America, in the Years 1780–1782* (Bedford, MA: Applewood Books, 2009), 162.

17. Peter Buckstaff (b.ca.1756) was a wheelwright in Captain Ledger's Company of Colonel McDougal's Regiment. *Documents of the Assembly of the State of New York*, XX: 271.

18. Letter 141.

19. Letter 143.

20. *Ibid.*

21. *Ibid.*

22. The camp was near Middle Brook twenty-three miles west of Perth Amboy. Harry P. Johnston, *The Storming of Stony Point on the Hudson, Midnight, July 15, 1779: Its Importance in the Light of Unpublished Documents* (New York: James T. White & Co., 1900), 53.

23. Lewis Du Bois (1728–1802) received a commission of captain in the Third New York Regiment in Jun 1775 and promoted to major in Nov the same year. He was assigned to Nicholson's New York Regiment in Mar 1776 and promoted to colonel on 21 Jun 1776. He took command of the Fifth New York Regiment on 21 Nov 1776. He was taken prisoner at Fort Montgomery on 6 Oct 1777 and resigned his commission on 22 Dec 1779. He subsequently served as a colonel of the New York Levies. Heitman, *Historical Register*, 205; Edward Hagaman Hall, *The Sons of the American Revolution: New York State Society*, 1893–94 (New York: Republic Press, 1894), 119.

24. Frederick Weisenfels (1728–1806) was appointed captain in the First New York Regiment on 28 Jun 1775. He was promoted to lieutenant colonel of the Third New York Regiment in Mar 1776 and transferred to the Second New York Regiment on 21 Nov 1776. He was promoted lieutenant-colonel commandant of the Fourth New York Regiment on 13 Jan 1779 and retired his commission in Jan 1781. He served subsequently as lieutenant colonel of the New York Levies. Heitman, *Historical Register*, 579; Schuyler, *Institution of the Society of the Cincinnati*, 340.

25. Philip Van Cortlandt (1749–1831) was appointed Lieutenant Colonel of the Fourth New York Regiment on 30 June 1775. He accepted a commission of Colonel of the Second New York Regiment on 21 November 1776 and served to the close of the war. On 30 September 1783, he was appointed Brevet Brigadier General. Heitman, *Historical Register*, 555; Emily Warren Roebling, *The Journal of the Reverend Silas Constant: Pastor of the Presbyterian Church at Yorktown, New York*, ed. Josiah Granville Leach (Philadelphia, PA: J. B. Lippincott Company, 1903), 429.

26. Haverhill, New Hampshire, in Grafton County, was originally known as Lower Coos. It was situated by the western branch of Connecticut River. Hamilton Child, *Gazetteer of Grafton County, N.H., 1709–1886* (Syracuse: Syracuse Journal Company, 1886), 339–340.

27. Jacob Bayley (1726–1815) was commissioned in Aug 1776 as brigadier general of Glouster and Cumberland Counties. He was assigned to construct a quicker route, known as the "Bayley-Hazen Military Road," from Newbury to St. Johns, Canada, a distance of about one hundred miles. In 1777, he was commissioned commissary–General of the Northern Department of the Colonial Army. During and after the war, he held various civil offices, serving as a delegate to the New York Provincial Congress (1777); a member of two Vermont General Assemblies (1777–1784); Chief Judge of the Supreme Court of Gloucester County (1778); Chief Judge of Orange County Court (1783, 1786–1791); a member of two Vermont Constitutional Conventions (1777, 1783); a delegate to the Continental Congress at Philadelphia (1777) and a member of the Vermont Governor's Council (1778, 1786–1794). Nathaniel Bouton, comp. and ed., *Documents and Records relating to the State of New-Hampshire during the period of the American Revolution, from 1776 to 1783* (Concord: NH: Edward A. Jenks, 1874), VII: 171; Heitman, *Historical Register*, 92.

28. The name Coos derives from the Algonquian Indian term meaning crooked, the Indian name of the Connecticut River, which rises in the northernmost end of the county. The largest county in New Hampshire, Coos County was first settled in 1763 at Lancaster. The northern part of Grafton County was set off to form the county in 1803. John A. Anderson and Stearns Morse, *The Book of the White Mountains* (Bowie, MD: Heritage Books, 2002), 92; James G. Carter, *A Geography of New-Hampshire, with a New Map of the State, for Families and Schools* (Portsmouth, NH: Nathaniel March; Boston: Hilliard, Gray, Little and Wilkins, 1831), 50.

29. Letter 144.

30. Built in 1756 by Sir William Johnson for the Onondagas, Onondaga Castle consisted of a 150-foot square with blockhouses on two corners. It was located six miles south of Onondaga Lake near the village of Onondaga Valley. Oscar Jewell Harvey, *A History of Wilkes-Barre, Luzerne County, Pennsylvania: From its First Beginnings to the Present Time; Including Chapters of Newly-Discovered Early Wyoming Valley History Together with Many Biographical Sketches and Much Genealogical Material* (Wilkes-Barre: Raeder Press, 1909), 117.

31. Letter 145.

32. Letter 146.

33. Located in Northampton County, Easton, PA sits on the confluence of the Delaware River and the Lehigh River. It was also one of the first three places the Declaration of Independence was publicly read. General Sullivan used the town as a rendezvous for the expedition in 1779. From Shute's Journal, there were about 150 houses with three elegant buildings among them. The settlers were very inhospitable, "all High Dutch and Jews." Frederick Cook, ed. *Journals of the Military Expedition of Major General John Sullivan against the Six Nations of Indians in 1779; With Records of Centennial Celebrations; Prepared Pursuant to Chapter 361, Laws of the State of New York, of 1885* (Auburn, NY: Knapp, Peck & Thomson, 1887), 268.

34. Letter 147.

35. William Maxwell (ca. 1733–1798) accepted a commission as a colonel in the Second New Jersey Regiment on 8 November 1775. He was promoted to Brigadier General in the Continental Army on 23 October 1776 and resigned 25 July 1780. Heitman, *Historical Register*, 385; Boatner, *Encyclopedia of the American Revolution*, 687.

36. Physician by profession, Edward Hand (1744–1802) began his military service as a lieutenant colonel of Thompson's Pennsylvania Rifle Battalion in Jun 1775. On 1 Jan 1776, he was assigned to the First Continental Infantry. He was promoted to colonel, serving from Mar to Dec 1776. On 1 Jan 1777, he commanded the First Pennsylvania and in Apr that same month, was assigned to the Continental Army with a rank of brigadier general. From Jan 1781 to Nov 1783, he served as adjutant-general of the Continental Army. On 19 Jul 1798, he was promoted to the rank of major general of the United States Army. Heitman, *Historical Register*, 272; Howard A. Kelly and Walter L. Burrage, *American Medical Biographies* (Baltimore: The Norman, Remington Company, 1920), 488.

37. Tuffin Charles Armand, Marquis de la Roueire, (1750–1793) was a colonel in the Third Cavalry of Pulaski Legion in May 1777; succeeding Count Pulaski in command of the Legion in Oct 1779 and on 21 Oct 1780, the designation of the command was changed to "Armand's Partisan Corps," which he commanded to the close of the war. On 26 Mar 1783, he was appointed brigadier general in the Continental Army. Heitman, *Historical Register*, 73–74; Fredriksen, *Revolutionary War Almanac*, 254.

38. John Paul Schott (1744–1829) was assigned to the Independent Pennsylvania Company as a captain in Sep 1776. He was attached to Ottendorff's Corps in Dec 1776. He was taken prisoner at Short Hills on 26 Jun 1777 and exchanged, serving to close of war. Heitman, *Historical Register*, 484; Elmer James Ferguson, ed., *The Papers of Robert Morris* (Pittsburgh, PA: University of Pittsburgh Press, 1977), III: 10.

39. William Butler (1745–1789) received a commission as captain in the Second Pennsylvania Battalion in Jan 1776. He was promoted to major in Sep 1776 and assigned to the Fourth Pennsylvania Regiment with the rank of lieutenant colonel on 30 Sep 1776. On May 1778, he was appointed aide-de-camp to General Alexander and promoted lieutenant colonel commandant of the Fourth Pennsylvania Regiment in Jan 1779. He retired his commission on 1 Jan 1783. Heitman, *Historical Register*, 138; Edward G. Lengel, ed. *The Papers of George Washington: May-Jun 1778, Volume 15* (Charlottesville: University Press of Virginia, 2006), 166.

40. Israel Shreve (1739–1799) received a commission of lieutenant colonel in the Second New Jersey Regiment on 31 Oct 1775. He was promoted to colonel on 28 Nov 1776 and served until his retirement on 1 Jan 1781. Heitman, *Historical Register*, 495; Frank E. Grizzard, *George!: A Guide to all Things Washington* (Buena Vista, VA: Mariner Publishing, 2005), 341.

41. Matthias Ogden (1754–1791) served as a brigade major in the expedition to Canada and was wounded at Quebec on 31 Dec 1775. He was promoted to lieutenant colonel in Mar 1776 and colonel in Jan 1777 of the First New Jersey Regiment. He was taken prisoner at Elizabethtown, NJ on 5 Oct 1780, exchanged in Apr 1781 and granted leave on 21 Apr 1783 to visit Europe and did not return to the army. Heitman, *Historical Register*, 418; DenBoer, *The Documentary History of the First Federal Elections,* III: 186.

42. Oliver Spencer (1736–1811) served as major and lieutenant colonel in the New Jersey Militia in 1776. He received a commission of colonel of the sixteen additional Continental Regiments on 15 Jan 1777 and served until his retirement on 1 Jan 1781. Heitman, *Historical Register*, 511; Sons of the Revolution in the State of New York, *Supplement to Year Book of 1899 of the Society of Sons of the Revolution in the State of New York* (New York: Francis E. Fitch, 1903), 126.

43. Joseph Cilley (1734–1799) received a commission of major in the Second New Hampshire Regiment, serving from May to Dec 1775. He was assigned to the Eighth Continental Infantry on 1 Jan 1776. In Nov 1776, he was promoted to lieutenant colonel and in Apr 1777, colonel of the First New Hampshire Regiment. He retired his commission on 1 Jan 1781. Heitman, *Historical Register*, 155; Sons of the Revolution. Pennsylvania Society, *Decennial Register of the Pennsylvania Society of Sons of the Revolution,* 276.

44. George Reid (1733–1815) was a captain in charge of a company of Minute Men in Apr 1775. He was appointed captain of the First New Hampshire Regiment, serving from May to Dec 1775. He was assigned to the Fifth Continental Infantry on 1 Jan 1776. In Nov in the same year, he was promoted major and re-assigned to the First New Hampshire Regiment. In Apr 1777, he was promoted to the rank of lieutenant colonel and transferred to the Second New Hampshire in Mar 1778. He was later retained in the New Hampshire Battalion in Mar 1782 and served to 3 Nov 1783. He was promoted to colonel on 30 Sep 1783. Heitman, *Historical Register*, 462; Cook, *Journals of the Military Expedition of Major General John Sullivan*, 360.

45. Alexander Scammell (1747–1781) was appointed a major in the Second New Hampshire Regiment in April 1775 and on 21 September 1775, was assigned as a Brigade Major to New Hampshire Brigade. He was

sent to reinforce the Continental Army units in the Invasion of Canada. On 14 August 1776, he was assigned as an aide-de-camp to General Sullivan and Brigade Major to General Lee's Division on 29 October 1776. On 8 November 1776, Scammell was promoted to Colonel of the Third New Hampshire Regiment. He commanded the regiment at Trenton, Princeton, Saratoga, the Sullivan Expedition and Monmouth. At Valley Forge, Scammell was appointed Adjutant-General of the Continental Army on the staff of General Washington from 5 January 1778 to 1 January 1781 when he resigned to assume command of the First New Hampshire. Scammell was mortally wounded and taken prisoner at Yorktown on 20 September 1781 and on 6 October 1781, died while in confinement. Heitman, *Historical Register*, 483; Boatner, *Encyclopedia of the American Revolution*, 988–989.

46. Letter 148.

47. Otsego Lake is the source of Susquehanna River. The nine-mile-long lake was known to James Fenimore Cooper as Glimmerglass and was a principal feature in several of his novels. Cohen, *The Columbia Gazetteer of the World*, II: 2316.

48. Probably Cornelius Van Dyck (1740–1792), the second-in-command of Van Schaick's First NY Regiment. Heitman, *Historical Register*, 43; Hanson, *A History of Schenectady During the Revolution*, 234–235.

49. Letter 151.

50. Colonel Jacob Klock (1708–1798) was the colonel of the 2nd regiment of the Tryon County militia. He commanded the regiment at the battle of Oriskany. Berry, A.J., *A Time of Terror*, 2005; Watt, *Rebellion in the Mohawk Valley*, 2002.

51. Robert McKeen was appointed captain in Wynkoop's New York Militia Regiment, serving from 1 Mar to Nov 1776. He received a commission of captain of the First New York Regiment on 21 Nov 1776, serving until his resignation on 29 Jan 1778. His wife had died and left eight children. Heitman, *Historical Register*, 371–372.

52. John Davis received a commission as first lieutenant in the Third New York Regiment on 28 Jun 1775. On 6 Feb1776, he was promoted to captain in the Fourth New York Regiment. He was wounded at Stillwater on 19 Sep 1777. He was later promoted to major on 11 Apr 1780 and retired on 1 Jan 1781. Heitman, *Historical Register*, 188.

Jonathan Titus (1751–1835) became his military service as a second lieutenant in the First New York Regiment in Nov 1775 and was promoted to first lieutenant in Jul 1776. He was assigned to the Fourth New York Regiment with the rank of captain on 21 Nov 1776. He retired his commission on 1 Jan 1781. Heitman, *Historical Register*, 545; Benjamin Homans, ed., *Army and Navy Chronicle* (Washington, DC: B. Homans, 1835), I: 256.

53. Letter 152.

54. *Ibid.*

55. Serving as Joseph Brant's headquarters, Oquaga or Ouaquaga was a large Iroquois village, located on the east branch of the Susquehanna River some twenty miles southwest of Unadilla. An expedition led by Colonel William Butler destroyed it in 1778. Boatner, *Encyclopedia of the American Revolution*, 817; Cook, *Journals of the Military Expedition of Major General John Sullivan*, 23.

56. Albert Pawling (ca.1750–1837) received a commission as second lieutenant in the Third New York Regiment on 2 Aug 1775. He was assigned brigade major of Clinton's Brigade from Nov 1775 to May 1776. He was promoted captain of Dubois' New York Regiment in Jun 1776 and major of Malcolm's Additional Continental Regiment in Jan 1777. He resigned his commission on 5 Mar 1779 and served as lieutenant colonel and colonel in the New York Levies from 1779 to close of war. After the war, he was appointed the first mayor of Troy, NY in 1816–1820. Heitman, *Historical Register*, 431; Arthur James Weise, *Troy's One Hundred Years, 1789–1889* (Troy, NY: William H. Young, 1891), 93, 326.

57. Fort Herkimer was a fort located on the southern side of the Mohawk River, opposite West Canada Creek. Built in 1740 around the homestead of the Herscheimer (Herkimer) family, it was originally known as Fort Kaouri (Fort Bear) and rebuilt during the American Revolutionary War around the Fort Herkimer Church. Roberts, *New York's Forts in the Revolution*, 216, 218.

58. Opposite the mouth of the East Canada Creek, Ga-ne-ga-ha-ga or the upper castle of the Mohawks was settled near the town of Danube in Herkimer County. Morgan, *League of the Iroquois*, 416.

59. Letter 153.

60. The lower castle of the Mohawks or Te-hon-da-lo-ga was situated on the west side of the Schoharie Creek. Fort Hunter was positioned near this settlement. Morgan, *League of the Iroquois*, 416.

61. Letter 154.

62. Letter 155.

63. *Ibid.*

64. Smith's Clove, named after William Smith, was located in Monroe, NY. The word clove derives from the Dutch word klove meaning a rocky cleft. William Smith, *Historical Memoirs of William Smith, 1778–1783*, ed. William H. W. Sabine (New York: New York Times, 1971), II: 114; French, *Gazetteer of the State of New York*, 507–508.

65. Peter's son was named Herman (1779–1862), who married Catherine Quackenbush (1774–1855). Kenney, *The Gansevoorts of Albany*, x.

66. John Beatty (1749–1826) was a physician and student of Benjamin Rush. In 1776, he was taken prisoner at Fort Washington and exchanged in 1778. He became commissary general for Prisoners. New Jersey Historical Society, *Documents relating to the colonial history of the state of New Jersey* (Newark, NJ: New Jersey Historical Society, 1904), 521.

67. Letter 158.

68. Meaning bright or clear mountain, Hellebergh was the west manor of Rensselaerswyck. Arthur B. Gregg, *Old Hellebergh: Historical sketches of the West Manor of Rensselaerswyck; including an account of the anti-rent wars, the Glass House and Henry R. Schoolcraft* (Altamont, NY: The Altamount Enterprise, 1936), 102.

69. *Ibid.*
70. Letter 159.
71. Letter 160.
72. Letter 161.
73. Letter 162.

Chapter Six

1. Letter 164.
2. *Ibid.*
3. Letter 165.
4. Letter 166; Letter 167.
5. Letter 168.
6. Letter 169.
7. *Ibid.*
8. Letter 170.
9. Letter 171.
10. John Post (1748–1830) served as the Commissary of Issues for the New York Brigade from 1776 to 1783. Heitman, *Historical Register*, 448; *DAR Patriot Index*, 2154.
11. Letter 174.
12. Alexander Webster was a colonel in the New York Militia from 1780 to 1782. Heitman, *Historical Register*, 578.
13. Alexander Webster to Peter Gansevoort, Jr., October 24, 1780. Military Papers of Brigadier Peter Gansevoort, Jr.
14. William Monsell to Goose Van Schaick, October 15, 1780. Military Papers of Brigadier Peter Gansevoort, Jr.
15. Peter Gansevoort, Jr. to James Gregg, October 26, 1780. Military Papers of Brigadier Peter Gansevoort, Jr.
16. Lewis Van Woert was a colonel in the New York Militia from 1775 to 1780. Heitman, *Historical Register*, 558.
17. Lewis Van Woert to Abraham Ten Broeck, October 26, 1780. Military Papers of Brigadier Peter Gansevoort, Jr.
18. Letter 175.
19. Jacobus Schoonhoven served as a colonel in the New York Militia from 1775 to 1779. Heitman, *Historical Register*, 484.
20. James Gregg to Peter Gansevoort, Jr., October 28, 1780. Military Papers of Brigadier Peter Gansevoort, Jr.
21. Marinus Willett to Peter Gansevoort, Jr., October 29, 1780. Military Papers of Brigadier Peter Gansevoort, Jr.
22. Letter 176.
23. Henry Watson Powell (1733–1814) came to Canada in 1776 in command of the Fifty-third Foot, became a Brigadier-General, and was successively in command at Ticonderoga, Montreal, Niagara, and Quebec He returned to England at the close of the American Revolutionary War. W. Stewart Wallace, ed., *The Encyclopedia of Canada*, Vol. V, Toronto.
24. Letter 177.
25. Christopher Carleton to Peter Gansevoort, Jr., November 3, 1780. Military Papers of Brigadier Peter Gansevoort, Jr.
26. John Chipman (1744–1829) participated in the capture of Fort Ticonderoga as second lieutenant of the Green Mountain Boys. He was promoted to captain in Aug 1777 and captured at Fort George in Oct 1780. He was exchanged in 1781. Heitman, *Historical Register*, 154; Freemasons. Grand Lodge of the State of New York, *Proceedings of the Grand Lodge of Free and Accepted Masons of the State of New York* (New York: Press of J. J. Little & Co., 1900), 303.
27. Cornelius T. Jansen to Peter Gansevoort, Jr., November 7, 1780. Military Papers of Brigadier Peter Gansevoort, Jr.
28. Jeremiah Van Rensselaer to Peter Gansevoort, Jr., November 8, 1780. Military Papers of Brigadier Peter Gansevoort, Jr.
29. Thomas Reed was appointed assistant paymaster-general in Mar 1778. He was then elected to the office of deputy paymaster-general at Albany in Jun 1779. United States. Adjutant-General's Office, *Legislative history of the General staff of the Army of the United States (Its Organization, Duties, Pay, and Allowances), from 1775 to 1901* (Washington: Government Printing Office, 1901), 449, 453.
30. James Black entered the war on 11 Mar 1777 and served to May 1779. He was appointed State Clothier for the Army on 26 Oct 1779 to end of war. New York State Archives, *New York in the Revolution Prepared Under Direction of the Board of Regents: Documents relating to the Colonial History of the State of New York*, ed. Berthold Fernow (Albany NY: Weed, Parsons and Co, 1887), XV: 239.
31. James Rosekrans was appointed captain of the Fourth New York Regiment on 3 Aug 1775. He was commissioned captain of the Fifth New York Regiment on 21 Nov 1776. On 1 Mar 1780, he was promoted to the rank of major and transferred to the Third New York Regiment and retired his commission on 1 Jan 1781. Heitman, *Historical Register*, 474.
32. Letter 181.
33. Letter 182.
34. Jacob G. Klock (1738–1814), the nephew of Colonel Jacob Klock (1708–1798), represented Tryon County as a member of the New York State Assembly from 1777 to 1778 and represented the western district in the New York State Senate from 1779 to 1786. Berry, *A Time of Terror*, 12; Hough, *The New York Civil List*, 472.
35. Letter 183.
36. Letter 184.

Chapter Seven

1. Letter 185.
2. Samuel Huntington (1731–1796) was a statesman from Connecticut who signed the Declaration of Independence and the Articles of Confederation. He also served as President of the Continental Congress from 1779 to 1781, chief justice of the Connecticut

Supreme Court from 1784 to 1785, and Governor of Connecticut from 1786 until his death. Kail, *Who Was Who During the American Revolution*, 17.

3. Letter 186.

4. Letter 187.

5. Harmanus Wendell served in the New York Militia, first as a captain in 1775 and then as a lieutenant colonel from 1780 to 1781. Heitman, *Historical Register*, 581.

6. Philip P Schuyler, son of General Philip Schuyler, was a major in the New York Militia in 1775. Heitman, *Historical Register*, 485.

7. Henry Quackenboss (1737–1813) served as a major and colonel in the New York Militia from 1775 to 1781. Heitman, *Historical Register*, 455; *DAR Patriot Index*, 2194.

8. John Blair (ca. 1722–1789) was a lieutenant colonel in the New York Militia from 1778 to 1780. Heitman, *Historical Register*, 105; *DAR Patriot Index*, 248.

9. Cornelius Van Veghten served as lieutenant colonel and colonel in the New York Militia from 1775 to 1781. Heitman, *Historical Register*, 557.

10. Ezekiel Taylor was a major in the New York Militia from 1775 to 1778. Heitman, *Historical Register*, 534.

11. Younger brother of General Philip Schuyler, Stephen J Schuyler (1737–1820) was a colonel in the New York Militia from 1775 to 1781. Heitman, *Historical Register*, 485; Stefan Bielinski, "Stephen J. Schuyler," *Colonial Albany Society History Project*. http://www.nysm.nysed.gov/albany/bios/s/stjschuyler1770.html.

12. Letter 188.

13. Abraham Cuyler (1742–1810) held the ranks of major, lieutenant colonel and colonel in the New York Militia from 1775 to 1781. He served as mayor of city of Albany from 1770 to 1778. Although he halfheartedly supported the patriot cause, he evidently became an avowed Loyalist and moved to Canada. Heitman, *Historical Register*, 183; Howell and Tenney, *Bi-Centennial History of Albany*, 661.

14. Letter 189.

15. Letter 190.

16. Letter 191.

17. *Ibid.*

18. Letter 191.

19. George Clinton to Peter Gansevoort, Jr., April 19, 1781. Military Papers of Brigadier Peter Gansevoort, Jr.

20. Anthony Van Bergen (1729–1797) was a colonel in the New York Militia from 1775 to 1780. Heitman, *Historical Register*, 554; *DAR Patriot Index*, 2771.

21. David Abeel (1727–1813) settled in Catskill as early as 1754 on the "west side of and adjoining the brook called the Caterskill, at a place called the Bak-Oven." He and his son, Anthony (1754–1822), were taken captive by Jacobus Rowe and another Tory. They almost died from hunger while reaching Fort Niagara. His son, Anthony, was made to run the gauntlet. In May 1781, the Abeels were confined in the Prevot at Montreal and after suffering great hardship, on the evening of 10 Sept 1782 they escaped and reached the headquarters of General Bayley upon Lower Coos or Haverhill, NH on the 29 Sept 1782. Henry Whittemore, *The Heroes of the American Revolution and Their Descendants: Battle of Long Island* (Brooklyn: The Heroes of the Revolution Publishing Co., 1897), 209–210.

22. Letter 193.

23. *Ibid.*

24. Richard Varick to Peter Gansevoort, Jr., April 28, 1781. Military Papers of Brigadier Peter Gansevoort, Jr.

25. *Ibid.*

26. Letter 195.

27. *Ibid.*

28. Letter 196.

29. *Ibid.*

30. Peter Vrooman (1736–1794) was a colonel in the New York Militia from 1778 to 1781. Heitman, *Historical Register*, 562; *DAR Patriot Index*, 2811.

31. Schoharie Lower Fort was a stockaded stone church with two bastions located near Schoharie Creek north of the village. Roberts, *New York's Forts in the Revolution*, 56–57.

32. Letter 198.

33. Thomas Chittenden (1730–1797) was Vermont's first governor from 1778 to 1789 and 1790 to 1797. Kail,. *Who Was Who During the American Revolution*, 171.

34. Letter 199.

35. *Ibid.*

36. Also known as Fort Plain, the fort was constructed in 1776 under the supervision of General Robert Van Rensselaer, it was situated near the confluence of Osquaga Creek and the Mohawk River. In 1781, Willett made it his headquarters. Roberts, *New York's Forts in the Revolution*, 384, 386.

37. Letter 200.

38. *Ibid.*

39. Letter 202.

40. Wawarsing, from the Indian word signifying "a black bird's nest," is situated on Rondout Creek, twenty-eight miles northwest of Newburg in Ulster County. On 12 Sep 1781, the town was plundered and some five or six dwellings, seven barns and a gristmill were burned down. Henry Kollock, ed., *State of New York: Embracing Historical, Descriptive, and Statistical Notices of Cities, Towns, Villages, Industries, and Summer Resorts in the Various Parts of the State, Together with a Complete List of the Post Offices, Counties, and County Towns, Lakes, Rivers, Railroads, &c.* (New York: Henry Pollock, 1882), 257; French, *Gazetteer of the State of New York*, 667–668.)

41. Johannes G. Hardenbergh (1731–1812) built his house in 1762 near the Rondout Creek, a mile southwest from Kerhonkson, a hamlet of Rochester in Ulster County. When the British ships sallied up the Hudson in Oct 1777, the Council of Safety of the State of New York chose Hardenburgh's house to store all the monies and property of the state, the papers of the council and the public records of New York City and of Ulster County. Helen Wilkinson Reynolds, *Dutch Houses in the Hudson Valley before 1776* (NY: Dover Publications, 1965), 202–203.

42. Letter 202.

43. Abraham Wempel was a colonel in the New York Militia from 1777 to 1779. Heitman, *Historical Register*, 581.

44. Peter Gansevoort, Jr. to Jacob C. Schermerhorn, August 19, 1781. Military Papers of Brigadier Peter Gansevoort, Jr.

45. Letter 204.

46. On 1 Sep 1781, a farm, owned by Lieutenant Johannes Dietz (ca. 1717–1781), was attacked by Indians led by a British soldier. The farm was situated in the Switzkill Valley, in Beaver Dam (now Berne). Lieutenant Dietz's son, Captain William Dietz (ca. 1747–1781) was taken captive but Lieutenant Dietz and his wife were massacred and scalped, as was Captain Dietz's wife and children, along with a Scottish servant girl. Captain Dietz was confined at Fort Niagara. He died in captivity in Oct 1781. Josiah Priest, *Stories of the Revolution, with an Account of the Lost Child of the Delaware; Wheaton and the Panther, &c.* (Albany: Hoffman and White, 1836), 3–9; Henry Z. Jones, Jr., *More Palatine Families: Some Immigrants to the Middle Colonies 1717–1776 and Their European Origins, Plus New Discoveries on German Families Who Arrived in Colonial New York in 1710* (Universal City, CA: Henry Z. Jones, Jr., 1991), 69–70.

47. *Ibid.*

48. On 7 Aug 1781, John Walden Meyers (1745–1821) was employed to abduct General Schuyler but failed. In 1782, he received a commission as captain in Edward Jessup's Loyal Rangers from Governor Haldimand. About 1787, he went up to the Bay of Quinte and settled near the mouth of Meyer's Creek (now known as Moira River). He built a sawmill, a distillery and a brick kiln and established a trading post. Benson J. Lossing, *Reflections of Rebellion: Hours with the Living Men and Women of the Revolution* (Charleston, SC: History Press, 2005), 152; William Canniff, *History of the Province of Ontario (Upper Canada): Containing a Sketch of Franco-Canadian History, the Bloody Battles of the French and Indians, the American Revolution, the Settlement of the Country by U.E. Loyalists, Trials and Hard-Ships Incident to Pioneer Life, Thrilling Narratives of Adventures with Indians and Wild Beasts, Struggles for the Establishment of Christianity and Schools, Agriculture and Manufactures, the War of 1812 Battle Scenes, Capture of Buffalo, Subsequent Growth and Prosperity of the Country, Including Biographies of Prominent First Settlers and the Census of 1871* (Toronto: A.H. Hovey, 1872), 112; Ontario Historical Society, *Papers and Records Vol VIII* (Toronto: Ontario Historical Society, 1907), 67–68; Robert J. M. Shipley, "John Walden Meyers," *Dictionary of Canadian Biography*, VI: 502–503.

49. Joseph Bettys (ca. 1754–1782), a native of Saratoga Co., NY, supported the American Cause and was captured during the naval battle of Valcour Island in the fall of 1776. While a prisoner in Canada he changed allegiance and was appointed an ensign. He was captured and was granted reprieve by George Washington before he was hung. In 1782, he was recaptured and hung as a spy and traitor at Albany. Due to his cold-blooded murders and plundering, the name, "Joe Bettys," spread fear throughout the region around Albany. Lossing, *Reflections of Rebellion*, 123–124.

50. Letter 207.

51. Succeeding the Committee of Correspondence, the Commissioners for Detecting and Defeating Conspiracies was a seven-member board created by the New York Provincial Convention. The Albany County board of this organization functioned from 1778 to 1781 to suppress the growth of loyalism among the community. Richard L. Blanco, ed., *American Revolution, 1775–1783* (New York and London: Garland Publishing, 1993), I: 356.

52. Letter 208.

53. Campbell LeFever (b. 1758) was taken in Virginia in Jun 1780. Chris McHenry, *Rebel Prisoners at Quebec, 1778–1783: Being a List of American Prisoners Held by the British During the Revolutionary War* (Lawrenceburg, IN: C. McHenry, 1981), 24.

54. John Angel (b. 1760) was taken from his Kentucky County Virginia home in Jun 1780. McHenry, *Rebel Prisoners at Quebec*, 26.

55. A Kentucky County Virginian, John Duncan (b. 1740) with his wife and eight children were taken from their farm on 26 Jun 1780. McHenry, *Rebel Prisoners at Quebec*, 27.

56. Letter 209.

57. William Heath (1737–1814) was a Colonel of a Massachusetts Regiment at Lexington and Concord from April to June 1775. He was appointed Major General of the Massachusetts Militia on 20 June 1775 and reassigned with the rank of Brigadier-General to the Continental Army on 22 June 1775. He was promoted to Major General of the Continental Army on 9 August 1776 and served to close of war. Heitman, *Historical Register*, 284; Kail, *Who Was Who During the American Revolution*, 119–120.

58. General Robert Van Rensselaer (1740–1802) served as a member of the New York Provincial Congress from 1775 to 1777. On October 20, 1775, he was received a commission of Colonel of the Eighth Regiment of the Albany County militia. On June 16, 1780, he was made brigadier general of the Second Brigade of the Albany County militia and served in this capacity until the close of war. This brigade included the Tryon County militia. He fought at Fort Ticonderoga and at the Battle of Klock's Field. Heitman, *Historical Register*, 557; Walter Whipple Spooner, "The Van Rensselaer Family," *American Historical Magazine* 2, no. 1 (January 1907): 195–196.

59. Derived from an Indian word signifying "Owl-hoot," Coxsackie lies upon the Hudson River in the northeast section of the Greene County. It was formed in 1772 as a district and a town in 1788. French, *Gazetteer of the State of New York*, 332.

60. Peter Gansevoort, Jr. to Robert Van Rensselaer, October 11, 1781. Military Papers of Brigadier Peter Gansevoort, Jr.

61. Letter 212.

62. Matthew Visscher (1751–1793) was appointed a lieutenant in Albany militia. He served in the Albany Committee of Correspondence, Safety, and Protection and as a member of the Albany Commissioner for Detecting and Defeating Conspiracies. He also served as

an Indian Commissioner and he was elected assistant alderman for the first ward, serving for ten years. He also was appointed Albany City and County clerk, serving from 1778 to 1790. Stefan Bielinski, "Matthew Visscher," *Colonial Albany Social History Project*, http://www.nysm.nysed.gov/albany/bios/v/mavisscher4062.html.

63. Letter 215.

64. Letter 216.

65. Letter 217.

66. *Ibid.*

67. Samuel Logan (1745–1825) was a major in the New York Militia from 1775 to 1776. He was assigned to the Fifth New York Regiment on 21 Nov 1776. On 6 Oct 1777, he was taken prisoner at Fort Montgomery and exchanged on 21 Dec 1780. He retired from service on 1 Jan 1781 and served subsequently as a major in the New York Levies. Heitman, *Historical Register*, 356; *DAR Patriot Index*, 1673.

68. George Clinton to Peter Gansevoort, Jr., October 18, 1781. Military Papers of Brigadier Peter Gansevoort, Jr.

69. Peter Gansevoort, Jr. to Philip P. Schuyler, October 21, 1781. Military Papers of Brigadier Peter Gansevoort, Jr.

70. Letter 219.

71. Letter 220.

72. Samuel Fletcher (1745–1814) started his military career as a first lieutenant in the Second New York Regiment, serving from Jun 1775 to Jan 1776. He was an orderly sergeant at the battle of Bunker Hill and commanded a company for the relief of Ticonderoga. He was at Bennington and served in the Burgoyne campaign. From 1779 to 1782, he was appointed colonel and brigadier general of the Vermont Militia. From 1788 until 1806 he held the office of High Sheriff of Windham County and during the years 1778, 1783, 1784 and 1786 was a judge of the county court. Heitman, *Historical Register*, 230; Benjamin H. Hall, *History of Eastern Vermont, from Its Earliest Settlement to the Close of the Eighteenth Century* (New York: D. Appleton & Co., 1858), 640–642.

73. Letter 221.

74. Letter 222.

75. Letter 223.

76. John N. Bleecker (1739–1825) was elected in 1775 to represent the second ward on the Albany Committee of Correspondence. He also held a commission in a militia company. He later became assistant deputy commissary general of stores and provisions in the New York Department. After the war, he served as alderman in the second ward for a number of years. He was actively involved in Albany city and county government serving as city and county treasurer, clerk of the board of supervisors and member of the Committee of Correspondence. Bielinski, Stefan, "John N. Bleeker," *Colonial Albany Society History Project*. http://www.nysm.nysed.gov/albany/bios/b/jnbleecker204.html.

77. Fort Hunter was situated at the confluence of the Mohawk River and Schoharie Creek, named after Governor Robert Hunter, who brought 3000 Palatines to America in 1709. Roberts, *New York's Forts in the Revolution*, 218.

78. On 26 Oct 1781, 450 British troops, with two hundred Tories and Indians, commanded by Major John Ross, penetrated Tryon County and destroyed thirty habitations. Colonel Willett with his regiment, some of the Massachusetts levies, Militia and a few Oneidas fought back the invasion. Maryly B. Penrose, *Indian Affairs Papers: American Revolution* (Franklin Park, NJ: Liberty Bell Associates, 1981), 278–79.

79. Letter 224.

80. Letter 225.

81. Samuel Safford (1737–1813) was a major with the Green Mountain Boys from 27 Jul to Dec 1775. He was promoted to the rank of lieutenant colonel of Warner's Continental Regiment in 5 Jul 1776 and served until 1 Jan 1781. After retiring, he served as brigadier general in the Vermont Militia from 1781 to 1782. Heitman, *Historical Register*, 479–480; Hiland Hall, *The History of Vermont, from Its Discovery to Its Admission into the Union in 1791* (Albany, NY: Joel Munsell, 1868), 468.

82. Letter 226.

83. Letter 227.

84. Letter 228.

85. *Ibid.*

86. Letter 229.

87. Letter 230.

88. Peter Yates to Peter Gansevoort, Jr., December 17, 1781. Military Papers of Brigadier Peter Gansevoort, Jr.

89. Ebenezer Walbridge (1738–1819) was a lieutenant in the regiment of Green Mountain Boys in 1775 and served as the adjutant of the regiment. He was promoted to lieutenant colonel in 1778, and in 1780 took command of the Bennington regiment. He also commanded a regiment of militia in that vicinity in 1781 and in Oct of that year was at Castleton to meet a threatened invasion by St. Leger. In 1782, he was appointed brigadier general of the militia. Jacob G. Ullery, et. al. *Men of Vermont: An Illustrated Biographical History of Vermonters and Sons of Vermont* (Holyoke, MA: Transcript Publishing Co., 1894), 52.

90. Letter 231.

91. Letter 232.

92. *Ibid.*

Chapter Eight

1. Letter 233.

2. *Ibid.*

3. *Ibid.*

4. Letter 234.

5. *Ibid.*

6. Charles Thomson (1729–1824) served as the secretary of the Continental Congress through its entirety from 1774 to 1789. Boyd Stanley Schlenther, "Thomson, Charles," *American National Biography, s.v.*

7. Letter 235.

8. Letter 236.

9. *Ibid.*

10. Letter 237.

11. Letter 238.

12. When the war began, Irish native Peter Fitzpatrick (b. 1752) was an indentured servant laboring for the superintendent for Indian Affairs in the northern colonies, Guy Johnson, in Tryon. In Apr 1775, he followed Guy Johnson to Canada and return to the Mohawk Valley in 1776. He served in the Kings Royal Regiment of New York under Sir John Johnson, serving as a spy. He was captured in 1781 and imprisoned in Albany. Although sentenced to death, he was reprieved and released after the war. He settled in Cornwall, Ontario. Jon Fox, "A Loyalist's History: Peter Fitzpatrick," *Loyalist Trails UELAC Newsletter* 2006–20 (May 14 2006). http://www.uelac.org/Loyalist-Trails/2006/Loyalist-Trails–2006.php?issue=200620#Fitzpatrick (accessed 24 Jun 2011).

13. John Ten Broeck served as sheriff from 22 Mar 1781 to 28 Nov 1782 and then again from 29 Sep 1786 to 28 Sep 1790. Howell and Tenney, *Bi-centennial history of Albany*, IV: 156.

14. Ezekiel Taylor to Peter Gansevoort, Jr., July 15, 1782. Military Papers of Brigadier Peter Gansevoort, Jr.

15. The Soldiers of the New York Militia to Peter Gansevoort, Jr., April 25, 1782. Military Papers of Brigadier Peter Gansevoort, Jr.

16. James Ashton (1728–1802) was a major in the New York Militia from 1777 to 1778. Heitman, *Historical Register*, 77; Daughters of the American Revolution, *Lineage Book*, LV: 114.

17. Letter 239.

18. Elias Boudinot (1740–1821) was appointed colonel and commissary-general of prisoners on 15 May 1777, resigning on 11 May 1778. He was a member of Continental Congress, serving as president from 1782 to 1783, the U.S. House of Representative from 1789 to 1895, and director of the U.S. Mint from 1795 to 1805. Boatner, *Encyclopedia of the American Revolution*, 99–100; Heitman, *Historical Register*, 111.

19. Letter 240.

20. Letter 243.

21. Letter 244.

22. Peter Gansevoort, Jr. to Peter Vrooman and Abraham Wempel, July 19, 1782. Military Papers of Brigadier Peter Gansevoort, Jr.

23. Nathan Denison (1740–1809) served as lieutenant colonel in the Connecticut Militia in 1777 and as colonel in the Connecticut Militia from 1777 to 1780. Heitman, *Historical Register*, 193; Daughters of the American Revolution, *Lineage Book*, XII: 112.

24. Letter 246.

Chapter Nine

1. Letter 249.

2. John Beekman was commissioned second lieutenant of the First New York, serving from 28 Jun 1775 to Jan 1776. After that, he served as captain and lieutenant colonel in the New York Militia. Heitman, *Historical Register*, 96.

3. Doc 250.

4. Letter 251.

5. *Ibid.*

6. Elisha Benedict (1736–1798) served as captain of the Second New York Regiment from Jun 1775 to Jan 1776. He served subsequently as captain in the New York Militia. Heitman, *Historical Register*, 98–99; Joseph Trowbridge Bailey, *Ancestry of Joseph Trowbridge Bailey of Philadelphia and Catherine Goddard Weaver of Newport, Rhode Island* (Philadelphia: The De Vinne Press, 1892), 18.

7. Elisha Benedict had three sons, Caleb, Elias and Felix. Bailey, *Ancestry of Joseph Trowbridge Bailey*, 18.

8. *Ibid.*

9. Letter 252.

10. The Treaty of Paris was signed on 3 Sept 1783 and ratified by the Congress of the Confederation on 14 Jan 1784 and by the King of Great Britain on 9 Apr 1784. Mary A. Giunta and J. Dane Hartgrove, *Documents of the Emerging Nation: U.S. Foreign Relations, 1775–1789* (Wilmington, DE: Scholarly Resources, 1998), 132.

11. Letter 253.

12. *Ibid.*

13. In early Jul 1778, a raiding party of approximately one thousand Tories and Indians under the command of John Butler invaded and destroyed homes and farms the Wyoming Valley of Pennsylvania. Colonel Zebulon Butler with 450 old men and youths who were stationed at Forty Fort tried to stop the destruction but fell into a trap and as many as 400 Americans were killed or captured. Most of the surviving settlers fled to the mountains or to the great swamp of the Poconos ominously known as the Shades of Death. Heard, *Handbook of the American Frontier*, II: 400.

14. Letter 254.

15. Peter Snyder served as lieutenant in the associated exempts company of Colonel Vrooman's Fifteenth Regiment of the New York militia (as known as Schoharie Militia). Simms, *Frontiersmen of New York*, I: 533–534.

16. Letter 255.

17. *Ibid.*

18. Letter 256.

19. *Ibid.*

20. Edward Dunscomb (1746–1814) was appointed second lieutenant of Lasher's New York Militia Regiment in Jan 1776. He was promoted to first lieutenant in May 1776. On 27 Aug 1776, he was taken prisoner at Long Island. On 21 Nov 1776, he was transferred to the Fourth New York Regiment. He was promoted to captain lieutenant on 23 Apr 1778 and captain 11 Apr 1780, retiring on 1 Jan 1781. After the war, he served as sheriff of New York City in 1810 and 1811 and as trustee of Columbia College from 1795 to 1814. Heitman, *Historical Register*, 207; Leonhard Felix Fuld, "Kings College Alumni—VIII," *Columbia University Quarterly* (Dec 1910): 81.

21. Letter 257.

22. *Ibid.*

23. *Ibid.*

24. Andrew Finck, Jr. (1751–1820) was commis-

sioned as a First Lieutenant of the Second New York Regiment on 15 July 1775. He was promoted to the rank of Captain on 16 February 1776 and transferred to the First New York Regiment on 21 November 1776. He retired on 16 January 1781 and subsequently served as Brigade Major of Militia and Levies from 1 September 1781 to 1 January 1782. Heitman, *Historical Register*, 226; John B. Koetteritz, *Andrew Finck, Major in the Revolutionary Wars: Address Delivered Before The Herkimer County Historical Society, June 8th, 1897* (Utica, NY: Press of L. C. Childs & Son, 1897), 1.

25. Letter 258.

26. *Ibid.*

27. Hendrick J. Wendell, the incumbent, was re-elected sheriff. Howell and Tenney, *Bi-centennial History of Albany*, IV: 156.

28. Gansevoort would serve as sheriff of Albany from 29 Sep 1790 to 28 Sep 1792. Howell and Tenney, *Bi-centennial History of Albany*, IV: 156.

Chapter Ten

1. Fort Stanwix (Fort Schuyler) Treaty of Sept. 22, 1788, https://courses.cit.cornell.edu/govt313/lc/texts/1788treaty.html.

2. For further information on earlier disputes between Oneida, Onondaga and other native nations with the state of New York, refer to Alan Taylor's *Divided Ground*.

3. Kenney, *The Gansevoorts of Albany*, 141.

4. Kenney, *The Gansevoorts of Albany*, 125; Jabez D. Hammond, *The History of Political Parties in the State of New-York, from the Ratification of the Federal Constitution to December 1840* (Cooperstown: H. & E. Phinney, 1846), I: 20–21; S. V. Talcott, compiler, *Genealogical Notes of New York and New England Families* (Bowie, MD: Heritage Books, 2001), I: 136.

5. *A Sesqui-Centennial Souvenir Describing One Hundred and Fifty Years of Progress With a Complete Story of the Sullivan Campaign of 1779 and a History of the Towns of the Finger Lakes Region Settled by Veterans of that Expedition by Harry R. Melone* (Auburn, NY: Harry R. Melone, 1929), 266, 290.

6. *Ibid.*

7. Kenney, *The Gansevoorts of Albany*, 122; Joel Tiffany, *Reports of Cases Argued and Determined in the Court of Appeals of the State of New York, with Notes, References and an Index* (Albany: Weare C. Little, 1885), I: 9–45.

8. For more information on New York political factionalism and anti–Federalist movements, read Jackson Turner Main's *The Anti-Federalists: Critics of the Constitution 1781–1788*.

9. Peter Gansevoort, Jr. to Marinus Willet, December 19, 1798. Military Papers of Brigadier General Peter Gansevoort, Jr.

10. Peter Gansevoort, Jr. to Marinus Willet, January 4, 1799. Military Papers of Brigadier General Peter Gansevoort, Jr.

11. *Ibid.*

12. Lois McClellan Patrie, *Descendants of Michael McClellan and Jane Henry of Colrain, Mass.* (Troy, NY: n. p., 1970), 115.

13. Hammond, *The History of Political Parties in the State of New-York*, I: 134.

14. United States. Army. Quartermaster's Department, *A Sketch of the Organization of the Quartermaster's Department, from 1774 to 1868* (Washington: Government Printing Office, 1869), 14; U.S. Congress, *Senate Exec. Journal*, 1st Cong., 20th sess., 27 April 1802.

15. Kenney, *The Gansevoorts of Albany*, 140–141; "Regent of the University of New York Appointment," *Otsego Herald*, March 12, 1808; Philip G. Hubert, Jr., *The Merchants' National Bank of the City of New York: A History of Its First Century Compiled from Official Records at the Request of the Directors* (New York: Merchants' National Bank, 1903), 192.

16. Colonel Anthony Lamb was nominated by President Madison on June 28, 1809, to replace Gansevoort as the military agent for the Northern Department of the United States. Kenney, *The Gansevoorts of Albany*, 143, 145; United States Congress, Senate, *Journal of the Executive Proceedings of the Senate of the United States of America* (Washington: Duff Green, 1828), II: 128; Peter Gansevoort, Jr. to Daniel Tompkins, March 25, 1809. Military Papers of Brigadier General Peter Gansevoort, Jr.

17. Gordon Wood, *Empire of Liberty: A History of the Early Republic, 1789–1815* (New York: Oxford University Press, 2009), 483.

18. Letter 261.

19. *Ibid.*

20. *Ibid.*

21. Irish-born Daniel Clark (1766–1813) was the first Delegate from the Territory of Orleans to the U.S. House of Representatives. In 1809, he published a long, well-documented diatribe against General Wilkinson, entitled "Proofs of the Corruption of Gen. James Wilkinson, and of his Connexion with Aaron Burr," accusing Wilkinson of being a paid Spanish agent while Wilkinson commanded the U.S. military. Junius P. Rodriquez, ed., *The Louisiana Purchase: A Historical and Geographical Encyclopedia* (Santa Barbara: ABC-CLIO, 2002), 71–72.

22. Thomas Power worked as an agent for Baron Francisco de Carondelet, governor of the Spanish-held territories of Louisiana and West Florida. Mann Butler, *A History of the Commonwealth of Kentucky* (Louisville, KY: Wilcox, Dickerman and Co., 1834), 321.

23. Other members of the court were Colonels Jonathan Williams, William Russell, Jacob Kingsbury, Lloyd Beall, Lieutenant Colonels Franklin Wharton, Alexander Macomb, T. C. Smith, Majors Amos Stoddert, Joseph Gardner Swift, George Armistead, Moses Porter and Nicholl. The defense attorneys were Roger Brooke Taney and John Hanson Thomas and Walter F. Jones, Jr. served as acting Judge Advocate. Thomas John Chew Williams and Folger McKinsey, *History of Frederick County, Maryland* (Baltimore: Regional Publishing Company, 1967), I: 163.

24. William Winthrop, *Military Law and Precedents* (Boston: Little, Brown and Company, 1896), 249–250.

25. Letter 264.

26. Letter 273.

27. Letter 274.

28. *Ibid.*

29. Gansevoort probably sent a substantial amount of financial support to his son Peter, who was at this time in the final phases of obtaining a law degree from Princeton.

30. Letter 269.

31. Letter 266.

32. Letter 267.

33. When Gansevoort opened the court on September 2, 1811, General James Wilkinson stood up and stated: "Mr. President, this sword (unclasping it from his side) has been the untarnished companion of my thigh for forty years, with a resolution never to surrender it dishonorably to an enemy, I am now by the order of the government of my country, ordered to place it in your hands." He handed his sword to Gansevoort, "who with much simplicity and dignity and uncommon brevity, replied, 'General, I receive your sword. These officers are assembled to try you, and with doubtless do you justice. Are you ready, General?' 'I am,' said Wilkinson. 'Mr. Advocate, General Walter Jones of Virginia, please to proceed with the trial.'" Harrison Ellery, ed., *The Memoirs of Gen. Joseph Gardner Swift, LL. D., U.S.A., First Graduate of the United States Military Academy, West Point, Chief Engineer U.S.A. from 1812 to 1818* (Worcester, MA: F. S. Blanchard, 1890), 96.

34. Letter 269.

35. Letter 270.

36. *Ibid.*

37. Walter F. Jones, Jr. (1777–1861), son of U.S. Congressman Walter Jones, was the District Attorney for the District of Columbia from 1801 to 1821. Winthrop, *Military Law and Precedents*, I: 270; F. Regis Noel and Margaret Brent Downing, *The Court-House of the District of Columbia* (Washington D.C.: Judd & Detweiler, 1919), 57, 59; Fanny Lee Jones, "Walter Jones and His Times," *Records of the Columbia Historical Society* Vol. 5 (Washington: Columbia Historical Society, 1902), V: 140; Bruce H. Harrison, *The Family Forest Descendants of Lady Joan Beaufort* (Kamuela, HI: Millisecond Publishing Company, 2005), 1779.

38. Letter 271.

39. Letter 272.

40. Letter 274.

41. J. C. A. Stagg et al., ed., *The Papers of James Madison*, Presidential Series, vol. 4, *5 November 1811–9 July 1812 and Supplement 5 March 1809–19 October 1811* (Charlottesville: University Press of Virginia, 1999), 168–170.

42. Letter 271.

43. Letter 277.

44. *Ibid.*

45. Kenney, *The Gansevoorts of Albany*, 144.

Bibliography

Books and Articles

Anderson, John A., and Stearns Morse. *The Book of the White Mountains.* Bowie, MD: Heritage Books, 2002.

Bailey, Joseph Trowbridge. *Ancestry of Joseph Trowbridge Bailey of Philadelphia and Catherine Goddard Weaver of Newport, Rhode Island.* Philadelphia: The De Vinne Press, 1892.

Bancroft, George. *History of the United States of America, From the Discovery of the Continent.* New York: D. Appleton and Company, 1885.

Barr, Daniel P. *Unconquered: The Iroquois League at War in Colonial America.* Westport, CT: Praeger, 2006.

Berry, A. J. *A Time of Terror.* Victoria, B.C.: Trafford, 2005.

Bird, Harrison. *Attack on Quebec: The American Invasion of Canada, 1775.* New York: Oxford University Press, 1968.

Blanco, Richard L., ed. *American Revolution, 1775–1783.* New York and London: Garland Publishing, 1993.

Bleeker, Leonard. *The Order Book of Capt. Leonard Bleeker, Major of Brigade in the Early Part of the Expedition under Gen. James Clinton, against the Indian Settlements of Western New York, in the Campaign of 1779.* New York: Joseph Sabin, 1865.

Boatner, Mark Mayo. *Encyclopedia of the American Revolution.* New York: David McKay Co, 1966.

Bouton, Nathaniel, comp. and ed. *Documents and Records Relating to the State of New-Hampshire During the Period of the American Revolution, from 1776 to 1783.* Concord, NH: Edward A. Jenks, 1874.

Bright, William. *Native American Placenames of the United States.* Norman: University of Oklahoma Press, 2004.

Brodhead, John R. *Documents Relative to the Colonial History of the State of New-York; Procured in Holland, England and France.* Edited by E. B. O'Callaghan. Albany: Weed, Parsons and Company, 1857.

Buell, Augustus C. *Sir William Johnson.* New York: D. Appleton and Company, 1903.

Butler, Mann. *A History of the Commonwealth of Kentucky.* Louisville, KY: Wilcox, Dickerman and Co., 1834.

Caliendo, Ralph J. *New York City Mayors, Part I: The Mayors of New York Before 1898.* Bloomington, IN: Xlibris, 2010.

Calloway, Colin G. *The American Revolution in Indian Country: Crisis and Diversity in Native American Communities.* New York: Cambridge University Press, 2009.

Campbell, William W. *Annals of Tryon County or The Border Warfare of New York, during the Revolution.* Cherry Valley, NY: Cherry Valley Gazette Print, 1880.

Canniff, William. *History of the Province of Ontario (Upper Canada): Containing a Sketch of Franco-Canadian History, the Bloody Battles of the French and Indians, the American Revolution, the Settlement of the Country by U.E. Loyalists, Trials and Hard-Ships Incident to Pioneer Life, Thrilling Narratives of Adventures with Indians and Wild Beasts Struggles for the Establishment of Christianity and Schools, Agriculture and Manufactures, the War of 1812 Battle Scenes, Capture of Buffalo, Subsequent Growth and Prosperity of the Country, Including Biographies of Prominent First Settlers and the Census of 1871.* Toronto: A.H. Hovey, 1872.

Carrington, Henry B. *Battles of the American Revolution, 1775–1781.* New York: Promontory Press, 1877.

Carter, James G. *A Geography of New-Hampshire, with a New Map of the State, for Families and Schools.* Portsmouth, NH: Nathaniel March; Boston: Hilliard, Gray, Little and Wilkins, 1831.

Chase, Franklin Henry. *Revolutionary Soldiers Resident or Dying in Onondaga County, NY: With Supplementary List of Possible Veterans.* Edited by Rev. W. M. Beauchamp. Syracuse: The McDonnell Co., 1913.

Chase, Philander D., ed. *The Papers of George Washington: 15 September–31 October 1778, Volume 17.* Charlottesville: University Press of Virginia, 2008.

Child, Hamilton. *Gazetteer of Grafton County, N.H., 1709–1886.* Syracuse: Syracuse Journal Company, 1886.

Cohen, Saul B. *The Columbia Gazetteer of the World.* New York: Columbia University Press, 1998.

Colbreath, William. *Days of Siege: A Journal of the Siege of Fort Stanwix in 1777.* Edited by Larry Lowenthal. [New York]: Eastern Acorn Press, 1983.

Colcock, Charles J. *Family of Hay: A History of the Progenitors and Some South Carolina Descendants of Col. Ann Hawkes Hay, with Collateral Genealogies, A.D. 500–1908.* New Orleans: Pelican, 1959.

Cook, Frederick, ed. *Journals of the Military Expedition of Major General John Sullivan against the Six Nations of Indians in 1779; With Records of Centennial Celebrations; Prepared Pursuant to Chapter 361, Laws of the State of New York, of 1885.* Auburn, NY: Knapp, Peck & Thomson, 1887.

Cowen, Phoebe Strong. *The Herkimers and Schuylers: An Historical Sketch of the Two Families with Genealogies of the Descendants of George Herkimer, the Palantine, Who Settled in the Mohawk Valley, N.Y., in 1721.* Albany: Joel Munsell's Sons, 1903.

Daughters of the American Revolution. *Ancestral Register of the General Society of the Daughters of the Revolution, 1896.* Philadelphia: The Bailey, Banks & Biddle Co., 1897.

Daughters of the American Revolution. *DAR Patriot Index.* Baltimore, MD: Gateway Press, 2003.

Daughters of the American Revolution. *Lineage Book.* Washington, D.C.: The National Society of the Daughters of the American Revolution, 1902–1908.

De Chastellux, Francois J. *Travels in North-America, in the Years 1780–1782.* Bedford, MA: Applewood Books, 2009.

DenBoer, Gordon, ed. *The Documentary History of the First Federal Elections, 1788–1790.* Madison: The University of Wisconsin Press, 1986.

Denslow, William R. *10,000 Famous Freemasons from A to J.* Trenton, MO: Missouri Lodge of Research, 1957.

Denslow, William R. *10,000 Famous Freemasons from K to Z.* Trenton, MO: Missouri Lodge of Research, 1957.

Derby, Samuel Carroll. *A List of the Revolutionary Soldiers of Dublin, N.H.* Columbus, OH: Spahr and Glenn, 1901.

Diamant, Lincoln. *Chaining the Hudson: The Fight for the River in the American Revolution.* New York: Fordham University Press, 2004.

Drury, Augustus W. *History of the City of Dayton and Montgomery County, Ohio.* Chicago and Dayton: S.J. Clarke Publishing Co, 1909.

Ellery, Harrison, ed. *The Memoirs of Gen. Joseph Gardner Swift, LL. D., U.S.A., First Graduate of the United States Military Academy, West Point, Chief Engineer U.S.A. from 1812 to 1818.* Worcester, MA: F. S. Blanchard, 1890.

Elting, John Robert. *The Battles of Saratoga.* Monmouth Beach, NJ: Philip Freneau Press, 1977.

Ferguson, Elmer James, ed. *The Papers of Robert Morris.* Pittsburgh, PA: University of Pittsburgh Press, 1977.

Fiske, John. *The American Revolution.* Boston and New York: Houghton, Mifflin and Company, 1891.

Ford, Worthington Chauncey. *The Journals of the Continental Congress. 34 Volumes.* Washington D.C.: Government Printing Office, 1904–1937.

Fredriksen, John C. *Revolutionary War Almanac.* NY: Facts on File, 2006.

Freemasons. Grand Lodge of the State of New York. *Proceedings of the Grand Lodge of Free and Accepted Masons of the State of New York.* New York: Press of J. J. Little & Co., 1900.

French, John H. *Gazetteer of the State of New York: Embracing a Comprehensive View of the Geography, Geology, and General History of the State, and a Complete History and Description Every County, City, Town, Village, and Locality.* Syracuse, NY: R. Pearsall Smith, 1860.

Frey, Samuel Ludlow, ed. *The Minute Book of the Committee of Safety of Tryon County: The Old New York Frontier, Now Printed Verbatim for the First Time.* New York: Dodd, Mead, 1905.

Fryer, Mary Beacock. *King's Men: The Soldier Founders of Ontario.* Toronto: Dundurn Press, 1980.

Fuld, Leonhard Felix. "Kings College Alumni—VIII." *Columbia University Quarterly* (Dec 1910): 77–86.

Gabriel, Michael P., ed. *Quebec During the American Invasion, 1775–1776: The Journal of Francois Baby, Gabriel Taschereau, & Jenkin Williams.* East Lansing: Michigan State University Press, 2005.

Gansevoort-Lansing Collection. Manuscripts and Archives Division. The New York Public Library. Astor, Lenox, and Tilden Foundations.

Giunta, Mary A., and J. Dane Hartgrove. *Documents of the Emerging Nation: U.S. Foreign Relations, 1775–1789.* Wilmington, DE: Scholarly Resources, 1998.

Glatthaar, Joseph T., and James Kirby Martin. *Forgotten Allies: The Oneida Indians and the American Revolution.* New York: Hill and Wang, 2006.

Graymont, Barbara. *The Iroquois in the American Revolution.* Syracuse, NY: Syracuse University Press, 1972.

Greene, Nelson. *The Old Mohawk Turnpike Book.* Fort Plain, NY: Nelson Greene, 1924.

Gregg, Arthur B. *Old Hellebergh: Historical Sketches of the West Manor of Rensselaerswyck; Including an Account of the Anti-Rent Wars, the Glass House and Henry R. Schoolcraft.* Altamont, NY: The Altamount Enterprise, 1936.

Grizzard, Frank E. *George!: A Guide to All Things Washington.* Buena Vista, VA: Mariner Publishing, 2005.

Hall, Benjamin H. *History of Eastern Vermont, from Its Earliest Settlement to the Close of the Eighteenth Century.* New York: D. Appleton & Co., 1858.

Hall, Edward Hagaman. *The Sons of the American Revolution: New York State Society, 1893–94.* New York: Republic Press, 1894.

Hall, Hiland. *The History of Vermont, from Its Discovery to Its Admission into the Union in 1791.* Albany, NY: Joel Munsell, 1868.

Halsey, Francis W. *The Old New York Frontier: Its Wars with Indians and Tories, Its Missionary Schools, Pioneers, and Land Titles, 1614–1800.* New York: C. Scribner's Sons, 1901.

Hammond, Jabez D. *The History of Political Parties in the State of New-York, from the Ratification of the Federal Constitution to December 1840.* Cooperstown: H. & E. Phinney, 1846.

Hanson, Willis T., Jr. *A History of Schenectady During the Revolution, to Which is Appended a Contribution to the Individual Records of the Inhabitants of the Schenectady District During that Period.* N.p.: Willis T. Hanson, Jr., 1916.

Harpster, Jack, and Ken Stalter. *Captive!: The Story of David Odgen and the Iroquois.* Santa Barbara, CA: Praeger, 2010.

Harrison, Bruce H. *The Family Forest Descendants of Lady Joan Beaufort.* Kamuela, HI: Millisecond Publishing Company, 2005.

Harrison, Keith G. *The Ancestry of Nathan Lewis Harrison, Revisited Nineteen Years Later.* Holt, MI: KGH Environmental, 2008.

Harvey, Oscar Jewell. *A History of Wilkes-Barre, Luzerne County, Pennsylvania: From Its First Beginnings to the Present Time; Including Chapters of Newly-Discovered Early Wyoming Valley History Together with Many Biographical Sketches and Much Genealogical Material.* Wilkes-Barre: Raeder Press, 1909.

Hayward, John. *A Gazetteer of Massachusetts: Containing Descriptions of All the Counties, Towns and Districts in the Commonwealth; Also, of Its Principal Mountains, Rivers, Capes, Bays, Harbors, Islands, and Fashionable Resorts. To which are Added, Statistical Accounts of Its Agriculture, Commerce and Manufactures; with a Great Variety of Other Useful Information.* Boston: J. Hayward, 1846.

Heard, J. Norman. *Handbook of the American Frontier: Four Centuries of Indian-White Relationships, Volume II: The Northeastern Woodlands.* Metuchen, NJ: Scarecrow, 1990.

Heitman, Francis Bernard. *Historical Register of Officers of the Continental Army during the War of the Revolution, April 1775 to December 1783.* Washington D.C.: The Rare Book Shop Publishing Company, 1914.

Hislop, Codman. *The Mohawk.* Syracuse, NY: Syracuse University Press, 1989.

Homans, Benjamin, ed. *Army and Navy Chronicle.* Washington, D.C.: B. Homans, 1835.

Hough, Franklin B. *The New York Civil List, Containing the Names and Origin of the Civil Divisions and the Names and Dates of Election or Appointment of the Principal State and County Officers, from the Revolution to the Present Time.* Albany: Weed, Parsons & Co, 1858.

Howell, George Rogers, and Jonathan Tenney, eds. *Bi-centennial History of Albany: History of the County of Albany, N.Y., from 1609 to 1886.* New York: W. W. Munsell & Co., 1886.

Hubert, Philip G., Jr. *The Merchants' National Bank of the City of New York: A History of Its First Century Compiled from Official Records at the Request of the Directors.* New York: The Merchants' National Bank, 1903.

Johnston, Henry P. *The Storming of Stony Point on the Hudson, Midnight, July 15, 1779: Its Importance in the Light of Unpublished Documents.* New York: James T. White & Co., 1900.

Jones, Charles Henry. *History of the Campaign for the Conquest of Canada in 1776.* Philadelphia: Porter & Coates, 1970.

Jones, Fanny Lee. "Walter Jones and His Times," *Records of the Columbia Historical Society* Vol. 5. Washington: Columbia Historical Society, 1902.

Jones, Henry Z., Jr. *More Palatine Families: Some Immigrants to the Middle Colonies 1717–1776 and their European Origins, Plus New Discoveries on German Families Who Arrived in Colonial New York in 1710.* Universal City, CA: Henry Z. Jones, Jr., 1991.

Jones, Pomroy. *Annuals and Recollections of Oneida County.* Rome, NY: Pomroy Jones, 1851.

Kail, Jerry, ed. *Who Was Who During the American Revolution.* New York: The Bobbs-Merrill Co., 1976.

Kelly, Howard A., and Walter L. Burrage. *American Medical Biographies.* Baltimore: The Norman, Remington Company, 1920.

Kelsay, Isabel Thompson. *Joseph Brant, 1743–1807, Man of Two Worlds.* Syracuse, NY: Syracuse University Press, 1984.

Kenney, Alice P. *The Gansevoorts of Albany: Dutch Patricians in the Upper Hudson Valley.* Syracuse, NY: Syracuse University Press, 1969.

Ketchum, Richard M. *Saratoga: Turning Point of America's Revolutionary War.* New York: Henry Holt and Company, 1997.

King, Dean, John B. Hattendorf, and J. Worth Estes. *A Sea of Words: A Lexicon and Companion for Patrick O'Brian's Seafaring Tales.* New York: Henry Holt, 1995.

Koetteritz, John B. *Andrew Finck, Major in the Revolutionary Wars: Address Delivered Before the Herkimer County Historical Society, June 8th, 1897.* Utica, NY: Press of L. C. Childs & Son, 1897.

Kollock, Henry, ed. *State of New York: Embracing Historical, Descriptive, and Statistical Notices of Cities, Towns, Villages, Industries, and Summer Resorts in the Various Parts of the State, Together with a Complete List of the Post Offices, Counties, and County Towns, Lakes, Rivers, Railroads, &c.* New York City: Henry Pollock, 1882.

Lengel, Edward G., ed. *The Papers of George Washington: May-June 1778, Volume 15.* Charlottesville: University Press of Virginia, 2006.

Logusz, Michael O. *The Saratoga Campaign and the Wilderness War of 1777.* Havertown, PA: Casemate Publishers, 2010.

Lossing, Benson. *The Life and Times of Philip Schuyler.* New York: Sheldon & Company, 1873.

Lossing, Benson J. *Reflections of Rebellion: Hours with the Living Men and Women of the Revolution.* Charleston, SC: History Press, 2005.

Lothrop, Samuel Kirkland. *Life of Samuel Kirkland, Missionary to the Indians.* Boston: Charles C. Little and James Brown, 1848.

Mahoney, Harry Thayer, and Marjorie Locke Mahoney. *Gallantry in Action: Dictionary of Espionage in the American Revolutionary War.* Lanham, MD: University Press of America, 1999.

McHenry, Chris. *Rebel Prisoners at Quebec, 1778–1783: Being a List of American Prisoners Held by the British During the Revolutionary War.* Lawrenceburg, IN: C. McHenry, 1981.

Melone, Harry R. *A Sesqui-Centennial Souvenir describing One Hundred and Fifty Years of Progress With a Complete Story of the Sullivan Campaign of 1779 and a History of the Towns of the Finger Lakes Region Settled by Veterans of that Expedition.* Auburn, NY: Harry R. Melone, 1929.

Mooney, James L. *Dictionary of American Naval Fighting Ships.* Washington, D.C.: Navy Dept., Office of the Chief of Naval Operations, Naval History Division, 1959–1981.

Morgan, Lewis Henry. *League of the Iroquois.* Secaucus, NJ: The Citadel Press, 1975.

Morrison, James F. *A History of Fulton County in the Revolution.* Gloversville, NY: Fulton County Bicentennial History Committee, 1977.

Mudge, Alfred. *Memorials: Being a Genealogical, Biographical and Historical Account of the Name of Mudge in America, from 1638 to 1868.* Boston: Alfred Mudge & Son, 1868.

Munsell, Joel, ed. *Collections on the History of Albany: From Its Discovery to the Present Time.* Albany: J. Munsell, 1871.

Neilson, Charles. *An Original, Compiled and Corrected Account of Burgoyne's Campaign, and the Memorable Battles of Bemis's Heights, Sept. 19, and Oct. 7, 1777, from the Most Authentic Sources of Information; Including Many Interesting Incidents Connected with the Same.* Port Washington, NY: Kennikat Press, 1970.

New Jersey Historical Society, *Documents Relating to the Colonial History of the State of New Jersey.* (Newark, NJ: New Jersey Historical Society, 1904).

New York. The Office of the State Comptroller. *New York in the Revolution as Colony and State.* Albany: J. B. Lyon Company, 1904.

New York State Archives. *New York in the Revolution Prepared Under Direction of the Board of Regents: Documents Relating to the Colonial History of the State of New York.* Edited by Berthold Fernow. Albany NY: Weed, Parsons and Co, 1887.

Noel, F. Regis, and Margaret Brent Downing. *The Court-House of the District of Columbia.* Washington D.C.: Judd & Detweiler, 1919.

Nugent, Lady Maria Skinner. *Lady Nugent's Journal: Jamaica One Hundred Years Ago.* Edited by Frank Cundall. Soho Square, London: Adam & Charles Black for the Institute of Jamaica, 1907.

Ontario Historical Society. *Papers and Records: Vol VIII.* Toronto: Ontario Historical Society, 1907.

Paltsits, Victor Hugo, ed. *Minutes of the Commissioners for Detecting and Defeating Conspiracies in the State of New York: Albany County Sessions, 1778–1781.* Albany: J. B. Lyon Company, 1909.

Park, Lawrence. *Major Thomas Savage of Boston and his Descendants.* Boston: Press of David Clapp & Son, 1914.

Patrie, Lois McClellan. *Descendants of Michael McClellan and Jane Henry of Colrain, Mass.* Troy, NY: n. p., 1970.

Penrose, Maryly B. *Indian Affairs Papers: American Revolution.* Franklin Park, NJ: Liberty Bell Associates, 1981.

Priest, Josiah. *Stories of the Revolution, with an Account of the Lost Child of the Delaware; Wheaton and the Panther, &c.* Albany: Hoffman and White, 1836.

Ranzan, David. "'Thus a war has begun': The Capture of Fort Ticonderoga and Its Influence on the American Revolution." MA thesis, East Stroudsburg University, 2002.

Reid, William Max. *The Mohawk Valley, Its Legends and Its History.* New York and London: G. P. Putnam's Sons, 1901.

Reid, William Max. *The Story of Old Fort Johnson.* New York and London: G. P. Putnam's Sons, 1906.

Reynolds, Cuyler, ed. *Genealogical and Family History of Southern New York and the Hudson River Valley: A Record of the Achievements of Her People in the Making of a Commonwealth and the Building of a Nation.* New York: Lewis Historical Publishing Co., 1913.

Reynolds, Cuyler, ed. *Hudson-Mohawk Genealogical and Family Memoirs: A Record of Achievements of the People of the Hudson and Mohawk Valleys in New York State, Included within the Present Counties of Albany, Rensselaer, Washington, Saratoga, Montgomery, Fulton, Schenectady, Columbia and Greene.* New York: Lewis Historical Publishing Co., 1911.

Reynolds, Helen Wilkinson. *Dutch Houses in the Hudson Valley before 1776.* New York: Dover Publications, 1965.

Roberts, Robert B. *Encyclopedia of Historic Forts: The Military, Pioneer, and Trading Posts of the United States.* New York: Macmillan, 1988.

Roberts, Robert B. *New York's Forts in the Revolution.* Rutherford: Fairleigh Dickinson University Press, 1980.

Rodriquez, Junius P., ed. *The Louisiana Purchase: A Historical and Geographical Encyclopedia.* Santa Barbara: ABC-CLIO, 2002.

Roebling, Emily Warren. *The Journal of the Reverend Silas Constant: Pastor of the Presbyterian Church at Yorktown, New York.* Edited by Josiah Granville Leach. Philadelphia, PA: J. B. Lippincott Company, 1903.

Sabine, Lorenzo. *Biographical Sketches of Loyalists of the American Revolution with an Historical Essay.* Boston: Little, Brown and Company, 1864.

Saffell, W. T. R. *Records of the Revolutionary War: Containing the Military and Financial Correspondence of Distinguished Officers; Names of the Officers and Privates of Regiments, Companies, and Corps, with the Dates of Their Commissions and Enlistments; General Orders of Washington, Lee and Greene at Germantown and Valley Forge; with a List of Distinguished Prisoners of War; the Time of Their Capture, Exchange, etc. to Which Is Added the Half-Pay Acts of the Continental Congress; the Revolutionary Pension Laws; and a List of the Officers of the Continental Army Who Acquired the Right to Half-Pay, Commutation, and Lands.* Third Edition. Baltimore: Charles C. Saffell, 1894.

Schuyler, John. *Institution of the Society of the Cincinnati, Formed by the Officers of the American Army of the Revolution, 1783, with Extracts, from the Proceedings of Its General Meetings and from the Transactions of the New York State Society.* New York: Douglas Taylor, 1886.

Scott, John Albert. *Fort Stanwix and Oriskany: The Romantic Story of the Repulse of St. Leger's British Invasion of 1777 Told for the First Time, in Chronological Order and in Detail—Mainly from Contemporary Reports, Letters and Diaries, with All Sources Indicated.* Rome, NY: Rome Sentinel Company, 1927.

Simms, Jeptha Root. *The Frontiersmen of New York: Showing Customs of the Indians, Vicissitudes of the Pioneer White Settlers and Border Strife in Two Wars.* Albany: Geo. C. Riggs, 1883.

Smith, William, *Historical Memoirs of William Smith, 1778–1783.* Edited by William H. W. Sabine. New York: New York Times, 1971.

Sons of the Revolution. Pennsylvania Society. *Decennial Register of the Pennsylvania Society of Sons of the Revolution, 1888–1898.* Philadelphia: J. B. Lippincott Company, 1898.

Sons of the Revolution in the State of New York. *Supplement to Year Book of 1899 of the Society of Sons of the Revolution in the State of New York.* New York: Francis E. Fitch, 1903.

Spafford, Horatio Gates, ed. *A Gazetteer of the State of New York.* Albany: B.D. Packard, 1824.

Spooner, Walter Whipple. "The Van Rensselaer Family." *American Historical Magazine* 2, no. 1 (January 1907): 1–212.

Stagg, J. C. A. et al., ed. *The Papers of James Madison,* Presidential Series, vol. 4, *5 November 1811–9 July 1812 and Supplement 5 March 1809–19 October 1811.* Charlottesville: University Press of Virginia, 1999.

Stone, William L., ed. *Orderly Book of Sir John Johnson during the Oriskany Campaign, 1776–1777.* Albany: Joel Munsell's Sons, 1882.

Sullivan, James, ed. *Minutes of the Albany Committee of Correspondence 1775–1778.* Albany: The University of the State of New York, 1923.

Talcott, S. V., compiler. *Genealogical Notes of New York and New England Families.* Bowie, MD: Heritage Books, 2001.

Thompson, Benjamin Franklin. *History of Long Island: Containing an Account of the Discovery and Settlement; with Other Important and Interesting Matters to the Present Time.* New York: E. French, 1839.

Thompson, Zadock. *History of Vermont, Natural, Civil and Statistical, in Three Parts, with a New Map of the State, and 200 Engravings.* Burlington, VT: Chauncey Goodrich, 1842.

Tiffany, Joel Tiffany. *Reports of Cases Argued and Determined in the Court of Appeals of the State of New York, with Notes, References and an Index.* Albany: Weare C. Little, 1885.

Ullery, Jacob G. et. al. *Men of Vermont: An Illustrated Biographical History of Vermonters and Sons of Vermont.* Holyoke, MA: Transcript Publishing Co., 1894.

United States. Adjutant-General's Office. *Legislative History of the General Staff of the Army of the United States (Its Organization, Duties, Pay, and Allowances), from 1775 to 1901.* Washington, D.C.: Government Printing Office, 1901.

United States. Army. Quartermaster's Department. *A Sketch of the Organization of the Quartermaster's Department, from 1774 to 1868.* Washington, D.C.: Government Printing Office, 1869.

United States. Congress. Senate. *Journal of the Executive Proceedings of the Senate of the United States of America.* Washington, D.C.: Duff Green, 1828.

Van Benschoten, William Henry. *Concerning the Van Bunschoten or Van Benschoten Family in America: A Genealogy and Brief History.* West Park-on-Hudson, NY: William Henry Van Benschoten, 1907.

Walker, Paul K. *Engineers of Independence: A Documentary History of the Army Engineers in the Amer-*

ican Revolution, 1775–1783. Honolulu, HI: University Press of the Pacific, 1981.

Walworth, Ellen Hardin. *The Life and Times of Kateri Tekakwitha: The Lily of the Mohawks, 1656–1680*. Buffalo: Peter Paul & Brother, 1893.

Watt, Gavin K. *The Burning of the Valleys: Daring Raids from Canada Against the New York Frontier in the Fall of 1780*. Toronto and Tonawanda, NY: Dundurn Press, 1997.

Watt, Gavin K. *Rebellion in the Mohawk Valley: The St. Leger Expedition of 1777*. Toronto: Dundurn Press, 2002.

Weise, Arthur James. *Troy's One Hundred Years, 1789–1889*. Troy, NY: William H. Young, 1891.

Whitney, David C., and Kay Lovelace Smith. *The Colonial Spirit of '76: The People of the Revolution: The Lives of Members of the Continental Congresses and Other Prominent Men and Women of the Period*. Chicago: J.G. Ferguson Pub. Co., 1974.

Whittemore, Henry. *The Heroes of the American Revolution and Their Descendants: Battle of Long Island*. Brooklyn: The Heroes of the Revolution Publishing Co., 1897.

Willett, William M. *A Narrative of the Military Actions of Colonel Marinus Willett: Taken Chiefly From His Own Manuscript*. New York: G. & C. & H. Carvill, 1831.

Williams, Thomas John Chew, and Folger McKinsey. *History of Frederick County, Maryland*. Baltimore: Regional Publishing Company, 1967.

Winthrop, William. *Military Law and Precedents*. Boston: Little, Brown and Company, 1896.

Wood, Gordon. *Empire of Liberty: A History of the Early Republic, 1789–1815*. New York: Oxford University Press, 2009.

Woodruff, Ceylon Newton, and Maurine R. Herod. *Woodruff Chronicles; A Genealogy: The Long Island-New Jersey Family of John Woodruffe, the Immigrant Ancestor to America*. Glendale, CA: A.H. Clark Co., 1967.

Wynkoop, Richard. *Wynkoop Genealogy in the United States of America*. New York: Knickerbocker Press, 1904.

Reference Works

Dictionary of Canadian Biography. Toronto: University of Toronto Press, 1966-.

Garraty, John A., and Mark C. Carnes. *American National Biography*. New York: Oxford University Press, 1999.

Johnson, Allen and Dumas Malone, eds. *Dictionary of American Biography*. New York: Charles Scribner's Sons, 1958.

Merriam-Webster, Inc. *Webster's New Biographical Dictionary*. Springfield, Mass: Merriam-Webster, 1988.

Wilson, James Grant, and John Fiske. *Appletons' Cyclopaedia of American Biography*. New York: D. Appleton & Co., 1898.

Newspapers

Connecticut Courant
Massachusetts Spy
Otsego Herald

Online Resources

Bielinski, Stefan. "Benjamin Egberts." *Colonial Albany Social History Project*, http://www.nysm.nysed.gov/albany/bios/e/beegberts4510.html.

Bielinski, Stefan. "Edward S. Willett." *Colonial Albany Social History Project*, http://www.nysm.nysed.gov/albany/bios/w/edwillett6905.html.

Bielinski, Stefan. "Harme Gansevoort." *Colonial Albany Social History Project*, http://www.nysm.nysed.gov/albany/bios/g/hagansevoort4662.html.

Bielinski, Stefan. "Johannes G. Van Schaick." *Colonial Albany Social History Project*, http://www.nysm.nysed.gov/albany/bios/vs/jogvschaick3963.html.

Bielinski, Stefan. "John N. Bleecker." *Colonial Albany Society History Project*, http://www.nysm.nysed.gov/albany/bios/b/jnbleecker204.html.

Bielinski, Stefan. "Magdalena Gansevoort Ten Eyck." *Colonial Albany Social History Project*, http://www.nysm.nysed.gov/albany/bios/g/maggans4668.html.

Bielinski, Stefan. "Matthew Visscher." *Colonial Albany Social History Project*, http://www.nysm.nysed.gov/albany/bios/v/mavisscher4062.html.

Bielinski, Stefan. "Robert Yates." *Colonial Albany Social History Project*, http://www.nysm.nysed.gov/albany/bios/y/ryates.html.

Bielinski, Stefan. "Stephen J. Schuyler." *Colonial Albany Society History Project*, http://www.nysm.nysed.gov/albany/bios/s/stjschuyler1770.html.

Bielinski, Stefan. "Volkert P. Douw." *Colonial Albany Social History Project*, http://www.nysm.nysed.gov/albany/bios/d/vopdouw2234.html.

Fort Stanwix (Fort Schuyler) Treaty of Sept. 22, 1788, https://courses.cit.cornell.edu/govt313/lc/texts/1788treaty.html.

Fox, Jon. "A Loyalist's History: Peter Fitzpatrick." *Loyalist Trails UELAC Newsletter* 2006–20 (May 14, 2006), http://www.uelac.org/Loyalist-Trails/2006/Loyalist-Trails-2006.php?issue=200620#Fitzpatrick.

John L. Bronk Family Bible, Rossi Records, Volume 34, p. 25 at the Durham Center Museum, http://www.rootsweb.ancestry.com/~nygreen2/john_l__bronk_family_bible.htm.

Revolutionary War Pension Application of John Ball (W5767); Bounty-Land Warrant Application of John Ball (1197–200).

Index

Numbers in ***bold*** italics indicate pages with photographs.

www.ingramcontent.com/pod-product-compliance
Lightning Source LLC
Chambersburg PA
CBHW081402090726
47908CB00012B/2763